God's Way From The Beginning

Theology of Grace for the Third Millennium

FROM THE LIBRARY OF
K & S HUGHES

God's Way From The Beginning

Theology of Grace for the Third Millennium

Father Al Lucking

PUBLISHING COMPANY
P.O. Box 220 • Goleta, CA 93116
(800) 647-9882 • (805) 692-0043 • Fax: (805) 967-5133

Library of Congress Number # 2004111865

Published by:
Queenship Publishing
P.O. Box 220
Goleta, CA 93116
(800) 647-9882 • (805) 692-0043 • Fax: (805) 967-5133
www.queenship.org

Printed in the United States of America

ISBN: 1-57918-226-7

Table of Contents

Chapter 4
CHAPTER THREE OF GENESIS

Chapter 5
CREATION IN THE NEW TESTAMENT

APPENDIX ONE

Reader's Expectations

This book concerns the creation chapters of Genesis. Billions of readers have read these three chapters. They have read and pondered them many times over in seeking their hidden truth. Many have written of their insights into their hidden meaning. This commentary seeks to manifest what those billions of readers have missed. That claim no doubt sparks readers to wonder how could anything have been missed by billions of readers? Surely any such claim must be just folly. In the past many individuals have duped themselves into believing they see what no one else has seen or known.

This assumption is now challenged by the facts presented here. This commentary is based on what others have seen and missed of the meaning of the creation chapters. It seeks to remedy the many not inconsiderable failures of reading and understanding correctly the creation chapters.

How many have not seen or ever recognized and pointed out the following regarding the format or structure of the first chapter. That format does not involve only God as all readers have thought. The second day, like the other days, involves three persons. Count them. "Then God said, 'Let there be a dome in the middle of the waters, to separate one body of water from the other'". And so it happened: God made the dome, and it separated the water above the dome from the water below it. God called the dome "the sky". Evening came and morning followed—the second day.

God who speaks is person number one. The person who says: "And so it happened: God made the dome, etc. is person number two. The person to whom he is speaking is person number three. Person number two is not talking to God or to himself. No reader has pointed out this second person and who he might be. Nor does anyone point out the third person. Who might he be or what is he doing? Commentators have said nothing of them. They are completely silent about them because they have not acknowledged their existence.

Six times the author says: "Evening came and morning followed." Why and how can he say evening came and morning followed? He and everyone must know that when evening comes night follows. Why do all ignore this oddity? Ignoring it means they do not need to offer an explanation.

Has anyone pointed out the formats of chapters two and three for the understanding of these chapters? It is obvious their formats are not at all like the format of the first chapter. No one points out how the author obtained information to write these chapters. No one seems to be telling him anything was happening in first chapter.

Why is Adam, after being alone in Paradise a day or two, expecting God to provide him with a wife? When he entered Paradise he knew he was the only human on earth. God had not said a word to him about a wife. Has he, in the meanwhile, discovered other humans on earth?

Adam, only days after his creation, speaks divine wisdom of the value and purpose of marriage and family. Why is it no one has ever pointed out how the text indicates Adam could have had such knowledge and understanding? Do they suppose the author put such divine understanding on the lips of Adam? If so, where did the human author get such divine wisdom?

At the end of chapter two the author informs his readers that Adam and Eve were naked. Has anyone pointed out that he states this before even Adam and Eve discover their nakedness. Who informed the author of their nakedness? What does this indicate about who the author might be? It in part identifies him.

When tempting Adam and Eve what better disguise for Satan to assume than that of a polished liberated gentleman? The billions of readers don't see or understand the predicament that forced Satan into disguising himself as a talking, caring serpent.

The fruit of two particular trees of Paradise are very effective agents. The tree of life effects good for their lives. The fruit of the tree of knowledge of good and bad effected great evil. How is it explained that God, after Adam and Eve sinned, would forbid and prevent them from ever again eating the fruit of the tree of life, the fruit that was so extraordinarily beneficial to them?

How unjust can God be in His punishments? Adam and Eve disobeyed by being misled by Satan. When God appears on the scene and after He learns the facts, He sends Satan back to hell. Adam and Eve are expelled from Paradise and must die. All their descendants are punished by being forever exiled and must die. They had no part in the disobedience of their parents, Adam and Eve.

The last sentence of the fourth chapter reads: "At that time men began to invoke the Lord by the name Yahweh. This means that never before that time did anyone invoke or call God by the name Yahweh Lord. Before that time men always used the name Elohim, God, when invoking God. No one has pointed out or explained how Yahweh, Lord, can appear nineteen times in chapters two and three of Genesis. Consequently no one has understood what implication the use of Yahweh has regarding the authorship of Genesis. More importantly what does this apparent contradiction or real contradiction imply regarding the reliability of the whole text of Genesis?

No one has seen the inconsistencies of contradictions between the first part and the second part of this translation of the protoevangelium: "I will put enmity between you and the woman, and between your offspring and hers; He will strike at your head, while you strike at his heel." (Gen 3:15.) No one has pointed out that those inconsistencies or contradictions do not exist in the translation the Catholic Church used several decades ago. "I will put enmity between you and the woman, between your seed and her seed; she shall crush your head with her heel." Translation taken from St. Jerome's Vulgate. What? You don't see the contradictions or inconsistencies either! Have patience. You soon will.

The eleven unperceived and unsolved problems presented here are a small fraction of many other unperceived and unsolved problems of the creation chapters. All have gone unnoticed by the billions who have read and pondered the creation chapters. All have gone unnoticed in the theology in the past millenniums. Welcome to the theology of the third millennium.

In this commentary is to be found the complete plan of the Father for everything *ad extra*—a theology of grace for man on earth and man's supernatural salvation.

Foreword

What I always wanted to know... is here.

Since this book will reveal itself as quite original, its content unheard of, readers could have questions or reservations concerning its orthodoxy. Have no fear; the author is a retired, conservative priest of the Archdiocese of Miami, Florida and is in good standing. Since 1 January 1995 he has been retired and is doing parish work in the Diocese of San Bernardino, California.

This study had already budded when its author was yet a young man. The bud was in the form of a resolution. It came to bud at a time when justification by faith was regarded a Protestant heresy. That was also a time when Catholics were publishing and studying apologetical pamphlets and articles in defense of the Catholic view of justification, the view that persons were supposedly justified by faith and works. A way of justification that was called justification by living faith and this living faith was frequently referred to as charity.

That Catholic view of justification in the eyes of this novice aspiring to be a priest could not be easily vindicated in the emphatic words of the apostle Paul that persons are justified by faith and not justified by the works of the Law. Nor could it be easily vindicated by the gospel of the apostle John that has Jesus teaching: "This is the will of my Father that whoever believes in the Son should have eternal life and I will raise him up on the last day." For years a certain Protestant evangelist was often heard preaching, "when a person believes in Jesus he is justified and saved forever."

The reality of the tension coming from the opposing Catholic and Protestant views led this young novice to form the resolution of spending whatever time and study would be needed to clarify the theology of justification. That resolution required at the very least as a starter the very special effort to gain total familiarity with justification in the writings of the apostle Paul. During ten years spent to gain familiarity with the sense of the apostle Paul's writings regarding justification there came a number of breakthroughs.

For nearly fifty years that familiarity has been the cause of joy. The joy of knowing what St. Paul knew of the great goodness and love of God the Father for his God-man and for all persons created and recreated in the image of the God-man.

Since the spirit of clarity remained alive after the triumph of clarifying the theology of justification, that spirit of clarity could not be satisfied with the trend of the then-current theology of grace, a theology and an apologetics that allegedly clearly explained points of Catholic belief, theology and passages of scripture. One point in particular was the documentary hypothesis as the source of Genesis. That hypothesis appeared to do nothing but destroy the inspiration and the truth revealed in Genesis.

What then is the true source of Genesis? Is Genesis a revelation and is it inspired by God? The spirit of clarity accompanying the reading of the creation chapters saw that its most literal sense implied consequences, consequences that had gone completely unnoticed by scholars or by anyone. Because they remained hidden, scholars found it necessary to invent symbolic senses to make the creation chapters meaningful.

The format of the first chapter manifests that the first chapter is an ongoing revelation to its author, who immediately and simultaneously writes down that ongoing revelation. The unnoticed consequences of the literal sense of the second and third chapters reveal also that the author of these chapters writes as an eyewitness to the creation of the first man and woman. The hidden consequences or implications found in the literal sense of the second chapter reveal the all-important creation covenant God made with the first man. That creation covenant reveals how the great disaster of the third chapter came upon Adam and Eve and all mankind.

Scholars could not help but find the literal sense of the creation chapters quite meaningless since they did not recognize the very important implications of the literal sense of the words of the creation chapters. The implications of the literal sense of the second chapter manifest the setting that makes sense of chapter three.

It became clear that the revealed truths of the creation chapters were in need of being rescued from burial under the symbolic senses of the speculations of scholars. In return, clarity has buried their speculative symbolic and valueless senses, along with the deadly documentary hypothesis. Readers of this study will be very pleasantly surprised to see the implied truths of the literal sense of Genesis' creation chapters.

The word day in the first chapter of Genesis has been for many a mystery, if not a true conundrum. Creationists vehemently disagree among themselves on the length of a creation day. Some believe it was a true day of twenty-four hours while others believe a day is a very long geological period of time. The author of Genesis certainly knew the difference between a day and a long period of time. Also why would he repeatedly write "evening came and morning followed" when he knew night, not morning, always follows evening?

Another conundrum is why scholars of scripture and theology can proclaim that man was created in the image and likeness of God, and why is it that their affirmations of that double likeness always dwindle to a single likeness when they attempt to explain man's creation in the image and likeness of God. Their explanations of man's creation in the image and likeness of God become either the image of God or the likeness of God.

If one were to ask those scholars "in what man's image and likeness to God," they answer that man was created a spiritual and immortal being like God or that man was created with spiritual faculties of intellect and free will like God. The conundrum becomes evident in the fact these scholars teach that by original sin man lost his image and likeness to God. If all that be true, than man after original sin was no longer a man, for he would have lost his essential spiritual faculties of intellect and free will, and was no longer a spiritual and immortal being. Something has to be wrong with their explanations. Obviously, a new and far better explanation is due.

The use of the divine names YAHWEH, Lord, and ELOHIM, God, in the creation chapters is another conundrum for everyone including the holders of the documentary hypothesis. Chapter four of Genesis ends with the declaration, "At that time men began to invoke YAHWEH by name." That means God began to be called by the name of YAHWEH at that time. If so, how does that explain the fact that YAHWEH appears in the earlier creation chapters that concern earlier times than at the end of the fourth chapter?

The source of Genesis, as proposed here, easily solves this mystery regarding the use of YAHWEH in these early chapters of Genesis. It solves as well the mystery of how the author could state at the end of chapter two that Adam and Eve were naked, when Adam and Eve discovered their nakedness later in chapter three.

The profound protoevangelium also suffers abuse. During the past fifty or more years new English versions of the Bible have been multiplying in the market. These new versions made from the Greek give a very different translation of the protoevangelium. Gen 3:15. Their meaning is very different from what Catholics have known from their English Latin Vulgate Versions. The correct sense of the protoevangelium is critical for Catholics. Hence it has become paramount to discover whether the new or the old translation is the correct translation of the protoevangelium.

Persons seeking truth and clarity have no difficulty seeing contradictions in the new translations of the protoevangelium. Any translation containing contradictions leaves the persons seeking the truth no choice but to reject a translation that is intrinsically contradictory. Happily, the discovery of those contradictions has led to the discovery of further implications in the profound protoevangelium.

The first article of the apostle's creed has Catholics professing to "believe in God the Father almighty, creator of heaven and earth." The current philosophy and theology of scholars make it impossible for Catholics to understand how the Father alone can be the Creator as the creed teaches. Why so? Thomistic philosophy and theology teach that all *ad extra* works of God are done by all three Persons of the Trinity. Hence it would seem that the Father alone could not be the Creator of all things as the creed states.

The solution proposed by modern theologians and catechists has been to invent what they call the attribution process by which *ad extra* works of God are attributed to one or other of the Persons of the Trinity. They teach that all the works of God's almighty power are attributed to the Father. Since those works are attributed to the Father, we profess to believe that the Father alone is the Creator of heaven and earth. They go on to teach that just as the works of God's almighty power are attributed to the Father, so the works of redemption are attributed to the Son, and for that reason we profess that the Son alone is the redeemer of mankind in the same way all the works of sanctification are attributed to the Person of the Holy Spirit.

Clarity objects and rejects this mere attribution of certain works to particular Persons of the Trinity. It is easy to see how false is this attribution solution when attempting to merely attribute man's redemption to the Son of God alone. If the redemption were the work of all the Persons of the Trinity but merely attributed to only the Son then all three Persons of the Trinity should have become man and died for our redemption or none of the Persons became man. That is contrary to Scripture and the teaching of the Church. Hence it cannot be that our redemption is merely attributed to the Son of God, the only God-man of our race. The truth is the Son alone truly became man and truly died on the Cross and truly redeemed us.

Readers will find this study putting forth clearly and completely a realistic solution to this nothing-more-than the attribution of certain works to particular Persons of the Trinity. The solution has nothing at all to do with attributing works to particular Persons of the Trinity as modern scholars and apologists would have us believe. The Father is Creator because He is really and truly the only Creator as the creed teaches.

The spirit of clarity continued to draw attention to other sayings of theologians that are not clear. That clarity makes one wonders how theologians or anyone can believe that Mary was untouched by original sin and at the same time assert "of course Mary was redeemed"? Doesn't man's redemption mean that men were first of all redeemed from original sin? Wouldn't Mary's redemption mean she was redeemed from original sin? How could she be redeemed from original sin if she had not been touched by original sin?

Hence clarity requires a new understanding of the basis by which all persons receive original justice and suffered original sin and the basis for Mary receiving the gift of Immaculate Conception and freedom from original sin. Understanding the bases for Mary's reception of the grace of Immaculate Conception is also to understand the bases for Mary being chosen to be the Coredemptrix and Mediatrix of all graces for mankind.

Our late Holy Father, John Paul, would like very much to declare the dogmas of Mary Coredemptrix and Mediatrix of all graces. He, along with the faithful, believes those truths but he has refrained for many years from defining and declaring them truths explicitly or implicitly revealed by God. It seems he refrains not because he is personally opposed to their definitions but because he does not clearly see a way of doing so on theological grounds.

What theological reasons oppose Mary being declared Coredemptrix and therefore Mediatrix of all graces? There is a principle of justice that demands any fruit of the redemption not be used to pay the price of redemption. For example, if Mary was redeemed how can she or anything she has or has done be used to pay the price of man's redemption? So how is it possible for Mary to be a coredeemer or coredemptrix in any true sense of redemption? This study shows how Mary can be a coredeemer.

What is the reason God created all things? The Baltimore Catechism has as one of its first questions, why did God create you? The answer given is that God created persons to love and serve Him in this life and to be happy with Him forever in heaven. The purpose or goal God has in mind for the life of each individual is not the reason why God created the person and all things. If the catechism had asked why did God create the universe and the earth it very likely would have answered that that is a mystery.

The basic premise of this entire book is that God the Father created the universe, the earth and man on it in order to incarnate His Son as the God-man of our race. This truth was not revealed during the Old Testament period for Genesis' account of creation reveals God's order of execution not God's order of intention in the creation of all things. The New Testament writings reveal what had first and highest priority in the Father's order of intention when creating all things. The truth that God created all things in order to incarnate his Son as a man does not appear to have been clearly or forcefully taught through the centuries. It certainly was taught in apostolic times as is clear especially from the letters of the apostle Paul. In this matter authors have not followed the leader.

Historically the Jews, Moslems and Christians have taught that Abraham offered his son on Mt. Moriah. A careful reading of chapter twenty-two of Genesis reveals he could not have done it on Mt. Moriah.

Commentators admire Abraham for his obedience to God's request to sacrifice his beloved son and his supposed willingness to suffer the loss of his son and all God promised to him through Isaac—"Through Isaac shall your descendants be called." The apostle Paul teaches that Abraham knew he would not lose his Son and what was promised to him through Isaac by his sacrificing of Isaac. Abraham believed that after sacrificing Isaac God would raise up Isaac alive from the ashes of the sacrifice. St. Paul wrote of Abraham, "He reasoned that God was able to rise from the dead, and so he received Isaac back as a symbol." Heb 11:18.

Abraham was at Beer-sheba when God commanded him to sacrifice Isaac and to do it on a height in the land of Moriah, a height God promised "to point out to you" once Abraham arrived in the land of Moriah. If that height were the prominent Mt. Moriah, God didn't need to point it out to him once he got to the land of Moriah. Abraham already knew of its location for many years. He did not know of the height God had chosen for the sacrifice of Isaac. If God intended nothing more by that sacrifice than to test Abraham's willingness to sacrifice Isaac, He could have ordered him to sacrifice Isaac at Beer-sheba without sending them on a three days journey to Moriah. That command to go to Moriah implied that Abraham's going to that exact location was indispensable to God's intention for the sacrificing of Isaac.

What would make a particular location necessary? God the Father intended Abraham's sacrifice of Isaac to symbolize his own sacrificing of his Beloved Son who would be sacrificed on Mt. Calvary not Mt. Moriah. As part of that same symbolism Isaac carried the wood of his holocaust to the location, just as Jesus would carry his cross to the same location, Mt. Calvary. If Abraham, in the sacrificing of Isaac, symbolized God the Father sacrificing his Son, the place God would have chosen for Abraham to sacrifice

Isaac would have been the same height He had chosen to sacrifice his divine Son. That was Mt. Calvary, not Mt. Moriah. Both locations were equally distant from Beer-sheba. This is Scripture's way of teaching that Jesus' Death on the Cross was a true sacrifice.

A criticism of many modern writers in the fields of scripture, theology and philosophy is that they are not critical students of their subjects. They tend to just follow the leader, even into his goofs. A perfect example of this has been pointed out in the designation of Mt. Moriah as the hill on which Abraham offered his son Isaac and Abraham's supposed losses in his willingness to sacrifice his beloved Isaac.

Another perfect example of this trend is the "creation of man in our image and likeness." In the original Hebrew there is no "and" between the word image and the word likeness. Here the leaders are the translators of the Septuagint. Apparently "image likeness" was a complete mystery to the translators. They thought it an equally great mystery to their readers, and so attempted to make the phrase meaningful by inserting an "and" between the word image and the word likeness. It was meaningful but the wrong meaning. Their first duty as translators was to believe not to understand.

Another example of writers following the leader concerns the two great signs St. John wrote about in the twelfth chapter of Revelation. No one ever asks when those signs appeared in the sky and who saw them? If they had, they would have known they wouldn't have known why they appeared.

The content of this study manifests the reason why the chosen title of this book is GOD'S PLAN FROM THE BEGINNING and why its subtitle should be THEOLOGY OF GRACE FOR THE THIRD MILLENNIUM.

Fr. A. Lucking

Introduction

EVERY MAN'S GREAT NEED TO KNOW HIMSELF, HIS ORIGIN AND DESTINY

"GNOTHI SEAUTON" "KNOW YOURSELF" These Greek words were engraved on a wall of an ancient Greek temple dedicated to Apollo. The words manifest that mankind has always had a great desire and need to know his hidden self, his true inner self. These words also hint at every man's great desire to know other things. Man desires to know with certainty his ultimate origin and his ultimate destiny. Man greatly desires to know his immense universe and their ultimate origin and destiny. For all men see their own destiny and their efforts to seek fulfillment inexorably involved in his world and his destiny.

"Know Yourself" suggests little of the manner the Creator-God produced the very first man or provided man with some ultimate destiny, nor does it suggest anything of what God has specifically in store or in preparation for man. The words suggest that the ultimate origin and destiny of man and his world are deep, dark mysteries, unfathomable to the sciences and intuitions of man. Since they are deep, dark mysteries to man, every man is in need of a clear and certain revelation from God regarding his ultimate origin and destiny. Man's all-knowing God and Creator is the only one who can reveal those mysteries to man. God, who made man, keeps man in existence and gives man an eternal destiny.

Modern man's proud boast that his universe and all things in it had their origin in a big bang is no longer so scientifically certain in view of the latest wonders revealed by the Hubble Telescope. Modern man has no reason to boast or rejoice in the ultimate destiny assigned to him by his own understanding of his physical sciences or his theory of evolution. Many understand that destiny to be complete extinction in a lost grave in a black hole of an eternal deep freeze of a burned out universe.

"Know yourself" for Christians means men should believe and recognize themselves as truly children of God. For Christians the words mean that men have been created by God in "our image likeness" and consequently share in the divine nature and are destined for eternal supernatural glory and happiness in new heavens and a new earth.

In spite of the fact that the ultimate origin of all things is a deep, dark mystery to man, nations and tribes everywhere on earth have always had very different wisdom and beliefs about the origin of man and his universe. However, it is only the revelations of the creation chapters of Genesis that were written with the intention of specifically informing men with the absolute truth and certainty that the Almighty Creator created all things from nothing and established an orderly and systematic world. He did it all by the power of His almighty command. Only the Creator of all things is able to inform man of the manner in which the entire universe, the world and man came to be.

The intention of the author of the creation chapters of Genesis was nothing less than that of informing fallen man with absolute certainty what was the true origin of the universe, the world and man. The most puzzling aspect of Genesis' account of creation is how its author or authors could have known about the ultimate origin of all things. All readers would naturally expect from the author or authors evidence for the facts presented in the creation chapters. They wonder whether those facts are based on a direct revelation from God. If they are indeed based on a direct revelation from God. Where or what is the evidence that the author or authors received any revelation? Readers would also want to know whether God intended those creation chapters to be the exclusive means by which all men of the last three millenniums should learn the absolute truth about the ultimate origin and destiny of man, the universe and man's world?

Men now question whether there is any outside or independent source for evidence that the creation chapters are direct revelations from God. Everyone can rest assured that the New Testament offers that independent evidence.

If the three creation chapters of Genesis were revealed or contain revealed information, it would seem that scholars should have no more difficulty attributing the authorship of the creation chapters to Moses than they have attributing the authorship of the other books of the Pentateuch to Moses. The big problem with attributing authorship of the creation chapters to Moses or anyone is the question of how any person living in the past could have known what happened at the beginning of time or at the creation of all things? How can any person know what truly happened at the origin or the creation of all things without a revelation from God regarding the origin of all things? Since scholars can find no evidence of such a revelation they hold the creation chapters to be nothing more than the accumulated wisdom of the ancients.

Readers of the creation chapters must know that the ultimate origin of all things is hidden from the sciences and intuition of man, and for that reason man is not competent to judge the accuracy of Genesis' account of the origin of all things. Many biblical scholars have judged that account and have rejected the literal meaning of the creation chapters. Biblical scholars are not ready to call the creation chapters a revelation of God to their author for two reasons. The first is that they do not find that the creation chapters manifest themselves to be revelations of God. The second is that the literal sense of the chapters does not make much sense to modern men and that the literal sense would seem to contradict reason and science. Divine revelation cannot contradict reason or true science. That opens the way for many to deny that the creation chapters contain divine revelation.

The reality and the truth that the ultimate origin and destiny of all things are mysteries hidden from the sciences and intuitions of man did not prevent ancient man from producing wisdom accounts or myths about the origin of things. Their wisdom accounts regarding the origin of the earth give mythical reasons for man's existence on earth.

The reality and the truth that the ultimate origin of the universe and mankind are deep mysteries hidden from the sciences and intuitions of men have not prevented modern man from speculating about the ultimate origin of his universe or of his own ultimate origin, nor prevented modern men from speculating about the ultimate ends of the world and of men. Modern men have engaged in much speculation and have developed two theories to explain the hidden ultimate origins of man, his universe and all living things on earth. Modern men have speculated that their universe began with a big bang and that all life on earth, including human life, began in the earth's and the universe's total evolutionary process.

With respect to the ultimate origin of all things the ancients were satisfied to think the earth or the cosmos always existed. The ancients were satisfied to think that matter could not come to be from nothing by itself and therefore matter or whatever are the ultimate components of the universe must have always existed. The ancients supposed the earth and everything in it were composed from four elements, and, as regards the origin of living beings on earth, they have always been reproducing their kind and will forever continue to do so. Every species reproducing it own kind. This process of every creature reproducing its own kind was seen as continuing indefinitely with respect to the past and with respect to the future. Nevertheless on occasion a god or the gods intervened in the process and changed a being of one kind into a being of another kind. Changed an immutable nature into that of another immutable nature!

It is true modern man knows what ancient man did not know about the origin and the substances of things. Man now knows that matter is indestructible except in an atomic reaction where matter is changed into energy. Matter is never annihilated completely. Material things keep changing form one form to another without ever suffering complete destruction or annihilation. Consequently whatever may appear to be new is new only in form. Modern men, except for believers in evolution and reincarnation, know that while the beings or substances of living things are mutable their natures are immutable.

There are reasons external to Genesis for holding to a very literal sense and understanding of the creation chapters of Genesis. The first is that it is unthinkable that our most loving and merciful Creator would have left us, the fallen descendants of Adam, floundering in the darkness of our inability to ascertain what He revealed regarding the mysteries of the origin of all things and of man himself. This is the reason that today's unbelieving scholars are floundering in the darkness of uncertainty regarding the origins of things even after studding the creation chapters of Genesis. It is unthinkable that the God, who made his most merciful plan of redeeming fallen man and of returning fallen man to the supernatural state, would have denied fallen man the certainty of divine revelation regarding the origin of all things and especially of man.

It is therefore unthinkable that He would have given that revelation in a language or a sense man could not readily understand. So if Genesis was given to fallen man as God's revelation regarding the origin of all things and of man, it must have been given in a language or a literal sense that fallen man would readily understand. God would not have given man an account of man's origin, his fallen condition and his divine destiny in terms that would not have been completely intelligible, comforting and encouraging to fallen man.

Why would God not have give fallen man his inspired written revelation in a sense that was primarily literal rather than mystical, figurative, symbolical or metaphorical? So why has God supposedly given fallen man his inspired written revelation of the origin of things and of man in a sense that is not primarily literal rather than mystical, figurative, symbolical or metaphorical?

God by his omniscience would certainly have known that any non-literal account of the origin of things would send fallen man on a speculative and frantic search for that knowledge. That is precisely the kind of speculative and frantic search for the ultimate origin of things that is to be found in commentaries on Genesis by authors who do not accept a literal sense for the creation chapters.

The second reason external to Genesis for thinking that God gave his inspired written revelation of the creation in a completely literal sense is the fact that the New Testament's authors understand Genesis' account of creation in a completely literal sense. For New Testament authors, when quoting the creation chapters, quote them in a sense that is completely literal. The New Testament does this quoting for the purpose of adding weight to or for confirming its own teaching about the origin of all things and of man in particular. The New Testament in this way affirms that the creation chapters of Genesis have the same literal sense. The New Testament's authentic interpretation of the creation chapters makes it mandatory that all understand Genesis in that same literal sense.

These are the two external reasons for holding that God inspired a literal sense for the creation chapters of Genesis. The intrinsic reason for holding that these chapters have a literal sense will become obvious where this commentary shows how the first chapter manifests that it is a new and direct revelation of God to its author.

Modern scholars seriously question, for example, how the word day, with respect to the six days of creation, can mean a day in a literal sense. This commentary will define the literal sense of such words, including the word day, which scholars find most troublesome or impossible to understand except in a symbolical sense. It will manifest that the literal sense of troublesome words like day, morning, evening, night, light and darkness have a true and certain literal sense that is completely consistent with the account's orderly creation of all things from nothing in six days.

Scholars likewise seriously question how the word light God used to create light on the first day could mean material light, for material light had already begun to shine everywhere with the creation of the heavens and the earth at the beginning of the first day of creation. There was no need and therefore no reason for God to create any material light by his command "Let there be light". Moreover material light never exists without a material source of light. By the mere command "Let there be light" it would appear that God was creating material light without creating some material source of that light, for there is no evidence in the text that God created something that was the material source of that light. Hence that creation of light could not be the creation of material light.

Some raise scientific objections to the truthfulness of Genesis for implying that Adam would have to pass on to all his descendants his supernatural state of original innocence through the natural sexual generation of his descendants. For the same reasons they question also how the New Testament or even the Catholic Church can teach that original sin is now passed on to everyone of Adam's race by natural sexual generation from Adam and all persons of his line. Since these persons consider these teachings scientifically impossible they feel free to deny that doctrine of the Church. They hold that these errors could not have been revealed and therefore Genesis could not literally teach or imply them, and any text that would appear to teach them literally must be understood in a symbolical sense.

It should be obvious that the author of the creation chapters manifests no more knowledge of the universe and our world than what a casual observer would need to observe and correctly describe happenings on earth and in the sky. Both scientists and casual observers see the earth as flat and that the sky over a flat earth appears to all as a huge dome or firmament to which the sun, moon and stars seem attached. Such a dome could be viewed by anyone as useful for storing great quantities of water. From that great store of water God could rain down fresh water for the growing of plants and potable water for men and animals.

The author of the creation chapters manifests no intention or desire to write otherwise than literally when declaring that the origin of all things was by creation from nothing at the command and power of an Almighty God. Since the mind of man cannot conceive of something evolving from nothing, the revelation of the origin of all things by creation from nothing by the power of an Almighty God rings true to men.

The creation of specific things from nothing at specific commands of God is unquestionably an origin that is ultimate. It is an origin that is also intelligible, comforting and in no way ominous. The revelation of the creation of things from nothing by God, unlike the ancient pagan myths, ends all but superfluous or merely speculative questions man might have concerning himself, his origin and his ultimate destiny.

In pagan creation myths some things come to be by the gods merely changing one thing into another. In those pagan myths impotent gods change the immutable natures of things into other immutable natures! Again, those myths about the gods causing new things to be through the gods merely changing one thing into another in no way reveal the ultimate origin of anything and remain completely silent about any real or specific ultimate destiny for man.

These ancient pagan myths have discredited themselves to all reasonable persons of the past. They do the same to all reasonable persons of the present and no doubt will be without credit to men in the future. It would be a shame if Genesis were to suffer the same discreditation if it implied the evolution of immutable species!

It should be obvious that the account of creation in Genesis manifests no thought or concern for what is called scientific, although the account is in everything very reasonable. Genesis' account supposes there are reasons for everything but makes no effort to manifest those reasons except to teach that an all-wise God planned, designed and caused all things. The concordism of today's commentaries attempts to conform even minor details of the account to a cosmology based on man's modern sciences and theories.

Readers of Genesis should not let themselves be confused by the concordism of today's scholars, for it should be obvious to readers that Genesis' account of creation has about as much astronomy and science as can be found in the minds of some of today's preschoolers. To scientists, casual observers, adults and children alike, the earth appears flat and the sky appears as a huge dome to which the sun, moon and stars are attached.

It is true Moses, an educated person, surely espoused the primitive cosmology of his day, but why should anyone suppose that Moses' espoused cosmology found its way into this account of the six days of creation, when Moses is not the originator of its content or its composition? For it will be shown that although Moses is the human author of the creation chapters, he is not its composer but merely the receiver and writer of that explicitly revealed literal account of the creation of all things and of man. The account of each day's work of creation is a word-for-word account of what a messenger of the Creator is telling another person. The format of the first chapter manifests that a messenger is delivering to someone a verbal account of the creation for the purpose of having the other write it down.

These creation chapters inform fallen men that God planned immortality for men and yet did not destine men to live eternally on earth. Hence Adam and Eve must have been informed early on by God of their planned departure from their Paradise on earth for that eternal heavenly Paradise that had already been prepared for them from the foundations of the world.

Also Adam must have been informed of the final judgment God would be passing on every individual at the completion of his or her allotted time in Paradise on earth. This divine judgment of every individual with free will is necessary if every individual is to be justly and individually rewarded by God for his or her every action while living in the earthly Paradise. Their entire reward at their entrance into the eternal glory of the heavenly Paradise will be in accord with the merits of their intentions and deeds while living on earth.

The exact times and circumstances of their departure from their earthly Paradise and the time of their final judgement and glorification were not part of the revelation Moses received when writing of Adam and Eve living in Paradise. It should not have been a part of that revelation for the very obvious reason that such a departure had long been canceled by original sin. God had planned an immortal and triumphant exit for man from Paradise. Adam's sin changed such a welcomed departure from Paradise on earth to an exit by death and a return to dust.

LITERAL ACCOUNT OF CREATION REVEALS THE CREATOR

The theory of evolution of species offers no evidence of the existence of God. Genesis presents all things as coming into existence out of nothing by the power of God's word. In the literal sense of Genesis God's command is the ultimate origin of all things. In this way the literal account in Genesis reveals the only real and true God. It reveals a God who is self-existent, preexistent to all things, eternal, transcendent, and possessed of universal and absolute sovereignty over the whole of reality, including man. The providence of such a God is capable of effectively predestining man to a specific destiny, the destiny of a life of eternal supernatural communion and fellowship with the Creator Himself.

A God who cannot create things out of nothing is a god who is not only not omnipotent but not a god. The God revealed in Genesis is the Almighty Creator, but also the designer, caretaker, provider and ruler of all things. A God able to create things out of nothing is also the prime mover and is therefore able to govern and guide all things to a final eternal divine destiny. As the only prime mover, God is able to bless man abundantly and gratuitously.

The creation chapters manifest a Creator who is the Supreme Lord and Master of man's very being and life. He gives men not only human life but also supernatural life along with a supernatural destiny when creating man in God's own image likeness. God is a real being, supreme in goodness, magnificent in majesty and deserving of exaltation above all his wondrous works. In the creation chapters God manifests Himself as freely and deliberately choosing to make man in "our image likeness". These chapters manifest that man's existence, his life and his destiny to an eternal glory are solely the fruit of the Creator's eternal infinite goodness, unconditional love and friendship for man.

The Creator of all things is revealed as a reality whose existence is knowable to man. At the creation of all things God is unseen. His words, his commands, his power and his works can do no more than reveal some of his eternal attributes. The Creator and his marvelous attributes cannot change or be changed. They remain the same and ever new though ever without a beginning. The Creator has his dwelling-place far beyond where man's vision can reach or man's strength can take him. The Creator is a hidden God who dwells everywhere dwelling in Himself things live and move in Him.

Without divine revelation the specifics of the Creator's free will choices, plans and particular judgments are hidden from man and from all creatures. By teaching explicitly that the absolute beginning of everything began with the creation of the heavens and the earth, the angels and finally all earthly creatures were created out of the dust of the earth. Genesis teaches the mutability of created beings and the immutability of created natures. The immutability of created natures is contrary to the creation myths of the pagan nations and the theory of evolution of species.

In Genesis the Creator never changes the substance of one being into the substance of another species. Plants are not changed into animals or animals into men. Every specific species retains its specific nature and all species are destined to remain specifically the same throughout endless generations. The changing of one species into another by a god or goddess is a favorite tactic of the dishonest pagan creation myth. Such changes cannot explain the ultimate origin of species. They merely promote the particular cult of a mythical god, who is neither real nor omnipotent nor immutable.

The creation chapters explain also the origin of things other than physical realities. Besides revealing the existence of angels they explain the origin of society, marriage, family life, sin, the reason for human suffering and death. They manifest that sin, suffering and death were not a part of God's original plan for man. They explain it was God's displeasure, not with man, but with man's misconduct that the life of man on earth was condemned to unremitting labor, unbearable sorrows, drudgery and even death; the full wretchedness of man having fallen from that most favored state in which he was created by God. Without the fullness of God's favors life leaves fallen man with unremitting burdens ending in death. The good news of Genesis begins with God creating man in order to have a race of humans on which He could bestow great and manifold blessings. The irony of Genesis is that God has had to impose death on fallen man to impede man's abuse of God's great gift of free will.

The revelations of the inspired account of the ultimate origin and eternal destiny of man, which God willed to be given to fallen man, is in general limited to the creation of all things from nothing and the creation of man "in our image likeness". By creating man in God's image man was created in a supernatural state with a supernatural divine destiny. The creation account of man includes the account of the shameful fall of man from the grace of God and God's gracious plan to return man to his lost supernatural favors and destiny through redemption.

The creation chapters manifest a God who is totally truthful, just, merciful and loving toward all his works. It manifests a God who freely chose to create all things and freely chose to initiate a very special communion of fellowship with Adam and his entire race. The existence of Adam and his race, man's transcendent humanity and eternal supernatural destiny, were solely the fruit of the Father's infinite goodness, unconditional love and friendship for Adam and his entire race. This commentary will clearly explain these truths by explaining that God the Father gave all gifts to Adam and his race in view of the Incarnation of his Beloved Son as the God-man of Adam's race.

After years of knowing God intimately and after forty years of faithful service as the leader of God's people, Moses could write of the character of the God he knew and served: "The Rock—how faultless are his deeds. How right all his ways! A faithful God, without deceit, how just and upright he is!" DT. 32:4. Indeed, unless God were such a rock, it would have been impossible for Moses or anyone to have absolute trust in God's promise of a supernatural destiny for the fallen race of man. Moses' complete trust in his God is the reason Moses could call his God the rock of his life. God was such a rock of Moses' life that with great confidence he could promise Pharaoh: "As soon as I have gone out of the city, I will stretch out my hands to the Lord; the thunder will cease, and there will be no more hail, that you may know that the earth is the Lord's." Ex 9:29.

Without such a concept of God how could Moses have written the creation chapters? By writing it for fallen man Moses wrote a divine adventure for man. Man would live an eternal adventure which man could never have imagined possible. Man's great adventure began with his divine origin in the 'image likeness of God". The adventure included a supernatural life and an eternal supernatural destiny for man. That greatest of adventures for man can be known, grasp and clearly understood only in the light of the faith and theology of the grace God had for all men from the beginning. Theology is man's best effort to use God's revealed words to understand God and man and the extent of God's eternal wisdom, omnipotence and limitless generosity to man.

This commentary will use the apostle Paul's writings for its guide on the great adventure God initially revealed to Moses. In Paul's writings this adventure is an adventure into a mystery hidden in God, which ends in the fulfillment of the glorious gospel in man. The glorious gospel is "that mystery hidden from ages and generations past but now revealed to his holy ones. God has willed to make known to them the glory beyond price which this mystery brings to the gentiles—the mystery of Christ in you, your hope of glory." Col 1: 26-27. "To me Paul...God's secret plan, as I have briefly described it, was revealed. When you read what I have said, you will realize I know what I am talking about in speaking of the mystery of Christ, unknown to men in former ages but now revealed to the holy apostles and prophets." Eph 3:2-4.

May this commentary produce in those who grasp its exegesis and theology some of the burning zeal St. Paul had for the mystery of Christ and the mystery of the gospel of salvation for man. May the brightness of the revelation St. Paul received be the light guiding readers and students through these faltering attempts to manifest the mystery of the glorious gospel of Christ. "Pray for me that God put his word on my lips, that I may courageously make know the mystery of the gospel." Eph 6:19.

Chapter 1

CREATION OF ALL THINGS

ERRONEOUS PERSPECTIVES REGARDING THE CREATION ACCOUNT OF GENESIS

The almost complete neglect and even the denial of the literal sense of the creation chapters in favor of accepting a highly symbolical sense has forced modern scholars to indulge in much pure speculation when trying to give some acceptable meaning to the creation chapters. They indulge themselves in pure speculation especially when attempting to manifest the mysterious ultimate origins and destinies of creatures.

The fact is that the meaning of these chapters remains as much a mystery to fallen men after reading the explanations of modern scholars as before reading those explanations. Symbolical senses are by nature quite unspecific and for that reason an account of creation given in some symbolic sense must leave fallen man with little or no certainty regarding himself, his ultimate origin and destiny as well as those of the material universe and earth.

An oriental author has written: "The account of the creation of the world and the story of Adam and Eve and the Garden of Eden, seem to be funny." They were funny to him for he thought he understood the story in its literal sense. How could he have read with enjoyment modern commentaries with their disconnected and convoluted speculations explaining its supposed symbolical sense? He found the text of the creation chapters to be a funny story. He would have found modern commentaries irritating, confusing and contradictory.

A much more tragic case of misunderstanding the creation chapters is that of a present day rabbi. The rabbi, after his long and arduous study of the creation chapters in their original Hebrew, with the aid of the exegesis of modern biblical scholars, found that he could not understand why the author of Genesis has God giving Adam and Eve the order not to eat fruit from the tree of knowledge of good and bad. Anyone, he says, knowing human nature would have known that such an order almost certainly would have guaranteed Adam and Eve would eat that fruit.

If the rabbi's view were correct, God would then defeat his own purpose for Adam and Eve. Therefore God, contrary to the text, should never have given such an order to them. Any such command and supposed guarantee of disobedience would in effect destroy certainty regarding any useful meaning for the text. This rabbi is very confused for he could not have been thinking of the kind of human nature Adam and Eve had during the time from their creation to their fall from God's favor and grace.

The rabbi explained that God should not have given that order also for the reason that God did not have to create that tree or its fruit. If such were the true reality of Adam and Eve's situation in Paradise, why would anyone ever take seriously anything God has revealed to man in these creation chapters or anywhere else? It forces one, as it did the rabbi, to wonder whether God could have had the best interests of man at heart by placing Adam and Eve in their situation. Moreover it seemed to the rabbi that the account of Adam and Eve had to be erroneous for other reasons. One such reason was that, in the end, God came down excessively harsh on Adam and Eve and all their descendants in consequence of merely eating some very good but forbidden fruit. All the fruit of all the trees in Paradise was very good fruit. The account would thus seem to indicate that God arbitrarily chose to prohibit them from eating some very good fruit while making that fruit very accessible to them.

Normally persons would find it much more sensible, in view of the fact that eating the fruit would give them knowledge of good and bad, that God should have commanded them to eat the tree's fruit instead of forbidding them to eat its fruit.

Like the rabbi's misunderstanding most commentaries by modern biblical scholars turn out to be obstacles rather than aids to a completely sensible understanding of Genesis' account of Adam and Eve in Paradise. The first reason for so much darkness is that the authors of commentaries, because of their refusal to recognize or accept the literal sense of the creation chapters, attempt to explain the story in a highly symbolical sense. The second reason is that these authors attempt to explain those chapters by applying the theory of evolution to them. How could anyone suppose the theory of evolution was on the mind of the human author of Genesis while he was writing those chapters?

The third reason is that the authors of these commentaries take for granted that the documentary hypothesis is a correct explanation of the origin, development, composition and preservation of Genesis' creation account. Thus the authors of these commentaries cannot begin without many implicit grave doubts about the correctness of the supposed edited texts found in Genesis.

Because of all the uncertainty regarding the creation of man and especially the fall of man, modern biblical scholars cannot explain, as will be shown, with any certainty what the protoevangelium promises in regard to man's redemption and salvation. They are found to have two different translations, which have very different meanings or senses. These different texts with very different senses are reason enough for great confusion regarding the redemption and salvation of mankind. These differences in the literal senses of the protoevangelium, to say the least, must be distressing to sincere Christians.

Scholars are embarrassed, as well they should be, to find themselves unable to identify the woman of the protoevangelium and what she is to do to whom and what her offspring is to do and to whom he is to do it. Their preferred translation of the protoevangelium implies that the mere crushing or striking the head of the serpent, Satan, will redeem mankind. Reason says there isn't anything anyone could do to Satan that could possibly redeem mankind. Also since they don't know what was the condition of man at his creation they are at a loss to know or explain what the New Testament means by God recreating or restoring fallen man to his pre-fallen condition. The reason is they don't have any certainty regarding what God meant by "our image likeness" when God said: Let us make man in "our image likeness."

This commentary's explanations will be found completely in line with the teachings of the New Testament, the Fathers of the Church and the Councils of the Church, for all of them accepted the literal sense of the creation chapters of Genesis. All of them taught that all things had their origin in a direct creation by God, that the reality and the identity of Adam and Eve was that of the very first two real individuals of our race and that from them all humans on earth have descended. They taught that the transmission of the state of original innocence from Adam to all his descendants has been by physical generation, just as the Catholic Church of today teaches that original sin is now transmitted to all men by their physical human generation.

Most persons, who reject the literal sense of the creation chapters, believe that all things had their origin in an interminable process of change. Because of that process of change man and all living things were essentially something else before evolving and will continue evolving into some thing different from what they once were and now are. Their belief is that all things are and will always be in a process of continuous change. That process they believe has been going on for many millions or billions of years and will continue forever. In that process the very substances or natures of living things change.

They believe also that process of change continues without anything giving that process any direction if it should have any direction. If it had any predetermined direction reality would have a specific destiny. Hence they cannot accept Genesis literal teaching that God created many specific kinds of creatures on earth and that all have immutable natures.

These scholars apparently have put their complete trust in what they think human science and especially the theory of evolution propose was the origin of all things. However science and the theory of evolution cannot reveal the ultimate origin of all things for that would suppose that there was some predetermined direction from which that development began. The ultimate origin of things remains a mystery to man's science and man's intuitions. Moreover an undirected and purely evolutionary origin for man unavoidably implies no special or ultimate meaning for human life and no value for human life on earth except the value a human chooses to give his own or another's life. They teach that men are free to do with their lives whatever they freely choose.

Many of today's commentators, in spite of the literal teaching of the creation chapters, enthusiastically agree almost completely with secular theoretical physicists in proposing that matter began from a big-bang and from that big-bang matter and ultimately all things came to be. Man came to be in consequence of that ever changing and evolving universe of matter. The coming to be of all things from some big bang obviously cannot be the ultimate origin of things.

The evolution of species is nothing more than the superstition of atheistic scientists who keep changing their theory as creation scientists continue to prove features of the process of evolution erroneous, impossible, nonexistent or irrelevant. Atheists believe in that superstition because they dread the inevitable accountability all persons must make to an all-knowing and Almighty Creator.

Modern scholars and commentators by accepting such an origin for all things must reject the literal sense of the creation chapters of Genesis. They must reject also the explicitly revealed truth of the formation of Adam's body from dust and reject most especially the explicit formation of Eve's body from a rib of Adam. Many explicitly reject the truths that Adam and Eve were real individuals and that they were the very first man and woman. They reject the reality of the tree of life and the tree of knowledge of good and bad growing in the center of the one and only Paradise on earth. They reject the truth of the reality of Satan disguising himself as a real serpent, the truth that Adam and Eve really eat some real fruit from the real tree of knowledge of good and bad, they reject the truth that its fruit was explicitly forbidden to them by God. They reject thereby the truth that Adam and Eve committed some specific sin by eating that fruit and that the eating of that fruit resulted in the fall of mankind from the state of original innocence.

This commentary on the contrary accepts the formation of Adam's body from dust and Eve's body from a real rib of Adam. It sees the specific origins of Adam and Eve as highly significant for their partnership in marriage. It acknowledges that Adam and Eve lived as husband and wife in a real Paradise on this earth for but a short time.

By accepting the literal sense of the creation chapters this commentary is able to point out a number of reasons why the evolution of man is incompatible with the account of the six days of creation and the first man and woman living in Paradise.

In the light of true science and Genesis' revelation of the true origin of man, all should wonder why commentaries on Genesis are still being produced that cling to the theory or opinion of evolution. Such commentaries are being produced and promoted at a time when the very validity of that opinion or theory cannot stand the test of true science. The theory has never been proven to be possible or to be fact. The theory is now more suspect than ever on the bases of the fossil record and the inability of the proponents of the theory to answer many questions true science raises in opposition to evolution of any species. All the early promoters of the theory confidently predicted that the fossil record would contain missing links and thus establish the theory of evolution of species. One of the most guarded secrets of evolutionists is the fact that the fossil record does not contain a single fossil of a missing link of any species.

According to the theory the evolution of species is a very slow process consuming millions of years in the development of a single species. In view of time limitations on the existence of the earth, the theory of evolution as the source of innumerable species would be much more believable, if only a very limited number of species were ever in existence. Instead the fact is there are many millions of species still remaining on earth after many millions of species have already become extinct. The existence of many millions of species makes it inconceivable that many millions of species could have come into existence by means of the very slow evolutionary process during the limited span of time the earth or even our solar system are know to have existed.

Hence it should be obvious that the theory of evolution of species, aside from the fact that revelation teaches the direct creation of every species of plant and animal, must be much more the product of wishful thinking, science fiction or pseudo-science than observable fact or pure science. It is no secret that the general promotion the theory of evolution has been given and its acceptance in educational systems has been motivated by persons anxious to free themselves and others form any direct accountability to God. Direct creation by God implies that every person is going to be held accountable by God for every deliberate though, word, deed and omission of a person's entire life. They rightly perceive that if there is no Creator of man there can be no Creator-Judge of man.

Readers of this commentary will find that the literal sense of the creation chapters is far more informative than the speculations of men based on a highly symbolical sense of Genesis. Reading those chapters in their literal sense enables every individual to better satisfy his or her desires to know self. At the same time the literal sense encourages individuals to live the specific kind of life God intends for all individuals. In general this commentary uses the literal sense to manifest the reasons for the special manner of the first man's origin, the first man receiving a transcendent humanity in his formation from dust, why and how Adam received his original supernatural state of innocence along with his supernatural destiny. It will manifest the meaning and the truth of St. Paul's teaching that mankind owes honor and praise and thanks for everything and owes them especially to God the Father, the Creator, rather than to the Son. Men owe God the Father specifically for limitless divine generosity in creating man, in establishing man in his original state of innocence and in reestablishing man, after his fall from grace, in God's favor through a redemption by his Son as the Redeemer God-man.

The New Testament teaches that the Father gave the God-man the mission of redeeming and saving mankind and that the God-man willingly accepted that mission. Understanding this commentary will make its readers much more aware of how gratuitously the Father created everything, established man originally in his supernatural favor by doing all things through the merits of the very Incarnation of the Son as the God-man of our race.

Fallen man can have much greater confidence, courage and comfort in the hope of receiving forgiveness of sins, knowing the graces of salvation and all other benefits came through the Father's generosity and love. Readers who come to know and understand the plan of the Father should become aware of God the Father's free choices regarding fallen man and his eternal salvation.

The inspired prologue of St. John's gospel details what options God chose when informing redeemed mankind of the reason God created all things rather than revealing again God's executive order when creating all things. The creation chapters of Genesis are limited primarily to God's executive order in the creation of all things.

THE TRUE ORIGIN OF GENESIS

Before beginning the presentation of the proofs for the true origin of the creation chapters of Genesis, it will be necessary to present a short preview of what the first chapter manifests in the way God chose to reveal the creation of all things to fallen man.

The way God chose to reveal the origin of all things is by way of visions given to an intermediary between God and the human author. God gives those visions to one particular person, perhaps an angel. This person, this visionary, becomes God's messenger to another person whom God has chosen also to be the writer or author of the inspired account of the six days of creation. The receiver of the visions communicates the content of those visions by words to the author and so acts as the intermediary between the Creator and the human author.

The visionary communicates by word what he hears and sees in those visions of the creation. He communicates them to the person he knows God has chosen to be the human author of the first chapter. The visions he receives of the creation are not visions of the actual creation but visions of a supernatural reenactment of the actual creation. It is in this way that the great length of time between the actual creation and the writing of the first chapter of Genesis is bridged.

In the three creation chapters of Genesis God has chosen to reveal his executive order of creation, not the order of the priority the things created had in God's intention at the creation. God's order of intention is revealed in the New Testament's accounts of creation, which is to say that in the first chapter of Genesis God does not reveal what motivated Him to create all things. The creation chapters do not reveal what had first and highest priority in God's order of intention.

Hence Genesis' first chapter can be described as the written account of the verbal messages God's visionary-messenger delivered by word to his author-collaborator, the inspired human author of the first chapter of Genesis. The messages of the visionary-messenger to his author-collaborator are exact repetitions of the very words the visionary-messenger heard God speaking when giving his commands for the creation of certain things and the exact words the visionary-messenger used to describe what he saw God doing to fulfill his own commands. Those commands besides bringing certain things into existence establish the particular order God intended among creatures at their creation and was intended to endure forever after their creation. The visionary-messenger, besides informing his author-collaborator of the exact words of the commands of God that created or did certain things also informs him of what he sees happening in the visions he is receiving of the creation. Therefore the author-collaborator's written account contains the very words he heard the visionary-messenger telling him of the creation. This is true of the whole account of the six days of creation except for the very last verse, which is exclusively the words of the author-collaborator. In that verse he is not writing something he heard from his visionary-messenger, but is writing on his own choice of words.

The above setup of the two persons communicating holds true for only the first chapter of Genesis. The setup for the writing of the second and third chapters is very different. In these chapters God has chosen the author-collaborator of the first chapter to be writer or author of the second and third chapters of Genesis. For the writing of these chapters, God has again chosen to reveal things by means of visions God gives to the author. Visions that reveal information regarding Adam and Eve. For the writing of the second and third chapters God has chosen to give those visions directly to the author of the second and third chapters of Genesis. God does not give them to some intermediary between Himself and the inspired author.

In the second and third chapters the author has the visions in which he sees and hears what God and other say and do. He sees and hears what God, Adam and Eve do and say. In later visions he will see Adam and Eve living in Paradise and witnesses their subsuming to Satan's temptation and their expulsion from Paradise to live in an area east of Eden. There they would be at a distance from Paradise and it would not be easy for them to return to Paradise to eat from the tree of life.

When writing the second and third chapters the author writes as an observer and in the main is using his own choice of words. In these creation chapters he writes almost exclusively of what he sees and hears in visions. In chapters two and three it is obvious that he writes as an observer for he is not receiving messages being relayed to him as is so obvious in the first chapter. In these chapters the author writes primarily of what he sees and hears in visions for he express also his own understanding regarding what he hears and sees in the visions.

In the first series of visions the author almost immediately witnesses the formation of the man's body from dust. This is followed by visions of the formation of Paradise. He then has visions of God taking the man He has just formed from dust into that Paradise. The author accompanies God and the first man into that Paradise and by means of visions witnesses God showing and explaining to the man the many wondrous features of Paradise.

On accompanying the man into Paradise, God immediately begins the making of the creation covenant between Himself and the man. While God and the man are together in Paradise the making of this creation covenant is the prime concern of God and the man and of the author. With the making of that creation covenant God settles the man in Paradise. God then withdraws and leaves the man in Paradise and in charge of Paradise. God will be returning to the man in Paradise to carry out the covenant's provision of providing the man with a wife.

When God returns to the man in Paradise, the author witness the formation of Eve's body from a rib of the man and observes God presiding over and witnessing the marriage of Adam with Eve. Again God withdraws from Adam leaving him and his wife to enjoy their life together in Paradise.

After the marriage of Adam and Eve the author continues to receive visions of them which show them living and working together in Paradise. He is able to sees and hears them interacting with one another and with their environment in Paradise. The author is secretly present and observing when God visits them in Paradise. These visions continue until after the author witnesses their succumbing to a temptation by the serpent, the promulgation of the protoevangelium and their expulsion from Paradise.

When God returns to the man and his wife after their fall into sin, the author first hears God questioning them. He then hears God curse Satan first. He then hears God curse Adam and Eve. This is followed by God's proclamation of the protoevangelium. In the last series of vision the author witnesses the permanent expulsion of the man and his wife from Paradise to live in a place east of Eden.

This protoevangelium, among other things, is a prophecy of Adam's race long and monumental struggle against Satan. It is a struggle against Satan in mankind's efforts to reach the destiny of a life in the Kingdom of Christ; the final and eternal destiny of human life is life in the God-man's eternal Kingdom of Heaven. From eternity man had been chosen by the free will of the Almighty Father to live only temporally on earth and thereafter live eternally in an heavenly Paradise, the heavenly Kingdom of the Eternal King, Jesus Christ, who is forever King of kings and Lord of lords.

These creation chapters with their protoevangelium can be viewed as God's first inspired history of man in a mysterious prophetic prehistory of mankind living on earth. That history begins with the man's creation from dust and continues on to tell of fallen Adam and Eve and their fallen race. A prophetic history of a race living a difficult life on a cursed earth while assured of the coming of the Son of God as the Incarnate God-man of their race. They believe He will be sent by the Father to be the redeemer and savior of their race. Men will live in hope of the fulfillment of God's plan of redemption and restoration of the human race to a lost supernatural state and to an eternal supernatural destiny.

According to the Father's eternal plan, the God-man's Eternal Kingdom would be a vast multitude of highly favored humans of the one race of Adam and each person a unique and true genetic brother or sister of the God-man. In that Glorious Kingdom mankind is to live eternally in the friendship and fellowship of the God-man and of his and their heavenly Father. In that eternal Kingdom all will enjoy perfect happiness gazing eternally on the face of their heavenly Father by means of the created grace of the beatific vision.

One of the fruits to be hoped for from the manner of the discovery of the true manner in which the revelation of the creation was deliver to the author should be a new great impetus to further study and research into the exact meaning of the creation chapters. Knowing the precise manner in which those revelations were given to the author of the creation chapters provides fallen man with a distinctly fresh interpretation and understanding of the creation chapters.

This commentary should bring readers and students of Genesis first to a better realization of the many options available to God with respect to time, place, persons, and manner of revealing to fallen mankind the mysteries of the origin of a vast and complex universe. Since it offers readers a far better understanding of the revealed mysteries of man's original state of innocence, the meaning of man's creation in "our image likeness" and the extent of man's sharing in the absolute fullness of the God-man's inheritance. The full extent of the unfathomable riches of the inheritance the Almighty Father has granted the God-man, the First-born of the Almighty Father.

It is especially in the first two chapters of Ephesians and of Colossians that St. Paul reveals what he calls the mystery of Christ—the mystery hidden for ages in God—the mystery of the fullness of the Father's intentions for mankind in relation to the Incarnation of the God-man. The mystery of Christ begins with the truth that God the Father, even before the creation of the heavens and the earth, intended first of all, and above all to incarnate his Beloved Son as the God-man of the race of Adam. God the Father, like all good fathers, intended also the most and the best for the God-man. It is the Father's will that the God-man have primacy in everything. This mystery of the Gospel of God is this mystery of Christ. It is the mystery that the entire race of Adam was from eternity chosen or predestined to share in the absolute fullness of Christ and that all men as brother of Christ share fully in the unfathomable riches of Christ's inheritance. That inheritance is the most and the best of all things the Almighty Father willing to do for the God-man.

When planing to incarnate his Son as the God-man, God the Father did not plan to create only one human nature and unite that human nature hypostatically to the Person of his Son. The Father willed to accomplish the Incarnation of his Son by having his Son being conceived and born of a woman. That woman too was not to be created out of nothing but was to have human parents from a race of humans on earth. Now it is obvious that the Father's will to incarnate his Son in this way would require that the Father create the universe, the world and create Adam and Eve. They would be the first parents of an entire race of humans on earth and from their race the Mother of the God-man would be born.

The Father would actually incarnate his Son by his virginal conception in the womb of Mary, a woman of the race of Adam. Then Adam and his entire race could and would truly become coheirs to the absolute fullness of Christ and coheirs with Him to the unfathomable riches of the Almighty Father's inheritance. The inheritance the Almighty and Eternal Father intended from all eternity for his First-born Son, the God-man of our race, Jesus Christ.

These are the reasons St. Paul could say that the Father created all things in, through, and for the God-man, Jesus Christ. "He [the Person of the God-man] is the image of the invisible God, the first-born of all creatures. In him everything in haven and on earth was created...all things were created through him and for him. He is before all else that is. In him everything continues in being " Col 1:15-16. St. John wrote the same: "He was present to God in the beginning. Through him all things came into being and apart from him nothing came to be." Jn 1: 2-3. This mystery of the Father's eternal plan will be explained in much greater detail in chapter four of this commentary. By accepting the understanding of Genesis to be found in this commentary persons will be adopting the mind of St. Paul regarding the mystery of the Incarnation of Jesus Christ and Christ's Divine Mission for redemption and salvation of mankind.

EVIDENCE THAT THE CREATION CHAPTERS ARE A NEW DIVINE REVELATION TO ITS AUTHOR

Happily for everyone, the format of the first chapter of Genesis manifests that the one and only source of information the author had and made use of when writing the account of the six days of creation was the special explicit divine revelation of the six days of creation. God is the only one who could have known the precise mysteries of the ultimate origin and destiny of all creation. God is the only one with knowledge of those mysteries and the one who could have make those mysteries known to the author of Genesis.

Persons who do not already know how the very prominent documentary hypothesis came to be and how it proposes that Genesis came to be compiled from several sources documents should turn to the appendix of this book for that information. Since the first chapter of Genesis in its entirety is an explicit revelation of God to its author the documentary hypothesis is completely in error and everything about the documentary hypothesis is without merit. The same is true concerning the second and third chapters. The hypothesis is full of demerit for it would decertify everything contained in the creation chapters.

Readers of Genesis can be assured that God intended that his revelation of the mysteries of creation be adequate so as to satisfy fallen man's many legitimate desires to know the material universe and himself, his origin and his destiny. The fact that the creation chapters are a new revelation to their author completely removes the documentary hypothesis and the innumerable enormous problems associated with it from any further concern for readers and students of Genesis.The Catechism of the Catholic Church still permits persons to believe that Genesis was compiled from source documents. However revelation and reason do not permit it.

The manner in which the direct revelations of God concerning creation were made known to the author for the purpose of writing Genesis differs for different chapters of Genesis. The format of the first chapter manifests that God's visionary-messenger gave his author-collaborator a day-by-day and a word-by-word account of the creation of all things. This visionary-messenger communicated a verbal account of the events of the creation to his author-collaborator as those events were being made known to him in visions.

In chapters two and three it is obvious that the human author writes as an observer. He can write as an observer because he himself is having the visions and writes what he hears and seeing happening or taking place in those visions. In chapters two and three the author is recording in his own words what he himself hears and sees God, Adam and Eve saying and doing. In the remaining chapters of Genesis, the author writes what an informant from God is verbally disclosing to him. The informant gives him the names of persons, their exact genealogy, the significant and pertinent words and actions of those persons, the principal events in the lives of Adam and Eve and of their immediate descendants and the legacy each has left to his fellow men. That revealed history begins in chapter four with Adam and Eve immediately after their expulsion from Paradise and ends just prior to the call of Moses and his mission.

The first three chapters of Genesis are to be considered history in the same sense that films, videos and sound recordings of past event may be considered history. The subsequent chapters of Genesis are history also for they are a reliable written account of the words, actions and events of earliest men recorded in the memory of the informant. In these subsequent chapters the author has recorded in writing the verbal communication he received from a messenger of God. This informer is recalling from memory the earliest of humans, their names, their genealogy, and the principal events of their lives and even their exact words. He is informing the author of them for the purpose of writing these chapters of Genesis. This informer was a witness and knew with certainty the words, actions and events he relates to the author of these chapters.

That a divine revelation of the creation could have been the source of the author's information certainty should not seem strange to anyone. In fact, divine revelations have often revealed past as well as future events. The fact that the creation chapters reveal past events should not be something strange or new to readers of Sacred Scripture. Daniel, Ezekiel, and others were given locutions and visions concerning future events. In these latter chapters of Genesis Moses is receiving locutions from one of God's angelic messengers who knew first hand the things he relates to the author. In these locutions Moses is informed of the most ancient words and actions of mankind.

The whole twelfth chapter of Revelation is a record that reveals past events. Those revelations were given to him by means of prophetic signs that he knew appeared in the sky on the first day of creation although he himself did not see them. They appeared in the sky on the first day of creation and were seen only by the angels—by all the angels. The first revelation was the great sign of a woman. The woman herself did not yet exist and that is the reason the revelation speaks of the sign of the woman appearing in the sky. In the revelation a woman appeared in the sky portrayed as the Glorious and Mighty Queen of the Universe. The sign itself makes it obvious that the woman is the great Queen of the universe for she is clothed with the sun, the moon is under her feet and she is wearing a crown of twelve stars on her head.

This Queen is pregnant. She is the Theotokos, the God-bearer, as the early Greek Church prefers to call the Virgin Mother of the God-man. The second revelation John speaks of is another great sign, the sign of a huge red dragon. Although this sign too appears in the sky the dragon appears to be on earth and doing outrageous things on earth. St. John does not record any sound coming from either sign except from the woman in the second sign. She cries aloud knowing her Son will come under attack from the huge red dragon as soon as he is born.

St. John says that signs appeared in the sky. It could be nothing more than a sign of that woman for that woman did not yet exist. For the same reason the second revelation is a sign. Satan existed but not his powerful evil kingdom. In the second sign the huge red dragon represents Satan's kingdom on earth which did not yet exist.

It is evident from Scripture that many authentic revelations have been verbal and very literal messages to persons while the persons were either fully awake or asleep and dreaming. When God wished that his authentic messages be deliver to unholy men, such as the cup-bearer and baker of the Pharaoh or to the evil king of Babylon, his messages were delivered to them in their dreams. God's messages to these evil persons were usually given in the form of symbols or signs that were very obscure and unintelligible to the persons receiving them. The persons would then need these symbols or signs interpreted for them by a prophet, a holy man or an authentic interpreter of dreams.

Not infrequently God gave very clear and specific revelations to holy persons in their dreams by means of messengers or angels coming to them. These verbally specific revelations were so explicit and obvious in their meaning that the persons receiving them did not need to seek their meaning from some prophet, holy man or interpreter of dreams. At least three such explicit revelations were given in dreams to St. Joseph, the husband of the Ever Virgin Mary. Cf. Mt 1:20; 2:13; 2:19. At the Annunciation, Mary actually saw and heard the Archangel Gabriel speaking to her. She really heard him give her the clear and specific message that she had been chosen by God to be the Mother of the Incarnate Son of God.

THE FORMAT OF THE FIRST CHAPTER OF GENESIS MANIFEST THAT THE FIRST CHAPTER IS AN ACCOUNT OF AN ONGOING REVELATION

The format of the first chapter of Genesis is the all-important clue to knowing the origin of Genesis. Because no commentator is remotely aware of the format for each day except the first day, it is most important that it be demonstrated. This is that format as manifest in the account of the second day of creation. After reading these three verses, the whole of the second day of creation, first answer the question, how many persons are involved in them. "Then God said, let there be a dome in the middle of the waters, to separate one body of water from the other." And so it happened: God made the dome, and it separated the water above the dome from the water below it. God called the dome "the sky". Evening came and morning followed—the second day."

How many persons do you think are involved? One? The second day and every day involve three persons.

The first person is God. God on each day says "thus and so".

The second person is the person who hears God say "thus and so" and sees God do "thus and so" and then always says that is exactly what happened. What happens is always what God commands each day.

The third person is the person to whom the second person speaks. He tells him first what God said and what God did immediately each day.

To whom is he speaking? Since he does not speak to God or himself he is speaking to a person who does not know what God said or what God did.

That third person is the person who is writing what the second person is telling him. He is telling him what God said and did on each of the days of creation. Since the third person is writing at the command of God he becomes the inspired author of the first chapter of Genesis.

Because this is the format for each day the first day could not begin by the second person telling what he heard God say. At the beginning of the first day nothing existed. There was no person to hear what God said or see the heavens and the earth come into existence. This format is also the reason the chapter ends with the second and third persons signing off their account.

The format of the first chapter clearly manifests that the writing of the first chapter involved three persons. The format manifests that the person is observing the creation of all things by means of visions. In those visions the person is hearing and seeing what God says and does. That person then relays to another person a verbal description of the creation he sees in his visions. That other person is therefore informed of all the happenings at the creation of all things for the purpose of writing the first chapter. What the person hears and sees in these visions he immediately and simultaneously communicates to the other person. That other person immediately begins to inscribe those messages being relayed to him and so writes the first chapter of Genesis.

This inscribing of the messages should not be imagined as having taken place over a period of six or seven days or many years but only over the length of time required for the visionary to verbally communicate them and for the author to inscribe those verbal messages. Perhaps the inscribing of the first chapter was accomplished in one sitting of an hour.

The person having the visions of the creation describes the creation as he observes the creation in the visions given to him by God. In these visions the visionary is seeing and hearing a supernatural reenactment of the creation, not the actual creation, for the actual creation occurred long before God gave these visions. The person having the visions becomes God's messenger to the other person, who becomes the human author of the inspired written account of the creation of all things or the inspired author of the first chapter of Genesis. That other person is the visionary-messenger's author-collaborator; for he writes what the visionary-messenger communicates to him by word for the purpose of producing this inspired written account of the creation of all things.

This ongoing communication by the visionary-messenger to his author-collaborator compares well to two persons communicating by means of a telephone. In this comparison the person on the phone is like a person in a stadium hearing and seeing directly a football game and at the same time is speaking to another person on the other phone at home. By listening to the other person he knows what is happening in the stadium.

In this format of the first chapter of Genesis only one person ever needs to speak, the person chosen by God to be given the visions of the creation. He is the one communicating verbally to the other person the words of God and sees what God does or causes to happen to fulfill his commands. In this format the visionary always first communicates in words what he hears God command or says and then communicates what he sees God doing to fulfill his command. What he sees God has done is always exactly what he heard God command to be done.

The person having the visions knows the person with whom he is communicating is totally dependent on him for information regarding the origin of everything. Both persons know that God has arranged for both of them to collaborate in this way and know that they are in this way about to produce an inspired account of the creation of all things. The person chosen by God to write the account of creation must write only the exact words the visionary-messenger communicates to him.

In this format the visionary-messenger on hearing the words God speaks immediately and simultaneously communicates them to his author collaborator just as the person on the phone watching the football game simultaneously describes and communicates to him the action of the game. On hearing the words of God being communicated to him, he begins to record or write them down. It is in this way that he becomes the inspired author-collaborator of the first chapter of Genesis.

The reality of this collaboration is the reason there is so much repetition in the first chapter of Genesis. The author-collaborator is not able to know anything of what the visinonary-messeenger hears and sees unless he tells him. The visionary-messenger tells him first what he heard God say or command. After hearing what God said or commanded the author-collaborator doesn't know what if anything happened, so the visionary-messenger needs to tell him whether or not what God commanded actually happened. Hence the visionary-messenger after telling him first the words of God's command he communicates to his author collaborator what happened. It turns out that what happens on each day of creation is always exactly what God said or commanded be done or happen.

This communicating of what happened is apparently very important to visionary-messenger and he has an empathic way of letting it be known. The empathic way amounts to telling it to him twice. He always uses the formula, "That is exactly what happened" and then using the words of God's command tells him what he saw happening.

The communication that took place on the third day most clearly exemplifies all of this. Then God said, "Let the water under the sky be gathered into a single basin, so that the dry land may appear. And so it happened: the water under the sky was gathered into a basin and the dry land appeared". Also on the third day. Then God said, "Let the earth bring forth vegetation: every kind of plant that bears seed and every kind of fruit tree on the earth that bears fruit with its seed in it. And so it happened: the earth brought forth every kind of plant that bears seed and every kind of fruit tree on earth that bears fruit with its seed in it."

For the purpose of revealing and writing the whole inspired account of creation, on the morning of each of the six days of creation, God gives a vision to the person He had chosen to receive the visions. In each vision the person first hears a command of God which specifies that certain things are to come into existence immediately. In that same vision he also sees God immediately fulfilling his command by causing those specific things to come into existence. Simultaneous with the continuing vision the visionary-messenger verbally communicates to the other person what he sees God does or causes to fulfill his command. If the observing of the creation was not simultaneous with the reporting of the creation the visionary-messenger should have said, "that was exactly what happened" but he instead says, "that is exactly what happened".

Some modern commentators consider the first chapter of Genesis to be poetry. They even go so far as to call it "The Creation Song". Their reason for calling it Hebrew poetry is the repetition that is so obvious in this first chapter. Ancient Hebrew poetry is not rhyme and rhythm as is our modern poetry. What is most charcteristic of Hebrew poetry is repetition. Repetitions that restate the same thought or concept but in different words. The repetitions found in the first chapter of Genesis do not fit the definition of Hebrew poetry. Its repetitions are repetitions of the same thought or concept in the exact same words not in different words.

There is reason for all the repetitions to be found on each of the six days of creation and why those repetitions are repetitions using the same identical words.

There is another reason for the repetitions in the first chapter. It is that when the things, which God commanded to come into existence, come into existence, the visionary-messenger needs to tell his author-collaborator that they came into existence for he has no other way of knowing. The visionary-messenger always informs him of this by first telling him, "that is exactly what happened" and then communicates to him precisely what it was he saw come into existence. He does this by telling him what he saw come into existence or saw happen by simply repeating to him the words of God's command that brought those things into existence.

It is always the same person, on the morning of each of the six days of creation, who is given a vision. In each of these visions he first hears a command of God specifying what certain things should come into existence. After each such command of God, what the visionary-messenger sees come into existence immediately is always precisely what that command of God commanded to begin coming into existence immediately. On each of the six days of creation, the visionary-messenger communicates verbally to the other person first what he hears God commanding and then communicates to him what he sees God causing to immediately fulfill his command.

On each of the six days of creation the person writing the account writes first what God commanded and then what God caused to come into existence in consequence of his command. The result of this divine arrangement and collaboration of the two persons an inspired written account of the creation of all things is produced.

The format of the first chapter is precisely the format that would be expected, if God were not revealing the creation immediately and directly to the author but to some other person. The person receiving the revelation then must communicate verbally the content of the visions he is having of the events in the creation of all things. This kind of communication between the persons is necessary since the author is not privileged to hear and see what the other hears and sees. The author merely writes down what the visionary-messenger tells him, what he is hearing and seeing in his visions of the creation.

The format of the first chapter of Genesis is obviously like that of two persons using telephones to communicate with each other. It is like that of one person, the person having the visions of the creation, speaking to the other through his telephone to the person and telling him what he is seeing and hearing in the visions of the creation of all things. This other person, with pen in hand, listens very intently and simultaneously records in writing the exact words he is hearing from him on his telephone.

It appears that scholars have completely overlooked this format of the first chapter. They have overlooked its great significance for the inspiration and authorship of Genesis. They have also overlooked its great significance for manifesting the precise literal sense of the first chapter.

The manner of the revelation of six days of creation is unique. It is revealed and recorded in a double format. The first part of the double format communicates what God said or commanded and second part of the double format communicates what God created or did. In the first part of the double format God communicates certain facts to his messenger by giving him visions in which he hears the words of God and sees what God causes to fulfill his commands. In the second part of the double format, the visionary-messenger communicates verbally to the other person, his author-collaborator, what he hears God commanding to come into existence and then communicates what he saw coming into existence in consequence of God's command that certain things come into existence.

The person on hearing God's commands and seeing what God caused immediately in order to fulfill his commands is not the person writing the account of the creation of all things. This latter person needs to be informed by the visionary of the events of the creation as they occur.

The visionary-messenger's way of reporting to the other that he actually saw the things God commanded to come into existence actually coming into existence is always the same on each day of creation. He first tell his author-collaborator, "And that is [exactly] what happened" he then always immediately tells him explicitly and exactly what things he saw come into existence. What he always sees come into existence is always exactly what God commands to come into existence.

The second part of the double format is identical to the format of two persons using their telephones to communicate to each other. It communicates a moment by moment account of what the visionary-messenger knows by hearing and seeing, for the other persons does not hear and see anything of what is occurring in the visions. Since the person having the visions is aware that the other person, his author-collaborator, is not privileged to hear or see what he himself is hearing and seeing, he is aware that the other person is totally dependent on him for information regarding the creation. He therefore knows he must report to him exactly not only what he hears God command but also what he sees God doing or causing to fulfill his own command.

The account of the second day of creation is typical of this chapter employing this double format that is employed on each of the six days of creation. The first part of the double is, "Then God said, 'Let there be a dome in the middle of the waters, to separate one body of water from the other.' The second part of the double format is, "And that is [exactly] what happened: God made the dome, and it separated the water above the dome from the water below it."

On this second day, the person having the vision states, in the first part of the double format, what God commanded to come into existence. Then, in the second part of the double format, states first: "And that is [exactly] what happened" and then specifies what things God caused to come into existence in consequence of his command that those specific things come into existence. What comes into existence immediately after he hears a command of God is always what God specifically commanded to come into existence in the first part of the double format.

In the first part of the double format, God reveals to the person by means of visions what He intends to create or do. What necessitates the second part of the double format is the fact that the other person, whom God has chosen to be only the writer or author of the creation account, does not receive any vision for hearing and seeing what God commands and does. Therefore in the second part of the double format the visionary-messenger must inform him what he saw coming into existence or was happening.

In this double format only one of the persons ever needs to speak. He is the person who is having the visions. The other person pays strict attention to the words the visionary-messenger speaks to him so he will be able to write down the exact words of the visionary-messenger describing the events of the creation of all things. The repeated use of this unique double format for each day throughout the first chapter manifests the existence of an ongoing communication and that ongoing communication is God's revelation of the creation of all things. This communication between the two persons, between these collaborators ends in the production of the inspired written account of the creation of all things. Thus the author-collaborator, by writing down the words of the visionary-messenger, has authored the inspired account of the creation of all things. The entire first chapter of Genesis is nothing other than the written account of the exact words the visionary-messenger of God has communicated to his author-collaborator, the author of the first chapter of Genesis. This double format of God revealing and doing and the persons working closely together in this way is indicative of an especially precise and important ongoing communication.

The visionary-messenger does not perceive the specific commands of God as addressed to him or to any particular person, but as efficacious operative divine decrees that cause specified things to come into existence. He perceives these commands or decrees as coming from God, for only God could have given such commands and fulfilled them. Hence the messenger could inform his author-collaborator of the fact that God was the one giving the commands and that God was the one directing him to inform his author-collaborator what he is to write.

In this situation, the visionary-messenger would necessarily want his author-collaborator to understand that the eight specifically different commands of God he had reported to him were actually fulfilled by God and that is precisely what he wants him to understand by his every "And that is [exactly] what happened".

If this is truly the format of the first chapter of Genesis, then the first chapter should begin on the first day as it does. No one heard the command of God that created the heavens and the earth and no one saw the heavens and the earth coming into existence. There was no creature in existence when that command was given. Hence the text begins simply, "In the beginning God created the heaven and the earth." This is the reason the visionary-messenger can say no more about the creation of the heavens and the earth than what he had been informed, namely that the heavens and the earth were created in the beginning or first of all. Since the visionary-messenger could not have heard that command or witnessed the creation of the heavens and the earth, he does not claim to have done so. He does not say after the creation of the heavens and the earth, "And that is [exactly] what happened" as though he saw it happen.

This is further evidence that the visionary-messenger must have intended his eight "And that is [exactly] what happened" to imply that he saw the coming into existence of all the specific things he heard God command to come into existence.

God arranged for these two persons to cooperate in the receiving, relaying and recording of the revelations of the creation of all things. The visionary-messenger nowhere in the text explicitly identifies himself to his author-collaborator, however the author-collaborator is aware that the voice he hears is not the voice of God, but that of a messenger of God speaking to him. Hence the visionary-messenger everywhere speaks of God saying and doing things in the third person.

After six days of communicating in this way the visionary-messenger wants to assure his author-collaborator that no more messages of God creating things would be coming to him, for God had permanently terminated his work of creating things. Since he is fully aware that his words to his author-collaborator have been his only source of information, he now feels the need to reassure his author-collaborator that his words to him were a complete and exact disclosure of all he heard and saw in the visions of the creation. The visionary-messenger therefore signs off with the words: "Thus the heavens and the earth and all their array were completed. Since on the seventh day God was finished with the work he had been doing he rested on the seventh day from all the work he had undertaken. So God blessed the seventh day and made it holy, because on it he rested from all the work he had done in creation." This is the first ending of the first chapter.

The second ending of the first chapter is that of the author-collaborator. He wants to end his written account by assuring his readers that what he has written is the whole of the exact information he received and that his written account is the exact words of God's visionary-messenger to him. He therefore fittingly ends his account with the words, "Such is (the written) story of the heavens and the earth at their creation."

Since translators, interpreters and commentators were not aware of the visionary-messenger and his author-collaborator they could not have suspected that the first four verses of chapter two could be the closing comments on their own account of the six days of creation. Their ignorance of these things lead them into mistakenly identifying these four verses as the beginning of another or second story of creation, even though no second story follows. In what follows there is no attempt of any kind to retell the origin of all things. Chapters two and three are limited entirely to the formation of the first man and the woman, their living together in Paradise for a very short time, their sin of disobedience and their expulsion from Paradise.

It is obvious that chapter two is a more complete and explicit account of what God did at the end of the sixth day when creating man male and female and in "our image likeness".

It was stated earlier that the visionary-messenger received his information about the creation by means of visions; visions that were supernatural reenactments of what God did on each of the six days of the actual creation. The visionary-messenger's only task was to faithfully inform his author-collaborator of what he heard and saw accomplished in those visions of the creation of all things.

The new problem to be pondered now is what evidence is there for stating that the visionary-messenger received his information of the creation of all things by means of visions? Why could it not be contended that the visionary-messenger received information verbally from God, which he then passed on verbally to his author-collaborator?

The answer is that the visionary-messenger on the morning of each of the six days hears nothing more than the command of God that certain specific things come into existence. On hearing that command he immediately informs his author-collaborator of the exact words of each command that certain things come into existence, then without hearing anything more informs him that the very things he heard God command to come into existence actually came into existence. The fact that the visionary-messenger was able to testify to the fact that those very things came into existence without hearing anything more from anyone about those commands was possible only because he saw those things come into existence. It was without hearing anything more from God, that the visionary-messenger informs his author-collaborator that what God commanded to come into existence actually came into existence. He could not do this unless he saw them come into existence. Seeing them come into existence implies he saw them come into existence which could only have been possible by him seeing them come into existence by means of visions.

Seeing them come into existence implies that the visions of them coming into existence were supernatural reenactments of the actual creation, for he saw them come into existence many thousands of years after their actual coming into existence.

Readers and students of Genesis should realize that God had many options available to Him with respect to the time, place, persons and manner for revealing to fallen man the mysteries of the origin of the vast universe and of man being made in the image likeness of God.

The manner in which the revelations of chapters two and three were given is very different from that of chapter one. The first reason for thinking so is the great differences in the format of these chapters. They do not have the format of an ongoing communication between two persons, as does the first chapter. The second obvious reason is that in chapters two and three the author writes as an observer and that implies the author himself is having the visions of those most ancient events he records in these chapters. The author can write as an observer for he himself is hearing and seeing what is happening by means of visions. He is therefore free to use his own choice of words to describe what he himself is seeing in those visions.

In these chapters, the author can write as an observer only because he was an observer of the formation first of Adam and then of the formation of the Garden of Eden or Paradise. He saw God lead the man into Paradise; he, unseen by the man, accompanies them into Paradise and witnesses the guided explanatory tour of Paradise, which God is giving to the man. He observes Adam interacting with God while they are busily engaged in making the creation covenant. Sometime later he observes the formation of Eve's body and observes Adam and Eve living together in Paradise. He could write of these things as an observer only after observing them and he could have observed them only by means of visions that were supernatural reenactments of those events, for he was observing them thousands of years after God actually created Adam and Eve in Paradise on earth.

Beginning with chapter four to the very end of Genesis, the author, Moses, is no longer having visions of the persons and events he is writing about. In these chapters the author is merely recording the words he hears from an informer, who is speaking from his personal knowledge and memory of all those persons and events. This person is perhaps the same person God had chosen to be the visionary-messenger for disclosing the words and happenings of the six days of creation.

In the latter chapters of Genesis God's informer is disclosing to the author his own precise memory of the names of persons, their genealogy and certain events in their lives. He begins that history with Adam and Eve shortly after their expulsion from Paradise and ends it with the beginning of the book of Exodus. He discloses the names of only the outstanding personalities involved in the earliest history of mankind. He gives exact information even to the extent of giving the exact words of these most ancient persons.

What evidence is there that in chapters two and three the author is writing a revelation he himself hears and sees in visions given to him by God for the purpose of writing his inspired account? What evidence is there that the second and third chapters are not only a new revelation but that his account is an account inspired by God?

This becomes evident from the first chapter's manifestation of the manner in which its revelation was given to the visionary-messenger and received by the author-collaborator. There the author is completely dependent on divine revelation for information about the creation of all things. Hence it must be supposed that the same author is still dependent on revelation for information at the time of his writing the second and third chapters, for he can have no personal or first hand knowledge of what he writes in chapters two and three. Therefore it must be assumed that the author continues to be in need of receiving divine revelation as his source for information about which he writes in chapters two and three.

Since he writes as an observer he must be receiving that information by means of visions which must be supernatural reenactments of what was happening for he is writing as an observer thousands of years after Adam lived on earth.

That the author received the information directly from God by means of vision is evident from the format. Since in the formats of the two chapters there is no evidence he is receiving his information verbally from God or that he is receiving information transmitted to him verbally by a messenger from God. Hence it must be that he is receiving information of what was happening by receiving visions from God. In these chapters there is evidence that Adam and Eve received information directly from God.

In the account of the six days of creation it is very evident that the author is receiving information from a visionary-messenger. The evidence in these chapters is that the author writes as an observer through receiving visions. There is no evidence he is receiving information by locutions from God or anyone. The author is obviously writing as an observer who hears and sees directly what he is writing about in these chapters. The only way he could possibly write as an observer of what occurred thousands of years before his time and thousands of years after their occurrence of those events would be by means of visions that were supernatural reenactment of those events.

Since the author himself was seeing and hearing what was happening, there was no need for any person or messenger to communicate verbally to him what was happening. No need for anyone to tell him what was said or done and no need for anyone to keep telling him, "And that is exactly what happened" as happened in the first chapter precisely because he was receiving information verbally. There is special evidence that the author heard and saw what he was writing about in certain peculiarities in the text of these chapters. What some of those peculiarities are and how they are evidence of the author actually seeing and hearing what he is writing about will be noted in the commentary on those texts.

It should be obvious that the three creation chapters are not an account actually written by God Himself, by the very hand of God so to speak, as some rabbis suppose and teach. A manuscript written by the very hand of God would of necessity do away with anyone being inspired by God for the writing of the creation chapters. An explicit divine revelation to an author would not necessarily require that God Himself address or speak to the author in the same way God spoke to Moses on Mt. Sinai or as the Father spoke to his Incarnate Son at his Baptism by John. In that revelation the voice of the Father was heard by all. The Father said of his Son: "You are my beloved Son. On you my favor rests." Lk 3:22.

God can reveal truths to a person by giving the person a vision in which that person hears and sees what God is saying

or doing. "He made it know by sending his angel to his servant John, who in reporting all he saw bears witness to the word of God and the testimony of Jesus Christ... Write down, therefore, whatever you see in visions—what you see now and will see in time to come." Rev 1:2-19.

ELOHIM AND YAHWEH ARE NOT USED RANDOMLY IN THE CREATION CHAPTERS

In consequence of the evidence that the first chapter of Genesis is a new revelation, the rather recent documentary hypothesis thankfully can be dismissed along with the many enormous problems that have followed in its wake. One of the enormous problems following in its wake is the placement of the Hebrew names ELOHIM for God and YAHWEH for Lord in the text of Genesis.

Persons who believe in the documentary hypothesis have attempted to uses the location of these names in passages of Genesis as a means of identifying those particular passages as lifted from one of several source documents used in the supposed compilation of Genesis. They can attempt this since they suppose that a particular divine name or some other peculiarity is more typical of a particular source document than of other supposed source documents.

The occurrence of the two Hebrew names, YAHWEH and ELOHIM, for deity in the text of Genesis, especially in its first three chapters, was the initial reason some scholars, since they did not know the true source of Genesis, became convinced that Genesis had been compiled from certain source documents. They then attempted to identify particular passages of Genesis as passages lifted from a particular source document.

These names for Deity cannot be used in this way to identify any passage of the creation chapters as a passage lifted from a certain particular source document for two reasons. The first reason is that these chapters, as is the whole of Genesis, are not compiled from source document for these chapters are new and originally inspired texts of God to only one person. The second reason is that the use of these names for Deity in the creation chapters invariably follow two definite rules that do not support the contention that these names can be used to identify any passage as lifted from any supposed source document.

The reason for this is that if Genesis were compiled from such source documents the result would be that these names would be used in a random pattern in the creation chapters. When either is used it always follows a pattern invariably circumscribed by two rules.

The rules for the choice of these particular names for Deity in the first three chapters of Genesis are these. The only name for Diety God's visionary-messenger speaks (he is the only person who speaks in the first chapter) is the name ELOHIM and that is the only name for Deity the author-collaborator hears from the visionary-messenger. He hears only ELOHIM and therefore writes only ELOHIM. He wrote ELOHIM twenty eight times in the first chapter. He never hears YAHWEH or YAHWEH ELOHIM. In chapters two, three and four where several different persons speak, Moses quotes all of them as using only the name ELOHIM. The name YAHWEH never appears alone in the first three chapters.

The names YAHWEH ELOHIM appear together for the first time in chapter two. It is only the author who uses them together and only when he is free to write his own choice of words, that is, when he is not quoting anyone, that is when as the author makes his own choice of names for Deity. An author would not have the freedom of choice of divine names when quoting someone.

The author of these chapters, when writing his own choice of names for Deity, writes the two names YAHWEH ELOHIM together. He invariably makes this choice nineteen times in chapters two and three. The above rules are followed in the first four chapters of Genesis without a single exception.

Genesis itself in the fourth chapter gives the reason these names for divinity are used in this way. The last verse of chapter four identifies the particular time at which men first began invoking God by the name YAHWEH. This historical note implies that only ELOHIM would have been used by anyone invoking Deity during the time of the first four chapters of Genesis. On checking back it was found that this historical note is true and accurate. ELOHIM is used forty one times by men, women and Satan in these first four chapters. Noah is the very first person in Genesis to use the name YAHWEH. Readers of

the NEW AMERICAN CATHOLIC BIBLE would find that in the first verse of chapter four the name Lord is used. But this is an error. Here Lord is an incorrect translation of ELOHIM.

In the creation chapters the two names YAHWEH and ELOHIM are used together only in the second and third chapters and then only when the author himself is making his own choice of names for Deity. The use of the name YAHWEH for Deity by the author writing the first three chapters of Genesis must not be seen as a violation of Genesis' historical note that the name YAHWEH had a late origin. The reason is that the author is writing centuries after the time the forth chapter dates man's first invoking Deity by the name YAHWEH.

In the first four chapters the person giving the author information always uses the name ELOHIM for he is always quoting someone who lived before the name YAHWEH came into use. In the fourth and following chapters the person narrating this history to the author is doing so centuries after the time the historical note dates men's first use of the name YAHWEH. He does so because he is giving exact quotation of persons.

These names for Deity are use fifty-four times in the first three chapters of Genesis and every use is in accord with these two rules without a single exception.

The person narrating the early history of man to the author of Genesis beginning in chapter four is speaking freely from his own personal knowledge and memory. It may be that the person narrating this history to the author should be identified with the guardian angel of the early community of man and that it was he who appeared from time to time to various persons during the early period covered by Genesis. He may have been one of the visitors Abraham entertained in chapter eighteen.

HOW THE AUTHOR RECEIVED INFORMATION FOR WRITING CHAPTERS TWO AND THREE

The author is dependent on the visions for receiving information to write the second and third chapters of Genesis. The second chapter begins with God giving the author first a vision of the creation or formation of the body of the first man. Some time after the vision of the formation of the first man, God gives the author a vision of a large area of earth. It is the area in which God created the first man and in which God will prepare a Paradise for the first man and woman.

God gave the author a vision of that area because He wanted fallen man to know what area of the earth God had chosen to create man and what area was the first or original home of man on earth. Any adequate account of the origin and history of man on earth must logically include the identification of the place that was man's origin and man's first home on earth.

When God has completed the formation of the man and the Paradise, He takes the man into that Paradise to show him the beauty and bounty of the place that would be his new home. God had a very special reason for introducing the man to the new home in the way He did. The reason is that God was concerned to prepare the man for the making of a most extraordinary deal God desired to make with the man.

The author sees God taking the man He had just formed from dust on a guided explanatory tour of Paradise. In writing of this tour the author is concerned about giving his readers a description of God in the process of making that deal with the man. Immediately after making that deal, the creation covenant, God leaves Paradise and when leaving God leaves the man in Paradise and in charge of Paradise. The last scene in this series of visions will be that of God expelling Adam and Eve from Paradise and of God securing Paradise against their returning to it to take fruit from the tree of life in Paradise.

FORMAT OF THE SECOND AND THIRD CHAPTERS

Apparently no commentator has been concerned to manifest that the author of chapters two and three is writing as an observer. The author can write as an observer because he is receiving visions of Adam and Eve he is writing about in Paradise. These visions are the only source for the author's detailed information regarding the mysterious origin of Adam and Eve. The author was given visions of Adam and Eve for the purpose of writing his inspired account of what God was doing for Adam and Eve and what Adam and Eve were doing while living in the Garden of Eden.

If the Mosaic account of the six days of creation, of Adam and Eve living together in Paradise and of their making a home for themselves in Paradise were compiled from written sources, is it not a great wonder that not a fragment of those supposed extensive source documents should not have survived more than a few centuries after Genesis was compiled? The reason it is no great wonder is that no such documents have ever known to exist except in the unfounded suppositions of some modern scholars. It is an even a greater wonder that Moses did not make further use of those source documents in his other extensive writings, if they ever existed, to give fallen men more information regarding Adam and Eve and their lives not already contained in the Genesis account. The fact the author never makes any such an attempt manifests that Moses, who understood well his own account, must have considered his account adequate for fallen man's understanding of the origin of the universe, the earth and of man himself.

If the author could have reasonably anticipated all the uncertainty and confusion his written account would cause in the minds of modern sophisticated scholars, it would have been incumbent upon him to write an account that would have eliminated that uncertainty and confusion. Since he didn't that itself indicates the fault is not with his account but with modern sophisticated scholars.

The author should then have written that much more un-

derstandable account of the creation of all things, of the creation of man and of the reasons for all he wrote of what scholars now consider mysterious happenings in the creation chapters of Genesis. The mysterious trees of life and of knowledge of good and bad, the reason for the command forbidding Adam and Eve from eating that fruit, the temptation presented by a serpent, the fall of Adam and Eve from grace and the precise reason for the apparent excessive punishment of expulsion from Paradise for so morally indifferent an act as eating good fruit from a particular tree. Why the author went through the difficult task of writing two chapters, which give so little light and caused so much speculation and confusion for fallen man. If those scholars understood well the literal sense of the account Moses had written for fallen man, that further writing they would know that it would have been superfluous

The writers of the New Testament, when writing of the origin of all things frequently quoted these creation chapters not only as proof of the truthfulness of their presentation but as adequate for fallen man's understanding of the origin of all things. These New Testament authors must have considered the content of these chapters as an adequate and certain description of the creation of all things, for they make no attempt to enlarge on the content of that account of creation. What the New Testament authors add to Moses' account of God's order of execution is God's order of intention when God created all things.

It appears that Moses would not have been adverse to taking further details from those supposed source documents to add them to his account for in the four other books of the Pentateuch; he does not refrain from giving very general summarizes of his account in Genesis. He wrote the following summaries. "For in six days the Lord made the heavens and the earth, the sea, and all that is in them, but on the seventh day he rested. That is why the Lord blessed the Sabbath day and made it holy." Ex 20:11. Later still, Moses repeats the same understanding more emphatically. "Think! The heavens, even the highest heavens, belong to the Lord your God, as well as the

earth and everything on it." Dt 10:14. "When God created man, he made him in the likeness of God; he created them male and female. When they were created, he blessed them and named them [both genders] man". Gen 5:1-2. In all of his further writings he did make explicit only one additional detail. It is God's calling the man a man; a detail not explicit in the creation chapters of Genesis.

One reason for thinking that Moses is the author of all chapters of Genesis is that when Moses, in his other writings repeats, interprets or quotes from his Genesis account he does so as though that account were his very own. Moses' authorship is implied also in the fact that his listeners and readers understood Moses to be saying that he had received all that information as well as other information by direct revelation from God.

A very good reason for thinking that Moses is the author of the creation account is what Jesus knew and taught about their authorship. "Do not imagine that I will be your accuser before the Father; the one to accuse you is Moses on whom you have set your hopes. If you believed Moses (including believing what he writes in Genesis) you would then believe me, for it was about me that he wrote. But if you do not believe what he wrote how can you believe what I say?" Jn 5:45-47. Since Moses wrote about much more than what he wrote about Jesus, the accusation Jesus makes implies that all the writings ascribed to Moses were indeed written by Moses. Twenty five times in the gospels Jesus, with respect to the five books of Moses, says, Moses said, Moses wrote, Moses gave, Moses prescribed and etc.

PREVIEWING THE VISIONS OF CHAPTERS TWO AND THREE

After the vision of the formation of Adam's body and before God takes the man into Paradise, Moses is given a vision of what is a bird's eye view of a large region of the earth. The vision is given to the author at that time because it is a view of the region of the earth in which God has created the man and is about to locate Paradise, the first home of man on earth. God gave him a bird's eye view of the region so that the author could identify for his readers the place on earth the man was created and lived, identify the place of the often-called cradle of mankind.

As God continues to give visions to the author he is given visions of God taking the man into Paradise and of God conducting the man on an explanatory tour of Paradise. God Himself gives this conducted tour of Paradise to the man because the tour will be necessary to prepare the man for making a most extraordinary deal between Himself and the man.

That entirely gratuitous deal, the creation covenant, gives the man the right to make a home in Paradise for himself, his future wife, family and leave it to all his descendants. After this tour of Paradise Genesis records God giving Moses a series of visions that include visions of the formation of the woman from a rib of the man and of the marriage of that woman to the man. In still later visions the author will see events that occurred during the short period the man and the woman were living happily as husband and wife in Paradise. With the beginning of the third chapter there are visions of the temptation, the fall of the man and the woman from God's grace and their expulsion from Paradise.

All of these visions are very clear or distinct visions of the persons and of what they are doing and saying. He hears the words of God, Adam, Eve and the serpent as though he was in their company but without anyone, except God, knowing of his presence. No one ever addresses him and he never says or does anything to anyone. The author writing as an observer and moving about them unnoticed is evidence that the author is

seeing and hearing everything by means of visions.

Thus, Genesis has sources, visions, but that is not the kind of sources the documentary hypostasis speculates about. St. Stephen told the Jews that angelic voices delivered the Law or the Torah to Moses. Cf. Acts 7:53. From the beginning of chapter four to the very end of Genesis, God's revelations are in the form of locutions, not visions. Someone, a messenger of God, is giving the author, Moses, a verbally precise history of early mankind.

That history includes in its account the exact names of persons, those persons' genealogies and the crucial events in their lives. The messenger's locutions begin with Adam and Eve starting off their lives in the cursed world after their expulsion from Paradise. It gives the names the of the first children of Adam and Eve, the story of Noah and the Great Flood, the Tower of Babel, and important events in the lives of the great patriarchs.

This account by Moses has the perspective of the Old Testament regarding the creation of all things. The perspective of the Old Testament is that of presenting fallen man with the details of God's order of execution in the creation of all things. The perspective of the New Testament is that of presenting the supreme priority the Incarnation had in God's order of intention when creating or doing all things ad extra. From the perspectives of these orders we learn that the Incarnation of the Son of God as the God-man of Adam's or our race, had first and highest priority in the Father's order of intention. We learn that God the Father's mental image "the our image likeness" of Genesis is John's Logos or Word.

DISQUALIFIED AS HEBREW POETRY

Because scholars were very uncertain of the sense of the first chapter of Genesis and found in that chapter many repetitions some scholars supposed this first chapter to be Hebrew poetry. It was even given the title "The Creation Song".

Ancient Hebrew poetry is not characterized by rhyme and rhythm, as is the poetry of modern languages. What characterizes ancient Hebrew poetry is repetition. When a person expresses a particular feeling, thought or truth in a phrase or sentence and immediately expresses that particular feeling, thought or truth in different words in a following phrase or sentence that repetition is considered poetic. It is necessary that the repetition be in different words not in the same words for it to be considered poetry.

The format of the first chapter is that of the visionary-messenger communicating with his author-collaborator and that necessitates repetition. The repetitions in the first chapter do not fit the definition of Hebrew poetry. The repetition found in the first chapter is the repetition of the same particular feeling, thought or truth in the very same words, while the repetition required for Hebrew poetry is that the repetition of the same feeling, thought or truth be in different words.

The first chapter's repetition is due to the visionary-messenger first stating what he heard God command and then having to communicate to the other person the very same words he heard God speaking.

Repetition of this kind is found in the account of each day of creation. A typical example of this extended repetition is found on the third day, but any day would do as well. Then God said, "'Let the earth bring forth vegetation: every kind of plant that bears seed and every kind of fruit tree on earth that bears fruit with its seed in it'. And so it happened: the earth brought forth every kind of plant that bears seed and every kind of fruit tree on earth that bears fruit with its seed in it."

Chapter 2

THE SIX DAYS OF CREATION

UNDERSTANDING THE ACCOUNT OF THE WORKS OF THE FIRST DAY OF CREATION

"In the beginning when God created the heavens and the earth, the earth was a formless wasteland, and darkness covered the abyss, while a mighty wind swept over the waters. God said, 'Let there be light,' and there was light. God saw how good the light was. God then separated the light from the darkness. God called the light 'day,' and the darkness he called 'night.' Thus evening came and morning followed—the first day." Gen 1:1-5.

With these words the visionary-messenger begins informing his author-collaborator, the human author, of the first works of the first day of creation. Already on this first day of creation a pattern is being established that will be followed on all the days of creation. According to that pattern the reporting of each day's work takes place in two steps. The visionary-messenger, the person God has chosen to be given visions of the creation and to be his messenger to the author-collaborator, hears the words of God's command. The words of these commands he immediately communicates to his author-collaborator. He communicates God's commands using the same words he heard God speak when giving his commands.

After communicating each day's command, the visionary-messenger sees the things God commanded to come into existence actually coming into existence and he immediately informs his author-collaborator of the fact that the specific things God commanded to come into being came into being.

The visionary-messenger on each day of creation informs his author-collaborator of the fact that the specific things God commanded to come into being came into being. He gives that testimony each day most emphatically in two steps. In the first step he always tells him "And that is exactly what happened". His every

"And that" always refers back to the command he reported to him moments before. The 'that' of "And that" always refers to the things God commanded to come into existence by the command he just heard from God. After every time saying to him "And that is exactly what happened" He then specifies to him precisely what things the "And that" indicated he saw come into being immediately in consequence of the command of God. For example on the fifth day, after saying "And that is exactly what happened" he immediately adds he saw "birds were flying in the air and fish were swimming in the sea."

The pattern is that every day he specify what things came into existence in consequence of each morning's specific command of God by repeating each specific command of God to his author-collaborator to inform him that the things specified in the command were the things that came into existence immediately.

In conformity with his position of visionary-messenger in the production of the account of creation he does not report hearing the command of God that created the heaven. He does not report it, as he cannot truthfully report, hearing the command or seeing the heavens and the earth come into existence. He could not truthfully report hearing that command or seeing the heavens and the earth come into existence for no creature existed when God gave that command. Hence as regards the creation of the heavens and the earth the visionary-messenger reports merely that the heaven and the earth had been created first of all or in the very beginning of creation.

The heavens and the earth were the first things created by God. They were first in God's order of execution. They had to be first in God's order of execution because living creatures need habitats in the heavens and on earth for their existence.

The words "In the beginning... and then God said" mean more than that the heavens and the earth were created first of all. The "In the beginning" along with "then God said" indicate that only after the heavens and the earth had been created could God proceed with his next work, the creation of light. The "then" indicates that the beings created in God's following works on the first day were in some way dependent on the

heavens and the earth being created first. Only after God had created the heavens and the earth could God proceed with the creation of other things.

The light created on the first day are the angels and their creation was dependent on the heavens existing for the heavens at their creation contained the eternal dwelling-place in which the angels were created and were to live. God did not want to create the angels until He had created the heavens with eternal dwelling-places for his angels.

This indicates that God intended that creation should proceed in that same order during the remaining days of creation. That order is that things on which other things are dependent be created first. In fact the account for the remaining days of creation, the dwelling-places or habitations of living creatures are always explicitly created before the creatures that would occupy them. Later it will be shown that this creation of light, which occurred on the first day after the creation of the heavens and the earth, was not the creation of material light but the creation of the angels. Material light already existed and there was no need to create material light. Material light is always in the presence of its material source of light.

The work of God that produced the heavens was distinct from the work that produced the creatures, which would inhabit the heavens. Just as the works of God that produced the earth and prepared it for occupancy by earthy creatures was distinct from the work of God that produced the creatures that would inhabit the earth.

When creating the heavens, God created dwelling-places in the heavens for angels and men and deposited in them the just rewards of all the angels and men who would inhabit those eternal dwelling-places forever. "In my Father's house are many dwelling-places." Jn 14:2. "Come. You have my Father's blessing. Inherit the kingdom prepared for you from the creation of the world." Mt 25:34. "Indeed, we know that when the earthly tent in which we live is destroyed we have a dwelling in the heavens, not made with hands but to last forever. We groan while we are here, even as we yearn to have our heavenly habitation envelop us." 2 Cor 5:1-2. It would appear that the abyss, God created and covered with darkness on the first day, was the hell God created to be the place of detention and punishment for all wicked spirits and men.

The first day of creation was the only day on which God created things out of nothing, ex nihilo. Thus all the angels as well as the heavens and the earth were created out of nothing on the first day. All living things on earth, whether plants, animals or men, were not created out of nothing, but were formed days later from the dust of the earth. Cf. Gen 1:19.

On the first day of creation, the visionary-messenger sees that the earth is a formless wasteland, that is, he could see that the earth was not in a condition which would sustain the life of plants or trees or animals. The very fact that he reports knowing that the earth was a formless wasteland and void of living creatures implies that he was informed that the earth was in that condition. God wanted men to know that that was the condition of the earth when He began his works on earth. From the beginning of the second day all of God's works are limited to the earth exclusively.

Since the author knew darkness covered the abyss but not the earth, even before God's special command that there be "light", cosmic light existed from the beginning. More importantly it implies that the specific creation of light on the first day could not have been the creation of material or cosmic light. Hence this creation of light has to be something other than the creation of material or cosmic light.

By stating "In the beginning God created the heavens and the earth" Genesis portrays the earth as something entirely distinct from the heaven or the dome of the sky, just as they are considered distinct entities by today's causal observers. Our sun is seen as dominating the earth, the moon and other heavenly bodies by causing changes in them at different times of the year. Those changes in the sky can be observed by persons on the earth. Since the air and the wind are earthly realities, God created them along with the earth and the water on the first day. "While a mighty wind swept over the waters". Air, water, and earth are three of the ancients' four elements. Fire being the fourth.

The earth had to be a formless wasteland and devoid of earthly creatures on the first day. This is in accord with Genesis informing us that it was not until the second day that God began works fundamental to preparing the earth to be a suitable habitat for living creatures. The actual creation of living things on earth began with God's second work on the third day. The order in which God creates and does things is always aimed at preparing suitable habitats for living creatures before creating living creatures in their suitable habitats. The only exception will be when God creates man. God creates the man immediately before forming the Paradise God intends to be man's permanent dwelling-place on earth.

THE CREATION OF THE ANGELS

The very first command of God, the visionary-messenger reports hearing is, "Let there be light". Immediately after hearing that command the visionary-messenger saw that light come into existence and informs his author-collaborator of that light coming into existence. He tells him, God said, "'Let there be light,' and there was light."

Some people do not believe that angels exist because, as they say, Genesis does not explicitly or implicitly state that God created any class of beings in the heavens called angels. They rightly point out that Genesis' account of creation makes explicit mentions of each of the various classes of beings as God creates each one of them. But, they say, Genesis makes no mention of the creation of any class of living beings in the heavens and that the author makes no explicit mention of the creation of angels in spite of his expressed intention of giving a full account of all beings created by God.

The creation of innumerable angels could not have been so insignificant as not to deserve any mention among all the works of God. Some believe that the omission clearly implies that God did not create any class of beings called angels and therefore angels do not exist. The Sadducees, who certainly knew these verses in Genesis, did not believe that there were angels or that God created any class of beings called angels.

The visionary-messenger manifested his intention of mentioning every class of beings created by God, when he stated: "Thus the heavens and the earth and all their array were completed." Here he clearly distinguishes between the heavens and their array. Without that heavenly array of beings, the heavens would be without any array. The heavens would have no reason for existing for no creatures would have been created to dwell in them.

The heavens didn't need to be created so God might have a dwelling-place, for God Himself. God has lived and dwelled in Himself from all eternity, before He created the heavens. The visionary-messenger could not have ended his communication with the expression of an array or host of creatures in the heavens, if he had not included in his account of the creation the creation of the angels. This is especially evident in the fact that no other class of creatures is known to make up or belong to that array of creatures dwelling in the heavens. The question remains, "where in the first chapter is there any mention or implication of the creation of angels?"

Some, when commenting on the explicit mention of light being created first after the creation of the heavens and the earth, propose that the reason light was created first is that light is the most sublime of all elements. They persist in that evaluation in their interpretation of the three verses that follow and in so doing turn to darkness the sublime truths of these verses. For it is obvious from the text that material light could not have been created first and that material light is not an element and not the most sublime element. Light is not employed as an element in the creation of anything nor is light an element in any usual sense of the term. Light is not known to be an element to modern chemistry or physics nor is it one of the four elements of the ancients. It is important also to remember that before there can be light there must be some material source of the light, such as a sun or star. To create light God must first create the material source of that light.

There was no need for a separate creation of light, for material light continuously radiates from the many sources of light in the universe, which God created when He created the heavens and the earth on the first day. Since light continuously radiates from many sources, if God were to separate light or move light from one place to the next, He would have to move the source of that light. If God intended to create material light by the command, "Let there be light", He could have done so only by first creating some new material sources of that light. The text does not indicate God created any new source of that material light when saying on the first day "Let there be light."

Most commentators, who believe God created angels, suppose that implicit in the command of God that created the heavens created also the angels, who would inhabit the heavens. Hence they believe that God created the angels simultaneously with the heavens. However, if the angels were created simultaneously with the heavens, that would mean God had departed from his routine of creating living beings only after He had prepared proper dwelling-places for them. In Genesis' account of creation these two different works are always separated in time and usually separated by one or more days. In the case of the angels God separated his work of creating the heavens from his work of creating the angels or that light. These works were not simultaneous even though both works occurred on the same day.

Both the Old and New Testament Scriptures often speak of the innumerable angels of God and of God giving specific duties or missions to certain angels. This certainly implies that God had created angels, for God could not be giving duties or missions to angels, unless they existed and unless they knew He was the one who created them. It is true that Genesis neither makes mention of angels by the specific term angels, nor does it offer any terminology that would make it immediately obvious that God created the angels on the first or any other day of creation.

The supposed complete lack of any special mention of God creating the angels has been reason enough for many persons of the past and of the present to deny or at least seriously question the very existence of angels or their creation on the first day. However is it really true that Genesis does not expressly mention the creation of angels on the first day? It will be presently shown that the text of Genesis gives many clues to the fact that the specific command on the first day "Let there be light" was not a command to create cosmic light or daylight, but something entirely different. The first chapter of Genesis gives many clues to the fact that the command "Let there light" was the command that created the angels and therefore the creation of the angels is not missing from the account of the creation of all things. Clues to the fact that the command "Let there be light" implies the creation of the angels can be discovered by a careful analysis of the text of the first chapter of Genesis.

The first clue is that Genesis does not explicitly state that the heavens, the supposed dwelling-place of angels, were empty or void on the first day, as it explicitly states of the earth. An empty heavens after the first day would imply that heavenly creatures or angels were not created on the first day, just as an empty or void earth implies there were no living creatures on earth on the first day. Genesis' complete accuracy and the fact that Genesis does not state that the heavens like the earth were empty or void must be due to the fact that angels were present in the heavens toward the end of the first day and therefore angel were created on the first day.

The second clue is why does Genesis have God creating light and then separating that light into light and darkness, after the heavens with its many great sources of light had been created already on the first day? What is this light that God creates and then almost immediately separates into light and darkness? It cannot be cosmic or material light for several reasons. On the first day of creation, when God said: "Let there be light" cosmic or material light already existed. If God had already created cosmic or material light on the first day when He created the sun, moon and stars, the natural sources of material light, why would he again create light on the first day and without creating any material source for the light? That existing natural cosmic light is the reason "Let there be light" cannot be the creation of light. The reason the visionary-messenger knew the earth was a formless wasteland was that that was part of the very first revelation given the visionary-messenger. That revelation was "In the beginning, when god created the heavens and the earth, the earth was a formless wasteland."

The third clue is that, if that light were some eternal great cosmic light or material light, God would have explicitly created that eternal great cosmic light without making any mention of the creation of some enormously great eternal material source of that eternal great light. Cosmic or material light always demands a material source of light. The creation of some great everlasting material or cosmic light would have required more than the creation of some great sun or group of suns as the source of that great and eternal light. So it would be very strange of the author of Genesis to omit reporting the creation of that everlasting great source of material light when the author though it necessary to explicitly mention that the sun was created to be the source of light for creatures on earth. Our human understanding and the otherwise completeness of the account of creation can not tolerate the omission of the creation of the source of that great material light independently created on the first day.

For the same reasons when separating light from darkness Genesis should have mentioned God moving some great source of light or the doing of something to that great source of light in order to separate light from darkness. These omissions imply that the great everlasting light God created separately on the first day could not have been cosmic or material light. Moreover, how could that great light be an everlasting great light, if its nature were material as is that of other cosmic lights?

The fourth clue is that in the very creation of the source of that material or comic light, God in his great wisdom would not have created that light in some inappropriate place but in its proper or right place or places. By doing that correctly in the first place God would have already permanently separated light from darkness and there would not have been any need for God to later separate light from darkness. Such an error is not possible to God. Implied in the fact that God found it necessary to separate light from darkness, if the light where cosmic light and not the angels, there must be some right places for light and for darkness. What is the right place for light? The only right place for material or cosmic light is in the presence of its radiating source. Also after creating that light with its source why should God have found it necessary, on the first day, so soon after their creation, to move at least some of that great light along with its source and so make darkness instead of separating the light from darkness?

The fifth clue is that Genesis portrays the creation of that light as the creation of a substance, as though that light was some substance. Light is not known to be a substance and this fact would imply a most disturbing kind of blunder on the part of the author. If light were a substance, then when light goes out or disappears a substance would be annihilated or at least would have to take on some entirely different form, but then it would no longer be light.

The sixth clue is that the text, immediately after the creation of that light, has God seeing the light as good. "God saw the light was good". Strange then isn't it that He need do anything to it if it were good! Why would God then separate that good light into light and into darkness! How is it possible to separate out from that good light some darkness! Also how is it possible to separate light into light and into darkness? Moses like other persons would normally speak of separating light from darkness in the sense of separating particular times and places of light and darkness from other times and places of light and darkness. But here God separates light into light and darkness! Just as though light were a substance!

If that light were all the angels, then on the first day after some of the angels sinned and became darkness, all the angels together would appear as a mixture of light and darkness. God could then separate darkness from light by separating the bad angels from the good angels.

The seventh clue is that the angels because they are spiritual and intellectual beings their substances are immediately intelligible to their own intellects and to the intellects of other intellectual beings. In this sense angels are self-illuminating substances. They live and know and understand by their own light, they are their own lights. God therefore could create all the angels using the analogous term light for all species of angels. Since angels are entirely spiritual beings and manifest or represent their presence by light, just as God, a spiritual Being, has often manifested his presence by light. Scripture often represents God's Being or presence by light. In Scripture God is said to dwell in unapproachable light. Cf. 1 Tm 6:16.

The eighth clue and best reason for believing that the command "Let there be light" did not create a great material light is that after there was no new source of material light separate from the light God had already created when creating the heavens with its sun and stars, is that we do not now see that light or the source of that light. That great light with its source of light should have been as lasting as any of the other sources of light God created on the first day. Why is it that we today do not see any light or source of light independent of the sun and stars created on the first day? Why is it that we today do not see that light which supposedly came into existence when God said, "Let there be light"?

The creation of the immaterial substances of angels was fittingly described to fallen man as the creation of light, for light seems the most immaterial of all material things. Here in "Let there be light" light is used as a symbolic as well as analogous term. The creation of angels was fittingly described as the creation of light because of their great intellectual light. The spirituality of these intellectual substances is the source of the light by which angels can know themselves and other spiritual substances as well as comprehend truth.

The creation of the angels' spiritual and intellectual substances along with their brilliant intellects was accompanied by an infusion of a great store of intellectual knowledge. That infused store of intellectual knowledge is the light by which angels understand reality and know the principles of the natural sciences and arts. In this sense Jesus could remind us that He is our truth and our light in this world and that we are to be the light of the world.

A much greater light than the angel's store of infused intellectual knowledge was the supernatural light of faith infused into their intellects at their creation, the light by which the angels know and understand revealed supernatural truths and mysteries.

Every angel's being represented these various kinds of light at their creation. All the angels were spiritual beings in possession of their spiritual faculties and of various kinds of knowledge including the infused knowledge they received at the moment of their creation. All these created realities have been repeatedly represented to fallen man by the very apt analogous concept and term of light.

Those angels who failed in their test of loyalty and obedience to God were no longer light but darkness later the first day. The separation of light into light and darkness on the first day was the separation of the evil angels from the good angels. For it was immediately after the separation of light from darkness that God calls the good angels day and the rebellious angels night.

This separation of the bad angels from the good angels included the separation implied in the bad angels being driven from their dwelling-places in heaven. It is also true that their darkness, compared with the light of the other angels, was especially due to there not receiving the created light of the beatific vision of God. The beatific vision is the created light or condition by which the good angels know God directly or intuitively by a permanent union of each angel's intellect with the Divine Nature.

This light, the created grace of the beatific vision, was a far brighter light than the combined lights of an angel's natural intellectual knowledge or the light of their store of infused intellectual knowledge or the light of their supernatural faith. The light of having their intellects united to the Divine Nature, the beatific vision of God, did not follow immediately upon their creation. It was later on the first day, that the light of the beatific vision was given everlastingly but only to those angels, who, after the consecration of themselves in total and eternal loyalty to the God-man, were eternally glorified. By the created light of beatific vision, the good angels know God face to face through the union of their intellects with the Divine Nature. It was primarily due to this created great light of the beatific vision, given permanently to the good angels after they made their total eternal consecration to the God-man, that God later on the first day calls those angels day. The absence of this created light in the other angels, Satan and his demons, is the primary reason God calls those angels night.

God's permanent separation of light from darkness did not make light and darkness alternate in time or place. That separation made both light and darkness eternal. The good angels entered an eternal day of light, while the evil angels entered an eternal night of darkness. On the first day of creation there began for all the good angels their eternal day of everlasting light, and on the first day there also began for the evil angels their eternal night of everlasting darkness.

The ninth clue is that if the light God created on the first day was the angels, then Genesis could rightly imply the creation of that light was the creation of a substance. It could as well speak of the separation of the bad angels from the good angels as the separation of darkness from light. In this way already on the first day of creation, God revealed that the ultimate divine destiny of intellectual creatures is either an eternal day of eternal light or an eternal night of eternal darkness in the abyss.

If the command "Let there be light" was in fact the creation of the angels, we might very well ask: Why wouldn't God have commanded "Let there be angels" instead of "Let there be light."

There are two reasons why God would not have chosen to create the angels by a command such as, "Let there be angels". No two angels can be of the same specific nature. If God were to create each species of angel by giving one command for creation of each species, then God would have had to give innumerable commands in order to create all the innumerable species of angels. The visionary-messenger would then have been required to report an endless series of such specific creation commands. To avoid this God has the messenger report the creation of all species of angels by one command using the analogous term light to signify all the innumerable species of angels. That analogous term light not only brought all the species of angels into existence but also gave all the angels all the natural and supernatural endowment as entirely free gifts except the gift of the created light of the beatific vision. The good angels would receive free the created light of the beatific vision later the first day when God called them day.

It might be noted that on the sixth day of creation God would do something similar when creating man in "our image likeness". By that one command God not only created man in the possession of a transcendent human nature but also in the possession of original innocence with a great store of infused knowledge and man had a supernatural destiny.

The tenth clue is found in the fact that Genesis, throughout the six days of creation, follows the pattern of God always looking at his work at the end of each day and declaring it good. The visionary-messenger reports at the end of each day that God saw his work of that day as good or very good. It is significant that Genesis records God doing this on all six day of creation except on the first day. On the first day, the visionary-messenger reports God seeing his work as good and declaring it good not at the end of the day, but immediately after He creates light. God does it before He separates the darkness from the light.

This indicates that there must have been an obvious reason

why God didn't follow his own chosen pattern of looking at his work at the end of each day and then declaring it good. The reason for this is found in the fact that the rebellion of some angels occurred at some time before the end of the first day. All the angels were good at their creation.

The rebellion of those angels was a very grave evil and their ejection from heaven reflected badly on the work of that first day. That was the reason God would not be able to declare at the end of the day that not all his work of that first day to be good and God would not be able to maintain that pattern of declaring his works of that day to be good at the end of the first day. God found it necessary to make his declaration regarding the goodness of the works of that day good after the creation of light; that is, immediately after the creation of all the angels—before God's work of separating the bad angels from the good angels and before expelling the bad angels from heaven.

This very change in the timing of God's declaration of finding his work as good immediately after the creation of light and before the separation of darkness from light is clear evidences that this creation of light was not the creation of material light, but the creation of something else. It was the creation of beings capable of changing from good to evil. This kind of change is not possible for material things, but is possible in spiritual beings. Hence the creation of light had to be the creation of spiritual beings. The only spiritual beings that would have existed on the first day were angels.

If this creation of light were the creation of cosmic light, and if God's separating of light from darkness were nothing more than the separation of areas or times of darkness from areas of material light, how could that be evil? If so, why couldn't God and Genesis have included the work of separating darkness from light among the good works of the first day?

HOW GOD TESTED THE LOYALTY OF THE ANGELS

All the angels were created in eternal heavenly dwellings and all in a degree of holiness, not sinfulness. The angels were not created in their ultimate degree of holiness and glory. Why then are there good angels and bad angels? Obviously some angels must have done something that was morally evil.

The twelfth chapter of Revelation informs us of something else happening on the first day of creation. It informs us that two great signs appeared in the sky on the first day. The first great sign was the sign of a pregnant woman clothed with the sun, having the moon under her feet and a crown of twelve stars on her head. The woman in this great sign is obviously the Great Queen of the Universe and she is pregnant with the Great Prince, the God-man, and the Supreme Lord of heaven and earth. The woman is manifestly "Full of Grace" and will be called such by the Archangel Gabriel at the Annunciation of the Incarnation of the God-man.

No commentary has ever asked and much less answered some very obvious questions regarding these great signs. When did these signs appear in the sky? Who saw these great signs? Apparently commentators saw no need to ask or answer those qestions. They were satisfied to suppose that St. John was the only one who saw them and that therefore they must have appeared in the sky some time while St. John was on the Island of Patmos. If so, why wouldn't someone besides John have seen them in the sky? The text does not explicitly ask or give answers to these questions. The text implies that the signs were seen by all the angels and seen by them immediately after their creation.

The text certainly has persons other than John seeing them. How does the text imply that it was the angels who saw the signs? Why would this Woman be seen on so huge a screen as the sky? Obviously the reason has to be that God intended a great number to see these great signs. Obviously, John was the only human to whom God revealed the fact that these signs really appeared in the sky. Why was it not necessary that John see them? God did not intend that these signs be seen by men for there is no record of any men having seen them. They appeared in the sky on the first day of creation before any man existed. The content of the second sign implies that at least Satan saw the first sign.

The time of the appearance of those signs cannot be fitted into the known history of man. At what period in human history would all men have seen them by looking at the sky? Surely the signs appeared so as to be seen by someone. If the signs did not appear in the sky to be seen by men then they appeared to be seen by all the angels. The signs appeared in the sky and filled the whole sky so all the angels could see them. If the signs were to be seen by some men it would not have been necessary that they fill the whole sky. The signs couldn't have been intended for men for the messages they contain were not the direct concern of men. What was the purpose of these signs? What do they reveal? The messages the signs contain are what all the angels needed to know immediately after their creation on the first day.

The first great sign manifests that the woman of the sign is the Queen of the Universe for the woman has the moon under her feet, twelve stars from the heavens form a crown for her head and she has the sun for her clothing. [This woman is Mistress of the sun as any woman would be mistress of her clothing]. She became Queen of the universe because she is pregnant with a Great Prince, the Son of God, King of kings and Lord of lords.

These great signs appeared in the sky on the first day of creation almost immediately after the creation of the angels. They appeared before God separates darkness from light. God placed the signs in the sky so that all the angels, who were created in the heavens, could see them. The first great sign was the very first revelation of God to any of his creatures. It revealed to the angels first of all the intention of God the Father to incarnate his Son as the God-man.

This sign signified to all the angels the Father's intention to make his Incarnate God-man the Supreme Head of all creation forever, the King of kings and Lord of lords. Therefore God's manifestation of this great sign to all the angels made it incumbent upon all the angels to immediately consecrate themselves forever in loyal service to the Incarnate God-man as their Supreme Head and Head of everything the Father intended to create. For by the will of the Almighty Father his Incarnate Son will be forever established their King of kings and Lord of lords and his Mother will be forever their Sovereign Queen sharing forever her Son's absolute sovereignty over all creation.

On seeing this great sign every angel was bound to exercise his freedom to acknowledge the God-man as his Supreme Head by consecrating himself forever to the service of the God-man. Lucifer coveted for himself the supreme dominion the Father willed for his Son, the God-man. He though his angelic nature vastly superior to the human nature of the God-man and that the superiority of his created nature made him more deserving and therefore entitled to supreme dominion over all creation. He therefore determined not to consecrate himself to the service of the God-man and immediately set about inducing other angels to follow him in rebellion against the Supreme Dominion God the Father would be giving to the God-man.

From the moment the first great sign appeared, even before the first man was created, Satan conceived and was consumed by a most intense hatred for the Incarnate God-man, his Mother and all humanity. Satan had a special hatred for the Woman of the sign because she would give birth to the God-man.

In retaliation for Satan's despising of his Son God the Father will give that woman an enmity for Satan by which she will destroy his pride. God the Father determined that the woman should be the one to crush Satan's head with her heel. In consequence of Satan's hatred for the God-man, Satan would have destroyed man as soon as man appeared on earth so the Son would not become the God-man. Satan would have killed the first man if God had permitted him to do so.

Satan was left with the choices of seducing all men into not acknowledging the God-man as their eternal Supreme Head and King and doing everything in his power to prevent men from ever benefiting from the God-man and his works.

Believers in evolution cannot conceive of spiritual beings or good angels and are equally incapable of conceiving of evil spirits. They disdain therefore the very thought that any spiritual beings could be determined to inflict the greatest of evils on men or be bent on destroying men. As the enemy of the God-man and of mankind, Satan would have killed the first man and woman immediately on discovering them in Paradise, if God had permitted him to do so. Therefore the most evil Satan would plot against the first man and woman is to have them doom themselves to death. He plotted to lead them and all their descendants into the rebellion of original sin. Satan is completely obsessed with taking revenge on all men for the God-man having been chosen for receiving Supreme Dominion over all creatures and especially over Satan himself.

Because of Satan's eternal hatred for all men Satan is always planning to lead men into committing inhumanities even against fellow men. Satan himself intends on inflicting by his own powers unlimited suffering on humans on earth and on souls in hell to the extent that God will permit him. All men should rejoice that God continues to deny Satan unlimited or unrestrained powers to inflict evils on men.

The eternal supernatural reward every angel received for consecrating himself in eternal total service to the God-man was the created grace of the beatific vision of God. This reward was given immediately on each angel entering upon his new status of a true and faithful servant of the Almighty Father's Anointed One, the Almighty Father's First-born. By their total consecration to the God-man each angel became an heir to sharing in the unfathomable riches of the Almighty Father's Son's inheritance.

The good angels immediately entered upon their new eternal day of loving service to their Supreme Head, the God-man. Their new eternal day is the reason God calls these consecrated angels "day" on the first day of creation. The angels who refused to consecrate themselves in total eternal service to the God-man placed themselves in the state of rebellion against the God-man. They entered immediately upon an eternal night of darkness and of hatred. This the reason God calls these rebellious angels "night" on the first day of creation.

These rebellious angels live in the eternal darkness of their interior enslavement to self and every evil. These rebellious angels, by refusing the goodness of serving the God-man, have dedicated themselves completely to evil. Therefore God immediately withdrew all supernatural favors from them and banished them forever from the eternal heavenly dwellings in which they had been created.

The second great sign that appeared in the sky on the first day of creation was that of the huge red dragon. Although the sign appeared in the sky, the sign shows the huge red dragon on earth. The huge red dragon is a violent perverted power on earth, Satan's kingdom on earth. The kingdom is headed by Satan and is dedicated to having men doing the most perverse things.

If none of the angels had sinned there would not have been this second great sign, for its content manifests that its appearance is in consequence of the failure of some angels to consecrate themselves in total eternal service to their Supreme Lord. This sign was a prophecy to both the good angels and the rebellious angels of what would be the consequences of Satan's rejection of God and Satan's leadership of the rebellious angels.

By this second great sign God manifested to all the angels Satan's secret intentions and unknown future. It revealed to all the angels the ultimate consequences of Satan's rebellion. Some of those consequences Satan himself did not know and others he would dread. The huge red dragon was a sign to Satan and to all the good and bad angels of Satan's future most perverse and powerful kingdom that would endure on earth only until the end times. At the time of the second great sign's appearance Satan had not yet formed his kingdom of rebellious angels and sinful men. Hence St. John rightly calls the huge red dragon a sign; a sign of that future reality. For what the sign signified did not yet exist.

The second great sign revealed to all the angels significant future events. The huge red dragon is first seen to sweep a third of God's stars from the sky. Satan will deprive the God-man of the loyalty of a huge portion of all men. The dragon then goes to stand before the pregnant Queen so as to be ready to devour her Son at the moment of his birth. The dragon, after his failure to destroy the Queen's infant Son, goes off determined to fight against the Queen and her other children. This second great sign reveals that Satan would be not only a very violent and inimical power working against men on earth, but also the chief adversary of the Great Queen of the Universe and of her divine mission.

The subsequent protoevangelium would inform Satan that the woman would in the end completely overpower him and his kingdom. The Great Queen will have her triumph over him in the world when she crushes his head with her heel in the end times.

The great Queen gives birth to a Son, the God-man, who is destined by his Almighty Father to be the only legitimate Eternal Supreme Head of all creatures and the entire universe. He will rule with unlimited authority forever over the angels and over all the nations of men. The realities indicated by these prophetic signs did not yet exist on the first day of creation and for that reason the realities themselves do not appear in the sky, but only their signs appeared in the sky.

All the angels were in their dwelling-places in heaven at the moment of their creation and at the moment they made their individual choices either to consecrate or not to consecrate themselves forever in service to the God-man as their Supreme Head, their King of kings and Lord of lords. On the same day the angels were created, God permanently separated the rebellious angels or demons from the consecrated angels by immediately and eternally glorifying the good angels and by decreeing the eternal banishment and immediate expulsion of the rebellious angels from their glorious dwelling-places in heaven. The good angels were eternally separated and glorified principally by being given the created light of the beatific vision of God. Thus the consecrated angels permanently secured for themselves supernatural divine life along with eternal happiness in their glorious dwelling-places in the God-man's Kingdom of Heaven.

Because the rebellious angels refuse to obey God's order that they immediately evacuate the marvelous eternal dwelling-places in which they were created, God orders the good angels to expel them from those marvelous dwelling-places. The good angels, because of their superior light of the beatific vision of God, were superior in battle to the rebellious angels and were able to expel them from their dwelling-places in heaven and from heaven itself.

The good angels, in accordance with the will of God, refrained from driving them into the abyss and confining them to the abyss forever.

The apostle St. Jude understood Genesis to teach literally that eternal darkness applied only to the evil angels and that their eternal darkness was God's punishment for their rebellion, for he wrote: "There were angels, too, who did not keep to their own domain, who deserted their own dwelling place. These the Lord has kept in perpetual bondage, shrouded in murky darkness against the judgment of the great day." Jude 1:6.

The twelfth chapter of Revelation explicitly states that the angels were driven out of heaven and fell onto the earth. Cf. Rev 12:7-10.

Satan and his demonic angels did not keep to their own places, that is, deserted their own domain, for by their deliberate rebellion they implicitly deserted their rights to their places and deserved to be forcefully expelled from their dwelling places. It was no surprise to the consecrated angels that Satan and his demons would refuse to leave and would forcefully resist expulsion from the marvelous and eternal dwelling in which they were created.

The bad angels or devils never received the created grace of beatific vision. These bad angels had darkened the natural light of their intellects through the influence their perverse wills had on their practical judgments. The great intellectual darkness of Satan is evident not only in Satan's deliberate perpetration of original sin on all mankind, but also in the draconian evil of eternally depriving the entire human race of every divine favor and the imposition of suffering and eternal death on mankind as something good. Satan and his demons, in their enormously perverse pride, considered their own eternal condemnation and damnation, in consequence of their rebellion against God, a good in comparison to eternally consecrating themselves to the God-man, their Eternal Supreme Head. Satan and his demons are always very much disturbed and frustrated by interior darkness and uncertainty. They can never have the certainty of success in their designs and efforts to secure a fulfilling and satisfying future for themselves.

In Scripture, good angels are often portrayed as beings of great light. The most beautiful and brightest angelic nature of all the angels at creation was the angel known by the name of Lucifer. Lucifer is Latin and means "Light-bearer".

In Scripture God's presence is sometimes manifested by a very bright light. God is described as a Being of Light and dwelling in unapproachable light. Cf. 1 Tm 6:16. Even though light can make visible only the visible properties of bodies and since God does not have a body, God can nevertheless manifest his presence in a particular place by making light appear in that particular place.

Lucifer, immediately after his own personal rebellion against God, began seducing other angels to rebel against God by making accusations against God and other angels. Lucifer's making of these accusations against God and other angels is the reason some angels immediately gave Lucifer the name Satan. The Hebrew word Satan means the Accuser. The fact that angels give names to each other in this way is evidence that the angels have some kind of language by which both good angels and bad angels can and do communicate among themselves.

In Scripture Satan is called a deceiver and is said to be a liar from the beginning. He deceives primarily by making false accusations and by making lying promises just as he did when tempting Adam and Eve in Paradise.

The very fact that Satan could set about making accusations against God and other angels in order to persuade them to join him in his rebellion against God indicates that all the angels did not immediately and simultaneously choose either to obey God or to rebel against God. God and their natures allowed them to deliberate for some time while they beheld the first great sign appearing in the sky on the first day of creation.

The Book of Revelation explicitly states that the demons lost their places in heaven. Cf. Rev. 12:8. This implies that God, when creating the heavens not only created dwelling-places for the angels but also created each angel in his own individual dwelling-place in heaven. Since every angel is specifically different in nature from every other angel, every angel required a dwelling-place designed for his uniquely different specific nature.

St. Michael and all the good angels when expelling Satan and his demons from heaven drove them from their dwelling places and from heaven without confining them in the abyss, the "bottomless pit" or hell, which had been created on the first day along with the heavens and the earth. "Out of my sight, you condemned, into that everlasting fire prepared for the devil and his angels". Mt 25:41. After Satan and his demons had been expelled from heaven, they made special choice of the earth, however unsuitable, for their principal dwelling-place. In the Book of Revelation it is revealed that they will be forced into the abyss forever in the end times in preparation for Jesus Christ establishing and ruling His Eternal Glorious Kingdom on earth and to await their final judgment. "The huge dragon, the ancient serpent known as the devil or Satan, the seducer of the whole world was driven out; he was hurled down to the earth, and his minions with him... So rejoice you heaven, and you that dwell therein! But woe to you, earth and sea, for the devil has come down upon you! His fury knows no limits, for he knows his time is short (before he is defeated and confined forever to the abyss)." Rev 12:9-12.

Satan, his minions of evil spirits and sinful men at the return of Christ to the earth to rule and reign in his glorious Church and Kingdom will not only be driven from the earth but will also be imprisoned in the abyss forever. They will be released for a short time at the general judgment of all creatures. "Then I saw an angel come down from heaven, holding the key to the abyss and a huge chain in his hand. He seized the dragon, that ancient serpent, who is the devil and Satan, and chained him up for a thousand years. The angel hurled him into the abyss, which he closed and sealed over him. He did this so that the dragon might not lead the nations astray until the thousand years are over. After this, the dragon is to be released for a short time." Rev 20:1-3.

The author of Genesis gives the impression that he intends to reveal the origin of all things. He manifests this intention by dividing all creatures into huge classes. Whenever God creates creatures or does things God always does those things by doing things for huge class of creatures. For example, God says, "Let the earth bring forth vegetation: every kind of plant that bears seed and every kind of fruit tree on earth that bears fruit with its seed in it."

"Let the water teem with an abundance of living creatures (fish of all kinds) and on the earth let birds (of all kinds.) fly beneath the dome of the sky. (That is exactly what happened.) God created the great sea monsters and all kinds of swimming creatures with which the water teems, and all kinds of winged birds."

If the creation of light was not the creation of the angels and if the separation of light into light and darkness was not the separation of the rebellious angels from the good angels, then the author of Genesis has failed to fulfill this impression he gave to his readers. For he has failed to explain the origin of angels. He therefore has failed to explain the existence of Satan, who disguised himself as a serpent when tempting Adam and Eve; failed to manifest the origin of the cherubim God stationed in Paradise to guard the way to the tree of life after God expelled Adam and Eve from Paradise. If God didn't create angels God created the heavens for angels that would not exist.

To the credit of Adam and Eve is the fact that they, unlike the rebellious angels, did not resist their expulsion from Paradise or threaten to return to it at any time for any reason.

The Paradise God formed on earth was never intended by God to be anything more than a transitory home for a transcendent race of men on their way to the eternal dwelling-place God had prepared for men in heaven from the foundations of the world. When creating eternal dwelling-places in the heavens for all the angels God created also an eternal dwelling-place for men. For almost immediately saints from Paradise on earth would begin arriving at the gates of that eternal Paradise of heaven and the eternal dwelling-place would have to be there and ready to receive them. All the angels of heaven now long for the day and the hour to see those dwellings occupied by the saints for whom God had prepared them from eternity. "In my Father's house are many dwelling places." Jn 14:2.

SOLVING THE ENIGMA OF THE WORD DAY IN THE SIX DAYS OF CREATION

One of the more obvious enigmas encountered by persons reading and studying the account of the six days of creation is surely the very perplexing problem of the meaning or meanings of the word day. Almost all modern commentators think that God did not work periods of only six twenty four-hour days. However their reasons for holding that view are based on their understanding of the physical science, rather than on reasons deduced from the text of Genesis.

For the purpose of completely unraveling the enigma of the six days of creation consideration must be given first to distinguishing the ordinary and extraordinary meanings of the word day and to understanding better the extraordinary meanings of the word day and of the word night. The first ordinary meaning of the word day is a period of daylight on earth; the period of about twelve hours; the time the sun shines and gives light to men on earth. The word day in this sense is opposed to night, the period of time when the sun is not shining on the earth. Another ordinary meaning of the word day is one complete cycle of light and darkness on earth, a period of twenty-four hour.

In literature the meanings of the word day and the word night are often used in their extraordinary meanings. Because of the common day and night in literature readers of Genesis must not limit or restrict Sacred Scripture's use or understanding of the word day and the word night to their ordinary meanings. Scripture often uses these words in their extraordinary meanings.

The extraordinary meanings of the words day and night are derived from things other than light and darkness being considered as light or darkness. That is when other things are considered as analogous to the light of day and to the darkness of night. The extraordinary meaning of the word day is had when good things or events are thought of as light and then the times of those good things or events are considered as a day. The same is true of the word night. When evil things or events are thought of as darkness then the times of those of those evil things or events are considered as a night. So for example salvation is a good thing and if salvation is though of as analogous to light, then the time of the coming of salvation is thought of as the dawning of a day, the dawning of the day of salvation. Likewise peace, gladness, joy, freedom, and life are good things and if thought of as analogous to light, then the time of the coming of those good things is thought of as the dawning a day; the coming of the day of peace, gladness, joy, freedom and life. It is in this way that Scripture speaks of the coming of the glorious Lord as the dawning of the great day of the Lord.

A day in its extraordinary sense or meaning has some properties that are the same as those of a day in its ordinary sense, but other properties are quite different. Days and nights in their ordinary sense are of the same length. A day in its ordinary sense is always necessarily followed by a night and a night is followed by another day. Both ordinary days and nights in their ordinary senses have a predetermined beginning and end and a predetermined length. Every ordinary day also has a predetermined morning and evening. Three hundred and sixty five such days make a year.

Properties of days and nights in their extraordinary sense are very different from those of days and nights in their ordinary senses. Days in their extraordinary senses are not necessarily followed by a night or night followed by a day. Nor do such days or nights have a predetermined length. That is the reason the first chapter of Genesis can state, "Evening came and morning followed". Genesis does not say of any of the six days of creation evening came and night followed. Three hundred and sixty five of these extraordinary days do not add up to a year. Days and nights in their extraordinary senses do not have a set duration, yet these days and night have beginnings and ends. An ordinary day begins with the rising of the sun and ends with the setting of the sun. A day in its extraordinary sense has no sun. The day begins with the coming of the anticipated good and ends when that anticipated good ceases.

The definition of a day in its extraordinary sense fits neatly and precisely the sense of a day as the word day is used in the first chapter of Genesis. So why wouldn't the author have used the word day in its extraordinary sense when writing the first creation chapter? The word day when understood in this extraordinary sense offers no difficult to readers of the first chapter of Genesis.

If the creation of things is thought of as good and if the work of creating is thought of as analogous to light, then the time of God beginning his work of creating is the dawning or the morning of a day, the dawning of a day of creating. Hence the six beginnings of the six separate works of creating are the dawning's of six days of creating. Then ending the work of each of the six separate works of God can be though of as the evening of each of the six day of God creating things. On each of the six days when God finishes creating things that day ends for evening has come. When God ends his work of that day, He looks at his work of that day and declares it is good.

Thus a creation day has a beginning and an end. A morning for beginning the work of the day and an evening for ending the work of the day. But the evening is not followed by a night. In this scenario there can be no night. That is the reason the text ends each day saying, "Evening came and morning followed." The text continuing with its extraordinary meaning of the word day could not say evening came and night followed.

Similarly the extraordinary meaning of the word night arises from times of great evils. Great evils are thought of as analogous to darkness, and the times of enduring great evils are thought of as night. The coming of those great evils is thought of as the coming of night and a night of evil. Hence times of evil are nights. There are nights of hatred, of war, of suffering, of destruction, of terror, of punishment, and of evils. This is the reason Scripture speaks of the evils of sin as darkness and their time the night of sin. These extraordinary meanings of the words day and night are the reasons the time of the good angels is called "day" by God while the time of the condemned and rebellious angels is called "night" by God.

There is even a day of darkness. It is a time when all expectations of men are for only evil and their occurring engulfs all time, not merely nighttime but the daytime as well. "Let all who dwell in the land tremble, for the day of the Lord is coming; Yes, it is near, a day of darkness and gloom, a day of clouds and somberness." Jl 2:2.

Some readers of Genesis have joined the enigma of the word day to that other enigma of the duration of each of the six days of creation and the duration of the combined six days of creation. Some persons, unaware of Genesis using the extraordinary meaning of the word day, think that the account of the creation would have been far less confusing, if the author would have simply chosen to call the time of God working or creating a period rather than a day. They think this because a day in its ordinary meaning is a time with a definite duration while a period is of indefinite duration. They suppose the duration of the days of creation must have been of various durations.

Since the author of Genesis was familiar with the extraordinary meanings of the words day and night, he most fittingly calls the time of God working a day. For the same reason he most fittingly calls the moment that begins the work of each work a morning and the moment God ended each work the coming of an evening, not a night.

Aware of the extraordinary meaning of the word day the author was not at all concerned about how long in duration was each day or how long in duration were the six days of creation. For that reason readers of the first chapter should not be concerned about them either. For in its extraordinary meaning the word day has nothing at all to do with any fixed or specific duration of time. Just as a day of rejoicing or gladness or happiness does not imply that the joy or gladness or happiness will last only twelve or twenty-four hours. Nor does it imply that the day of joy or gladness or happiness will necessarily and immediately be followed by a night sadness or unhappiness.

If the author had called the day a period his account would be minus all the life qualifications of work implied by calling the time of that work a day. A day is the time for work to secure some good or self-fulfillment. Hence the author had an added reason for calling the time of his working a day. The word day implies a striving or a progressing toward a goal or purpose, which the word period does not imply. The word period doesn't imply anything human, as does the word day. The critics of Genesis' use of the words light and day and the words darkness and night are not quite up to the class of author of Genesis.

Some creationists believe that each creation day was merely twenty-four hours in duration and have written chapters of books to show or prove creation days were only twenty-four hours in duration. Other creationists cannot believe they were so short in duration. They have written chapters to show or prove they were much longer even a thousand years in duration. In support of their opinion they quote 2Pt 3:8. "In the Lord's eyes, one day is as a thousand years and a thousand years as one day." Peter could have just as well said one day is as a billion years. Would a day of a billion years be any more satisfactory to them? Peter could have said one day is as one day with the Lord. Would any creationists have opted for that truth!

These creationists by their thousand-year day have merely added something unheard of to the mix of the enigma of a creation day without salving anything! God dwells in inaccessible or unapproachable light. That light is uncreated light. God's eternal light is identical with God. God's one eternal day is eternal because of the immutability of God. God's light is without beginning or end and God's day, not his ad extra day, is without morning or evening. It is only God's ad extra days that can have a beginning and an end, a morning and an evening. An ad extra day for God begins and ends when God begins and ends doing something ad extra. Creating things is a work outside God and is measured by an ad extra day. Any of God's ad extra days has a beginning and an end, a morning and an evening, just as God's ad extra work of creating had a beginning and an end. The seventh ad extra day had a beginning but does not have an end, because God's resting on that seventh ad extra day had a beginning but will not have an end. God has no intention of ending his rest by beginning another work. God's ad extra days are not necessarily followed by another day. The evening of an ad extra day of creation is the cessation of God's work, not the coming of darkness or the beginning of a night. Hence Genesis always says "evening came and morning followed" not that night followed.

As regards the number of creation days, when they began and ended and their duration are directly determined by the will of God.

An ad extra day begins when God wills to begin working or doing something ad extra. The day lasts as long as God wills to continue doing whatever God is doing. Each of these days began with a morning, with God beginning his work of that day, and each day ended in an evening when God willed to quit working. When God ended his work "evening came and morning followed" if there were to be another ad extra day.

Whenever the text states "Evening came and morning followed" it is indicating that a new work has begun and that new work began a new day. At the end of each of the six days of creation the text states "Evening came and morning followed". It does this at the end of the sixth day even though the sixth day was the last day of creating because the seventh day of God resting from work followed. It will be an eternal day for God's resting and that rest will continue forever.

The seventh ad extra day began immediately after the evening of sixth day. God began his rest on the morning of the seventh day and since God's rest will never end the seventh day will never have an evening or end. Hence there can never be an eight ad extra day. All of us now living on earth and will be living eternally in heaven live in God's eternal seventh ad extra day.

The sixth "evening came and morning followed" of God's ad extra days cannot be used as evidence that days for men on earth are intended by God, as is the tradition among Jews, to begin at sundown or evening rather than with its morning. If each of God's ad extra six days began with God's work, man's days also should begin with work, with man beginning his activity. Men begin their work or activity of the day with the coming of light, with morning light not with the darkness of the coming night. With the coming of darkness men cease their day's activity and begin their rest from work. "At the rising of the sun they (animals) steal away and go to rest in their dens. Man goes forth to his work to labor till evening falls." Ps 104:22-23.

The author of Genesis gives readers ample warning of his use and meaning of the word day, the word night and the duration of each. The author five times describes or defines a creation day as having a morning and an evening, not as a day and a night. A creation day is the length of time God works ad extra by his own eternal light. God's working or resting ad extra is always a day, never a night. God is always in the light, He is light. He is never in darkness or in nighttime.

Genesis begins defining the meaning of the word day by defining a day for the angels. After creating light, that is the angels, God on the first day separates that light into light and into darkness. God's separating of darkness from light resulted in light and darkness existing simultaneously. It did not result in light and darkness continuing to alternate. Both light and darkness became eternal. Their separation made the day for the good angels eternal and made the night for Satan and his demons eternal. By that separation of darkness from light God accomplished the eternal separation of the good angels from the bad angels.

For the angels consecrated to the God-man, life is unending light, their eternal day. For these angels there is no darkness or night, only one endless day. For the rebellious angels life is unending darkness, no light or day, only eternal night. After the separation of darkness from light God calls the good angels day. Day for them is a lifetime of light in service to the God-man. God sees the existence of the rebellious angels as darkness; an existence shrouded in eternal murky darkness. ''There shall be one continuous day (it is known to the Lord), not day and night, for in the evening time there shall be light." Zec 14:7. "There were angels, too, who did not keep to their own domain, who deserted their dwelling place. These the Lord has kept in perpetual bondage, shrouded in murky darkness against the judgment of the great day." Jude 1:6. It is in this way that we find the meaning Genesis gives to the word day and to the word night.

God's ad extra day does not end in darkness because there is no ad extra night for God. There is no need for an ad extra night for God to refresh Himself after his work. God is never diminished in any way by his works and there is no need for God to refresh Himself. "And the night shall be no more [the kind of night men experience on earth]; they need no light of lamps or the sun, for the Lord God will be their light, and they shall reign for ever and ever." Rev 22:4-5.

How long in duration was a creation day? How long is a day in its extraordinary meaning? How long is a day of peace, a day of hope, or a day of freedom? The length of a creation day as well as the number of creation day is completely and directly under the control of God's will. Since each of these ad extra days begins, not with the coming of light but with God beginning his working of creating. Since each day ends when God has completed his predetermined work an ad extra day can have no set duration. The evening of a creation day is followed by the morning of the following day, not by a night. Ad extra days do not come by the necessity of some cycle, but by God freely choosing to begin another work or begin resting. That new work or rest begins the morning that begins a new day.

The interval between the evening of the previous day and the morning of the following day of creation has no name in Genesis. It cannot be a night. In Genesis that interval is treated as an ad extra period of inactivity. The length of each of these intervals is not specified, but obviously, like a day, their duration is completely under the control of God's free will and therefore can be of any duration.

With these definitions and examples in mind it can be seen that Genesis makes no attempt to specify the length of any creation day or the length of any interval between creation days or the total span of time of the six days of creation. On the morning of the seventh day God began his rest and that rest and day has continued even until now and will continue throughout eternity

The duration of a particular day of creation measured in terms of time for man on earth might be discovered indirectly by discovering the time or duration God took to do the work of that particular day. Men could discover that duration if men could determine how much time would naturally be consumed doing the work of that particular day. If it could be proven that the animals began roaming the earth a hundred million years before men began to live on earth and if the animals were created on the morning of the sixth day, then if men were created at the end of the sixth day, that would then be hard evidence that the sixth ad extra day of creation was a hundred million years in duration.

The duration of the days God designed for man on earth was established on the fourth of God's ad extra day when God made the final adjustments in the positions of the earth, moon and sun. "God set them in the dome of the sky, to shed light upon the earth, to govern the day and the night and to separate the light from the darkness." In the time system God designed and established for man on earth, a day is not a morning and an evening, but a period of light followed by a period of darkness; a day followed by a night. A day for man begins with the coming of light for it is then that man begins his work or activity of the day. The light of the day for man on earth is ordered to work and leisure activity, for light both greatly aids and limits man's activity on earth; aids and limits the work to be accomplished by men on earth.

A day on earth must have a period of light, because the very life of some creatures is directly dependent on light while other living beings require light more indirectly. A day on earth must have a period of darkness to bring about the cessation of activity, for many living beings, such as animals and men become exhausted by their daily activity. These living beings must come to a rest to allow themselves to be refreshed physically and mentally. Hence in the time system for living things on earth, light and darkness must alternate and keep on alternating to permit life to flourish on earth.

On earth one complete cycle of light and darkness is called a day. On earth a cycle of light and darkness is continually being added to a completed cycle of light and darkness. For saints in heaven a day will be one eternal day of continuous light and activity. Their day will be like the eternal day enjoyed by the good angels. For unrepentant sinners from among men confined to the abyss, the "bottomless pit", there will no longer be earthly days. Sinners in the abyss will suffer in unending darkness; in the eternal darkness of an unending night of hopelessness and frustration. The same eternal hopelessness envelops Satan and his demons in the darkness of the unending night of the abyss.

Time and the passage of time on earth are not in the control of man, but in the control of God. Man does not start or stop the clock of time; speed up or slow down the clock of time, men merely use a clock to divide mentally the passing of time and dividing days and nights into hours or watches. In moving systems time slows down and that makes it possible at least in theory for men to travel in time but only forward in time.

It seems necessary that both good angels and devils, since they are creatures, would need to devise some unit of duration to measure and divide their eternal day and their eternal night at least conceptually, if they are to act in any unison and on any schedule. They might also have divided their eternal day and eternal night into a before and after Christ's Incarnation just as most men now do on earth or into a before or an after their condemnation.

The author of Genesis was fully aware of the various meanings of the word day and could not have had any intention of implying that the creation of all things was accomplished in one continuous period equal in duration to six days for man on earth. We should realize that the author of Genesis was aware that God's ad extra six days of creation began before God on the fourth day made final adjustments in the positions of earth and the moon in relation to the sun. He knew God did this to divide time on earth into days and nights and before man began dividing days into hours and nights into watches

UNDERSTANDING THE WORKS OF THE SECOND DAY OF CREATION

Then God said, "Let there be a dome in the middle of the waters, to separate one body of waters from the other." And that is exactly what happened: God made the dome and it separated the water above the dome from the water below it. God called the dome 'the sky'. Evening came, and morning followed—the second day." Gen 1:6-8.

The works on the second day of creation are the subject of the visionary-messenger's second report to his author-collaborator, Moses, the author of Genesis. Of this second report the author-collaborator writes of hearing the visionary-messenger telling him that he heard God command first that certain specific things come into existence and second of seeing all the very specific things God commanded to come into existence actually coming into existence. The visionary-messenger always gives compound assurances to his author-collaborator of what he sees God doing in his visions. He tells him first, "And that is exactly what happened" and secondly tells him exactly what it was he saw happen or come into existence by assuring him: "God made the dome, and it separated the water above the dome from the water below it."

The format of all six days manifests that the visionary-messenger was not satisfied merely to tell his author-collaborator, "And that is exactly what happened" for after telling him that he always goes on to specify exactly what he would see happening after hearing each specific command of God that cause certain things to come into being.

The forces at work in nature during the first day of creation left or caused the earth to be in a state of chaos. Genesis states that at the end of the first day the earth was without form and was empty or void. Those forces were unable to produce conditions on our earth or on other planets, for that matter, suitable for any creature to live on earth much less permit life to evolve on earth. In this respect the earth was like the other planets. For we know them to be such even to this day by our modern capabilities for observing conditions on other plants.

Both Viking probes to Mars proved conditions there were anti-life. That was a big disappointment for evolutionists and it was not freely admitted to the public. Mars has been from its beginning in chaos and completely void of living things even though water may have been abundant. Mars was like the earth at the end of the first day of creation.

Many wonder why God created so enormously large material universe if He created life only on this earth, if there is no extra terrestrial life. Our enormously large material universe is prophetic of and slightly revealing of the material aspects of the life God has planed for his glorified saints. The glorified saints will have bodies that will require a home in a material universe. The many billions of saints enjoying the fullness of a glorified life without end will require an enormous material universe for a home. The saints in heaven do not have bodies and are not in need of a home in a material universe.

On the second day and on all the following days of creation God's work is limited to our earth as we should expect for God's intention was limited to creating life on earth. On the second day God begins causing those changes and conditions on earth that would be needed to prepare the earth to be a suitable habitat for living creatures. At the end of the first day our earth was completely covered by water.

The first thing God does on the second day is a reduction of the excess of water on earth. God does not move the excess water over the edge of a flat earth, but raises a dome over the flat earth and moves the surplus water onto that dome. Then God gathers the remaining water into a basin by raising mountains, ridges and hills so the dry land could appear. On the fourth day God will make adjustments in the relations of the earth to the sun and the moon in the sky.

On this second day, God wills not only to establish order on earth but also wills that the order be permanent. He makes it permanent by creating creatures with immutable natures. A nature acts in only one way. The specific nature of a being is the cause of its specific set of actions. Its nature causes its life to be of a specific kind. On following days God will make the earth fertile and make living creatures fertile so that the earth's void will be always filled with all kinds of living creatures.

Genesis teaches that the absolute beginning of all things in time was the creation of the heavens and the earth from nothing; reality coming into being from nothing. The absolute beginning of living things on earth was their formation from dust by God. Here Genesis is teaching or implying the immutability of created natures. Genesis is unlike and contrary to the myths of the ancient pagan nations; the Creator never changes the nature of one thing into that of another. This impossible kind of change is a favorite tactic of the ignorance and dishonesty of the pagan myth fabricators and perveacators. Their myths often tell of the gods changing one species into another species. Consequently, their myths can not truly explain the ultimate origin of anything or even of any species. Such myths merely promoted the particular cults of mythical gods, who are neither omniscient nor omnipotent.

The immutability of the natures of all creatures is the basis for the eternal stability of the order God established on earth. Immutable natures can never change or be changed and since immutable natures are the causes of the specific kinds of actions or kind of life of every specific kind of creature, immutable created natures will always and everywhere cause only those actions that are proper to their specific natures. In this way every species can and will continue to fulfill its particular specific function on earth and so preserve until the end of time the order God established among creatures. The apostle Paul saw the need for the stability of a right and good order for all living creatures on earth. He wrote to the Corinthians: "As it is, God has set each member of the body in the place he wanted it to be... God has so constructed the body... that there be no dissension in the body." 1 Cor 12:18-25. God's construction of an orderly universe is evident in the created material universe.

Permanent order among non-living things is due to the forces of their self-maintenance. God has established two principles for stability in creation. The first is: all non-living things, things not having any living nature, from rocks down to atoms and subatomic particles, have no ability to act or cause change contribute to stability in realty. Non-living things always, in every way and every respect resist change to the extent of the physical energy within them. The second principle for stability in creation is that living things are limited to acting in accord with their nature and their natures are immutable. God hung the sun, moon, and stars in the dome of the sky to shed their light on the earth and to be permanent causes of certain motions on earth besides causing the ongoing change of cycles of the earth's seasons. "Let them mark the fixed times, the days and the years, and serve as luminaries in the dome of the sky, to shed light upon the earth." Gen 1:14-15.

The first day is the only day on which God created things from nothing, ex nihilo, for it was on that day only that God created the heavens, the earth and the spiritual angels out of nothing. On the third, fifth, and sixth days God will cause living things to appear on earth, but they will not be created from nothing. Genesis has God forming the animals from dust. God would form only the first man, Adam, from the dust of the earth. Eve was formed from a rib of Adam. God also made the earth fertile and that fertility enables all the various kinds of plants and trees to grow, mature, bear fruit and multiply according to their kind.

When in the beginning God created the heavens and earth, He created the original elements and compounds from nothing, ex nihilo. Once God had created these original elements and compounds ex nihilo, God was free to use them in the composition of greater non-living things and in the substances of living beings. God did not need to create cosmic light everywhere for the sources of cosmic light radiate their light into distant places. Light like the wind was not one of the elements or substances God created from nothing on the first day or any other day. Light can be seen when the electrons of that source of light leave or are forced out of their orbits around the nucleus of elements. This is the reason even the crushing of ice produces noticeable light in a very dark room or place.

From the beginning of creation and during the days of creation all of God's actions were directed toward making the earth, its dry land, its seas and its air suitable habits for living creatures. God's works from the first day of creation to the end of the sixth day were directed to preparing the earth a suitable dwelling-place for a race of humans from which the God-man would take his human nature. God, already on this second day of creation, began remedying the earth's bleak and inhospitable conditions for living beings. God's intention was to produce conditions on earth that would make it possible for man to live on the earth in great style. He first remedies conditions that make the earth unsuitable for all plants and animals. When that was complete God prepares a special place for man, a Paradise to be the home of the first humans.

All of God's actions during the early days of creation were directed to remedying all adverse conditions on earth and making the earth fertile. He first makes a dome high above the earth and moves earth's excess water onto that dome and then, on the fourth day, He repositions the earth into a proper position in relation to the sun and moon.

By means of this dome God permanently diminished the amount of water on the surface of the earth and, at the same time, makes fresh rainwater available for making the earth fertile and plants fruitful. Genesis implies that the water falling as rain on the earth from the dome ultimately finds its way back to the dome. If it did not God would have to continually create water on the dome for rain and continually annihilate surplus water on earth to prevent the rainwater from again flooding the entire surface of the earth. The author of Genesis is very much aware that this dome explains how plants and trees on earth get the fresh water they must have to live, grow, bear fruit and be of use to all animals and especially to man.

The apostle Peter, when confronting certain false teachers, takes literally Genesis' statement that certain things or conditions that existed in the heavens and on earth on the first day were later changed. Peter teaches that it was an error on the part of certain persons to think that the heavens and the earth, as they saw them in their day, were, as they said, in that same condition at their creation. Peter tells them they are in error, because on the second day, God made the dome, which formerly did not exist, and on the third day made changes on earth to make the dry land appear. Cf. 2 Pt 3:5-7. Peter warns also of the coming great day of the Lord with its further changes "on that day the heavens [of Peter's day] will vanish with a roar; they will be destroyed by fire, and the earth and all its deeds will be made manifest." Pt 3:10.

The dome or the sky must not to be confused with the heavens created on the first day. The heavens are above the dome of the sky. It was on the fourth day that God hung or repositioned the sun, moon, and stars in their relation to the earth.

UNDERSTANDING THE WORKS OF THE THIRD DAY OF CREATION

Then God said, "Let the water under the sky be gathered into a single basin, so that the dry land may appeared." And that is exactly what happened: the water under the sky was gathered into its basin, and the dry land appeared. God called the dry land 'the earth', and the basin of water he called 'the sea.' God saw how good it was. Then God said, "Let the earth bring forth vegetation; every kind of plant that bears seed and every kind of fruit tree on earth that bears fruit with its seed in it." And that is exactly what happened: the earth brought forth every kind of plant that bears seed and every kind of fruit tree on earth that bears fruit with its seed in its fruit God saw how good it was. Evening came, and morning followed—the third day". Gen 1:9-13

On the morning of the third day, the third ad extra day, God's visionary-messenger first reports hearing God's command that certain things come into existence. He immediately informs his author-collaborator of that command of God that certain specific things come into existence. After reporting that command, the visionary-messenger sees the specific things God commanded to come into existence coming into existence before his very eyes and reports: "That is exactly what happened" and then explicitly tells him what specific things just came into being. On all the six days of creation what comes into being after every specific command of God is always what God specifically commanded to come into being. That is the reason the visionary-messenger can always say, "And that is exactly what happened".

The author-collaborator, on each day of creation, after being informed what God commanded, hears the visionary-messenger testify to the power of that specific command of God. The visionary-messenger always does this by using his formula "And that is [exactly] what happened." The visionary-messenger's "And that is exactly what happened" is always followed by the visionary-messenger specifying to him what things he saw happen in consequence of every specific command of God. What he saw happen was what he heard God command to happen or to come into existence.

On the third day the visionary-messenger finds God continuing to improve on the inhospitable conditions on earth. God reforms the surface of the earth in preparation for the creation of living plants and animals. God will be creating them during the next two day. God gathers the remaining waters on the surface of the earth into a basin and thus forms the sea. God calls the newly formed dry land "the earth" and the water gathered into the basin, God calls "the sea".

During the next two days God will be creating living creatures on earth. Some specifically designed for swimming in the sea or walking on the dry land or flying in the air. God makes all of the newly created creatures fertile so they will eventually fill the sea, the air and the dry land with their kind. The sea became the habitat for all kinds of aquatic plants and fish, while the dry land became the habitat for innumerable kinds of plants, trees, winged-creatures and all animals, wild and domestic.

During the six days of creation God always follows the same program or order of separating his work of preparing suitable habitats for live creatures from his work of creating or forming creatures that will be living in those suitable habitats. God creates dry-land creatures on three different days, the third, and fifth and sixth days. He begins creating them immediately after the division of the surface of the earth into sea and dry land.

In God's judgment a perfectly suitable habitat or dwelling-place for man, the master to be of the earth and the master piece of God's creative activity on earth, did not yet exist on earth even after all kinds of living plants and animals had found the earth fertile. On the sixth day, God will make a small portion of the dry land into a Paradise to be the home for man, earth's master. That Paradise will be the very first home of the first man on earth.

The suitable dwelling-place God intends for transcendent man will come about by a very special work of God. God will make the Garden of Eden a spectacular and unique Paradise for man. God prepares that Paradise for man only after creating the first man, Adam. God has a very special reason for forming the man from dust and then have the man witness the formation of that Paradise.

On the third day, when God makes the earth fertile his works are beginning to manifest the special order He intends to establish for all non-living and living creatures on earth. In God's order for his creatures animal life is dependent on plant life and therefore on the third day before God creates any animals creates many kinds of plants. Which is one day before God creates animals on the forth and fifth days of creation.

Making the earth fertile required establishing ecological systems by which certain areas of the earth have the ability of hosting and supporting different kinds of plant and animal life. Fertility of living things is their ability to reproduce living beings of their same kind. That fertility belongs to only mature living beings of their kind. It does not belong to the inanimate earth or to inanimate things on earth. That is the reason God did not give to the earth the blessing for the multiplication of living things but to mature living creatures. Part of the order God established on earth is maintained by the fertility blessings God gives to living creatures by which they can reproduce only their own kind. This blessing made every species capable of filling the earth with its kind.

In this way God established the law of biogenesis: the law that new life comes from only living beings and only from living beings of the same specific kind or species. The very fact that the text states God created the different species and made each species fertile, giving to each species the specific ability of reproducing its own kind, implies that the fertility God gave to the earth did not empower the earth to bring forth life or living beings. The earth has no ability to evolve different species or a species the ability to evolve other species.

Evolutionists have never manifested any interest in any order for the development of species. But now when it has become obvious that a proper order on earth is necessary for the maintenance of species they have begun to show an interest in a proper order of things on earth.

It was in view of the dependency of animal life on plants that God ordered the earth to bring forth many different kinds of vegetation—plants, grasses, vines and trees before God creates live animals on earth. The plants produce seeds primarily for their own reproduction but also for food for animals. Many animals eat plants while many others, like birds, eat only the seeds of plants.

It was in view of the creation of man, however, that God gave the special and specific command and blessing that the earth bring forth plants that have their seed in their fruit. God intended that such fruit be reserved as the special food for man even when trees having such fruit are found growing outside Paradise. The last thing God does on the sixth and last day is give man dominion over the earth and everything on the earth. Cf. Gen 1:29-30.

On the third and forth days, when God creates many kinds of plants, there is no explicit mention of either the tree of life or the tree of knowledge of good and bad! These two trees will come into existence on the sixth day when God forms the Garden of Eden. Each of these trees was the only tree of its kind. They could not be found growing anywhere on earth except in the center of Paradise.

On the sixth day God will conclude his work of creating various kinds of land animals from dust, but in deference to man does not create man along with or at the same time He creates other animals. God creates man, as the text indicates, in a second creation on the sixth day.

Part of the good order God established on earth for the sake of all living creatures was the cycle of light and darkness, the ever recurring seasons of the year and the rhythmic life cycles inherent in the very natures of living creatures. God made many kinds of plants critically dependent on the cycles of light and darkness, seasons of the year, the fertility of the earth's ecosystems for the germinating, growing and maturing of plants. God made mature plants capable of producing seed for the reproduction of their own specific kind and each species ability to perpetually reproduce its kind.

God intended that the fertility of the earth, the different seasons of the year and the fertility of plants would permit plants to continue flourishing on earth and flourish so abundantly that they would supply food and shelter for animals and for man.

Genesis' account of creation manifests an order of interdependence among all living creatures that corresponds in a very remarkable degree to the interdependence modern science has discovered among living things. However, there is in the text what appears to be a glaring violation of that interdependency and order. It is such violation that it does not seem possible that Moses, who obviously knew of the dependence of plants on the fertility of the earth and on the sun for seasons and conditions necessary for life on earth, could have written it into his text. Because of that divinely established interdependence and good order, God's creation of plants should not have preceded God's placing of the sun and the moon in the dome of the sky. It seems necessary that God should have completed all preparations on earth for the earth's hosting of living beings before creating any living beings on earth.

The author has God preparing the earth for its hosting of all kinds of living creatures in two steps. In the first step, he has God making the dome of the sky and then moving the excess water on earth onto that dome. That makes possible the permanent division of the surface of the earth into sea and dry land. In the second step, he has God placing lights in the dome of the sky for the purpose of shedding light and heat on the earth and for causing cycles of days and nights and for establishing or marking the fixed times or seasons of the year. However the earth could not possibly host living creatures before the sun existed in the sky. Therefore it would seem that the author should not have God creating vegetation and trees on earth on the third day, one day before placing the sun in the dome of the sky.

A possible solution to this problem would be for readers to understand Genesis implying that the sun and the moon were already in the heavens from the first day of creation. After the first day God had completed all his works in the entire universe except for his works on earth. Hence what God is doing here on the fourth day can be nothing more than give the earth a position that would be more favorable for living creatures on earth. The text of the fourth day does not say God made the sun and the moon, but God "made the sun and the moon mark the fixed times, the days and the years." This would require that God give the earth a particular tilt to its axes.

UNDERSTANDING THE WORKS OF THE FOURTH DAY OF CREATION

Then God said: "Let there be lights in the dome of the sky, to separate day from night. Let them mark the fixed times, the days and the years, and serve as luminaries in the dome of the sky, to shed light upon the earth." And that is [exactly] what happened: God made the two great lights, the greater one to govern the day and the lesser one to govern the night; and he made the stars. God set them in the dome of the sky to shed light upon the earth, to govern the day and the night, and to separate the light from darkness. God saw how good it was. Evening came, and morning followed—the fourth day." Gen 1:14-19.

The earth itself does not produce any or enough light and heat for living things to exist on earth. Living creatures on earth require an abundance of controlled natural light and heat. Here God is providing that abundance of light and heat by adjusting the positions of the earth and moon in their relation to the sun. Here Genesis explicitly recognizes the fact that the sun and the moon, besides shining down on the earth to provide light and heat for life everywhere on the earth, have the additional functions of controlling seasonal conditions necessary for life on earth.

The author knows that these heavenly bodies divide time on earth into days and nights, they accommodate to the life cycles inherent in living creatures by causing the ever-recurring seasonal conditions. They even influence the free actions of men, for men have no choice but to accommodate themselves, their activities and living to the change of conditions caused by the sun and moon. However, it was God's decree regarding the Sabbath rest that divided time for man on earth into weeks of seven days—six days for labor and one day for rest from labor.

Moses understood these things clearly for he would later comment on the stability of the order God's work of this fourth day produced and permanently established on earth. He wrote, "As long as the earth lasts cold and heat, seedtime and harvest, summer and winter, and day and night shall not cease." Gen 8:22. Here in Genesis God wants to assure mankind that the good order He established on earth and in the sky will never permit the earth to fall back into the inhospitable conditions it was after its creation on the first day.

The false worldly wisdom prevalent today says that the only thing men can be certain of and plan for on earth is the constancy of change. However, prudence and true science teach that change on earth is very limited. The sciences of the present times assure men that the potential and kinetic energy in the material universe can continue to cause orderly change but only until their energy runs out. Before the sun and all other material bodies run completely out of energy, they will continue causing only what they have always been causing throughout all their ages.

The teachings of philosophers put limits on the changes possible in nature and in the world. First, they teach that nothing can move itself or act of itself. Second, they teach that only those things that have natures are capable of action. Third, they teach that beings with natures never act in any way except in accord with their natures, for their natures are the causes of their actions but their natures are not what act. Hence creatures are capable of only those actions that are in accord with their specific natures. Dogs cannot roar like lions and snakes cannot jump like deer. Since the natures of living beings are immutable, the immutability of their natures guarantees that their specific natures will always be capable of certain specific actions. Natures cannot act except in accord with their specific natures.

The immutable natures of living beings are not the subject of their own actions. A being's immutable nature merely causes its actions to be of a specific kind and its immutable nature can continue causing actions proper to its nature ad infinitum. Hence the particular actions any immutable-created nature causes are the actions it has been causing throughout all past ages and will continue to cause in all future ages including those ages men will live in heaven.

These are some of the reasons why Ecclesiastes could truly observe: "What has been is what will be; and what has been done is what will be done; and there is nothing new under the sun." Eccl 1:9.

UNDERSTANDING THE WORKS ON THE FIFTH DAY OF CREATION

Then God said: "Let the waters teem with an abundance of living creatures, and on earth let birds fly beneath the dome of the sky". And that is exactly what happened: God created the great sea monsters and all kinds of swimming creatures with which the water teem, and all kinds of winged birds. God saw how good it was, and God blessed them, saying, 'Be fruitful and multiply and fill the water in the seas, and let the birds multiply on the earth'. Evening came and morning followed—the fifth day." Gen 1:20-23.

The first animals God created on earth were the fish of the sea and the birds (literally beings with wings—that includes flying insects) of the air. The fish may venture anywhere in the sea and winged creatures may venture anywhere above the earth and below the dome of the sky. After their creation God in blessing the fish and the birds took them under his providential care to assure their well being, multiplication, and perpetual existence on earth.

On this fifth day, God limits his work to creating only two classes of living creatures, the fish of the sea and the winged creatures of the air. God commands the fish to multiply and fill the sea and the birds to multiply and fill the air. These combined commands indicate that God did not create the sea crowded with fish and the air crowded with birds and other flying creatures.

UNDERSTANDING THE WORKS OF THE SIXTH DAY OF CREATION

The order events have on the sixth day is not quite the same order events had on other days of creation. The order events for the first five days always has God commanding that the earth bring forth all kinds of living creatures: cattle, creeping things, and wild animals of all kinds. When on the sixth day God came to creating man, God first declares his intention to create man and then declares his intention to create man in a particular state or condition. God intends to create man in the condition of "our image likeness" and intends to give man dominion over all creatures on earth. God explicitly manifested his intention not to create man in a purely human condition but in a grand preternatural condition and even in the much grandeur supernatural condition. God begins executing his declared intentions concerning man.

Before God begins his work of creating man He states his intention of creating man in "our image likeness" [what our image likeness means will be explained in this commentary beginning with verse seven of chapter two]. After creating man in "our image likeness" God bestows on man dominion over all creatures on earth: over the birds of the air, the fish of the sea and the animal that roam the earth. God then designates all seed-bearing plants and every tree that has seed-bearing fruit to be man's special food. This was the last creative work of God. The very last work of God was to bless the man and the woman. This last blessing is "Be fertile and multiply; fill the earth and subdue it."

The whole of chapter two of Genesis, which describes the creation of the man and the woman, must have occurred on the sixth day of creation, for it was on the sixth day that God created man. Hence this entire second chapter must be read and understood as a much more explicit and detailed account of the creation of man than that found on the sixth day in the first chapter of Genesis. Chapter two is a more detailed account of what God did when creating man in our image likeness, "in his image; in the divine image he created him; male and female he created them." Gen 1:27.

This second chapter contains the account of God making the

extremely important creation covenant with Adam immediately after his creation. Awareness of the difference between God's order of intention and God's executive order will be critical later in manifesting the making of the creation covenant with Adam on this sixth day.

The first work of God on the sixth day was the creation of certain animals for it was only then that the earth had been adequately prepared to host those animals. "Then God said: Let the earth bring forth all kinds of living creatures: cattle, creeping things [creeping things are not only snakes, but ants, bugs, worms and insects], and wild animals of all kinds. 'And that is exactly what happened. God made all kinds of wild animals, all kinds of cattle, and all kinds of creeping things of the earth. God saw how good it was.' Then God said, 'Let us make man in our image, after our likeness. Let them have dominion over the fish of the sea, the birds of the air, and the cattle, and over the wild animals and all the creatures that crawl on the ground.' God created man in his image; in the divine image he created him; male and female he created them. God blessed them, saying: 'Be fruitful and multiply; fill the earth and subdue it. Have dominion over the fish of the sea, the birds of the air, and all the living things that move on the earth.' God also said: 'See, I give all the green plants for food. I give you every seed-bearing plant all over the earth and every tree that has seed-bearing fruit on it to be your food.' And so it happened. God looked at everything he had made, and he found it very good. Evening came, and morning followed—the sixth day." Gen 1:24-31.

On the previous five days God had completed everything necessary to prepare the earth, the sea and the dry land in ways that would enable them to host all species of plant and of animal adapted to live in them. Then on this sixth day God creates from dust other kinds of animals adapted for life on the land. Genesis records specifically that God created the wild animals, cattle (domestic animals) and all kinds of creeping things on the sixth day. "Both [men and beasts] go the same place; both were made from dust, and to the dust they both return." Eccl 3:20.

When creating the various species of plants and animals, God creates many of every species but when God comes to creating the human species God creates only one male and one female. That God should have created only one male and only one female is entirely consistent with the second chapter's account of God preparing a relatively small Paradise rather than the whole earth as a fit dwelling-place for the man and his wife. That is consistent also with God giving the man dominion over the whole earth and commanding him to multiply and fill the earth.

The fact that God when creating man creates only one man and one woman, who are to populate the earth with their race of humans, indicates that God intends something special for the whole race of man; has planned something special for the entire race of Adam and Eve. God's plan for the man was not to put man's multiplication on any fast track. The Incarnation of the Father's Son as the God-man of Adam's race was the governing factor in the rate of man's progress through history. In the fullness of time only would God the Father incarnate his Son as the God-man.

The truths that God would create only two humans in a separate creation on the sixth day and form the special Paradise for them are some of the means used in Genesis to indicate to fallen man that God had a very special predilection for man even before man's creation. The reason is that from eternity God intended to create man vastly superior to all other creatures on earth. Hence with the creation of man God's creative work reached completion and ends. That plan for the human race will reach its glorious culmination in the Incarnation of the God-man and in his communicating his eternal glory to man.

The fact that God deliberately creates only two humans, creates a fertile male a short time before forming a fertile female from the male, and prepares a relatively small Paradise for them clearly indicate that man did not evolve along with all the other animal species or in some similar way. If man had evolved or could have evolved, there would not have been any reason or need for a second creation on the sixth day in which God creates in quick succession one man and one woman and then unites them in a permanent and indissoluble marriage bond.

Another means employed in Genesis to manifest to fallen man

man's great superiority to all other creatures on earth is God's predetermination to give man dominion over all plants and animals on earth. Still another means employed by Genesis to manifest to men fallen man's superiority to all other creatures on earth, was God's designation and reservation of the seed of certain plants and the fruit of certain trees as man's special earthly food. God reserved the fruit of trees that have their seed in their fruit as the special food for man.

If the animals roamed the earth for many millions of years before man existed on earth, as archaeologists and anthropologists contend and if the sixth day began with the creation of certain animals and ended with the creation of man, then there is reason for thinking that the sixth day of creation was millions of years in duration. However this creation of man late on the sixth day does not constitute adequate reason for holding that man evolved from some specifically different form of life after the millions of years of the sixth day.

One reason God did not create man along with the other animals is that, even after the earth had proved a suitable habitat for the land-animals, the earth in the judgment of God was not yet the suitable dwelling-place He intended for his most highly favored creature, man. The earth was not the kind of place, in which man might live and enjoy the preternatural life and the supernatural life God intended for Adam and his race.

How greatly favored and highly honored man was at his creation Genesis makes evident to fallen man by informing fallen man that man had been created a man but a man in "our image likeness". Man's creation in that "our image likeness" was one reason for the superb preternatural physical and mental condition the first man and woman enjoyed at their creation. It was also the reason man was created in a supernatural state of original innocence which would bring men the blessings of a supernatural destiny.

Part of verse twenty-six is: "Let us make man in our image likeness." These words manifest not only that God freely chose to create man but also chose to freely create man the most highly favored and honored of God's creatures on earth. The "our image likeness" was the reason for all God had already worked in man, making him very fertile and giving him dominion over all creatures on earth. God had created special plants and trees bearing fruit designed to be man's special food.

In verses twenty eight through thirty of the first chapter, God has spelled out not only the favors already bestowed on the male and the female at their creation but also the favors God intends to bestow on all descendants of Adam's race at their conception. God would bind Himself to do all these things for all persons of Adam's race by the entirely gratuitous creation covenant or contract He made with Adam. In accord with that entirely gratuitous covenant, God would create all the descendants of Adam in "our image likeness" and give all of them dominion over all things on earth. God would give the seeds of plants and the fruit of trees everywhere to be man's food (especially the fruit of those trees that have their seed in their fruit). God would give the man and his entire race rights to Garden of Eden, Paradise, with all its wonders and bounty for their permanent home on earth.

The dominion God gave to man was a subordinate kind of dominion over all the animals, plants and the earth. God kept to Himself and to the God-man supreme or absolute dominion over all creation. Man's subordinate dominion permits man to use all animals and all living things on earth as man pleases, but in ways consistent with the Creator's absolute dominion over all things the Creator had kept to Himself.

When giving man dominion over all living things on earth God uses the strong verbs "radah" which means to trample and "kabas" which means to tread down. He used those verbs in order to express the kind of dominion He was giving man over all living things on earth. God gave man this kind dominion over the animals and plants to indicate that it would be morally right for man to use them in any way for man's welfare.

This original grant of dominion permitted man to domesticate animals, use them for beasts of burden, sport, and pets. If Adam were to use their flesh for food, their skin for clothing and their life-blood for sacrifice that would have been inconsistent with man's needs and the favorable conditions Paradise afforded man. Right to this original grant of dominion was a part of the creation covenant and therefore they did not survive man's breaking of the creation covenant. Other rights Adam received in being created in "our image likeness."

After man's fall from grace God gave man, living in the harsher conditions of the world outside Paradise, an extended dominion over animals which permits man to use them for food, clothing and sacrifice, but does not permit any abuse of animals or creatures. Cf. Gen 3:21; 9:2-4.

Already on the sixth day of creation Genesis uses the word cattle; a term for domesticated animals and stands in opposition to animals or wild animals. The implication of the use of the words cattle and wild animals is that from the beginning God had given the man knowledge of how to domesticate and care for animals and plants and their use for man's benefit. The second chapter informs us of God settling Adam in Paradise and records the activity of Adam and Eve in Paradise. It supposes Adam and Eve had knowledge that made them competent in the sciences and arts needed to properly care for the plants and animals of Paradise. Just as Genesis makes explicit mention of God giving man dominion over plants and trees, it also makes explicit mention of God giving man dominion over the birds of the air and the fish of the sea. Just as God expected Adam to harvest the plants and trees of Paradise, so God expected Adam to do the same with all plants and animals living outside Paradise.

Traditional Catholic theology teaches that Adam, while in his state of original innocence, had such extraordinary knowledge of natural things that Adam was immune to error. These traditional theologians believe that this extraordinary knowledge was infused into Adam and Eve. However they appear completely unaware of when or what or how great was the store of knowledge God infused into their minds. Was their store of infused knowledge so great that it include knowledge of all the sciences and arts?

Even modern theologians could not be aware of the reason for these things because they had accepted the incorrect translation of "our image and likeness". The first man's great store of infused knowledge must have included the sciences and arts, not only for the reason that God required that the man rightly and successfully cultivate the plants and trees of Paradise and harvest their fruits. The great store of knowledge was infused into the minds of Adam and Eve at their creation because they were created in "our image likeness". "Our image likeness" is the reason the man was created mentally as well as physically in the likeness of the God-man, who was destined to have a limitless store of knowledge that included knowledge of all the arts and sciences.

During the six days of creation God had been creating things in an order that indicated God's work of creating would be completed with the creation of man. Hence it was obvious to the visionary-messenger and his author-collaborator that the sixth day of creation was destined to be the last and greatest day of creation. On each of the previous days, God saw his work of each day as good, but on the sixth day, after the creation of man, God saw his work as very good. So pleasing and satisfying to God was the man's and the woman's creation in "our image likeness".

Once the visionary-messenger was aware that God had finished doing for man all God had promised to do for man, the visionary-messenger knew that God had completed all his works on earth, so he proceeds to inform his author-collaborator that God had completed his work and that the sixth day was about to end. "God looked at everything he had made and found it very good. Evening came, and morning followed—the sixth day."

God chose to begin the whole human race with a single pair, the man, Adam, and the woman, Eve. After creating that single pair and making that pair into a marriage partnership, God declares to that partnership: "Be fruitful and multiply, and fill the earth and subdue it". Here God is again manifesting that He held supreme dominion over man. Man was not to be his own master. God gave every individual the right and obligation to marry and multiply the human race on earth. God intended by his supreme dominion to hold men accountable for the right use of their sexual fertility. By this blessing and implicit command God gave everyone the right to marry. In giving this blessing and its accompanying command God manifested his intention to assist marriage partnerships and so insure the propagation of an entire race of humans filling the earth from that one couple.

This blessing and command manifest that God had no intention of multiplying the human race more quickly in some other way—by, for example, some mass creation of humans. Any such mass creation of humans, as will be seen, would have frustrated a significant element of the Father's plan for his God-man; his plan to leave to the God-man a race of brethren genetically intact. It was always the absolute will of the Father to incarnate his Son as the God-man by having Him conceived and born of a woman of the race of Adam. The Father's plan for man assures the God-man of Adam's race the joy of having a whole race of humans true genetic brothers and sisters of his. It was never the intention of the Father that the Most Sacred Humanity of his Incarnate Son originate out of nothing or that his Sacred Humanity originate from a race of humans genetically distinct from the race of Adam. Nor was it ever the intention of God the Father that humans of another race, an alien race having an evolutionary origin, for example, should have any share in the inheritance of his First-born, the God-man of Adam's race.

When describing the creation of the animals, Genesis does not explicitly state that animals were created male and female, yet God does command them to reproduce according to their own kind. By this omission sex in the case of the animals and its explicit mention in the case of man, God wanted to manifest and explicitly emphasize to fallen man the divine origin of both human sexes. The different sexes are of God's deliberate design, that persons of either sex are equally human and that the complementary nature of the different sexes makes possible marriage partnerships. God by drawing up his marriage covenant for man put into effect his divine standard of morality for all human sexual activity.

God's deliberate creation of only one man and one woman, his command that they begin the propagation of their race and the provisions of God's creation covenant suggest that from the beginning God intended that sexual generation, besides being the means of propagating a whole race of humans from Adam and Eve, was God's chosen means of extending the original state of innocence and divine destiny to every person of their entire race. From the beginning, God intended that the original state of innocence, the supernatural justice or holiness Adam and Eve received at their creation, be the birthright of every person of Adam's entire race. Therefore God made sexual generation from Adam and his line the condition in the creation covenant for the giving or passing on rights to the state of original innocence to every person of Adam's race. The fact that God willed originally to accomplish the original sanctification and salvation of Adam's entire race in this way, that is by means of human sexual generation, will become clear as Genesis' account of Adam and Eve unfolds. "For those he foreknew [of the race of Adam] he predestined to be conformed to the image of his (Incarnate] Son, in order that he [Incarnate Son] might be the first-born among many brethren." Rom 8:29.

MARRIAGE IS A DIVINE INSTITUTION

When God gave man a subordinate kind of dominion over all creatures on earth, God kept to Himself supreme dominion over man, human life, human activity, and in particular the sexual activity of men. God's supreme dominion over newly generated humans would not be as clear to fallen man, if God had not reserved to Himself complete control over the source of human lives; if God had not imposed his standard of sexual morality by making his marriage covenant or contract the only valid marriage covenant or contract for the use of sex.

God, by making his marriage covenant binding on all men, manifested that He fully intends to permanently maintain his sovereign dominion over mankind, human life and the destiny of individuals and of society. Therefore God intends to keep a vigilant guard over newly generated human life by the imposition of his marriage covenant or contract on individuals.

The marriage covenant God drew up would be valid for humans only while persons are living on earth. That is the reason marriage partnerships, since the fall of man are made to last only until death. God intends that human sexual activity be the only legitimate source of new human life. This excludes any mass creation of humans, any non-sexual generation of humans or cloning of a human whether cloning causes life or merely makes use of a life already in existence.

Because God willed and mandated marriage for humans on earth, God drew up a marriage covenant or contract for persons dwelling on earth. That divine covenant makes marriage a divine institution in the case of all humans. God's marriage covenant gives each marriage partnership exclusive rights which can be exercised only mutually. Such mutual use of sex is not only completely compatible with God's dominion over man, but also completely compatible with human freedom and every person's desire for offspring and happiness while on earth.

God has drawn up only one marriage covenant or contract. God has not approved a plethora of alternative marriage contracts to suit the desires of fallen men's erroneous or perverse beliefs and theories regarding man, human life, human sexuality, the family and family life. Consequently, persons engaging in sexual activity without having received rights to engage in that activity by agreeing to God's one and only marriage covenant, are committing grave violations of God's sovereign dominion over men, human sexual activity, the family, human life and human society. Homosexual orientation is opposed to all of these divine goals for human sexuality.

God intends that his one and only marriage covenant or contract be respected and scrupulously observed by all men for all time. When persons marry they must agree to God's one and only marriage covenant otherwise their marriage is no marriage at all and their agreed upon partnership is not a marriage partnership. The complementary nature of the sexes and God's one and only marriage contract make wedded life essentially the same for every marriage partnership in any age, everywhere on earth and anywhere partners may travel away from the earth.

Since the fall of man, God is not willing that his marriage covenant give the rights of marriage to persons except on an until death bases. Hence in God's intention there cannot be such a thing as a trial marriage partnership. God has such an overriding interest in every marriage partnership that provision for his interests affect the very validity of the marriage partnership. God's approval of a marriage partnership is implicit in the persons agreeing to live God's one and only marriage covenant. This is the reason it is no exaggeration to say that valid marriage partnerships are made in heaven.

Persons living in the Garden of Eden would not die and since persons in heaven do not marry, God intended to dissolve marriage partnerships of persons living in Paradise at the termination of their specified period of living in Paradise. In Paradise marriage covenants would not have been made "until death do us part", but until departure from Paradise for heaven. For this reason it would seem that both persons of a marriage partnership would have departed paradise at the same time.

Marriage will not exist among humans after their resurrection, even though each individual will retain his or her identity as a male or female after resurrection from the dead and supernatural glorification. The truth that all persons will retain their sexual identity as a male or a female after their resurrection and glorification is evident from the resurrected and glorified body of Jesus Christ. Jesus' Body clearly retained its masculinity, for the apostles continued to think of and refer to Jesus as a male after his glorious resurrection from the dead. The Mother of Jesus in her many apparitions to persons on earth always appears as a woman and a virgin. God's purposes for marriage partnerships will no longer exist in heaven. "For in the resurrection they neither marry nor are given in marriage, but are like the angels in heaven." Mt 22:30.

At the moment of the making of every marriage partnership on earth God always blesses that marriage partnership with his providential care in a way that will enable it to do its part to fulfill God's command to subdue the earth and fill the earth with descendants.

When placing the earth with all its plants and animals under man's dominion and giving man the command to subdue the earth, God did not give man the ready means for controlling all material things. God merely subjected the entire earth to man's radical ability to change and direct things through man applying his knowledge and physical strength and endurance to things. In man's pursuit to subdue the earth, man will experience the wonders of the inexhaustible possibilities of discovery. Everything is ordered to the honor of man and the praise of the Designer and Creator of all things. Only by God's design and man living by God's law can man live in freedom, master himself and subdue the earth.

God created every individual person autonomous and superior to the civil state and civil laws not in the sense that individuals or marriage partnerships do not owe obedience to civil authority, but that every individual is superior in the sense that the civil state must justify its every law in the rigor of the individual's inalienable rights and the true demands of the common good of society. A person's public profession of belief in God, his trust in the providence of God, his esteem for divine law, his honoring of the Lord's Day and his respect for the inalienable human rights are indispensable elements of the common good of society. Hence the practice of the denial of an individual's freedom by the state, an individual's public denial of the existence of God and any public contempt for

God, his law and his day are grave sins against the common good of society. In our times all-powerful and godless states feed on vital individual rights. Human societies are being replaced by a regimentation of peoples that is so complete and so absolute that true civil societies no longer exist.

God created man permanently blessed with human freedom. Every man has the freedom to acquire private goods and the obligation of serving the common good of society. One of the principal causes of civil unrest, mistrust, contention and strife in democratic societies today is the inability of its citizens to define correctly the true nature of the common good of society. Most sociologists today erroneously define the common good of society as the greatest good for the greatest number. Today that erroneous definition goes unchallenged in spite of the fact that it has civil strife; the struggle for minority rights, built into the very definition of the common good. That erroneous definition gives the majority the right to oppress minorities and that makes internal strife and the struggle for minority rights a permanent feature of life in society. That erroneous definition justifies subduing other individuals or even society itself to an individual's ambitions.

Other sociologists define the common good as the goods all individuals of the society possess in common. The entire infrastructure of that society, its roads, bridges and public buildings are considered the common good of society. That erroneous definition would turn every society into a socialistic or even a communistic society.

The common good is rightly defined as anything that makes it possible or easier for all persons of the society to work together. From this definition it may not be immediately obvious what makes up the common good of society and how every law must be for the good of every person in that society. The lack of knowledge and an understanding of the true nature of the common good are the principal reasons that men in highly developed societies are enduring much strife even when there appears to be much good will in the individuals. It is the reason that many think or believe that the government that governs least is the best. Because citizens cannot define the common good they can not know what is the function of national, state or local governments.

If the six days of creation had ended without the creation of man, the work of creating would have been without a climax or ultimate purpose. God would not have accomplished something most extraordinary by not creating man in "our image likeness". By creating man in "our image likeness" God not only created man but also established man in the most extraordinary state or supernatural condition of the most highly favored, honored and perfect of all creatures on earth.

This "our image likeness" has proved to be very enigmatic not only to readers of Genesis but also to translators and commentators. The unraveling of the enigma or mystery of "our image likeness" is a problem for both language and theology. The task of unraveling this enigma will be taken up after consideration is given to the meaning and importance of God's seventh day of rest.

THE PURPOSE AND SIGNIFICANCE GOD'S REST FROM LABOR

"Thus the heavens and the earth and all their array were completed. Since on the seventh day God was finished with work he had been doing, he rested on the seventh day from all the work he had undertaken. So God blessed the seventh day and blessed it, because on it God rested from all his work he had done in creation." Gen 2:2-3.

At the end of the sixth day of creation God found all his works, especially his work of forming man, to be very good. On the morning of the seventh day, the visionary-messenger, to whom God had been manifesting his commands and works by means of visions, doesn't hear any command coming from God, but finds God completely at rest. After blessing the marriage partnership of the man and the woman nothing more needed to be created or blessed on earth, so God begins on the morning of the following day his rest from all the works He had been doing. All the works God intended to do for man had been completed by the evening of the sixth day.

God's ad extra seventh day of eternal rest would become a symbol for man that makes every seventh day for man on earth a day of rest from man's own labor. Through the gracious assistance of divine providence man will not need to labor every day to provide for his livelihood. God has made his own eternal seventh day of rest a symbol or sign not only of one day rest a week for man on earth but also a sign of the total rest from labor men will enjoy throughout eternity in the heavenly Paradise God has already prepared for man.

Time belongs to God alone and is under his dominion alone. Only God could grant to men the time of the first six days of every week for laboring in the pursuit of personal growth in perfection of supernatural life and pursuit of perfection of mind, soul, body and temporal welfare. Only God could require that every seventh day of the week be set aside for every man to rest from the pursuit of his temporal welfare. Thus the seventh day became a special day in the pursuit of public worship of God and works dedicated to the service of God.

After man would have completed his life on earth God would invite man into the eternal rest of his ad extra eternal seventh day. All creatures capable of worship, friendship and fellowship with the Father and his Incarnate God-man are invited by the Father into eternal rest. St. Paul explicitly teaches that God welcomes all men into his eternal rest. "It is we who have believed who enter into that rest, just as God said 'Thus I swore in my anger. They shell never enter my rest.'" Heb 4:3. God has sworn never to let sinners enter into his eternal rest. This does not mean that sinners can never find any rest on earth. The fact that only good men can enter God's eternal rest is the Scriptural reason persons may rightly say: "There is no rest for the wicked."

There is no day of rest of any kind in the abyss, for in the abyss there is no day and no day for the enjoyment of any kind of rest. In the abyss there is always the struggle against eternal confinement and punishment; punishment for eternal rebellion against an almighty and most gracious God.

When giving men the command to rest from temporal pursuits every seventh day, God was fully aware of fallen man's inability to supply even his temporal needs entirely by his own labor. By giving this command to fallen man God implied his willingness to employ his powerful providence to assure men an adequacy of temporal goods for life on earth. Only by men putting complete trust and confidence in God's goodness, wisdom and providence can fallen men find it possible to live in abundance and in peaceful tranquility on earth. God is man's assurance of freedom, happiness and the strength to master himself and to subdue the earth.

Compulsory rest from labor on every seventh day implies man's obligation to publicly acknowledge his Creator-God, to trust in his almighty providence and to make the seventh day a special day for works of social or civic dedication done with religious motives. The seventh day is therefore called the Lord's Day. Society no less than an individual is dependent on God's providence for its prosperity and tranquillity in a peaceful land. Cf. Ex 20:11.

Genesis, in stating that God began an eternal rest from all the work He had been doing, implies that God does not have any intention of ever again creating any more worlds or universes. Since

God intends that his rest be eternal, God prepared in advance for that eternal rest by creating an eternally adequate universe for everything He planned to accomplish for man throughout eternity. If God has any intention of creating other worlds or universes, it would be necessary that He intend to end his eternal rest and end his seventh day of rest. He would then end his eternal seventh day not by ending time but by an evening of the seventh day followed by the morning of an eighth ad extra day.

God has predestined men to participate forever in the eternal rest of his eternal ad extra seventh day and for that reason God can not intend to end his eternal rest by another round of ad extra days in which other universes or worlds would be created. During the ad extra eternal seventh day of God's rest man will be sharing in God's eternal rest and will be enjoying most of all his all-sufficient beatific vision of God. During that eternal seventh day of rest the God-man and men will be living off of the unfathomable riches of the God-man's Almighty Father's inheritance. The source of the unfathomable riches of that inheritance is the Almighty Father's willingness to employ his almighty power to do anything and everything for man's eternal natural and supernatural happiness. Cf. Eph 3:8.

Another round of ad extra days of creating would suppose that something other than the Incarnation would be given highest priority in God's order of intention. The Incarnation's priority in the intention of the Father having already produced all its consequences. The truth that the Incarnation had highest priority in the intention of the Father at the creation of all things is the eternal source for stability of the entire created universe. If anything new would be created something new would have to be given highest priority in the intention of the Father as the final cause of the new or second round of creating things. It may be that the new final cause of that new work of creating would be another hypostatic union, just as the hypostatic union of the incarnate God-man was the final cause of the creation of our universe and of our race. For the New Testament teaches, as we shall see, that the creation of our universe was in, through and for the sake of incarnating the Son of God as the God-man of our race. The hypostatic union of the Person of the

Son of God with a human nature taken from our race was the final cause of the creation and of the continuing existence of this universe and everything in it.

The making of the new heaven and the new earth, prophesied in the New Testament, will not end God's eternal rest from his work of creating. For the new heavens and the new earth will not be the result of the complete annihilation of the old heavens and old earth and the creation of new heavens and an entirely new earth out of nothing. It will be the result of God transforming the old into the new. Cf. 2 Pt 3:1-13. What men have recently learned from astronomy indicates that parts of our material universe are still in their earliest stage of their development. The planets of our solar system except for our earth are still without form and are still void just as our earth was formless and void before the second day of creation.

Some persons have been saying wouldn't it be wonderful if men discovered Noah's ark. That find they say would be wonderful proof of the truth of the Bible. Modern technology of photography and space probes to the moon and elsewhere have proven or shortly will offer men convincing proof that all extra-terrestrial places are still as empty and void as the earth was at the end of the first day. All the days of creation except for the first were days God worked only on our earth.

The visionary-messenger, when speaking to his author-collaborator on the morning of the seventh day, informs him of the impending ending of all communications to him. There would be nothing more to report for the Creator God had finished his works and has begun his eternal rest. Hence the author-collaborator must not expect to hear from him any new commands of God or information of any new works of God. The visionary-messenger gives his author-collaborator that assurance by stating: "Thus (as I have reported) the heavens and the earth and all their array were completed. Since on the seventh day God was finished with the work he had been doing, he rested on the seventh day from all work he had undertaken." Gen 2:2.

Likewise the author-collaborator felt a need to assure his readers of the accuracy of his written account of the creation. He writes that assurance in words that imply that he had recorded all the words of the visionary-messenger just as he received them. He therefore signs off or ends his written account with the words: "Such is the story (as I have written it) of the heavens and the earth at their creation." Gen 2:4.

Since all translators of and commentators on the first chapter of Genesis were not aware that the first chapter had the format of a visionary-messenger of God communicating with his author-collaborator, they could not have understood verses one through four of the second chapter. For they could not have been aware of the fact that the entire first chapter was the communication of the visionary-messenger to his author collaborator. They could not have been aware that by these words the visionary-messenger was signing off to his author-collaborator and that the author-collaborator was assuring his readers in his own words that in writing his account of creation he faithfully inscribed only the words of God's visionary-messenger to him.

Translators and commentators have perceived these verses to be instead the beginning of another or second story of the creation. These verses cannot be the beginning of a second story of the creation, because there is no attempt in what follows to retell the story of the six days of creation. What follows is a fascinating account dedicated exclusively to the telling of the creation of the man and his wife and their living only for a short time in Paradise before their expulsion from Paradise by God.

Beginning with Genesis 2:4b, Moses begins to compose and write on his own, instead of merely recording what he hears a messenger from God telling him what he is to write. Hence it is at this point that the author of Genesis begins writing as an observer. For this reason chapters two and three, unlike chapter one, do not have the format of God and two persons communicating. These chapters do not contain a single "And that is exactly what happened" by which a person is being informed of what has been happening. This phrase occurs eight times in the first chapter.

In chapters two and three the author, Moses, is an observer and writes as any author able to choose his own words to describe what he himself sees and hears in the visions God gives to him. Consequently chapters two and three are the composition of the author and for that reason these chapters can and do contain explanatory notes of the author. By his explanatory notes the author informs his readers of how he understood what he heard and saw happening in the visions he has described.

THE GREAT ENIGMA "OUR IMAGE LIKENESS"

The Hebrew text of the creation of man quotes God saying: "Let us make man in our image likeness", not "in our image and likeness", not "in our image after our likeness", and not "in our image, in the likeness of ourselves". Here the ancient Hebrew text literally has the word image and the word likeness, but does not have an "and" or any conjunction between them. This Hebrew "our image likeness" has proven to be an inscrutable enigma even to this day to translators and commentators alike. But translators have compounded its inscrutability by choosing to place an "and" between the word image and the word likeness in their Greek translations of the Hebrew text.

The translators, who produced the ancient Greek Septuagint or Greek LXX, apparently thought the "our image likeness" of the Hebrew devoid of a definite or obvious meaning and for that reason attempted to give it a meaning in their Greek LXX translation by placing an and between the word image and the word likeness. A meaning they apparently thought, as time has not demonstrated, less mysterious or enigmatic then the Hebrew's literal "our image likeness". Their erroneous translation apparently sits well with modern translators for they keep it in their latest modern language translations. It apparently sits well with commentators as well for they do not reject or correct that error in their commentaries.

This error in the Greek LXX has been carried over into the modern critical Greek text. From that modern critical Greek text this error has spread to nearly all modern language translations, since nearly all modern language translations are made from the critical Greek text. St. Jerome's ancient Latin Vulgate too has "our image and likeness" and that is the reason the Douay-Rheims Translation and the Confraternity Translation, which are translations made from the Latin Vulgate, have the same erroneous "our image and likeness".

It is evident that the translators of the most recent English translations of this phrase are very well aware of the fact that the conjunction "and" does not appear in the original Hebrew. For they prefer to translate the phrase in various ways to mean the same as "our image and likeness" but without an "and". That is the reason two such alternative translations read: "Let us make man in our image after our likeness", and "Let us make man in our image, in the likeness of ourselves".

The inclusion of this non-existent "and" in all modern language translations make it evident that the Hebrew "our image likeness" is as inscrutable and incomprehensible to modern language translators as it was to the ancient translators making the Greek LXX. That makes it appear the translators of the latest modern language versions of this phrase apparently have no better understanding of the enigmatic Hebrew "our image likeness" than did the ancient translators. For that reason they have gone the same route as the ancient translators. They have adopted the same sense by inserting a hidden "and" in their translations instead of the visible and explicit "and" of ancient Greek translation. In this way modern translators might save themselves from making some other error and at the same time achieve having their elders share blame for their erroneous translations. In effect, they chose to let the conjunction "and" of the LXX and the critical Greek text stand by deliberately avoiding explicitly translating the "and" by giving a round about "and" through inserting equivalents of the conjunction in their translations. They variously translate that nonexistent "and" by inserting an "after" in the phrase "in our image, after our likeness" or by inserting an "of ourselves" as in the phrase "in our image, in the likeness of ourselves".

These errant phrases are in fact nothing other than non-suspicious disguises for a nonexistent "and", a nonexistent "and" for it is not to be found in the original Hebrew they are supposedly faithfully translating. These latest modern language translations make it obvious that their translators know very well that the conjunction "and" is an addition in the LXX and in the critical Greek since they can see for themselves that it cannot be found in the original Hebrew. Competent translators might then, for the benefit of readers and students of Genesis, have footnoted that what they have done has no bases in the Hebrew. A notation no translation makes. The refusal of ancient and modern translators to translate the Hebrew "our image likeness" by "our image likeness" may also be due to the fact that they, without saying so, considered the Hebrew text faulty rather than inscrutable or both. In the minds of translators creating man in "our image likeness" looms a greater mystery or enigma than creating man in "our image and likeness".

This "our image likeness" has proven to be as much an enigma or mystery to commentators as it has to translators. For commentators have been completely silent about the addition of that "and" in the Greek LXX and in the translations made from the Greek LXX or the critical Greek text.

It is to be noted that it is not only translators but also commentators who find even the "our image and likeness" of their translations quite confusing or unintelligible. For they find it impossible to agree philosophically on what in man's being or nature could rightly be thought of as some special reflection or likeness of God's Being or Nature. The attempt of many theologians to specify what in man's nature is the image and likeness of God will be shown unable to stand the test of faith or reason.

Most catechetics and catechisms, following the lead of theologians, have been asserting or explaining that "our image and likeness" means that man was created with an eternal spiritual and immortal soul or that man was created with the godlike spiritual faculties of intellect and freewill. Some commentators object to image and likeness having any reference to man's eternal spiritual and immortal soul. These contend the Semites knew of no dichotomy in man for Semites did not think of man as a real composition of a really distinct soul with a really distinct body. Semites thought of man as one whole as an undivided substance or person. It was the Greeks who thought of a man as a dichotomy, a substance composed of a soul and a body.

A few commentators have taught that God's creation of man in our image and likeness means that God gave man a share in his dominion over created things or that man is immortal for at his creation man was immortal. A small number prefer to think that "our image and likeness" consists in man being God's representative on earth. This last opinion leads inevitably to the question: To whom on earth would man be God's representative? Later it will be shown that not one of these opinions is even close to identifying God's intended meaning of "our image likeness".

These erroneous translations along with their interpretations ultimately leave unexplained what precisely in man is the image of God and what in man is the likeness of God. The Hebrew words in this phrase are "selem" meaning an image or an exact copy or reproduction, and "demut" meaning merely a likeness, a resemblance or similarity.

The use of these two words and the placing of an "and" between them certainly implies that there should be some significantly specific difference in the meaning of each when used in this way to describe the creation of man. It would seem that the use of each of these words would require that each signify something specific in man that also represents or signifies something specific in God. No commentator or expositor has attempted to point that out by explicitly comparing what in man is the likeness of God and what in man is the image of God.

Why would the Hebrew Genesis use both words together, when either word apparently would adequately signify whatever might be it meaning? This very difficulty seems to be the reason commentators, after stating that man was created in the image and likeness of God, immediately forget all about "image and likeness" and speak and write only of man being created in the likeness of God or only of man being created in the image of God.

Unless there are two significantly different aspects of man's being, one aspect being the image of God and the other the likeness of God there would seem to be no need for the use of the word image and the word likeness. If these words signify some certain specific and significant differences in God or in man intended by the author, why would the author then fail completely to indicate or explain what those specific significant differences might be? It would appear fallen man has never been able to comprehend those differences.

The truth seems to be that the Hebrew author felt no need to explain any such mysterious differences. Why is it that no modern translator has attempted to justify what he has done by pointing out the reasons or the differences for translating the Hebrew phrase "our image likeness" by "our image and likeness" or by "in our image, in the likeness of ourselves" or by "in our image, after our likeness"?

Happily nothing of this, as will be shown, has anything at all to do with this enigma of "our image likeness". What is truly amazing about the speculations of commentators regarding the meaning of "our image and likeness" is that there is never any attempt to explicitly identify anything of the supernatural order, in which Adam was created, with man's creation in "our image and likeness". The fact that modern commentator have not done so is in line with their otherwise complete indifference or silence regarding the supernatural gifts Adam and Eve received at their creation; supernatural gifts they would be passing on to all their descendants. This is not to say that they should have identified "our image and likeness" with the supernatural in man, but merely to point out that modern commentaries are completely silent about anything of the supernatural Adam and Eve received from God at their creation. This lack is to be expected since they view the creation account from the points of view of a scientist or of scientific evolutionist.

WHAT "OUR IMAGE LIKENESS" CANNOT MEAN

To get to the true meaning of "our image likeness" persons must understand first of all that if man's creation in God's image and likeness consisted in man being created with an intellect and freewill or created with a spiritual and immortal soul, then if by original sin man lost this "our image and likeness" there is no escaping the conclusion that by original sin man lost his intellect and free will as well as his spiritual and immortal soul. That means that after original sin man didn't have an intellect and a free will, no longer had a spiritual and immortal soul, which means that after original sin man was no longer had what made him a true man. Scholars seem completely unaware of this entirely valid conclusion that necessarily results from their explanation of what they contend "our image and likeness" means.

Before beginning a systematic investigation and explanation of the meaning of "our image likeness", it will be helpful to eliminate certain other extraneous things beclouding the meaning of the entire phrase "Let us make man in our image likeness". First, the phrases: 'Let us make man in 'our image and likeness' or 'in our image after our likeness' or 'in our image, in the likeness of ourselves' cannot represent any consultation, deliberation or decree to create man. Instead it represents a deliberation on the part of God to create man in a certain very special state or condition. At the beginning of creation God was already fully committed to creating man, for God had created the earth for the specific purpose of making it the dwelling-place of man.

Second, the phrases "Let us make man in our image and likeness, or in our image after our likeness" or in our image, in the likeness of ourselves cannot represent God deliberating whether to create man with a spiritual and immortal soul or with the spiritual faculties of intellect and free will. The reason is that if God chooses to create a man, He has no choice but to create man a man. If God intends to create a man He has no choice but to create a being with a spiritual and immortal soul which must have the spiritual faculties of intellect and free will. Hence any explanation of let us make man in "our image and likeness", or "in our image after our likeness" or "in our image, in the likeness of ourselves" as representing God deliberating about whether to create man a spiritual and immortal soul having the spiritual faculties of intellect falls far short of good sense. Such explanations would have the effect of rendering God's words redundant. God could say, "Let us make something with a spiritual and immortal soul without being redundant. God could say let us make man a spiritual and immortal soul without being redundant; without the ultimate redundancy of saying let us make man a man. A redundancy unworthy of the good sense of men and infinitely more unworthy of the wisdom of God.

The phrase: "Let us make man in our image and likeness or in our image after our likeness", has to refer first of all to something about which God could deliberate; something about creating man God could have some meaningful deliberate free choice. One such free choice might be the choice to create true humans endowed with supernatural divine life. It should be evident that creating man in a supernatural state or with supernatural divine life—a state theologians of the Church call original innocence—would be something of very special concern to God at the creation of man. Doing that would require a very deliberate free choice on the part of God and therefore something about which God could deliberated when about to create man. From eternity God had determined that He would create man and create man in the very special state or condition of original innocence—create man living a supernatural divine life; having a share in the divine nature. It will become ever more evident that by the divine declaration, "Let us create man in our image likeness" God intended to do much more for man than create man in the state of original innocence.

When seeking a solution to this enigma persons should keep in mind that the word image and the word likeness have very different points of reference. In English the word "like" means a close or exact correspondence in appearance of one real thing to another real thing. The word likeness indicates that two or more real things are identical in nature or quantity or in some quality. On the other hand the word "similar" suggests a resemblance that is only a partial correspondence of one real thing with another real thing.

If the words like and similar mean a correspondence of one real thing to another real thing, the word "image", on other hand, has reference to what is mental and therefore indicates the likeness of some real thing to some mental image or idea. Therefore the words image likeness indicates the "likeness" of some real thing to a mental image. When a person is said to be imagining something it is because the person has in his mind a mental image of that real thing and that the person is contemplating or dwelling on his mental image of the real thing.

In this terminology there can be two real objects, both of which are alike; one is like the other. Therefore in the case of one real thing being like the other real things, one of those real things may be said to be "like" the other but it cannot be said that the is the "image" of the other. Two real things are said to be completely alike when both have been made from the same mold or according to the same mental "image". A real thing can be unique but it will always be represented by a unique image in the mind of the person who made it.

When telling of the creation of the animals and other living creatures, Genesis does not make explicit the fact that in creating all of them God created all of them according to his exact eternal mental images of their specific natures; their image likenesses. Genesis informs us that when God came to creating man and he is determined to create man a very special kind of man, a transcendent kind of man—man in the state of original innocence and with a supernatural destiny—God did not use his eternal exact image of the species man as his model. God would have to use a different image as his model to produce that very different kind of man He intended to create.

Therefore God, as Genesis states, used his "our image likeness" as his working model when creating man. Creating man in "our image likeness" God created that very different man He intended to create.

Parenthetically it might be noted that God did something similar on the first day of creation when creating the angels. God had very many eternal exact image of every species of angel, but, as Genesis states, God used the analogous concept of light to create all the innumerably different species of angels and at the same time create them in their supernatural state of original innocence. When creating all the innumerable angels God created all of them by the one command: "Let there be light". God did not will to create all of the innumerable specifically different angels by a series of innumerable commands-–one command for each specifically different angel.

Since commentators failed to discover or to identify God's intended meaning and function of "our image likeness" in the creation process, they falsely supposed that "our image likeness" had to be something in man or in man's nature that bears a likeness to something in God's substance or nature. Commentators by making that supposition showed they were overlooking completely God's need for some mental image to be used as a model of the kind of man God intended to create. That oversight led them to misread the clear literal sense of the Hebrew "Let us make man in 'our image likeness'". Hence it is clear that commentators had the creation process backwards or reversed in their minds and in their attempts to explain Genesis' meaning of "our image likeness".

When the process of creation is not viewed backward or in reverse, it is clear that "our image likeness" is not something in the being or nature of the man, but something in the mind of God. That something in the mind of God was the image or idea God used as a working model in the creation of man. That "our image likeness" in the mind of God it turns out was the exact image or mental likeness God the Father had of his Incarnate God-man. It is also what John's gospel calls the Logos or Word.

God undoubtedly had an eternal exact image of the species man—an image that contained all that was essential for a being made according to it to be a true man. Here the literal sense of Genesis is telling us God rejected his eternal exact image of the species man as his working model when creating man. Genesis is telling us that God chose to use his "our image likeness" as his working model when creating man. God intended to use that same image likeness also as his working model in the creation of all the descendants of Adam so that all men would be transcendent humans at their conception and birth.

In this writing it has been stated that several different kinds of arguments from Scripture would be given to prove that God the Father from all eternity absolutely intended to incarnate his Son as the God-man. Since the Father unconditionally intended to incarnate his Son as the God-man, that implies that God the Father would have incarnated his Son as the God-man of Adam's race even if Adam would not have sinned. The Father intended to incarnate Him even if there would not have been any need for the God-man of the race of Adam to redeem Adam and his race.

God the Father had many "our image likeness" of the God-man in his mind from all eternity. God the Father, like all human fathers, intended the most and the best of everything for his Son the God-man. Hence God the Father destined the God-man to be the most perfect and glorious of men and destined him to live forever and living a most glorious mission among men on earth and in his Kingdom of heaven.

Since the Father intended to incarnate his Son by having Him conceived and born of a woman, the Father necessarily had many images of Him as a pre-born child, an infant, an adolescent, an adult and also images of Him in the activities of his life on earth and in heaven.

It is of utmost importance to understand that God the Father had a certain particular exact idea of the incarnate God-man in every particular state or condition He would have in life. Any one of them the Father could use as his working model when creating Adam and Eve or the Woman that would be the Mother of the God-man. The Father always wanted all men to be like the God-man and therefore God always intended to use one of his mental images of the God-man as his working model in the creation of man and in the forming of the most holy Mother of the God-man.

The proofs of the fact that the Father willed and decreed absolutely or unconditionally the Incarnation of his Son as the transcendent God-man of the race of Adam will be given in the fifth chapter of this book. It is not important for the understanding of this study of the God-man whether the Father willed his Incarnation either absolutely or conditionally. What is more necessary for readers to understand is that there are important consequences to the Father's willingness to incarnate his Son whether absolutely or conditionally

In the past theologian didn't get beyond discussing whether the Incarnation was willed either conditionally or absolutely. They did not discuss at all the fact that the Father willed his Son's Incarnation for the sake of creating all things. They have not discussed the Incarnation in relation to Scripture stating that the Father created everything "in, through, and for" the God-man and that the Father willed that all things "continue in existence in, through and for" the God-man. This will of the Father St. Paul calls the mystery of Christ. It implies the mystery that the Father likewise is most pleased to accept the praise and thanks of all creatures "in, through and for" the God-man and that the Father is most pleased to answer all our petition "in, through, and for" the sake of the God-man. "Truly, truly, I say to you, if you ask anything of the Father in my name, he will give it to you." Jn 16:23.

God chose not to use his eternal exact idea of the species man as his working model when creating Adam and when creating all the descendants of Adam. God intended man to be superior to the forces at work in the world. St. Paul would teach the Colossians that fallen man even in his recreated life must not be thought of as eternally subject to cosmic powers at work in the world or in the universe. "If with Christ you have died to cosmic forces, why should you be bound by rules that say, 'Do not handle, Do not taste, Do not touch!' as though you were still living a life bounded by this world? Such prescriptions deal with things that perish in their use. They are based on merely human precepts and doctrines." Col 2:20-23. In his second letter to the Corinthians, St. Paul has a list of expectations Christians must have for themselves. The things on that list run contrary to the expectations the world has for Christians. Cf. 2 Cor 4.

The Father willed to decree the most and the best of everything for the God-man and therefore his images of the God-man were images He formed according to his desires for the God-man. Since it was one of those images of the God-man that the Father chose to be his working model when forming the first man the first man was a man of great perfection. Hence it is obvious that the first man Adam was far superior to any man that process of evolution could produce. This predilection is the reason fallen mankind must face the fact that his creation in "our image likeness" is ultimately the only explanation of his greatness and the reason for the great quandaries and dilemmas fallen man must now face in his alien world.

The most perfect of all the eternal exact "our image likeness" in the mind of the Father represents the God-man's transcendent Sacred Humanity in its glorified state as the Eternal Supreme Head of all creation and enthroned at his Father's right hand in Heaven. This exalted state of the God-man St. Paul calls the absolute fullness of Jesus Christ. "He has put all things under Christ's feet and has made him, thus exalted, head of the church, which is his body: the fullness of him who fills the universe in all its parts." Eph 1:22. This "our image likeness" is the image likeness of the God-man living on high in his Glorious Eternal Kingdom of Heaven; Jesus Christ living and reigning eternally with great power over all creation.

The will of God the Father to incarnate his Son as the God-man of the race of Adam was absolute or unconditional. However the decrees of the Father regarding the different possible states or conditions of Son's Most Sacred Humanity and the different possible divine missions the God-man would have at his conception were conditional. In the intention of the Father his Incarnate Son's Most Sacred Humanity at his conception and birth would be in one state or condition if man did not sin and in a less perfect state or condition if man sinned.

In one state or condition the God-man would have been unable to redeem mankind if the God-man were to redeem mankind by suffering dying on the Cross. If man sinned the God-man would have to take on a less perfect state or condition. Hence to redeem man the God-man at his conception and birth would empty Himself of his fullness to become like us in everything except sin. In this less perfect or emptied state or condition the God-man could suffer and die for man's redemption.

It was necessary that the Father have an "our image likeness" that would represent the Sacred Humanity of the God-man in whatever state, condition or mission the God-man would have at his conception and birth and at all time of his life on earth and in heaven. A little reflection on certain truths taught in the New Testament concerning the God-man and his possible missions will show that the Father must have had innumerable different "our image likeness" of the God-man in his mind and had them of Him from all eternity. Each of the possible states or conditions or missions the God-man might have was represented in the mind of the Father by a like "our image likeness".

Hence God the Father from eternity had a whole series of "our image likeness" that represented all possible states and conditions and mission of the Most Sacred Humanity of his Incarnate God-man. The Father did not will that every image likeness He had of the God-man should come to reality or be manifest in the Incarnate God-man. From eternity one or more of those many eternal "our image likeness" in the mind of the Father represented the Sacred Humanity of the God-man in a state or condition of absolute perfection or of Him in his absolute fullness. From eternity there were "our image likeness" of the Incarnate God-man suffering ignominious crucifixion on Calvary for man's redemption.

Among all these many "our image likeness" was the particular "our image likeness" of the God-man which the Father chose and used as his model in his work of creating Adam and Eve in their transcendent state. It was that "our image likeness" that gave man in his transcendent state of having a supernatural divine life and an eternal destiny of supernatural happiness in the company of the Incarnate God-man reigning as Head of all creation at the right hand of his Almighty Father.

In the intention of the almighty Father the state or condition of the Sacred Humanity of the God-man at his Incarnation was not to be as perfect as the state It would have eternally glorified and seated at his Father's right hand in heaven. There was in the mind of the Father an "our image likeness" that represented the state of the Incarnate God-man at his conception if man did not sin and another less glorious or less perfect "our image likeness" that represented the state or condition of the Incarnate God-man at his conception if man sinned.

This first "our image likeness" was an "our image likeness" that represented the transcendent Most Sacred Humanity of the God-man in a state or condition with a life and mission among men which was that of Supreme Head and supernatural Savior, but not that of man's Redeemer. He was always predestined to be the Savior of all men for we must know that before original sin Adam and all men needed to be supernaturally saved {not redeemed} by the God-man. It was the will of the Father that all men be justified and glorified in, through, and for the sake of the God-man. Adam and Eve before they sinned were created and justified in, for and through the God-man, Jesus Christ.

From eternity the Father had an "our image likeness" of the Incarnate God-man that would be the model for the Incarnate God-man as He would live among sinners on earth in need of redemption by Him. This "our image likeness" was the "our image likeness" of the God-man in a condition which theologians term a passable state or condition. This is the "our image likeness" of the God-man that is the Father's image of his suffering servant. It represents the God-man as He was actually conceived, born and lived on earth two thousand years ago. It was the state or condition of the Most Sacred Humanity of the God-man prepared for his mission among sinners as their Redeemer, Savior and Lord—the God-man prepared for the mission of redeeming and saving fallen mankind by the Sacrifice of his Life on the Cross of Calvary.

This is the "our image likeness" of the God-man St. Paul has in mind when he teaches that Jesus Christ emptied Himself to become like us. Jesus Christ did not empty Himself of his divinity or of his humanity but emptied Himself of the fullness the Father and the Son initially and conditionally willed or intended from all eternity for the God-man at his Incarnation if man sinned.

From all eternity the Father intended that all men be like the transcendent God-man. But at the time of the creation of Adam and Eve the God-man was not as yet a reality. Hence the Father could not use the God-man Himself as his working model in the creation or formation of Adam and Eve. In that situation if God the Father wanted to create man like the God-man, the Father would have no choice but to use one of his many eternal exact "our image likeness" of his transcendent God-man as his working model in the creation of Adam and Eve. Therefore, Genesis states the situation most precisely when it states that God said: "Let us make man in our image likeness."

It cannot be too strongly emphasized for our understanding of God's goodness to man that embedded in the eternal plan of the Father to incarnate his Son as the transcendent God-man was the Father's plan to create, sanctify and finally glorify an entire race of transcendent humans. According to the Father's eternal plan to incarnate his Son as the transcendent God-man, the transcendent God-man's human nature was not to be created out of nothing and then that newly created human nature be united to the Person of his Son. It was always the Father's intention that his Son receive his Most Sacred Humanity through being conceived and born of a woman, the most holy Virgin Mary.

The woman chosen to be the Son's Ever-Virgin Mother too, in the plan of the Father, was not to be created out of nothing, but was to receive her human nature through being conceived and born of a woman of a race of humans on earth. Because the Father willed to incarnate his Son in this way, the very Incarnation of his Son merited or was the meritorious cause of the creation of the universe, the world or earth, the angels and a race of men on earth. The Incarnation of his Son was the specific motive of the Father for creating all things and for creating a transcendent race of humans on earth. It was also the meritorious cause of man's original state of innocence and subsequent eternal glorification. This is what Scripture means by God creating and doing all things "in, for, and through Him [the God-man]."

The Father planed that his Son's Incarnation as the God-man should last forever and that He should live first for some time among transcendent humans on earth and then forever in the Eternal Glorious Heavenly Kingdom the Father was pleased to prepare for Him. The Father planned that all transcendent humans of his race consecrate themselves to the service of his God-man as their Supreme Head, just as all the angels were created for a life of consecrated service to the same God-man as their Supreme Head.

Just as the eternal generation of the Son and his Incarnation as the God-man found their origin in the Divine Paternity of the Father, so also the creation and salvation of the transcendent race of Adam found their origin in the same Divine Paternity. Modern man should realize that just as there is no maternity in God for the eternal generation of the Son, so there is no maternity in God for the creation, salvation and eternal glorification of man. The Father's plan for the creation of Adam and his race and their achieving eternal salvation are entirely dependent and motivated by the Father initiating the Incarnation of his Son as the God-man of that race of transcendent humans on earth.

When Genesis states that God said: "Let us make man in our image likeness" Genesis is implying that God has deliberately chosen to use one of his eternal exact "our image likeness" of the God-man as his working model in the creation of Adam and Eve. It is also implying that the same "our image likeness" is the reason Adam and his entire race was created having transcendent human natures like the human nature the God-man would have at his Incarnation if Adam did not sin. "Our image likeness" is the reason Adam shared in the God-man's fullness and shared in the unfathomable riches of the God-man's Almighty Father's inheritance.

The creation of man in "our image likeness" is also the reason Adam and Eve had the very special natural and preternatural gifts and the reason God intended that those gifts be given to all their descendants. For the Father intended to use the "our image likeness" He used in the creation of Adam and Eve as his working model in the conception and birth of every descendant of Adam.

The creation of all men in "our image likeness" was the way God the Father planned to make Adam and Eve and every individual of their race transcendent humans and having a beginner's share in the natural, preternatural and supernatural fullness of the God-man, Jesus Christ. "Of his fullness we have all had a share—love following upon love." Jn 1:16. "It pleased God to make absolute fullness reside in him." Col 1:19. "In Christ the fullness of deity resides in bodily form. Yours is a share in this fullness... who is the head of every principality and power." Col 2:9. If it resided in Christ it also resided in his "our image likeness".

Because God used one of his eternal exact images of the God-man as his working model in the creation of man, Scripture could exalt man with the words: "When I behold your heavens, the work of your fingers, the moon and the stars which you set in place... What is man that you should be mindful of him, or the son of man that you should care for him? You have made him little less than the angels, and crowned him with glory and honor. You have given him rule over the works of your hands, putting things under his [man's] feet..." Ps 8:4-6.

If this psalm were speaking of the transcendent God-man, its author should not have expected to find the God-man made little less than the angels. The men made a little less than the angels are none other than Adam and Eve and their race.

The Father had a great number of different exact "our image likeness" of the God-man in his mind from eternity. When about to create man the Father chose that "our image likeness" of the God-man which would result in Adam and Eve and everyone of their race being conceived and born like the God-man would have been conceived and born if Adam had not sinned. They were not to be created with the attributes the Son's Glorified Sacred Humanity; the kind of humanity the God-man would have after his resurrection and glorification.

The Father's planned destiny for man, St. Paul explicitly informs us, was that man would ultimately share in the absolute fullness of Christ; share fully in the attributes of Christ's transcendent glorified Sacred Humanity and in Christ's Life on High in the Kingdom of Heaven. "He called you through our preaching of the good news so that you might achieve the glory of our Lord Jesus Christ." 2 Thess 2:14. "Dearly beloved, we are God's children now; what we shall later be has not yet come to light. We know that when it comes to light we shall be like him." 1 Jn 3:2

The Father's plan was that the transcendent natures of Adam and Eve and all persons of their entire race would omit at their creation and conception be transformed by another "our image likeness", a more glorious "our image likeness" of the God-man. God would provide this transformation when humans would arrive at the Gates of Heaven for their final judgement and eternal glorification. That perfect and glorious "our image likeness" of the God-man would transform men into copies of the perfect and glorious transcendent Sacred Humanity of the God-man. That "our image likeness" would give men a share in Christ's life on high; the life the God-man now has seated eternally at the right hand of his Almighty Father. It was always the absolute will of the Father that all men should ultimately share in the absolute fullness of the God-man. "Thus you will be able to grasp fully the breadth and length and height and depth of Christ's love and experience [experience, not merely witness] his love which surpasses all knowledge, so that you may attain to the fullness of God himself." Eph 3:19. "He [the Father] has put all things under Christ's feet and has made him, thus exalted, head of the church, which is his body: [his body is his members] the fullness of him who fills the universe in all its parts." Eph 1:22-23.

Chapters two and three of Genesis give clear evidence that Adam and Eve were not created according to God's eternal exact idea of the species man, but were created according to a model that produced far more perfect and splendid human beings or persons. In chapters two and three of Genesis, Adam and Eve are not merely highly developed humans, they are manifestly endowed with many special natural and preternatural gifts besides being superhuman, transcendent humans with supernatural life and a supernatural destiny. The very "our image likeness" God used when creating Adam and Eve is the very reason they were endowed with all God's special gifts of body, mind and soul.

That same "our image likeness" is the reason Adam and Eve were manifestly endowed with the gift of a profound knowledge of themselves and all natural things (knowledge Adam manifests at his marriage to Eve) and gave Adam immunity from error and freedom from interior tensions and strife. That "our image likeness" is the reason Adam was raised to the state of original innocence at his creation; a state in which he possessed supernatural divine life and a supernatural destiny, a destiny to a life on high in Christ's eternal Kingdom of Heaven.

By their creation in that "our image likeness" Adam and Eve were completely at peace and enjoyed tranquility with God, with each other and with all their descendants. They were in a state or condition far superior to any state or condition men on earth cannot even dream of enjoying.

Some modern scholars believe that the Church Fathers and theologians of the past ascribed too great a state of perfection to Adam and Eve when sinless and living in Paradise. If modern scholars and theologians had correctly identified and understood the meaning of "our image likeness" and its function in the process of creation they would never have thought such a thing.

That the above understanding of "our image likeness" must be God's and Genesis' intended meaning and function of "our image likeness" in the creation process is evident in the New Testament's teaching that fallen men need to be recreated in the image or likeness of the God-man for man's sanctification and salvation. In that teaching fallen men even in the very best and highest condition naturally achievable by man, must undergo a rebirth or recreation in the image of the God-man. Men must undergo that rebirth to have the justice and holiness God promised men in the Old and New Testaments. "You must put on that new man created in God's image, whose justice and holiness are born of truth." Eph 4:24. "Put on a new man, one who grows in knowledge as he is formed anew in the image of his Creator." Col 3:10. "Just as we resemble the man from earth, so we shall bear the likeness of the man of heaven [Jesus Christ]." 1 Cor 15:49. "All of us, gazing on the Lord's glory with unveiled faces, are being transformed from glory to glory into his very image by the Lord who is the Spirit." 2 Cor 3:18. "Of his fullness we have all had a share—love following upon love." Jn 1:16.

Ever since the fall of man, persons who are reborn or recreated in the image of Jesus Christ, no longer receive transcendent human natures, but do receive eternal life or supernatural divine life and are given a supernatural destiny.

God the Father, by using a specific "our image likeness" of the God-man as a model when incarnating his Son a transcendent God-man of the transcendent race of Adam made it possible for the God-man to be the First-born of many brothers. In this way the Father could destine all men to share in the fullness of the God-man and to share in the God-man's inheritance; share in his unfathomable riches by all men being coheirs to the inheritance the Almighty Father intended for his First-born, man's Supreme Head, Jesus Christ.

The apostle St. Paul revealed this intention of the Father when he wrote: "Those he foreknew he predestined to share in the image of his Son, that his Son might be the first-born of many brothers." Rom 8:29.

If more Scriptural evidence is desired which indicates that "our image likeness" was the Father's eternal mental image or likeness of the transcendent God-man, that evidence may be found in the writings of the apostles, especially St. Paul. He wrote: "He will give a new form to this lowly body of ours and remake it according to the pattern of his glorified body [the God-man's glorified transcendent Sacred Humanity], by his [almighty] power to subject everything to himself." Phil 3:21. "We are God's children now; what we shall later be has not yet come to light. We know that when it comes to light we shall be like him, for we shall be as he is." 1 Jn 3:2. We can be sure that it is not merely Christ's glorified body that will serve as a pattern for man's final glorification, but every aspect of the glorified transcendent human nature of Christ will serve as the pattern for the glorification of all the saints.

St. Paul prayed that all men would understand and act upon this most wondrous plan of the Father for mankind. "May the God of our Lord Jesus Christ, the Father of glory, grant you a spirit of wisdom and insight to know him clearly. May he enlighten your innermost vision that you may know the great hope to which he has called you, the wealth of his glorious heritage to be distributed among the members of his church, and the immeasurable scope of his power in us who believe. It is (almighty power) like the strength he showed in raising him from the dead and seating him at his right hand in heaven." Eph 1:17-20. The "in us" of this passage is very significant. St. Paul wrote that the immeasurable scope of his power would be manifest "in us" not merely manifest "to us". "Therefore I bear with all of this for the sake of those whom God has chosen, in order that they may obtain the salvation to be found in Christ Jesus and with it eternal glory. You can depend on this: If we have died with him, we shall also live with him; if we hold out to the end, we shall also reign with him." 2 Tm 2:10-12. "He called you through our preaching of the good news so that you might achieve the glory of our Lord Jesus Christ." 2 Thes 2:14.

The whole of the plan of the Father for mankind is the whole of the glorious and mysterious gospel of Jesus Christ. "Announced by the Lord, it was confirmed to us by those who heard him. God then gave witness to it (the gospel) by signs, miracles, varied acts of power, and distribution of the gifts of the Holy Spirit as he willed." Heb 2:4.

The Father destined all men to share in the very glory He intended for Christ. "I have come to rate all things as loss in the light of the surpassing knowledge of my Lord Jesus Christ. For his sake I have forfeited everything; I have accounted all else as rubbish so that Christ may be my wealth and I may be in him, not having a justice of my own based on observance of the law. The justice I possess is that which comes through faith in Christ. It has its origin in God and is based on faith." Phil 3:8-9. "Be intent on things above, rather than on things of earth. After all, you have died! Your life is hidden now with Christ in God. When Christ our life [now hidden in God] appears, than you shall appear with him in glory." Col 3:2-4. "Of his fullness we have all had a share—love following on love." Jn 1:16. "When Christ our life appears, then you shall appear with him in glory. [Not in his glory, but in a glory like his.]" Col 3:4. "It is not that I have reached it yet, or have already finished my course; but I am racing to grasp the prize if possible, since I have been grasped by Christ Jesus. Brothers, I do not think of myself as having reached the finish line. I give no thought to what lies behind but I push on to what is ahead. My entire attention is on the finish line as I run toward the prize to which God calls me—life on high in Christ Jesus". Phil 3:12-14. "Andronicus and Junias, my kinsmen and fellow prisoners; they are outstanding apostles, and they were in Christ before I was." Rom 16:7.

It was ever the Father's absolute intention, even before the world began, to incarnate his Son as the God-man of the race of Adam and to bestow all grace on that entire human race through the God-man, Jesus Christ. "God has saved us and has called us to a holy life, not because of any merit of ours but according to his own design—the grace [He] held out to us in Christ Jesus ***before the world*** began but now made manifest through the appearance of our Savior." 2 Tm 1:9-10. The New Testament teaches: "Those he foreknew he predestined to share the image of his Son, that the Son might be the first-born of many brothers." Rom 8:29.

If the Father intended that Adam and Eve and all persons of the race of Adam be created in the image likeness of the God-man yet did not intend that the Sacred Humanity of the Incarnate Son be born from a woman of the race of Adam, how could Jesus Christ be the First-born of many brothers? How could Jesus be a true brother to everyone of the race of Adam if He were not born of a woman of the race of Adam? How could all men of the race of Adam be coheirs with the God-man, unless all men were true genetic sisters and brothers of the God-man?

God the Father always willed absolutely his Son's Incarnation as the God-man of the race of Adam, hence the Father could not condition the Incarnation of his Son on the fall of Adam from grace or on the race of Adam needing redemption by the Incarnate God-man. Nevertheless some very eminent theologians of the past have held the contrary opinion. St. Thomas is among those who have held that the Son would not have become the God-man if Adam had not sinned. This opinion is often incorrectly stated. It is often stated that the Son became man in consequence of man's fall from grace, when in fact it was not the Father's decree that mankind be redeemed that determined the Incarnation of the Son as the God-man of the race of Adam.

The apostles John and Paul teach clearly, as will be shown in chapter five, that Jesus Christ, the God-man, was in the beginning or before everything else in the intention of the Father. The God-man was not first or before everything in the order of created reality, hence it must be that He was first in the order of the Father's intention. This means the Incarnation of his Son had first priority in the intention of the Father; first in the Father's plan and decrees. These texts of the apostles imply that the intention to incarnate the Son, as the God-man of the race of Adam, was absolute for it was intended and decreed already before God decreed the creation of the world, man or the sin of Adam occurred. The incarnation was not conditioned by or dependent on the Son having or receiving the mission of redeeming mankind.

WHAT "OUR IMAGE LIKENESS" SIGNIFIED FOR THE HUMANITY OF THE GOD-MAN

From all eternity, the Father for the love of his Son willed absolutely to incarnate Him as the God-man of the race of Adam, and willed absolutely that the God-man be ultimately supremely glorified at his right hand forever in heaven as the Supreme Head of all creation. God the Father, just as all fathers, desired and planned the most and the best of everything for his Incarnate Son, the God-man. From all eternity the Father willed to communicate to the God-man every created and uncreated grace and goodness possible to that Most Sacred Transcendent Humanity and Person of the God-man.

For this reason the Father, when making his eternal plans for his Son, decreed that the God-man should be incarnated having the most perfect transcendent Sacred Humanity and having the most glorious of missions while on earth and also while in heaven. In the Father's plan the God-man should have Supreme Headship over all creation and that He rule and reign over all creation forever. The Father planed that the God-man rule forever as King of kings and Lord of lords on earth and forever at the right hand of his Father in the glorious Kingdom of Heaven. This most glorious state or condition of the God-man as Supreme Head of the Church and all creation is what St. Paul calls the absolute fullness of Christ.

Hence it is that the Father willed ultimate goodness for man by his will that all men be created like the God-man and that all men have a life like that of the God-man. The Father willed that all men share completely and forever in that absolute fullness of Christ. Ultimately every person will be judged and destined eternally by God the Father on the bases of every person's likeness to the God-man.

The Father originally intended that the God-man have the fullness and perfection of every natural, preternatural and supernatural gift at his Incarnation. Already at his Incarnation the God-man's human will would have the perfection of every virtue; his human intellect have the greatest possible store of infused knowledge and that He be perfectly competent in the fields of every human science and art. The Father originally willed that the God-man have this fullness of perfection at the moment of his Incarnation on earth, and that He should live among men on earth in that condition but only for a limited time. After Adam sinned however for the redemption of man the Father willed that the God-man empty himself of his fullness at his Incarnation.

The Father originally intended to bestow on the Person of the Incarnate God-man at his Conception Supreme Dominion over all creation and that He be the Savior [not redeemer] of angels and all men. The Father willed that man's original supernatural salvation and destiny be due to the Incarnation. In the plan of the Father the God-man would be the Savior of all angels and men because his Incarnation would be the meritorious cause of the creation of the angels, their being created in the state of supernatural eternal life and their being destined to a supernatural destiny. According to that original plan of the Father the God-man would not be the Redeemer of all men for all men were created in a supernatural state and were to remain faithful and so were not in need of redemption. After his incarnation and after living for some time with men on earth the God-man would enter heaven forever and as Supreme Head of all creation ruling as King of kings and Lord of lords forever. The Father, when decreeing the bestowal of Eternal and Supreme Dominion over all creation on the God-man, decreed an Eternal Kingdom for the God-man. He was not to be King without a Kingdom. In imitation of the God-man's Supreme Dominion over all of creation, the Father willed to give Adam, at his creation, a subordinate kind of dominion over all creatures on earth.

The Incarnation of the Son as the God-man of the race of Adam would be accomplished by the union of a Sacred Transcendent Human Nature, taken from a woman of the race of Adam, with the Divine Person of the Son. In this hypostatic union the human intellect of the God-man would necessarily be united with the Person of Son and therefore the God-man's intellect would necessarily know his Divine Person and his human intellect could never be without the beatific vision of God. For human intellects necessarily know their person or being.

No one should think that God the Father, when creating Adam

and Eve in "our image likeness", used as a model that "our image likeness" which represented the God-man in his supreme glory. Such an "our image likeness" would have created Adam and Eve having the perfection of the glorified Sacred Humanity of the God-man. The Father did not have any intention of creating the transcendent human natures of Adam and Eve and all their descendants in a state equal in perfection to that of transcendent humans in the glory of heaven. Also God the Father certainly never intended that Adam and all descendants be created with the fullness of grace God the Father had most singularly designed and intended only for the Most Holy Virgin Mother of the God-man.

The Father intended that every individual of the race of Adam at conception should, besides being created with transcendent human natures, have a beginner's share in the fullness of the God-man, Jesus Christ. The Father intended that all the saved from among men possess a much greater share than a beginner's share in the absolute fullness of Christ when glorified upon entrance into the glory of heaven.

When creating Adam and Eve the Father chose for his working model that eternal exact "our image likeness" in his mind of the God-man which would create Adam and Eve with transcendent human natures like the transcendent human nature the God-man would have at his Incarnation. Creation in that "our image likeness" would likewise have given every descendant of Adam's race the same beginner's share in the fullness of the God-man Adam and Eve received at their creation. For the almighty Father willed that everyone of Adam's race be a coheir with his First-born Son and therefore share in the unfathomable riches of the inheritance the Almighty Father willed for his First-born Son.

It is precisely because the Father used that eternal exact "our image likeness" that Adam was not created the kind of man God's eternal exact idea of the species man would have made Adam—the homo sapiens of the evolutionist. Because God created man according to the eternal exact "our image likeness" man was created what God planned on man to be. "Then God said: 'Let us make man in our image likeness. Let them have dominion over the fish of the sea, and over the birds of the air, and over the cattle, and over all the earth, and over every creeping thing that creeps upon the earth.'"

In God's plan for incarnating his Son and for the creation of the universe we see that God's way of setting goals and pursuing them is not unlike man's. A musician may have heaven as his ultimate end or goal, but performances at the MET may nevertheless be the immediate goal of his planing, studies and training. The glorification of the God-man of the race of Adam and of the Most Holy Trinity were the ultimate end or goal of the Father's creative activity and of his master plan for all of creation. The God-man's life, his mission, his work and his functions as Supreme Head of all creation had for there ultimately goal the glory of the most Holy Trinity. The creation of the universe and the race of Adam were the more immediate goals in the plan and intention of the Father leading to the ultimate goal of eternal glorification of the Most Holy Trinity. Cf. Col 1:15.

It should now be obvious that the Father's love for the God-man and his welfare and glory were what held the Father's attention and interest above everything else ad extra. The fact that the Father, as St. Paul wrote, was willing to deliver the God-man up to death for the salvation of us all manifests how great must be the love and desire the Father has for the sanctification and salvation of each one of us. "Is it possible that he who did not spare his won Son but handed him over for the sake of us all will not grant us all things besides?" Rom 8: 32.

The truth is that the Father's attention and greatest interest above every other interest ad extra was and still is the Incarnate God-man and that the Incarnation of the God-man is the reason the Father willed to create all things. The truth and the fact that the Incarnation is the reason the Father wills to keep all things in existence add further meaning and significance to our celebrations of all the Solemnities of the Lord Jesus, especially his Annunciation and his Birth at Christmas. The same would be true of the Solemnities the Church celebrates in honor of the Virgin Mother of the God-man.

REASON FOR BELIEVING THAT THE INCARNATION WAS THE REASON THE FATHER CREATED AND KEEPS THE UNIVERSE, THE EARTH AND MAN IN EXISTENCE

What the Father intended and planned for his Son's Incarnation and Supreme Glorification was inseparable from what the Father intended and planned for all men. This can be clearly seen and understood in the Father's determination that the Most Sacred Transcendent Humanity of the God-man not be created out of nothing, but that his Incarnate Son receive his Most Sacred Transcendent Humanity by being conceived and born of a transcendent woman. The Father planned that this woman too not be created out of nothing but that she be conceived and born of a woman of the transcendent race of Adam.

Since God the Father planned to incarnate his Son in this way, it is very evident that the very Incarnation of the Son as a God-man merited the creation of the material universe, the earth and a race of transcendent humans on the earth. For it would be from that race of transcendent humans that the Ever Virgin Mother of the transcendent God-man was destined by God to be conceived and born. In the plan of the Father the very Incarnation of His Son as the God-man merited the creation and eternal existence of the universe and the supernatural salvation of all creatures capable of supernatural salvation; angels and men. The Sacred Passion and Death of the God-man, on the other hand, merited something entirely different. It did not merit the creation of anything. It merited the redemption and salvation of fallen mankind. The Sacred Passion and Death did not merit for mankind the state of original innocence the Father planed for Adam and all his descendants.

It is also evident that what the Father planned, decreed and executed made possible a multitude of humans that were true genetic brothers and sisters of the God-man. The God-man, the Firstborn of Father, would have many brothers sister and would be their Supreme Head forever. "For he who consecrates and those who are consecrated have one and the same Father. Therefore he is not ashamed to call them brethren, saying, 'I will announce your name to my brothers, I will sing your praise in the midst of the assembly.'" Heb 2:11-12.

In the plan and intention of the Father there would never be more than one race of humans, the race that began with Adam and Eve. Any origin of some men besides those having an origin from Adam would tear up the Scriptural birth certificate showing Adam and Eve to be the only true genetic brother or sister of the Lord Jesus Christ. "Those whom he foreknew he predestined to share in the image of his Son, that the Son might be the first-born of many brothers." Rom 8:29. "He will give a new form to this lowly body of ours and make it according to the pattern of his glorified body, by the power to subject everything to himself." Phil 3:21. "Dearly beloved, we are God's children now; what we shall later be has not yet come to light. We know that when it comes to light we shall be like him, for we shall be as he is." 1 Jn 3:2.

Even the fallen members of the race of Adam by their generation from Adam and his line still unavoidably inherit the Father's planned natural or physical genetic kinship to the God-man. Everyone born to the race of Adam is irrevocably a genetic brother or sister of the God-man by the very fact that he or she is born of the race in which the conception and birth of the God-man has taken place.

The New Testament teaches that men have this a far more valuable spiritual and supernatural kinship with the God-man. For according to the Father's original plan and covenant for man all the descendants of Adam would inherit supernatural divine life along with human life from Adam. This supernatural life is a participation in the divine nature. Cf. 2 Pet 1:4. This spiritual kinship is the result of the supernatural divine life the Father willed for everyone of the race of Adam. In the terminology of the Church of Christ regarding this doctrine, persons are truly the adopted supernatural children of God only when in the state of sanctifying grace. Fallen men no longer inherit the sanctifying grace of this spiritual adoption, the spiritual supernatural kinship of original innocence by their human generation from Adam and his genetic line.

However persons of the fallen race of Adam can regain the supernatural divine life and their supernatural kinship as a child of God by the requirement of doing the will of God and on condition that they believe in the God-man. "Someone said to him, 'Your mother and your brothers are standing outside there and they wish to speak to you.' He said to the one, who had told him, 'Who is my mother? Who are my brothers?' Then extending his hand toward his disciples, he said, 'There are my mother and my brothers. Whoever does the will of my heavenly Father is brother, and sister, and mother to me.'" Mt 12:50; cf. Lk 8:21. "See what love the Father has bestowed on us, in letting us be called children of God! Yet that is what we are. The reason the world does not recognize us [as children of God] is that it never recognized the Son [to be the natural Son of God]. Dearly beloved, we are God's children now; what we shall later be has not yet come to light. We know that when it comes to light we shall be like him, for we shall be as he is." 1 Jn 3:1-2. It is this sonship to God that St. Peter has in mind when he states that Christians share in the divine nature. "By virtue of them he has bestowed on us the great and precious things he promised, so that through these you who have fled a world corrupted by lust might become sharers of the divine nature." 2 Pt 1:4.

Surely human persons can never possess any higher dignity or have greater honor, in the eyes of God and of creatures, than that of being true genetic brothers or sisters of the God-man and true spiritual supernatural children of God. The highest, best and truest image any human person can have of himself or herself is that he or she is a true genetic brother or sister of the God-man and a true supernatural child of God the Father. No one by physical or spiritual death can any more loose his or her identity as a true genetic brother or sister of the God-man than a person who dies looses his membership in the race of Adam. Hence no individual is totally depraved by original sin. It is only by more and graver personal sins that persons become more and more depraved. St. Paul wrote: "God chose us in him (Jesus Christ) before the world began, to be holy and blameless in his sight, to be full of love, he likewise predestined us through Jesus Christ to be his adopted sons—such was his will and pleasure— that we might praise the glorious favor he has bestowed on us in his beloved Son." Eph 1:4-5.

Before time and before the world began, the Father destined all men in Christ Jesus to live forever and forever destined to pray, worship, love and praise the Father because of and in Jesus Christ. "God has saved us and has called us to a holy life, not because of any merit of ours but according to his own design—the grace held out to us in Christ Jesus before the world began but now made manifest through the appearance of our Savior." 2 Tm 1:9-10.

Contrary to myths of quarrelsome and immoral gods abusing men by changing men into beasts and beasts into men, Holy Scripture reveal an Almighty Creator-God. A Creator-God who willed to create Adam and his race out of pure paternal love that was for the sake of incarnating his Son as the God-man of Adam's race. All men of Adam's race were destined, at the creation of Adam, to become true genetic brothers and sisters of the God-man and to a life that is a true participation in the divine nature. Consequently, it was the beloved Son's true genetic brothers and sisters that the God-man willed to rescue from enslavement to Satan and from the eternal damnation their sins deserved. He rescued them by freely accepting for Himself the roles of redeemer and mediator on behalf of his fallen genetic brothers and sisters.

To accept the role of redeemer, Jesus Christ freely willed to empty Himself at his Incarnation by not assuming an impassible human nature and instead assumed a passable human nature, so He could suffer death, even death on the Cross, to redeem his fallen and enslaved brethren. The Son by assuming a human nature from Adam's fallen race made himself the God-man and emptied his Person and human nature of their fullness. He became a human in the likeness of God's eternal exact "our image likeness" that made Him like us in all things except sin. Cf. Heb 4:15. That "our image likeness" was essentially like God's eternal exact idea of man. The God-man willed to become the Father's prophetic suffering servant. The God-man freely emptied Himself of the fullness, the most and the best of everything the Father originally destined for him at his conception and birth to become like his fallen brothers and sisters. In that emptiness He would be able to suffer and die on the Cross for the redemption and salvation of his genetic brothers and sisters.

Man's physical or genetic brotherhood and sisterhood with the Incarnate God-man is very different from what pagans, complete secularists and even some Christians contend when they say all men are the children of God. Man's genetic brotherhood and sisterhood to the Incarnate God-man is real and man's sharing in the divine nature and divine life is also real. These are not the reasons pagans and secularists give for men being the children of God or for loving one another. Jesus Christ's new and supreme commandment that men love one another as He loves everyone. That is not the same as the old commandment found in Leviticus 19:18. His new command is that they love one another as He loves them. Cf. Jn 13:34.

One of the eternal exact "our image likeness" in the mind of the Father represented the transcendent Most Sacred Humanity of Jesus Christ in his absolute fullness. If the Father chosen to predestine the human natures of men to conform to that same eternal exact "our image likeness", the absolute fullness of the transcendent Most Sacred Humanity of Jesus Christ, then why should St. Paul not declare: "When Christ our life appears [in glory] you shall appear with him in glory." Col 3:4 "He will give a new form to this lowly body of ours and remake it according to the pattern of his glorified body, by his power to subject everything to himself." Phil 3:21. Why would St. John not declare: "We know that when it [our glory] comes to light we shell be like him, for we shell be as he is." 1 Jn 3:2. It is not only man's body but also man's whole being that will be remade in the pattern of the Glorious God-man. For Christ has power to subject everything to himself and He intends to use that almighty power to make us like him in glory.

Because the "our image likeness" of Genesis was neither correctly identified nor its function as the model God used in the creation of man, "our image likeness" has been completely misunderstood by theologians and commentators. Moreover commentators are unaware of the fact that the words "Let us" can be understood as a clear reference to the Persons of the Most Holy Trinity. This phrase necessarily supposes that it was God the Father who planned and decreed the Incarnation of his Son as the God-man of the race of Adam. By this "Let us" and "our image likeness" Genesis is clearly implying the reality of the multiplicity of Divine Persons in the Godhead.

At the end of the sixth day God saw the transcendent Adam and Eve as his very good, but apparently not as yet his very best work. If transcendent man had been found to be very good and all other creatures found to be no better than good, why was transcendent Adam and Eve not seen as God's best work? An incorrect answer would be that God saw Adam and Eve in their supernatural state and therefore saw them to be very good, while the other subhuman creatures on earth were seen in their purely natural states and therefore could be seen merely as good.

This understanding is incorrect not because the angels also were created in a supernatural state and yet were seen as merely good on the first day. They could not be seen as the perfect work of God because God the Father saw only man in the likeness of his Incarnate God-man who was most pleasing to the Father. The transcendent Adam and Eve in the likeness of the God-man was especially pleasing in the eyes of the Father. If this is true God had reason not to declare man his best work. The eternal exact image the Father had of his God-man glorified was destined to become a reality and therefore loomed much more pleasing in the Father's mind and intention. That glorious eternal exact "our image likeness" of the God-man was only temporally an unfulfilled reality. The reality signified by that glorious eternal "our image likeness" would one day become the God-man in his absolute fullness and would be most pleasing to the Creator as his best work. That glorious eternal exact "our image likeness" when it becomes a reality will be God's very best, most exalted, and most glorious work of all time and eternity. God's second best or second most glorious work of all time and eternity will be the God-man's Immaculate Mother, Mary full of grace, by her Immaculate Conception. These more perfect and glorious works were always in the mind of the Father and their reality was still in the future.

After God said: "Let us make man in our image likeness" Moses surprisingly records the messenger giving his usual affirmative witnessing statement: "And that is exactly what happened." Cf. Gen

1:30. The reason for surprise is that there was no way any messenger could see directly that eternal exact "our image likeness" hidden in the mind of God. Therefore he could not have known whether the Adam and Eve God had just created in fact conformed to that eternal "our image likeness". He could not assert "And that is exactly what happened" unless he were a creature with the beatific vision of God, an angel with the beatific vision of God. This is another reason for thinking that the visionary-messenger who spoke to his author-collaborator, Moses, during the six days of creation. was a glorified angel. For only glorified angels possessed the beatific vision of God. Only such an angel could have had direct access to the mind of God and could have seen that Adam and Eve had indeed been created in that "our image likeness" in the mind of God.

Earlier it was pointed out that the visionary-messenger knew more about what God was doing during the six days of creation than what he heard God command and what he saw God doing in consequence of his commands. On the first day, he knew, for example, that in the beginning God had created the heavens and on the seventh day he knew that God had begun his eternal rest without hearing God inform him that He had begun his rest. Hence it appears that a source of the visionary-messenger's greater knowledge was his beatific vision of God. This is one reason St. Stephen could have said that the law, the Torah, the writings of Moses, was delivered to Moses by an angel.

Jesus testifies to the fact that Moses is the author of Genesis and other books of the Old Testament. "Do not imagine that I will be your accuser before the Father; the one to accuse you is Moses on whom you have set your hopes. If you believed Moses you would then believe me, for it was about me that he wrote. But if you do not believe what he wrote, how can you believe what I say?" Jn 5: 45-47. In these texts Jesus is accusing the Jews of not believing what Moses, the author of the entire Pentateuch, wrote of him. Therefore Moses is the human author of Genesis.

DIFFERENT SETS OF "OUR IMAGE LIKENESS" IN THE MIND OF GOD

There were several main sets of eternal exact "our image likeness" in the mind of God the Father from eternity representing the God-man, his Mother and mankind. The first set concerned the Incarnation of his Son as the God-man. There were many sub sets belonging to this set of "our image likeness" representing the God-man. Only three of these subsets are of particular concern for this study, for they are easily identified in the actual Incarnation of the God-man and in their function in the different works of creation. There was one set for each of the two possible known states or conditions, which the God-man might assume at his Incarnation or Conception. A third set with its subsets represent the God-man's Sacred Humanity in glory and in its ultimate glorification at the right hand of his Father.

Since it was the Father's absolute will that the Most Sacred Humanity his Son would assume was not to be created out of nothing, but that He receive It by being conceived and born of a Virgin Mother, it was inevitable that there would be a set with sub sets of "our image likeness" in the mind of God the Father that represented the Mother of the God-man. There were subsets of "our image likeness" representing the different states or conditions of the humanity of the Mother of the God-man. Conditions of her humanity and missions that corresponded to the different states or conditions of the Sacred Humanity of the God-man. In this set representing the Mother of the God-man there were at least three subsets of eternal "our image likeness" representing the Virgin Mother. One "our image likeness" to represent each of the two possible conditions the Mother of the God-man might assume at her conception and birth. Another represented Mary as the Mother of the Redeemer of mankind. These sub sets of "our image likeness" represented Mary's humanity and missions in either of her two different divine missions. A final subset of "our image likeness" concerned Mary in her glorified heavenly fullness—Mary sharing to the fullest extent possible in the absolute fullness of her Son's Royalty and Supreme Headship. This "our image likeness" represents

Mary Mother of the God-man ruling and reigning in Heaven as Queen of the universe at the right hand of her Son, the King of kings and Lord of lords.

Another set with subsets of "our image likeness" in the mind of the Father concerned mankind. If the God-man were to receive his Sacred Humanity by being conceived and born of a woman from a woman born of a race of humans on earth, it was inevitable that there would be a set of "our image likeness" in the mind of the Father that would represent the race of men God would create. This set contained at least three different subsets of "our image likeness". One subset of "our image likeness" represented the state or condition of man at his creation. It was this "our image likeness" the Father used as his working model in the formation of the first man, Adam. It represented man in his state of original innocence with special natural, preternatural, supernatural gifts and enjoying the eternal supernatural destiny of sharing in the absolute fullness of the God-man. A second subset represented man in his fallen state, man in a state or condition in which he was without his original innocence; man without special natural, preternatural and supernatural gifts and without his supernatural destiny.

From eternity the set of eternal "our image likeness" in the mind of the Father representing the Virgin Mother of the Incarnate God-man was ever inseparable from the set of eternal "our image likeness" representing the Incarnate God-man. In the mind and intention of God the Father the humanity and divine mission of the Virgin Mother of the God-man were ever associated with the Most Sacred Humanity and missions of the Incarnate God-man living in this world. For the Mother of the God-man was always predestined to be like Him in his Most Sacred Humanity and always associated with the God-man in the different possible missions He would have on earth and in his glorified state in heaven.

Another set with subsets of eternal "our image likeness" in the mind of the Father concerned the first man and the woman and everyone of their race in their state of original innocence, their fallen condition and their reborn condition. This set of "our image likeness" with its subsets represented the condition of Adam and Eve at their creation; the condition all persons of their entire race would have at their creation or conception if Adam and Eve did not sin. A second subset of "our image likeness" represented all humans in their fallen condition. A third subset represented man's condition in his rebirth in likeness of the God-man. A fourth subset represented the condition of men glorified in heaven sharing in the absolute fullness of Christ. This "our image likeness" represented the condition men have as coheirs with Christ and enjoying the unfathomable riches of the Almighty Father's First-born's inheritance.

FURTHER EVIDENCE FROM GENESIS THAT ADAM DID NOT EVOLVE

God needs and uses some eternal exact idea or mental likeness as a working model in his work of creating or making anything. The first chapter of Genesis makes no explicit mention of God using his eternal exact ideas or images of the natures of creatures as his working models in creation of all the specifically different creatures He created during the six days of creation. The author of Genesis expected that all his readers would be aware of the fact that God always needed and used his eternal exact idea or image as his working model when He created each species.

Hence readers of Genesis would naturally suppose that God used his eternal exact idea or image of the nature of the species man as his working model when creating man. If God had used his eternal exact idea or image of the nature of the species man, then the first man, Adam, could have been like some kind of prehistoric man; the supposed homo sapiens of evolutionists and archaeologists. Genesis forestalls our making that mistaken assumption in the case of man by explicitly stating that God used his "our image likeness" as his working model when creating man.

If God had used his eternal exact idea or image of the species man—an idea or image of man that contained only what was essential or necessary for a being to be a true man—as his model in the creation of man, then Adam and Eve, the first parents of our race, might have been primitive humans. They might have been humans in the first stage of man's supposed evolutionary development. Adam and Eve might have been like the prehistoric cave dwellers of modern evolutionists, archaeologists and others, who believe man evolved from some subhuman species. Adam and Eve might then have lived like the first humans of pseudo-science and science fiction, instead of living the transcendent life Adam and Eve are displayed as living in the second and third chapters of Genesis.

Since God created Adam and Eve using his "our image likeness" of the transcendent God-man as his working model, Adam and Eve were created transcendent humans in imitation of the God-man's coming Incarnation. If the transcendent Adam were the progenitor of a whole race of transcendent humans, then there is no possibility that the human race had an evolutionary origin. Adam and Eve, instead of being primitive and undeveloped, their minds, wills, souls and bodies were free from every defect or imperfection. Adam and Eve from the first moment of their existence had all the special natural, preternatural and supernatural gifts the Father originally intended for God-man at his Incarnation.

Genesis makes it clear that Adam and Eve at their creation were without any defect and were incapable of any error, any suffering, any sickness and death or disfunction of any faculty of soul or body. Their intellects had been enriched with a great store of infused knowledge of things natural, preternatural and supernatural. They were endowed with competence in all human sciences and arts. That is the reason Genesis portrays Adam and Eve, from their very beginning, with the ability to speak and understand an audible language, with perfect understanding of their sexuality, their marriage partnership along with all the rights and duties of their marriage partnership. In Genesis Adam proclaims that family and family life must have dominant value forever for their entire race and that marriage is the only legitimate reason for a man to leave his father and mother and cling to his wife. He proclaims that by marriage the two persons became one body. Cf. Gen 2:15-24. From the beginning Adam and Eve manifest a knowledge no evolutionists would ever have ascribed to the first evolved man and woman. If a man may leave father and mother only to cling to his wife, then he may not leave father and mother to cling to his homosexual partner.

In particular, Genesis manifests that Adam from his beginning possessed an understanding of the nature of contracts, for he understood and accepted the creation contract or covenant God made with him as the head of the human race. He understood the limited dominion God gave him over all things on earth. Adam understood and accepted the contract God made with him for ownership of Paradise and for maintaining Paradise as a permanent home for himself and his family and his race. He understood that God was giving him Paradise as a permanent dwelling place on the bases of his taking care of Paradise by maintaining and cultivating its plants and harvesting their fruit and not eating fruit from the tree of good and bad.

Adam understood and accepted also the creation covenant's provisions for receiving and retaining his own and his family's original innocence and eternal supernatural destiny, for he understood the creation covenant was God's means for the salvation and the eternal glorification of himself, his wife and his entire race. Genesis implies that Adam understood clearly his and his family's rights to eat freely fruit from all the trees of Paradise and in particular he clearly understood God's command that he and his family abstain from ever eating fruit from the tree of the knowledge of good and bad. Adam understood that his loyalty was to God even when being tempted by Satan. Adam was not deceived by Satan as was Eve. Cf.1 Tm 2:14.

PRINCIPLES FOR PRE AND POST FALL THEOLOGY OF GRACE

Scripture reveals that the Incarnation of the Son of God as the God-man of the race of Adam was the final cause or only motive of God the Father for creating, for doing everything God had already done and would continue doing forever ad extra. The Incarnation was the final cause of the making of the creation covenant with Adam. The creation covenant would be the instrumental cause for all of Adam's descendents receiving transcendent human natures, the state of original innocence and the eternal destiny of sharing forever in the absolute fullness of Christ, the unfathomable riches of Christ's inheritance.

Particular consideration must be given to these truths and facts and their implications for knowledge and for understanding the principles of the pre-fall theology of grace. In the post fall proclamation of the protoevangelium God revealed his intention to reestablish or recreate fallen man in the likeness of another image of the God-man through redemption and to establish the New, Eternal and Universal Covenant as his only covenant for the rejustification and salvation of mankind. By revealing the creation covenant, the protoevangelium and the New, Eternal and Universal Covenant God clearly manifested truths that reveal the principles of the pre-fall theology of grace and the principles of the post-fall theology of grace.

The New, Eternal, and Universal Covenant was established by God as the only justifying covenant for the rejustification of the entire fallen race of Adam including Adam to the last man to be born of his race. Hence the new covenant was established immediately after the fall to confer on Adam and Eve and everyone of their entire fallen future race the only graces available to fallen man; the graces to be merited in redemption.

Chapter 3

CHAPTER TWO OF GENESIS

OH MAN! HAVE YOU FORGOTTEN HOW AND WHY YOU WERE CREATED? LISTEN! I WILL DECLARE THAT TO YOU AGAIN

CHAPTER TWO IS AN EYEWITNESS ACCOUNT OF THE CREATION OF THE FIRST MAN AND WOMAN

The third chapter of Genesis is the logical outcome of the truths taught in the second chapter. Readers should know that with the fourth verse of chapter two of Genesis the author begins composing and writing on his own the account of the creation for the visionary-messenger from God is no longer giving the author of Genesis information. Here in chapter two Moses himself is privileged to witness by means of visions the formation of the bodies of Adam and Eve and to observe them living the events of their lives. It should be clear that in chapter two Moses is writing of persons he actually sees, words he actually hears and certain happenings or events he sees taking place in the visions God is giving to him. These visions are supernatural reenactment of past events. They are not visions of the actual happenings, which occurred thousands of years earlier.

The second chapter of Genesis really begins midway in the fourth verse of chapter two. Verses one, two and three belong to chapter one of Genesis. Moses' first vision is a vision of a quite barren landscape where God first forms the man from dust and then the Paradise. Next he is given a vision of God forming the man's body from dust and of God leading the man into that Paradise. Once in Paradise God immediately begins proposing the making of the creation covenant with the man He has just formed from dust.

In the visions that follow Moses is shown a very large area of the earth. It is the area of the earth in which God has chosen to create or form the first man from dust and prepare a Paradise to be the permanent home on earth for the man, his wife and their descendents. After completing the creation covenant with Adam God leaves Adam and leaves him in charge of Paradise. In the next sequence of visions days later when God returns to the man in Paradise, Moses observes God forming the first woman's body from a rib of the man and God instituting marriage for mankind when marring Adam and Eve to each other. Moses will see the man and the woman enjoying life together in their Paradise.

The third chapter of Genesis is Moses' account of his witnessing, by means of a vision, Adam and Eve being enticed and succumbing to the deceitful temptation of Satan. These visions are followed by visions of God coming on the scene of Adam and Eve's fall from the grace of God. God learns from Adam and Eve what had happened and why. Moses hears God curse Satan for his great crime and hears God proclaim the protoevangelium. He then witnesses the expulsion of Adam and Eve from Paradise.

In these two chapters Moses not only composes and records in his own words what he hears and sees but also gives a few pointers on how to understand what is happening. The visions are so realistic that Moses clearly hears and understands what God, Adam, Eve, and Satan say and sees what they are doing. Moses incorporates this into his account, for our better understanding; the reason for Satan appearing as a serpent and why certain things are said and done. For example, in verses four through nine of chapter two, Moses records seeing that the earth is in a condition quite inhospitable for man. He then states the reasons for the earth's inhospitable conditions. The reasons he gives are a lack of rainfall and no man on earth to till the ground.

GOD BEGINS TO REVEAL AND IMPLEMENT HIS ETERNAL MASTER PLAN FOR MAN, THE CREATION COVENANT

It might seem incredible to many, especially to those who believe in the evolutionary origin of man, that God should have planned to create humans with transcendent human natures and in the most highly favored and privileged condition or state of original innocence. Genesis reveals that man was created in a state in which the man had not only a superb transcendent human nature, living a supernatural life and having a predestination to an eternal supernatural destiny which were totally beyond the abilities of man to conceive or achieve.

The author of Genesis had informed his readers that on the sixth day of creation God created man in "our image likeness". This creation of man in "our image likeness" necessarily resulted in Adam and Eve being created in the likeness of the transcendent humanity of the Incarnate God-man and being given a life that was like that of the God-man. Their creation in "our image likeness" made them fit for an eternal destiny, a life on high in the eternal Heavenly Kingdom of the God-man. In the Father's plan the ultimate destiny of all mankind was to live forever in the company, friendship and fellowship of the Most Holy Trinity and of the God-man, creation's Supreme Head.

From observing Adam and Eve by means of visions Moses concludes that the intellects of Adam and Eve must have been infused with a great store of knowledge. They had been infused with knowledge about the nature of all things and the principles of all sciences and arts. Their human wills had been infused with the cardinal moral virtues and the theological virtues. Moses observes Adam making use of his infused knowledge in the exercise of his God-given dominion over all the earth, its plants, birds, fish and animals. His God-given dominion made Adam the Monarch of the entire earth.

Everything commanded by God and implied in the creation of man in "our image likeness" on the sixth day is evident to Moses as he continues his observations of Adam and Eve. For in chapter two of Genesis, Moses sees and writes of Adam and Eve as transcendent humans living transcendent lives, living in the splendid abundance, in peace and tranquillity of a Paradise on earth.

In the third chapter Moses witnesses and describes their fall into sin. He will tell of how and why Satan as the serpent planned and succeeded in tricking Adam and Eve into committing the sin that would be the cause of their and their entire race falling from the favor and grace of God. He tells of the curses God imposed on Satan, Eve, Adam and the earth, and of God proclaiming the protoevangelium.

This profound protoevangelium implied much to Adam and Eve. Among the many things implied was the hope of God restoring their fallen race to the supernatural through its redemption by the God-man.

In chapters two and three, Moses writes as though anyone observing Adam and Eve in Paradise would have thought them more godlike than human. Creation in "our image likeness" translates, in the language of St. Paul, into Adam and Eve and everyone of Adam's race being created in the likeness of the fullness of the God-man, Jesus Christ. The Apostle Paul understood that at the beginning of the human race everyone was to receive from God a beginner's "share in the fullness of the God-man, Jesus Christ". From the beginning everyone was to be a coheir with Jesus Christ to the Almighty Father's inheritance of unfathomable riches. Everyone was to have the divine destiny of "a life on high in Christ" in the eternal Kingdom of Christ in Heaven. Cf. Col 1:19; Phil 3:14.

In the eternal plan and decrees of God the Father Adam and his entire race at their creation were coheirs with the First-born Son of the Almighty Father. All humans at their creation would have the status of being true genetic brothers or sisters of the God-man and for that reason coheirs with the God-man to the Almighty Father's inheritance of unfathomable riches. Those riches included special natural, preternatural and supernatural riches. "God chose us **in him before the world began**, to be holy and blameless in his sight and to be full of love; he likewise predestined us through Christ Jesus to be his adopted sons—such was his will and pleasure—

that all might praise his glorious favor he has bestowed on us in his beloved." Eph 1:4-6. "Praised be the God and Father of our Lord Jesus Christ, who has bestowed on us in Christ ever spiritual blessing in the heavens!" Eph 1:3. Cf. 1 Cor 6:9; Heb 1:2. "He [the Father] called you through our preaching of the good news, so that you might achieve the glory of our Lord Jesus Christ." 2 Thes 2:14.

St. Paul frequently expresses his great admiration, thanks and love for God the Father, for St. Paul sees himself and all men gratuitously predestined by the Father to sharing in the unfathomable riches of the absolute fullness of Christ. "Now to him who is able to strengthen you in the gospel which I proclaim when I preach Jesus Christ, the gospel which reveals the mystery hidden for man ages but now manifested through the writings of the prophets, and, at the command of the eternal God, made known to all the Gentiles that they may believe and obey—to him, the God who alone is wise may glory be given through Jesus Christ unto endless ages. Amen." Rom 16:25-27.

The author of Genesis requires of all his readers that they understand his account of Adam and Eve in the context of all the privileges, favors, and blessings the Father or God explicitly decreed for man on the sixth day of creation in addition to their creation in "our image likeness". He wants his readers to understand that it was precisely because Adam was created in "our image likeness" that Adam was created with a transcendent human nature and especially shared in God's spiritual and supernatural favors. He wants all to understand that Adam and his entire race were destined by God's creation covenant to have the rights to many great privileges, favors, blessings and an eternal supernatural destiny that were theirs by their creation in "our image likeness".

St. Paul understood it was in accordance with the Father's will and the creation covenant that all humans be "created in his own image, in the divine image he created him; male and female he created them. God blessed them saying: 'Be fertile and multiply; fill the earth and subdue it'". Gen 1:28. Moses wants readers of chapter two to understand also that God the Father's intention to create man in "our image likeness" was joined to an entirely gratuitous creation covenant between God and the man. A covenant made with the man as the male progenitor of his entire race. That creation covenant was the means by which everyone of Adam's race was to become a beneficiary of all that God intended for man. It was evident to Adam also from the creation covenant God had made with him that God would provide him with a wife and that not only he and his wife but also all his descendants would permanently possess Paradise as their permanent earthly home.

Adam and his wife would begin life's venture together with God assisting them while they would be living in their God's earthly Paradise. God intended that his creation covenant should be in effect from the moment of Adam's creation and remain in effect so long as Adam his wife Eve and their descendants refrained from eating the forbidden fruit. By eating that fruit they would repudiate God's dominion over them and break their most gracious creation covenant with God.

MOSES SEES AND IS ABLE TO IDENTIFY THE REGION OF THE EARTH WHERE MAN WAS CREATED, THE PLACE OF MAN'S ORIGINAL HOME ON EARTH

Chapter two has God showing Moses, not the man, by means of a vision, the area on earth in which man was created. The intention of the Father to create man a magnificent and highly favored creature presented God with a special problem. The special problems of finding on earth a permanent and perfectly suitable dwelling-place He intended for a transcendent race of humans, Adam and his race.

In Genesis Moses, after writing of God resting from all his work on the morning of the seventh day and after telling of God forming Adam's body from dust, reports seeing a very large area of the earth. That area, it turns out, is the area God has chosen for the creation of the first man and the area for preparing a Paradise to be the permanent and perfectly suitable dwelling-place on earth for the transcendent man, his wife to be and their entire race. In this vision of an area of the earth Moses sees that the earth is barren of both field shrubs and even grasses.

Moses, without being informed of the reasons for that bareness of the earth, volunteers two reasons for its barren condition. The first reason is that God had sent no rain on the earth and the second is that there was no man on earth to till the soil. Moses tells of what he then saw God doing to remedy that barren condition. God causes water to well up out of the earth and that water waters the surface of the ground. The next thing God does to remedy that barren condition is to create man, who will till the soil.

Before the creation of man the earth was without its master and caretaker and it was therefore to be expected that the earth be in a barren condition. "The Lord God then took the man and settled him in the Garden of Eden, to cultivate and care for it." Gen 2:15. One of the God-given tasks for man on earth is that of tilling the soil to make it productive and more productive.

Genesis explicitly states that there were no humans on earth at the time prior to the creation of Adam. This absence of any humans on earth is a given for the understanding Moses' entire account of the formation of Adam and Eve, their life together in Paradise, their expulsion and their permanent banishment to live permanently in the world outside Paradise. If, as Genesis states, there were no men on earth to till the soil for the growing of shrubs and grasses, then obviously there were no pre-Adamites, Adamites or real men, on earth at the time of the creation of Adam from whom Adam or man could have evolved.

This simple statement of Genesis directly contradicts the belief of many that there were in fact pre-Adamites, Adamites or true humans on earth at the time of the creation of Adam. It was from them Adam and Eve supposedly evolved. These humans or sub-human creatures supposedly evolved and lived on earth prior to the appearance of Adam and Eve on earth. Here Genesis explicitly contradicts what many commentators today have thought and are still proposing and teaching about the origin of man on earth.

Commentators who believe in the evolution of man have no choice but to believe that there were pre-Adamites, Adamites or even true humans on earth at the time God supposedly created Adam and Eve. For they believe that Adam and Eve were the product of that universal evolutionary process, which had been going on for many millions of years before Adam and Eve evolved. They prefer to believe that man evolved rather than believe that Adam and Eve were immediately and directly created by God. They suppose that pre-Adamites and Adamites were very primitive creatures and that the condition of the first man, Adam, having evolved from them, had to be almost identical to that of those sub-humans or most primitive of humans.

Believers in the evolution of man believe or suppose that pre-Adamites, Adamites or even true humans were widely dispersed over the earth long before Adam existed. They believe all of them died off since none have remained on earth. They suppose that this is what happened to the Neanderthal man or that the Neanderthals perished in the great flood, leaving Adam with lineal descendants only through Noah.

In his visions Moses saw that God provided a source of water which watered the surface of the ground and then wild field shrubs and grasses began growing on earth. But that water remedied only partially the inhospitable conditions for a race of human to live on earth. Moses knew that God still did not have a perfectly suitable dwelling-place on earth for the transcendent race of humans He was about to create on the earth. Man was the missing factor for more hospitable conditions on earth. God was not about to put the Adamites to work preparing a more suitable place for Adam and Eve. God was left with no alternative but that He Himself prepare a perfectly suitable dwelling-place on earth for transcendent man. God would prepare such a dwelling-place by preparing a very unique Paradise for transcendent man.

God wished to reveal to Moses and mankind the precise place on earth He had chosen to create man and locate Paradise. God reveals that place by presenting Moses with a vision first of the topography of that chosen region of the earth. On seeing it Moses was able to identify that region of the earth by means of his personal knowledge of geography and history. That region had four rivers. Among those rivers were the Euphrates and Tigris Rivers. Moses had knowledge of these well-known rivers and of their exact locations on earth and therefore knew the place God had chosen to be the place He would create the first man and the place of man's Paradise on earth.

In the vision of that area, Moses could see "A river rises in Eden to water the garden; beyond there [the border of Eden] it [the one river] divided and becomes four branches [or four rivers]. The name of the first is Pishon; it is the one that winds through the whole land of Havilah, where there is gold... The name of the second river is the Gihon; it is the one that winds all through the land of Cush. The name of the third river is the Tigris; it is the one that flows east of Asshur. The fourth river is the Euphrates." Gen 2:10-14.

By means of the vision Moses could view that whole region of the earth. Moses' description of the topography of the region makes it obvious that in this vision Moses was looking upstream from Eden for the river begins to rise from Eden. All rivers rise from their mouth and divide into branches upstream. Two or more rivers flowing down from their source converge downstream to form one river or stream. These facts recorded by Moses and the fact that rivers flow and merge in this way makes it possible for readers of Moses' account to determine that Eden and Paradise were located on or near the mouth of a large river, on or near the delta of the Euphrates and Tigris Rivers. The fact that the rivers named by Moses form one stream before entering the Persian Gulf indicates the exact location of Paradise was on that one stream before it entered the Persian Gulf. At the points where large rivers flow into large bodies of water or sea, a protruding landmass forms in the sea. It is called a delta because its shape is much like that of the Greek capital letter delta.

Now it was not possible for Moses, unless he were many miles above the earth's surface, to view with the natural vision of his eyes with one glance that whole region of the earth. If Moses were to view that whole basin of the Euphrates and Tigris Rivers, as the text indicates, he would have had to view it by means of a vision for that whole region, a thousand miles in length, is much too large to be viewed with one glance from the low vantagepoint of Eden on or near that delta.

This way of viewing a whole region of the earth by a vision must have been what happened to Moses in Deuteronomy 34:1. There Moses ascended Mt. Nebo and from its summit surveyed the whole land God had promised to the Israelites. That whole promised land is larger than the entire basin of the Tigris and Euphrates Rivers. Deuteronomy states that from the summit of Mt. Nebo Moses saw, for example, the coastal plain. That plain was fifty to sixty miles away and was on the far side of a high ridge of mountains that would have cut off his view to that coastal plain. The only way Moses could have seen that whole area from the summit of Mt. Nebo would have been in a vision of it given to him by God. "That very day the hand of the Lord came upon me and brought me in divine vision to the land of Israel, where he set me down on a very high mountain. On it there seemed to be a city being built before me." Ez 40:2.

Here another question arises. If Paradise in Eden was the first place on earth where men lived how could a vision of that region at a time just prior to the creation of Adam have shown Moses the old city of Asshur and that its location was on the west bank of the Tigris? Commentators do not attempt to solve this problem for they never get to the problem. If on the other hand Moses was given a vision of that whole region as it existed at the time of Moses, Moses would have had no problem giving his account of the area in which he locates Eden on a great river about to enter the gulf. By giving Moses these realistic visions of the area with its well known rivers, God revealed to Moses and mankind the exact place on earth He created the first man, the place that was to become the so-called cradle of mankind.

In any scenario of events leading to the creation of Adam, it would seem that God, following his usual procedure should have prepared the Paradise for the man, Adam, before creating the man. For in the account of the six days of creation God, whenever creating living creatures on earth, always prepare dwelling-places for living creatures before creating the creatures that would be living in them. In such a scenario Genesis' account of the events of the creation of man the proper place for verse seven, which tells of God forming Adam's body from clay, would be after verse fourteen. Then God would not have created Adam knowing full well there was no suitable dwelling-place for him on earth.

God would then have formed Adam's body from dust outside Paradise and, as Genesis indicates, could lead Adam into that Paradise. The obvious question arises, why would God have departed from his usual procedure by creating Adam before forming the Paradise for him? The Paradise God intended to give gratuitously as a permanent suitable home for him, his wife and his race.

As a solution of this problem it would be rather easy to suppose that some copyist had altered the text by transposing verse seven, which tells of the creation of Adam outside Paradise. However, if only this verse were transposed by some copyist, then the tenses of the verbs in verses eight through fourteen would be incorrect and readers would then be forced to suppose that some copyist also deliberately changed the tenses of all the verbs in verses eight through fourteen. Since both cannot be plausible, there must be some overriding reason, in the moral of the story of the creation of Adam, that required God to deliberately create Adam before forming the Paradise He intended as a permanent home for him and his race.

MOSES IS GIVEN VISIONS OF THE CREATION OF ADAM AND OF THE MAKING OF THE CREATION COVENANT BETWEEN GOD AND MAN

When creating living creatures on earth God created many of the same kind or species, but when God comes to creating the man He proceeds according to an entirely different plan. God planned to begin the human race by creating only two humans, one male and one female. He would create or form the male first. Why would God create a person of the male sex first and not create one person of each sex at the same time? What could be the reason that God created Adam before forming Paradise and before creating the female?

Consider the fact that God was about to make a deal that would be of enormously great benefit for the man and all men. We know that some deals between persons appear unbelievable because they are too good to be true! God is about to present Adam with a permanently great deal that appears too good to be true! What is that incredibly good deal God was about to offer Adam?

That incredible deal is the creation covenant. Here in chapter two God is about to make a covenant with Adam as the very first male progenitor of an entire race of humans. God wants Adam to accept his totally gratuitous and marvelous creation covenant and for that reason Adam needed to be prepared to accept the credibility of God's too good to be true creation covenant. Adam needed to know what God truly intended to do for him in order for the deal to be a true deal. In the totally gratuitous creation covenant God, after creating Adam with a transcendent human nature, offers Adam nothing less than a wife, with a transcendent human nature like his, a Paradise as a permanent home for them on earth, supernatural divine life and an eternal supernatural destiny. God intends that these two be the very first parents of a whole race of transcendent humans and that they and their children would live in their God-given Paradise of abundance and leisure as their permanent home on earth.

Before the man could reasonably accept the covenant of God's extreme generosity Adam had to understand clearly that only God could offer him and his entire race all the many marvelous things contained in God's creation covenant.

What better way of making the creation covenant a credible and acceptable deal for the man than for God to create the man as an adult with mature understanding, appreciation and capable of full responsibility and accountability. So God arranges to have Adam witness God forming that Paradise. For the sake of Adam believing the offer and agreeing to accept the creation covenant Adam needed to observe that it was God who caused Paradise to come into existence and that God had the right to offer it to him as an entirely free gift. God wanted Adam to know that God caused all the various beautiful and delightful plants and trees to spring out of the ground in that desert wasteland and that it was He who had the right to offer Paradise and everything in it to him as an entirely free gift. After the man witnesses Paradise coming into being, God immediately takes the man into that Paradise to point out and explain to him all its beautiful plants and tree with their abundant luscious fruits.

While guiding Adam about Paradise God explains to him how the Garden of Eden was designed to provide abundantly for all the human needs of those living in it. God, by forming that Paradise before the very eyes of Adam, made it obvious to Adam that Paradise was entirely the work of God and therefore God's to freely offer to whomever He chose and to offer it under whatever conditions He might choose to offer it. Also what better way to demonstrate Paradise's divine origin and its benefits to man than for the man to witness its formation in a barren region of the earth and be shown all its wonders by God its designer and maker? By introducing Adam to Paradise in this way, God was clearly manifesting to the man his intention of giving Paradise to him. The man understood that God could rightly contract with him for the benefit of his wife, his children and everyone of his race with respect to anything God wanted to give them as entirely free gifts.

By means of visions Moses had observed how God formed a human figure or body from dust and brought it to life by breathing a soul into it. At the breathing in of that soul Moses saw that the figure became a living human being. Immediately on creating the man, God anticipates the man's desire to know immediately how he came to be. God wills to satisfy that desire.

The man is most pleased to meet his Creator and supernatural Father and he immediately manifests a childlike trust and confidence in his Creator and Father. The man's creation in the "our image likeness" of the God-man and the creation covenant destined the man and all men to be true genetic brothers and sisters of the God-man.

God wants the man to be acutely aware of the completely gratuitous nature of everything God had already done to and for him and what He wanted to continue doing to and for him and his entire race. God does this by making the man aware that as his Creator He had already freely and deliberately chose to create him and to create him in the marvelous condition he found himself. The man realized that by freely choosing to create him in "our image likeness" God gave him a transcendent human nature, adopted him as his son and was disposed to give him many more things of great interest and value to him.

How might God best demonstrate to the man his true origin? God would begin with the man's awareness of his very first instant of his existence and of succeeding moments of his existence including his rising to his feet alive from the earth in the very place he knew he came to be. Only then and there could God show him the fresh depression in the earth right in front of the man, the very spot from which he arose to stand on his feet. Since the size and shape of that depression was of the same size and shape as his body, it was obvious to the man that God had formed his body from the clay of that depression.

In these ways God manifested Himself to the man as his Creator and that He had freely created him and just as freely created him in his present condition. In addition to creating the man in his marvelous physical condition the man's mind at his creation or formation was infused with a great store of knowledge regarding all natural, preternatural and supernatural things. Hence the man could truly understand and appreciate all that God was doing to him and for him.

The man is most pleased to meet his Creator and supernatural

Father and he immediately manifests a childlike trust and confidence in his Creator and Father. From the first moment of his existence, the man was supernaturally disposed through his infused knowledge and the infused theological virtues of faith, hope and charity to immediately accept his Creator as his true supernatural Father. God the Creator and his creature, man, immediately establish their very loving father-child and son-father relationships.

After the man's joyful recognition of his Creator as his most benevolent supernatural Father, the man and Moses witness the actual coming into existence or formation of Paradise. Moses writes of seeing God forming that Paradise. "Out of the ground the Lord God made various trees grow that were delightful to look at and good for food, with the tree of life in the middle of the garden and the tree of the knowledge of good and bad." Gen 2:9. The man saw God doing the same.

If the man and Moses had not witnessed the actual formation of Paradise, Moses should have used the past tense of the verb grow, he uses instead the present perfect tense.

When writing chapters two and three of Genesis, Moses was aware of the fact that he was not a witness to the actual formation of Adam and Eve, but was receiving visions of the true origin of Adam and Eve which had occurred a few thousand years earlier. The visions he received were authentic supernatural reenactments of these and other events of that most distant past.

After the formation of Paradise, a series of visions begins in which Moses sees the man being taken by God into Paradise and given a guided explanatory tour of Paradise. Moses, unseen, accompanies the man on this guided tour. Moses sees everything and hears all the words of explanation God gives the man regarding the plants, trees, animals and all the accommodations Paradise would offer as a permanent home for the man and his family. The man, as well as Moses, saw that Paradise had many kinds of animals, trees and plants beautiful to behold and the fruit of the trees delightful to eat. God wants the man to scrutinize everything in Paradise and sample the fruit of all various trees, especially those with their seed in their fruit. The man finds everything beautiful and all the fruit pleasant to his senses of sight, taste and smell.

Moses, judging from the reactions of the man, sees that the man is very pleased with everything in Paradise. The fruit of the various kinds of trees of Paradise would bear fruit during the different seasons of the year. "Out of the ground the Lord God made various trees grow that were delightful to look at and good for food." Gen 2:9.

Moses learns many things from this explanatory tour. He learns that, "Out of the ground the Lord God made various trees grow that were delightful to look at and good for food, that the tree of life was in the middle of the garden and beside the tree of the knowledge of good and bad." Moses realizes that the trees and their fruit were just as he heard God decreed on the sixth day of creation. It was obvious to Moses that anyone living in Paradise would have easy access to the fruit of all the various trees and would have easy access to whatever fruit anyone desired at any time.

While on this guided explanatory tour of Paradise, the two last things God points out to the man are the two particular fruit trees growing in the middle of the garden—the tree of life and the tree of knowledge of good and bad. They were so conspicuously placed in the center of the Paradise that they could not go unnoticed by anyone. The reason God had for placing these two trees in the center or heart of Paradise was for the sake of the very unique function the fruit of each of these trees would have in the daily lives of individuals living in Paradise.

While on the explanatory tour of Paradise, God explained to the man what very different results would result from eating the fruit of the tree of life and eating fruit of the tree of knowledge of good and bad. Moses learns of the purposes and very unique functions of the fruit of each of these trees listening to God inform the man of their purposes and functions for those living in Paradise. The man and Moses learned that by eating the fruit of the tree God called the tree of life persons would preserve themselves in a constant state of perfect health, vigor, strength, and perpetual youth.

Both the man and Moses understood that persons in a constant state of perfect health, vigor, strength, and perpetual youth would be free from any physical weakness or sickness and would never face the fear of death, for persons in perfect health cannot die from natural causes. Thus the eating of the fruit of the tree of life would bestow on Adam, his wife and all their descendants this kind of immortality. This real tree of life was the only fountain of youth that has ever existed for mankind on earth. The fruit of no other tree growing inside Paradise could have this very great beneficial effect on the life of anyone. The outcome of the story of Adam and Eve necessarily supposes no other tree of life grew outside Paradise.

After this guided tour the man, as well Moses, clearly understands that the Paradise God designed and prepared for the man would serve as the ideal permanent dwelling-place on earth for the man, his family, and his descendants.

Adam understood that God, by taking him into this new Paradise immediately after his creation and by giving him this explanatory tour of Paradise, was manifesting his intention of offering Paradise and everything in it as a permanent home for him, his family, and his race. Adam realized that God was offering a contract or covenant that would permanently give Paradise with everything in it as entirely free gifts and as a permanent home for him, his wife and his entire race.

The man could not but rejoice to know that God was at that time prepared to make Paradise perpetually available to him, his promised wife, his family and his entire race as their home on earth. Adam rejoiced to realize that Paradise was nothing less than an ideal place for him and his promised wife to live in perfect freedom, leisure, comfort, perpetual youth and peace on earth.

After Adam learned of the purpose of fruit of the tree of life growing in the middle of Paradise, he must have wondered what was the specific purpose or function of that other tree growing beside it in the center of Paradise. It was to end this wondering of the man that God informs the man that neither he nor anyone may eat the fruit of that tree, the tree of knowledge of good and bad. God plainly tells the man that if he or anyone would ever eat its fruit they would doom themselves to death!

Why would they be dooming themselves to death if they ate the fruit of that tree? Surely its fruit was not poisonous, for the fruit of all the trees of Paradise was good to eat. The reason persons would be dooming themselves to death is that by eating fruit from that tree they would be breaking the creation covenant God was making with Adam. Abstinence from eating that fruit was the condition in the will of God and of the creation covenant for the creation covenant to continue in effect. The consequences of breaking the creation covenant were that Adam and everyone of his race would lose not only their rights to everything given to them by the creation covenant, but also in consequence they would be immediately expelled from Paradise and would never be permitted to return to dwell in it or eat fruit from its trees. Since persons expelled and living outside Paradise would not have access to fruit from the tree of life and without eating fruit from the tree of life, would not be able maintain themselves in the state of perfect health, vigor, strength, and perpetual youth. Hence these persons were doomed to die from natural causes.

God had decreed death as the wages of sin. In God's law the penalty for sin is death. Therefore God would have to order the immediate expulsion of Adam and Eve from Paradise and never permit them or anyone to reenter Paradise to take and eat fruit from the tree of life to live forever. There were no other humans on earth to enter Paradise to bring out fruit of that tree to them.

Unless God had informed Adam neither Adam nor Moses could have known the unique benefits of eating the fruit of the tree of life nor could they have known why God was requiring complete abstinence from eating fruit from the tree of knowledge of good and bad. God revealed that He was requiring complete abstinence from eating fruit from the tree of good and bad because He had made eating fruit from that tree the invalidating condition of the creation covenant between God and the man as the head of his race. It was essential that Moses include in his account God's informing Adam of the purposes and functions of both of these trees.

The unique function of the fruit of each of these trees in the lives of persons living in Paradise explains also God's purpose for placing them in the center or heart of Paradise. In view of their purpose it would not due to have them growing in some obscure and inaccessible spot in Paradise.

Many modern commentators do not want to accept literally

either the reality of these trees or their functions or their purposes as Genesis literally states or implies them to be. These commentators prefer to consider these trees something purely mystical or symbolical in the lives of the first man and woman living in some equally mythical or symbolical Paradise. They also consider the sin of eating the fruit of the tree of knowledge of good and bad to be symbolical of something early men failed to learn or do early on in their lives on earth or while living in that symbolical Paradise. But why should persons not believe the literal sense of Moses' account of these two real trees growing in a real Paradise for man on earth? Why not believe the trees had these special functions for man according to the creation covenant God was making with the man, Adam? The stated functions of the fruit of these trees make perfect sense in the plan of God for man according to Moses' account of what would later happened to Adam and Eve in Paradise.

After the making of the creation covenant with the man God departs from the presence of the man. God as could be expected leaves the man in charge of the marvelous Paradise he has just acquired as an entirely free gift by agreeing to God's entirely gratuitous creation covenant. God's departure from the man and leaving the man in Paradise and in charge of Paradise are evidences that the creation covenant had been consummated to the satisfaction of God and the man. The satisfactory consummation of the creation covenant gave the man great assurance that God would be returning to him to fulfill his promises of giving him a wife and the vocation of becoming the sole male progenitor of a whole race of transcendent humans on earth. The man was rejoicing in his conviction that God was completely sincere in his promise of giving him a wife, children, and many descendants and that the marvelous Paradise would be their wonderful permanent home on earth.

Readers must realize that the garden Paradise, which God prepared as a permanent home for man on earth, could not have been a true Paradise for man, if persons living in it were not completely free from pain, fear of infirmities, sickness and death. Hence it was necessary that God's Paradise for man have this tree of life which would maintain them in a state of perfect health, vigor, strength, and perpetual youth. Also this Paradise could not be a true and perpetual Paradise for Adam, Eve or their descendants, if, while living in it, they would not be completely free from fear of a violent external attack by persons wanting to exploit their Paradise for themselves. In the complete absence of any explicit or implied provision for the external security of Paradise, Adam and Eve and their descendants could have been completely free from external attack by an alien people is that Adam and Eve and their descendant would always be the only humans on earth.

If the man and the woman had evolved then pre-Adamites or Adamites or even true humans, from whom Adam and Eve supposedly evolved, would still be roaming the earth outside Paradise. They at any time could be expected to attack Adam and Eve in their home Paradise for the purpose of taking possession of Paradise and exploiting it for themselves. Hence the complete lack of any provision for the external security of Paradise for the complete happiness and freedom of those living in Paradise implies that there were no other humans living on earth and that implies Adam and Eve had not evolved. All of this is just as Genesis states that before the man was created "there was no man to till the soil." Gen 2:5.

For the purpose of securing the external security of Paradise, Genesis does not state that God "stationed the cherubim with a fiery revolving sword" to protect Paradise as Genesis states God stationed in Paradise a cherubim for the sake of keeping Adam or anyone from returning to Paradise to take fruit from the tree of life. Cf. Gen 3:24.

At the very moment Adam's body received its life giving principle, Adam was given also the principle of his supernatural divine life. Moses had an understanding of a principle of life. This is true if for no other reason than that Moses observed God breathing into the lifeless figure of a human body the breath of life and that the man immediately became a living being. The Creator is also a giver of life, something evolutionists would seem to deny, for the theory does not recognize a specific principle of life.

Moses must have known of something immaterial intrinsic to the human person that gives life to the human body. Moses would also have understood death as the separation of such an immaterial or spiritual life-giving principle or soul from its body. Moses, from his eighty years of experiences with life and death, would have learned that at death a lifeless body begins to decompose while the life principle goes to the special place for departed persons. This is the principle reason the Hebrews and other peoples believed in a place called Sheol, which the Greeks and others called Hades.

Moses understood that at the moment Adam's body received its human principle of life, the man also received from God the principle of his supernatural divine life. Since Moses understood the meaning and function of "our image likeness", he therefore knew Adam was given supernatural life at his creation by being created in "our image likeness". Thus Moses understood that Adam possessed supernatural divine life along with human life from the first moment of his existence. In the terminology and theology of the New Testament, this principle of supernatural divine life has the name of sanctifying grace. It gave Adam eternal divine life or supernatural life.

The supernatural life or eternal life God gives to man St. Paul frequently refers to as the "justice of God" or "the justice of faith". The same is true in the terminology of the theology of the Catholic Church where this "justice of God" is better known as sanctifying grace. Unless a person posses the principle of supernatural life a person cannot live a supernatural life and the person is not justified.

This principle of supernatural life or divine life is always accompanied by the theological virtues of faith, hope, and charity to facilitate the actions of a person's supernatural life or eternal life. Adam was supernaturally disposed at his creation by the infused theological virtue of faith, to believe all the truths God was teaching him.

The principle of supernatural life or the divine life of grace must be recognized as the greatest of the many entirely free gifts Adam and Eve received from God at their creation. This must be true for the simple reason that supernatural life or eternal divine life is something supernatural to all created nature. God bestowed supernatural life on Adam and his wife at the moment of their creation, for from the first moment of their existence they were created in "our image likeness". In the plan of God this principle of supernatural life was to be bestowed on all the descendants of Adam and Eve at the moment of their conception and creation.

Adam and all mankind owe their creation, their creation in the likeness of the transcendent God-man, their genetic kinship to the God-man and their predestination to an eternity of complete happiness, friendship and fellowship with the God-man to the Father's eternal determination to incarnate his Son as the God-man of Adam's race. They owe thanks to the Father also for the Father's intention to permit man to live forever in his God-man's Glorious Kingdom and there enjoy to fullest the unfathomable riches of the inheritance the Father left to his First-born. The natural, preternatural and supernatural gifts God gave to Adam and Eve at their creation and intended for everyone of their entire race at their creation were merited by the very Incarnation of the God-man as a member of Adam's race. Those gifts were merited in the same way that the existence of the universe and man's creation were merited by the very Incarnation of the God-man. Fallen mankind's restoration to the supernatural was merited by the incarnate God-man, but merited by the Sacred Passion and Death of the God-man in the redemption of mankind, not by or in the very Incarnation of the Son as the God-man of our race.

Genesis' account of Adam and Eve living in Paradise manifests that God, besides giving them Paradise, lavished many natural and preternatural gifts on them from their very beginning, from their creation. For example, Adam and Eve had knowledge of a language by which they communicated verbally with God and with one another. Genesis manifests that Adam and Eve had the cognitive ability of understanding and speaking at least one language fluently. Since Adam and Eve were able to do so from their very beginning, they realized that they could have that ability only by God infusing that knowledge and ability into their minds at their creation. They knew they had no opportunity for learning it at any time from anyone after their creation.

This should be no surprising to us since God created Adam and Eve in the "our image likeness" of the God-man. That implies that God intended and infused Adam and Eve, like the God-man, with the fullness of all human knowledge including the knowledge and ability of speaking many languages. Since they were created in "our image likeness" it was to be expected that God would have formed many languages for them and would have infused them with knowledge of those languages along with the skill of understanding and speaking them fluently.

Genesis manifests that from the beginning Adam had a great store of knowledge and understanding of many things. In the second chapter of Genesis Adam deals competently with many subjects immediately after his creation. Almost immediately after his creation Adam intelligently comments on such matters as: property rights, marriage, marriage relationships, human sexuality, parenthood and family life. He manifests that he has an understanding of the different roles of a husband and a wife, what good family life should be and implies that physical health is important for life. He understood his need for food and that death was not impossibility for him and others. He knows what sickness, pain, beauty and pleasure are and what they imply for his own life and the life of other humans. If Adam would not have had a great store of infused knowledge and an understanding of all these subjects, how could Adam have appreciated what God was telling him, doing for him, and promising to do for him and his entire race through all generations forever?

Adam's and Eve's possession of a great store of infused knowledge is an additional reason for thinking that creation in "our image likeness" must be understood as man's creation in the likeness of the God-man. Adam and Eve had a store of knowledge that was like that of the God-man as is obvious from the gospels. There Jesus asked everyone to agree with Him on the subject of marriage and especially the indissolubility of marriage by agreeing with what Adam said in Genesis on the same subjects.

It was necessary that God should have given Adam and Eve an adequate store of knowledge and competence in all sciences and arts for them to live the very good life God intended for them in God's design of a marvelous Paradise for them. God gave them the competence to give a specialist's care for the plants, trees and animals of Paradise. Adam had the understanding of the utility of cultivating and harvesting the seeds of plants and the fruit of the trees of Paradise. In the making the creation covenant Adam agreed to cultivate the plants and harvest the fruit and seeds of all the plants and trees of Paradise.

By their creation in "our image likeness" Adam and Eve had at their creation the same kind of transcendent life the transcendent God-man would have had while living among men on earth, if man would not sin.

Genesis' account supposes that anyone who would have seen Adam immediately after his creation would have known that Adam was created in "our image likeness", because Adam appeared more godlike than human, more like the God-man than any mere human. The words "You have made him little less than angels, and crowned him with glory and honor" are spoken of Adam and Eve. Ps 8:6.

MORE PRECISE EVIDENCE FROM GENESIS OF THE MAKING AND THE EXISTENCE OF THE CREATION COVENANT

Today's theologians and commentators on the first chapter of Genesis acknowledge speculatively at least the need for some covenant between God and Adam, but fail to point out any evidence of either its making or existence or of its effects in the lives of Adam and Eve. In their writings even the fall of man into original sin is not seen as an effect of the breaking of the creation covenant God made with Adam. The result of the sin of Adam and Eve is seen or understood as the result of any other sin they could have committed. They do not attempt to offer explicit evidence of any covenant much less any application of the creation covenant to the lives of Adam and Eve and of their descendants. The expulsion of Adam and Eve from Paradise is not seen as a foreseen consequence of the breaking of the creation covenant. In their interpretations of these chapters of Genesis there is no evidence that the presence of Adam and Eve in Paradise or their living in Paradise are due to the creation covenant Adam made with God at the beginning of the second chapter. They offer no evidence that the covenant is the reason Adam and Eve are so fortunate as to live in God's Paradise. They offer no evidence that the covenant is Adam's reason for expecting a wife from God. They are silent about Adam and Eve not having any agreement with God permitting them to live in God's unique and most extraordinary Paradise.

The very fact that Adam and Eve knowingly lived together in God's Paradise is evidence they were keenly aware that God had lavished many different kinds of great and noble gifts on them from their beginning and had reason for expecting God would continue doing so.

God's gifts had transcendentalized Adam's and Eve's natures and faculties. What is the reason Adam and Eve rightly expected God would do for all their descendants what he had done for them? They could rightly expect that God would do for their descendants what He had done for them only because of the explicit agreement God had made with Adam for all his descendants. Hence Adam and Eve understood that God intended to preserve them also in their ideal situation and would continue indefinitely giving the same great and noble gifts to everyone of their entire race at their creation and conception.

Persons readily understand that there was a need, on the part of man, that Adam's and his race's ideal situation, freely bestowed by God, would continue to be bestowed by God and would continue to be bestowed according to an agreed upon covenant. For human reason demands that whenever anything is given that there be some explicitly or implicitly agreed upon gratuitous contract that acknowledges and specifies who is the giver, what is given, to whom it is given, and under what conditions or circumstances, if any, it is given. Reason demands that there be an explicit agreement especially if the gifts could be withdrawn and under what conditions the gifts could be withdrawn.

If explicit or implicit gratuitous contracts are necessary among humans when giving or receiving even token gifts, then surely a precise explicit contract is in order for the granting of very great and noble gifts to every individual of a whole race over the entire history of that race. This is especially true when those gifts are so great that they transform individuals into transcendent humans, giving those persons the ability to live supernatural lives while giving them also an eternal supernatural destiny.

By being aware of that contract any individual of that whole race at any time could be assured of receiving what God promised in perpetuity to every individual of that entire race by means of that covenant. It is necessary that persons have the assurance of a contract that would specify God as the giver, specify the good things God was promising to give, specify the persons to receive them, the means by which God would give them and under what conditions, if any, God would be obliged to give them, or withhold them or even withdraw them. We would expect that God and the man had agreed on all these important matters when God settled the man in Paradise and the man took permanent possession of Paradise.

We would expect that the text of the creation chapters would give clear evidence for the benefit of fallen man that God made such a covenant with Adam for his entire race. There is solid evidence of just such a comprehensive covenant between God and the man where the text explicitly states: "The Lord God gave the man this order 'You are free to eat from any of the trees of the garden except the tree of knowledge of good and bad.'" There is evidence of just such an agreement also in the words of God to Adam: "Be fertile and multiply; fill the earth and subdue it. Have dominion over the fish of the sea, the birds of the air, and all the living things that "move on the earth." God also said: "See, I give you [the man] every seed-bearing plant all over the earth and every tree that has seed-bearing fruit on it to be your food, and to all the animals of the land, all the birds of the air, and all the living creatures that crawl on the ground, I give all the green plants for food."

From the moment of Adam's creation to the completion of the guided tour of Paradise, the author of Genesis was permitted to observe God and Adam together in Paradise. Adam's acceptance of the covenant is the reason God on departing from the man in Paradise could leave the man in charge of Paradise. The man, Adam, could only wonder and be overwhelmed by what God showed him explained to him and under a covenant with him was promising to give and do for him and his entire race.

Everything about Adam's encounter with God in God's Paradise was very pleasing to the man. He must have loved his transcendent human nature, the prospect of a wife and children and the permanent home he and they would have or make for themselves in such a Paradise. In Paradise they would have an abundance of fresh fruit, enjoy a perpetual springtime of life and anticipate the supernatural destiny their entire race would enjoy forever in heaven.

If God forms a Paradise before the man's very eyes and after forming the Paradise takes the man into Paradise for an explanatory tour of Paradise during which He shows its wonders to him and then when the tour is complete departs leaving the man in charge of Paradise, would that not clearly indicate to the man that God is making an agreement that would give Paradise to him? That agreement was God's creation covenant with Adam. Adam's consent to God's covenant is certainly implicit in God permitting the man to remain in Paradise while God departs with no further instructions for him except the command that he not to eat the fruit of a certain tree.

While on that tour the author does not indicate that Adam had any explicit words with God about a wife. Yet after the tour why is it that the man is expecting a wife? While on the tour the man saw that Paradise was not designed for him alone, for he saw it was designed to be the home of a husband and a wife. That implied to the man that the person to whom God would give the Paradise would be receiving a wife from God. The man was partially motivated to make the agreement with God for ownership of Paradise for the sake of obtaining a wife from God.

The man understood that by consenting to God's creation covenant he would secure for himself a wife and a home in Paradise for himself, his wife and his children. Adam understood that consenting to the creation covenant would enrich him and his entire race with ownership of Paradise and to everything else God was promising to give him.

Only by God giving the man true ownership of Paradise could the man be rightly expected to cultivate and care for Paradise, gather and use its fruits for food, continue enjoying its abundance, comforts, beauty, pleasures and its provision for a life of leisure while raising a family. All of this is confirmed by the text stating, "The Lord God took the man and settled him in the Garden of Eden, to cultivate and care for it." Gen 2:15.

God settling the man in Paradise surely cannot mean that God led the man into the Garden of Eden and locked Adam in it, but that Adam had freely chosen to remain in the Garden even though he knew he would die if he ate its forbidden fruit.

Moses does not indicate that God was requiring anything of Adam at that time or at any time in the future in return for the Paradise or for anything God had already given him and had promised to do for him and his future family and race. Both Adam and Moses realized that the only condition explicit or implicit in the creation covenant for receiving and retaining everything was that the man, his wife, and his descendants always refrain from eating fruit from the tree of knowledge of good and bad.

Adam realized that he could not have made Paradise with its

trees and animals or the entire earth and that he had done nothing to deserve anything he had already received or was to continue receiving from God. Consequently Adam was fully aware that he acquired rights to Paradise and everything God was offering him only by God gratuitously giving him rights to them by means of God's entirely gratuitous creation covenant. Adam had no opportunity to make, earn, pay for or merit any of the things he had already received and what his wife and his entire race would be receiving in the future. Consequently, Adam realized that if he was to lose Paradise or God's other gifts there was no way he could get them. God would not be obliged to return them as entirely free gifts.

Adam rejoiced that Paradise was far more than an adequate home for himself, his wife and his children. Hence he was only too willing and happy to accept God's creation covenant with God's demand that neither he nor anyone eat the fruit from the tree of knowledge of good and bad.

While persons are reading and studying the second creation chapter, they should read and study it fully aware that God and Adam are in the process of making the creation covenant. Adam gladly approves of God's every offer and agrees to accept every offer of the gratuitous creation covenant in its entirety including its invalidating or terminating condition. Adam knew full well that eating the forbidden fruit would mean the loss of everything for himself and his entire race. Adam knew that the penalty for eating that fruit would mean immediate expulsion from Paradise and that that expulsion would in effect doom him and everyone of his race to death from natural causes.

Moses, writing thousands of years after God made the creation covenant with Adam, was able to know and write about the creation covenant, because by means of visions he accompanied the man and observed God and the man. He observed what they were saying and doing all the while God and the man were together on Adam's introductory tour of Paradise. Moses writes implying that he understood that God was offering Adam ownership of Paradise and many other wondrous gifts by means of the creation covenant, for Moses wrote: "The Lord God then took the man and settled him in the Garden of Eden, to cultivate it and care for it." Gen 2:15.

In this sentence the sense of the word settle is crucial for its understanding. Moses makes it clear that God took the man on an explanatory tour of Paradise for the purpose of settling him in Paradise. This implies that the author wants all his readers to understand that God took Adam into Paradise not merely to impress him with the wonders of Paradise, but to make an agreement with him, the progenitor of his entire race, for the perpetual ownership and use of the Garden as a home for himself, his wife and his race. Readers must understand that it would only have been after Adam had agreed to accept God's offer that Moses would have heard God tell Adam that he may freely eat fruit from all the trees of Paradise except from the tree of knowledge of good and bad. God then reinforces the prohibition of not eating fruit from the tree of knowledge of good and bad by telling him he would be doomed to die if he ate its fruit. All should understand that it could have been only after God and Adam had mutually agreed to the creation covenant that Moses would have heard what he calls an order God gave to the man. "The Lord God gave the man this order: 'You are free to eat from any of the trees of the garden except the tree of knowledge of good and bad. From that tree you shall not eat; the moment you eat from it you are surely doomed to die.'" Gen 2:16-17.

This order or command of God signified to Moses that God had accepted Adam's consent to the creation covenant. Moses reporting God's order implied to his readers that both God and Adam had agreed to the creation covenant's condition that made abstinence from the fruit of the tree of knowledge of good and bad an invalidating or terminating condition of the creation covenant.

This explicit command assured the man that God surely intended to keep his promise to give him a wife and that his family would have the right to live in Paradise and the right to freely eat fruit from all the trees of Paradise, except fruit from the tree of knowledge of good and bad. Adam clearly understood that he would be dooming himself and his race to expulsion from Paradise and to death if fruit from that tree were eaten.

The word "freely" in this order God gives to Adam has nothing at all to do with free will, as though God here, as some contend, God gave man the faculty of free will. Here freely means that God placed no restrictions on anyone living in Paradise taking and eating fruit from any tree except that one tree, the tree of the knowledge of good and bad.

With the giving of this command Moses ends his account of God forming the man from dust, taking him into Paradise, the making of the creation covenant with Adam and God departing from Adam while permitting Adam to live in Paradise while having charge of Paradise. In this way Moses ends the second chapter. Moses clearly intends to leave his readers to suppose Adam took up residence in Paradise intending to keep it as a permanent home for himself, his promised wife and descendants.

God departs from Adam in peace for God knew Adam intended to keep the creation covenant and live in Paradise. Adam begins to take fruit from the trees of Paradise in accord with his understanding of the provisions of the creation covenant. He feels no restraint on wondering anywhere inside or outside Paradise for he was the Monarch not only of Paradise but of the whole earth as well. The birds and animals with free access to Paradise are subject to the will of Adam.

Although Moses knew and understood the creation covenant in its entirety, he writes of it only to the extent his readers will find necessary to adequately understand the situation of Adam and Eve in Paradise. For without a correct and adequate understanding of that creation covenant there is no understanding the words and actions of Adam and Eve. Understanding it is especially necessary to understand what Moses is about to report happening to Adam and Eve in the third chapters of Genesis.

Readers of chapter two and three must constantly bear in mind the fact of the reality of the creation covenant, its entirely gratuitous nature and, especially its one invalidating or terminating condition, abstinence from eating the fruit of the tree of knowledge of good and bad. Without that terminating condition there can be no understanding of the reason Adam and Eve can be justly expelled from Paradise and their willing acceptance of their expulsion. The covenant, the purpose of the two special trees in the middle of

Paradise and the invalidating condition of the creation covenant are the setting for the tragedy that befalls Adam and Eve in the third chapter.

Commentaries on chapter two of Genesis completely ignore its account of the making of this creation covenant. Without an awareness of its existence and its terms and conditions there can be nothing in their commentaries to justify Adam and Eve living permanently in God's splendid Paradise or to justify their expulsion from it. Without that creation covenant there is no justifying reason for Adam and Eve finding themselves doomed to death if they merely ate that fruit. No reason Satan should have been so insistent on Adam and Eve immediately eating the fruit of that one particular tree and no reason for Satan disguising himself as a serpent. No reason Satan should have intended to deceive them about that fruit to the extent of trying to make a villain of God. Without the existence of the creation covenant and a proper understanding of the creation covenant, nothing can make intelligible the conduct of Adam and Eve and justify the very severe punishment God imposes on them and everyone of their race for merely eating a single fruit from that one tree. Their descendants are severely punished for a sin in which they had not the slightest part or given any consent.

Any commentary on Genesis' account of the lives of Adam and Eve must be based on the reality of the creation covenant if that account is to give any understanding of the function of either the tree of knowledge of good and bad or the tree of life. No understanding for the account to state that the two trees were located or grew in the middle of the Garden and for God so solemn warning against Adam, his future wife and his descendants eating fruit from the tree of knowledge of good and bad. Commentaries must give evidence for the fact that Adam and Eve were justly deprived of everything and why they would eat that fruit under the penalties of immediate expulsion from Paradise and being doomed to death.

Genesis makes it clear that Eve from the beginning didn't have any difficulty understanding God's one prohibition. It was only after Satan appeared on the scene that she could no longer believe eating the fruit would lead to their deaths, to their immediate loss of all their rights to Paradise and to everything else, especially their rights to supernatural life and an eternal divine destiny. Cf. Rom 5:12.

Commentaries presently in circulation regarding the account of Adam and Eve living in Paradise, their fall from grace and the protoevangelium do very little to give an understanding of the literal sense of Satan's plot against them and the entire story of chapters two and three. The authors of these commentaries are unaware of the creation covenant and their lack of understanding of these chapters reflects that ignorance. Because those authors are unable to completely rationalize the whole literal account of creation they are forced into symbolizing so much of the creation account.

Moses wants all his readers to understand that the creation covenant belongs to the very substance of chapters two and three. He wants his readers to understand these chapters exactly as Adam and Eve understood them. Moses wants all to understand how aware Adam and Eve were of the tree of life and how extremely important it was to them. It was so important for the eating of its fruit daily or frequently would have the very beneficial effect of preserving anyone eating its fruit in a state of perfect health, vigor, strength, and perpetual youth. Persons always in perfect health are free from pain, suffering and sickness and are incapable of dying from natural causes.

That this was the true function of the fruit of the tree of life is confirmed in Moses' reporting the details of the dialogue God had with Adam and Eve after eating the fruit and just prior to their expulsion from Paradise. For that dialogue clearly indicates that the time of Adam's free access to the fruit of all the trees of Paradise and especially the fruit of the tree of life had ended and that Adam would be returning to the dust from which he came.

Adam knew that the tree of life grew only in the center of Paradise. If he and Eve were expelled from Paradise neither they nor anyone of their descendants would ever be permitted to return to Paradise to take fruit from the tree of life to eat it and so live forever. They knew they were not to take that fruit for planting its seed outside Paradise. If Adam could in any way continue to secure that fruit he, his wife and descendant would live forever.

"Therefore, he must not be allowed to put out his hand to take fruit from the tree of life also, and thus eat of it and live forever. The Lord God therefore banished him from the Garden of Eden." Gen 3:22-23. The word "also" in the phrase "The tree of life also" refers to Adam again deliberately disobeying God by eating fruit from the tree of life as he disobeyed God by eating fruit from the tree of knowledge of good and bad.

No one should rhetorically ask or assert as someone has: "Why did God forbid the fruit of the Tree of knowledge of Good and Evil. If the 'tree of knowledge' was a good tree—and we dare assume it was because God created it—why was it singled out by God to be 'out of bounds' for Adam and Eve? Could it be because the gift of free will to our first parents (and us) could and would unwisely pervert attained knowledge? Misuse knowledge? Is it not tremendously significant that the 'tree' was not identified as the 'tree of wisdom'".

The creation covenant did not give anyone the right to existence or to life, otherwise Adam and Eve would have deprived themselves of the right to life at the moment of their breaking the creation covenant. Their breaking of it deprived them of their rights to transcendent natures and immortality, not to life itself. Obviously, Adam and Eve would not die from ingesting poison if they ate that fruit. Later in the temptation by Satan, when they ate that fruit, they do not become sick and die soon afterward from poisoning themselves.

This analysis of Genesis' account of Adam and Eve living in Paradise reveals that it was by means of the creation covenant that God intended to give every descendant of Adam and Eve rights to a transcendent human nature, to the state of original innocence and to a supernatural destiny. In this way the creation covenant would make it possible for Adam and Eve and all their descendent to attain the eternal divine destiny God had prepared for everyone of their race.

Under the creation covenant only Adam and persons of his race are eligible to receive anything from God by means of the creation covenant. Other humans, people who supposedly evolved from subhumans and persons supposedly living on other planets, could not benefit from the creation covenant God made with Adam as the head and only male progenitor of his race.

When the first three chapters of Genesis are analyzed in this way, a complete understanding of mankind's original state of innocence and its loss by sin emerges. That understanding clearly conforms to the New Testament revelations and Christian Doctrine regarding original sin and its propagation to all men until the end of time through their physical sexual generation by Adam and his line of progenitors.

The creation covenant alone conferred on Adam and Eve and their descendants rights to special natural, preternatural, supernatural gifts. It conferred the right to live in Paradise, so long as they abstained from eating fruit from the tree of knowledge of good and bad. This is evident from the fact that Adam and Eve lost all those rights as soon as they ate the forbidden fruit. All this is evident also from our Catholic belief that all men would have been born in Paradise, in the same transcendent condition as Adam and Eve and possessing the original innocence Adam and Eve had at their creation, if it were not for the original sin of our first parents.

All this is possible only if all God's favors were bestowed on everyone of Adam's race by means of the creation covenant and if eating the forbidden fruit were the one and only condition of the creation covenant that would terminate that creation covenant. It was for the very reason of bring about the fall of all mankind that Satan, in chapter three, had to be so insistent on Adam and Eve eating the fruit of that one specific tree, the tree of knowledge of good and bad.

The apostle St. Paul obviously understood that Adam's eating the fruit was a violation of that kind of command, the creation covenant. He wrote: "I say, from Adam to Moses death reigned, even over those who had not sinned by breaking a precept as did Adam, that type of the man to come." Rom 5:14. "Therefore just as through one man sin entered the world and with sin death, death thus coming to all men in as much as all sinned." Rom 5:12.

Since Genesis explicitly states that God took Adam and settled him in Paradise, no one should think, as many apparently do, that after certain pre-humans evolved into true humans or homo sapiens, Adam, one of those humans or homo sapiens, just happened to wander into that Paradise and took it over or occupied it for the purpose of exploiting it for his personal advantage. If Adam and his wife had just wandered into Paradise, they would have been obliged in justice to exit Paradise immediately and permanently, for they could not have rightly supposed that God or someone had prepared it as a permanent home for them and their family exclusively. If Adam had acquired Paradise for himself in that way, he would have stolen Paradise and Adam would have been a crook and a sinner before committing original sin.

The creation account of Adam and Eve and the reality of Adam and Eve being created in "our image likeness" make it clear that Adam and Eve from the beginning were far from being in the very primitive human state or condition of cavemen or tree-dwellers of science fiction. Genesis reveals also that Adam and Eve were far from being the primitive humans the theory of evolution would dictate that the first man and woman must have been. Genesis reveals that they had transcendent immortal natures and that their minds were infused with a great store of knowledge of all natural things and even of supernatural things.

With Adam giving his consent to the creation covenant, including consent to its invalidating condition not to eat the fruit of the tree of knowledge of good and bad, Moses ends the episode of the explanatory tour of Paradise. The next epic will be that of God providing the man, who had taken up residence in Paradise, with a helpmate like himself, a marriage partner.

GOD CREATES EVE AND GIVES HER IN MARRIAGE TO ADAM

When God returns to the man He left in charge of Paradise God finds that the man is still very much interested in keeping the creation covenant and that he wants God to fulfill the as yet unfulfilled promises of the creation covenant. God finds that the man has committed himself to the creation covenant for several reasons. Adam has remained in the Paradise; he has been eating fruit of its trees and has properly cared for Paradise and everything in it. He has not destroyed the tree of the knowledge good and bad even though he was not to eat its fruit. If the man had no concern for keeping the creation covenant in order to live in Paradise but wanted to live out side Paradise, he certainly would have first of all taken the tree of life and planted it outside Paradise. He could then continue eating its fruit and in that way retain his perpetual youth and vigor and so live forever.

God designed and made Paradise as a permanent home for both Adam and his wife. The tour of Paradise revealed to Adam God's intention of giving Paradise to him and of giving him a woman for a wife and of giving him the specific vocation of being the sole male progenitor of a whole race of transcendent humans on earth. Adam knew that he had not evolved and that he did not have a father or mother. Consequently Adam knew he did not belong to any family or race and that there was no race of humans on earth from which he himself might obtain a wife. The author knew the same for he had seen the man being formed from dust of the earth. Moses knew Adam was the only human on earth for he knew the earth was barren precisely because there were no humans on earth to till the soil.

The author also knew there was no race on earth from which the man or God might obtain a woman to be his wife. Hence Adam and Moses knew it was up to God to make a woman if He would provide the man with a marriage partner, if the man were going to be the male progenitor of a race of humans on earth.

On the sixth day God had created the animals from dust and decreed man's dominion over everything on earth. "Both [men and beasts] go to the same place; both were made from dust, and to the dust they both return." Eccl 3:20. God now causes all the animals to come before the man to be scrutinized by him and to be given names by the man.

God had given Adam dominion over all the animals, so Adam had the right to give names to all the different kinds of animals. Only to owners of things belongs the right to give names to thing that are his. Only the master of a pet has the right to give a name to his pet. There has always existed the practice of only parents having the right to give names to their children and of owners of animals to give names to their domesticated animals such as horses and cows or even pigs. Because of man's dominion over the entire earth, man has the right to give names to rivers, mountains, bodies of water and various places. God gave the names sun, moon and stars to those heavenly bodies over which Adam was not given dominion. Persons have rights to name things they have made, to things such as cars, locomotives, boats, ships, machines, roads, bridges, engineering projects and etc. Persons who are not the parents or the owners of things may give only nicknames to persons or things.

Lack of dominion over God is the reason neither Adam nor Moses nor any of the patriarchs ever attempted to give a name to the God who appeared to them or spoke to them. On those occasions the persons either asked God for his name or God volunteered his name to them. "I am, who am" of the Vulgate or "He who is" of the Greek is the name God gave Himself when Moses at the burning bush asked God for his name. God is identified but not named by persons calling God "the God of Abraham" or "the God of our fathers". God, who has absolute dominion over man, exercised that dominion over the first humans when He called the man and the woman, man. "He created them male and female. When they were created, he blessed them and named them 'man'". Gen 5:2.

Since God gave them the name "man" it is not right for humans to go by any name other than man. Any other name would imply the rejection of God's dominion over man. This right does not prohibit parents from giving identifying personal names to each of their children. But parents are not permitted, for example, to give their children names that would intentionally identify them with any kind of beast. For example, the name Leo, the Latin word for a lion, might be given to a person to manifest the person's real or imagined fearlessness or stouthearted like that of a lion. Adam had the dominion and right to give a name to the woman, his woman, because she was made from his rib and was given to him by God to be his wife. Persons in love or married feel free to give nicknames or endearing names to each other.

In the first chapters of Genesis, God always calls the male "the man". God built the rib he had taken from the man into a woman and when she was brought to the man he declares, " this one [as opposed to all the animals he had already named] shall be called woman for out of her man this one has been taken". Outside Paradise when the woman is about to have a child, the man, now Adam, gives his wife the identifying name, Eve. He chose for her the name Eve, because she would be the mother of all the living. Cain is called a man and the man is for the first time called Adam in Genesis. Cf. Genesis 4:25.

Mary and Joseph were told the name the Heavenly Father intended for his Incarnate Son, the God-man. They were to give Him the name, Joshua or Jesus, which means Savior. "Because He will save his people from their sins". Mt 1:21.

Today's radical feminists indignantly reject names for persons of their sex that imply or in the slightest identifies a person of their sex with anything male. So today's radical feminists, in the insanity of their extreme sexism, do not want a woman to be called a chair-man or even chair-woman, a business-man or business-woman, police-man or a police-woman. These feminists see these hyphenated names making persons of their sex subservient to men in that same professional occupation in spite of the fact that it was God Himself who called persons of both complementary sexes by the name "man". They like instead chairperson, businessperson, and etc.

These feminists consider the language regarding the gender or sex of persons, in use ever since God gave it in Genesis, sexist and are intent on changing the so-called sexist language of Scripture.

Person with the mentality of a sexist female cannot bear to be called a fe-male or a wo-man.

God, who formed all the animals from dust, knew there was no human other than the man arranged a parade of all the animals to be reviewed by Adam. God did this to impress on Adam the fact that among all the animal made from dust he was the only human. God wanted Adam to know by this empirical demonstration that no humans existed on earth and that there were no suitable marriage partners for him to be found on earth. In this way God reveals to the man and even to us fallen men that man was God's most special and most favored of all beings on earth. Since Adam knew he was the only human on earth, Adam was expecting God to provide a woman in some extraordinary way to be his marriage partner. Perhaps God would do so by forming a woman from dust. The fact that no humans showed up in this parade of all the animals was certain evidence to the man that he did not have parents.

This parade of all the different kinds of animals was not conducted specifically for the purpose of discovering a suitable marriage partner for the man. It was conducted, as the text states, to let the man see all the various kinds of animals God had made from dust and to have Adam give a name to each species. God had given the man dominion over all the animals so he alone had the right to give a name to each species. This parade of all the animals is further evidence that Genesis teaches the absolute uniqueness of the man and that absolute uniqueness of the man presupposes a non-evolutionary origin for the man.

Adam's reviewing, scrutinizing and naming all the animals God had formed from dust manifested to the man the vast verity of the domain God had given the man on the sixth day of creation. Moses is implying that he saw God form Adam's body from dust and that he saw God form the bodies of all the various species of animals from dust. Moses, the author, did not choose to put into his account of the creation of all things any description of God forming the animals from dust, which he witnessed.

From Adam's reviewing, scrutinizing, and naming the animals it was obvious to Moses that the man had been given infused knowledge for his mental capacity to distinguish the nature of one animal from that of another and what possible used his dominion could make of each species. Adam gives names to all the different species of animal and does not name any one of them man. There was no man or woman among them. During that review, Adam was judging whether any animal was or was not "bone of his bone or flesh of his flesh". That is the reason that God needed to form the woman and bring the woman to the man. When He does the man rejoices declaring, "This one, at last, is bone of my bone and flesh of my flesh". This review of all the various species of animals and God making the woman made it obvious that God and the man considered only a human person of the female sex a suitable marriage partner for the man.

After making of the creation covenant with the man and settling the man in Paradise God departs from the man leaving him alone and in possession of Paradise, Adam knew God would be returning to him in Paradise. God did return at a suitable time to provide him with a promised suitable marriage partner. In his short solitude in Paradise Adam found great joy in his expectations of a wife and children.

Adam must have wondered just when and especially how in the circumstances God was going to provide a suitable marriage partner (a woman) for him. This temporary solitude of the man, in view of the man's divine vocation to being the sole male progenitor of a race of humans on earth, is the reason God says on his return to the man: "It is not good for the man to be alone. (Now) I will make a suitable partner for him."

Here in the second chapter, God begins implementing his further promises of the creation covenant. The promise of providing the man with a marriage partner for the sake of generating ultimately a whole race of transcendent human as descendants to fill and subdue the earth.

Many persons have great difficulty understanding God's declaration that it is not good for the man to be alone. Some see in this declaration some opposition to the New Testament's teaching regarding the greater personal good of virginity when that virginity is consecrated to God. This problem results from not reading this second chapter in the light of God's intention, expressed on the sixth day of creation, to generate a whole race of humans from only one fertile couple. It results also from not understanding it in the light of the tour of Paradise, which manifested that God would provide the man to whom he would give Paradise the great blessing of a wife.

God had always intended that the man be the sole male progenitor of a race of humans, so when God saw the man alone in a Paradise designed for a husband and a wife why would God not say, 'It is not good for the man to be alone. I will make a suitable partner for him'". Gen 2:18.

This declaration manifested God's impending action of providing a suitable marriage partner for the man. God always intended that there be only one race of humans on earth, the race to be generated by this man and from the woman. He would provide for Adam as his suitable marriage partner. Hence for this man to be left permanently without a suitable marriage partner was not right or good according to God's plan for the man. God's plan for that man included the Incarnation of his Son as the God-man of the race of Adam. This was the hidden reason God declares it was not good for this man to be alone. Before there was any creation, God the Father desired most of all and above all to incarnate his Son as the God-man by his Son being conceived and born from a virgin of the race of Adam.

By a suitable partner for the man God could have meant only a person of the complementary female sex, a true marriage partner. That was precisely the kind of partner the man was expecting and was most willing to accept in view of what the man saw in the design of Paradise. With the formation of the woman, Eve, and God's giving her to the man, God had fulfilled his promise to the man and his own intention, expressed on the sixth day of creation, to create man male and female. He would bless them and command them to multiply and fill the earth with descendants, one of whom would be the incarnate God-man.

God would make the woman in the likeness of the man for in making her He would again use the same working model God used in the making of the man. The "our image likeness" He used when making of the man. "Let us make man in "our image likeness".

"God created man in his image, in the divine image he created him; male and female he created them." Gen 1:27.

God has excluded barren homosexual conduct forever from his plan for mankind. Clearly God intends only monogamous heterosexual marriages, for He created only one male and one female and unless they mated there could never be other males or females. Only a woman can be a suitable complementary partner for a male. Sexual generation produces males and females in equal numbers and this is necessary if God is to give everyone a right to marry and generate children.

God said He would "make", not "find" or "obtain" or "choose" a suitable partner for the man for there were no women on earth from whom God might find or obtain a partner for the man. The partner God will make and bring to the man would need an origin consistent with the man's uniqueness. It would have been sacrilegious to make anything but another human from the rib of the man and even more sacrilegious to make or evolve a woman from any subhuman species. God's declaration that He would make a partner for the man implies that in this situation only by God making a woman could the man have a suitable partner. The necessity of God having to make a partner also implies that the man had not evolved otherwise God would not have had to make a partner for him.

God's continuous use of "the man" and "the woman" with respect to Adam and Eve in the three creation chapters is another implication in Genesis that Adam and Eve were the only male and female on earth. It is only after the man is no longer the only male on earth that the man changes to Adam in Genesis. Whenever the sense of the word man, in the creation chapters, means any man the word man is used without a definite article in the Hebrew text. Cf. Gen 1:26; 1:27; 2:24; 2:25.

God designed all humans to be either one of two complementary sexes. God did not design persons of opposite or adversarial sexes, anti-male or anti-female persons, but persons whose sexuality is complementary in every respect to the person of the other complementary sex. A complementary sex always cries out for and seeks its complementary sex. The complementary sexes are designed to be attracted to each other not to a person of the same sex. Persons of complementary sexes are attracted to each other for the purpose of forming marriage partnerships, not merely friendships or companionships.

The declaration that it is not good for the man, this particular man, to be alone without a marriage partner, implies that God intended from the beginning to create only one male and one female. God intended that men be male and female of complementary sexes for the specific helps complementary marriage partners can give each other besides propagating the human race. Sexual propagation of the human race is also God's chosen means for propagating the state of original innocence in the race of Adam. "God created man in his image; in the divine image he created him; male and female he created them. God blessed them, saying: 'Be fertile and multiply; fill the earth and subdue it.'" Gen 1:27-28.

Humans, whether male or female, share a common dignity for persons of either complementary sex were created using the same "our image likeness" as a model in their creation. This shows that the "our image likeness" use as a working model in the creation of both Adam and Eve was not so specific that it did not allow its subject or material object to be either a male or a female. Consequently all men live in similar family units in a society and have the same ultimate divine destiny. God created the male first so He could give the female to the male who rightly functions as the head of the marriage partnership and family. Cf. 1 Cor 11:8-15.

God let the man, Adam, know that He is about to "make" a suitable partner for him, first by declaring it is not good for the man (the only man) to be alone. He does it also by letting the man know that He will be taking out one of his ribs for the purpose of building it up into a woman. God informed the man that for the purpose of making the procedure for removing one of his ribs painless He would be putting him into a deep sleep. This implies that Adam in his transcendent condition knew such a procedure would be painful and that he could suffer pain by that kind of violence to his body. By telling of that deep sleep Moses implies that he had previously observed Adam sleeping and that implies that resting and sleeping were a part of the daily routine of transcendent man.

God apparently did not let Moses know ahead-of-time how He would provide a suitable partner for the man. Moses is an author who is only an observer and was not expecting that God would cast the man into a deep sleep and would be removing one of the man's ribs for the purpose of building the man's rib into a woman. Moses perhaps was expecting to see God form the body of Adam's partner from the dust of the earth, just as he had seen God form the body of Adam from the dust of the earth.

Moses learns the price origin of the woman by observing the man in a deep sleep and seeing God remove one of the man's ribs. He then observes God building up that rib [not magically changing the rib] into a woman and then taking care of the man's surgical wound.

Many modern commentators consider the story of God taking a rib from Adam and building it up into a woman something merely mythical or symbolical in the story of God providing the man with a wife. Some modern commentators consider the making of the woman from a rib another incident of the author of Genesis being influenced by ancient pagan myths for in pagan myths the gods do such things. This happens in the mythology of gods who are incapable of creating anything from nothing and incapable of doing anything more than merely changing one thing into another.

"You made Adam and you gave him his wife Eve to be his help and support; and from these two the human race descended. You said, It is not good for the man to be alone; let us make him a partner like himself." To 8:6.

The man himself explicitly acknowledges the reality of God forming the woman from the physical flesh and bone of his own body when God brings the woman he had formed from the man's rib to the man. The man rejoices: "At last, this one [unlike all the animals Adam scrutinized and named] is bone of my bones and flesh of my flesh [her nature is the same as my nature]. This one shall be called 'woman', for out of 'her man' this one has been taken." Gen 2:23. This building up of a rib into a woman recalls those miracles of Jesus when He several times built up a few loaves of bread and a few small fish into enough food to satisfy the hunger of thousands of people.

The apostle Paul obviously did not consider the idea of God making the woman, Eve, out a rib of the man something symbolical or mythical. St. Paul considered it a reality, even an amazing prophetic reality, for he wrote: "Man was not made from woman, but woman from man [as Eve was made from Adam's rib]. Neither was man created for woman, but woman for man [as Eve was created for Adam]." 1 Cor 11:8-9. God created the woman and gave her to the man for the man and the woman to fulfill their God-given vocation of becoming the very first progenitors of the whole human race on earth.

Since Adam believed that he was the only human among all the creatures God had formed from the dust of the earth, Adam knew that any woman brought to him by God could not be the pick from a number of women from somewhere on earth. If she were, Adam would have been deceived into thinking that he was absolutely unique. In fact any woman brought to Adam would have raised questions in his mind regarding what was her exact origin and how that origin was consistent with his uniqueness as the only human then on the earth.

One possible way of preserving Adam's belief in his absolute uniqueness and of satisfying Adam's concern that the woman had an origin consistent with his absolute uniqueness would have been for Adam to witness God forming her body from clay or dust and seeing her body coming to life. God however does not desire that kind of origin for the man's perfectly suitable marriage partner. God had more in mind than merely preserving Adam's belief in his absolute uniqueness. God intended her origin be one of special significance to both the man and the woman and to all mankind, just as the origin of the man's body from dust has been of great significance to Adam and mankind.

The man's origin from dust signifies the radical mutability and mortality of man. The man, when still in his state of original innocence, knew he would die if he did not eat the fruit of the tree of life and would doom himself to death if he ate the fruit of the tree of good and bad.

The very special origin God had chosen for the man's marriage partner was one that would manifest not only the oneness of their flesh but also the oneness of their entire race. The origin of the woman's body from the man's body would also marvelously signify the complete oneness and the indissolubility of their marriage partnership. God intended that the origin of the woman's body from her man's body would induce husbands and wives to love each other as each loves his or her own body. God willed that marital love should have its origin in the oneness of their flesh.

The man loved his own body and the building up of one of his loved ribs into the flesh and bone of the body of his wife was a powerful incentive for the man to always love his wife as his own body. "Husbands should love their wives as they do their own bodies. He who loves his wife loves himself. Observe that no one hates his own flesh; no, he nourishes it and takes care of it as Christ cares for the church—for we are members of his body." Eph 5:28-30. No doubt Eve, as any woman, much preferred that she be formed from Adam's rib than from the dust of the earth. St. Paul taught that we know God loves the body since He wills to raise the human body from the dust of the grave and to glorify it. Cf. 1 Cor 6:13.

All of the man's concerns for the woman that God would give him for his wife were alleviated by God informing the man that He would be taking out one of his ribs, make that rib into the woman and she would be the most suitable marriage partner for him. This pleased Adam very much for when he sees her he rejoices: "This one, at last, is bone of my bones and flesh of my flesh; this one shall be called 'woman,' for out of 'her man' this one has been taken." Gen 2:23. Adam manifested that he believed God's promise of a woman for a wife and what precise origin she would have from him, Adam rejoiced, for when God brings the woman to him, Adam immediately declares her origin from his body. He was her man since she was formed from his rib and given to him by God for his suitable marriage partner. They would live together in Paradise.

The complementary nature of the sexuality in humans leads to attraction and attraction leads to love and love leads to marriage. The orientation of a marriage partnership is life together for mutual assistance with the purpose of generating new life and the nurturing of that new life. Every marriage partnership is oriented to the generation of new life by their partnership receiving from God the rights to engage in sexual activity. God gives these rights to every marriage partnership at the moment the partnership is formed. God gives the right to engage in sexual activity directly to the partnership not to the individual persons of the partnership. The partnership itself not the individuals of the partnership are free to choose either to engage or not to engage in sexual activity.

Now on this earth when one person of the partnership dies the partnership ceases to exist. When the partnership ceases so do the rights and duties of the partnership. Thus the Virgin Mary and her spouse, St. Joseph, chose to form a true marriage partnership, but that partnership agreed not to use their marital rights by making perpetual vows of virginity. They accepted the duties of their partnership.

For a better understanding of the oneness of the flesh of the two persons of the marriage partnership, everyone should know that sex is not just another function of a human body, as many contend in their attempts to justify their trifling with human sex, sexual activity and marriage. The flesh and bone of a body form many diverse complete organs of a body and each organ has its own function. The function of each organ is limited to that organ of the body. However, the genital organs are designed to be complementary to the persons of the partnership. The sexual organs of bodies are design to be complementary in their functions also. These complementary organs though of different bodies are designed to function as though they were organs of one body. When these organs function they unite the two bodies in one function. The two bodies become one functioning unit. The complementary sexual organs function as though they were one body.

Human sexuality, because it is bisexual and complementary in design and function, necessarily orders persons to heterosexual activity. "Can you not see that the man who is joined to a prostitute becomes one body with her? Scripture says, 'The two shall become one flesh.' But whoever is joined to the Lord becomes one spirit [not one body] with him." 1 Cor 6:16-17. A homosexual marriage is an impossibility because a marriage partnership must involve persons of complementary sexes for complementary sexual activity.

Since the actual functioning of sex requires the simultaneous acting together of two persons, the functioning of sex, if it is to be nonviolent, requires a loving agreement of the two persons to engage in sexual activity. Hence sexual activity requires the existence of a marriage covenant between the two persons.

There is a great difference between a suitable helpmate and a suitable partner. Two or more persons of the same sex or different sexes can join as helpmates in a partnership. Their partnership is always the result of an agreement. It is agreements that make persons partners not helpmates. The nature of any partnership is dependent on the nature of their agreement and the particular goal the persons will be perusing together in the same way or even in different ways. God when intending to make a partner for the man intended a woman for the man who would be his wife.

The covenant in the case of a marriage partnership can involve only two persons, two persons complementary in sex. The marriage covenant unites the persons into a partnership for life's activities and when the partners have children those activities must include the rearing and educating of their children.

Since persons do not have complete sovereignty over themselves, their bodies or their sexual activity persons are not completely empowered or competent to make a binding marriage covenant for themselves by themselves alone. The designer and creator of the human bodies of different sexes, their fertility and their sexual function are designed to be the efficient cause of a particular conception, not the efficient cause of the being or the person they conceive by their sexual activity. Consequently every sexual union of marriage partners involves at least the possibility of a creative act on the part of God. Partners cause the conception of a particular person but God, according to his predetermined plan, causes or creates the being of the person the partnership causes to be conceived. God, by designing and causing the fertility of sexual activity, has bound Himself to cooperate with that fertile sexual activity to create the particular person the partnership causes to be conceived. Because of this essential involvement of God in the creation of the person sexual activity causes to be conceived, the two persons are not completely competent to establish their marriage partnership by themselves. Substantially more is involved in making a marriage covenant than the two persons agreeing to establish their marriage partnership. Only God can, by means of his supreme dominion over man, establish persons permanently in their marriage partnership. "Therefore let no man separate what God has joined." Mk 10:9. Only by the persons agreeing to the terms of the marriage covenant or contract God drew up for the purpose of establishing marriage partnerships, can a couple form a marriage partnership for themselves. The partnership secures from God rights to live together and to engage in sexual activity. God blesses any such partnership as He did Adam's and the partnership is thereby assured of obtaining from God the graces and blessings necessary for the welfare of the partnership and family.

God intended that the oneness of the flesh of the partnership, manifest in the sexual function, signify also the permanence and indissolubility of the marriage partnership. This is the reason Adam in lovingly accepting the woman as his own body also lovingly gave himself completely and permanently to her, and declared: "That is why a man leaves his father and his mother and clings to his wife, and the two of them become one body." Gen 2:24.

Many may wonder how Adam could have known these and many other truths he speaks of almost immediately after his creation. This has been reason enough for many commentators to doubt or even deny Adam ever spoke what he is reported to have spoken. They believe Moses or the author, whomever he may have been, was the one who put words on the lips of Adam. How can these commentators do such violence to the story and to the format of the chapter and then expect the literal sense of the text to make sense?

No one could expect Adam, who did not have parents, to have such critical and certain knowledge of the marriage partnership, unless God infused that knowledge when creating Adam. The question that comes to mind is, what evidence can be found in the text of the creation chapters that would justify anyone thinking God infused so great a store of knowledge into the mind of Adam at his creation? The text gives that assurance when it states that God created the man in "our image likeness". To be created in "our image likeness" means, as has already been shown that Adam was created in the likeness of the transcendent God-man Jesus Christ. The creation of Adam in the likeness and fullness of the God-man, Jesus Christ, implies that Adam was infused with the same store of knowledge with which the God-man's human mind was infused at his Incarnation!

Only God's indissoluble marriage covenant can establish indissoluble marriage partnerships in which the concerns of one partner become the concerns of the other—the concerns of both partners as though they were truly the concerns of one flesh or of one body. In a marriage partnership a spouse views the concerns of his or her partner as the concerns of his or her own flesh or body rather than the concerns for some other flesh or body. Married partners are to promote the welfare of their partnership by an unreserved commitment that directs all efforts or actions to the welfare of their partnership.

By the marriage commitment, a partner is no longer free to consider himself or herself any longer a completely free and autonomous individual, but a partner completely committed or bound to another partner. A marriage partner is always bound to give the best of self to one's partner. This commitment obliges a partner to give his or her best to his or her partner. True marital love always gives the most and the best while demanding the most and the best in return. Only by a partner's complete and unconditional commitment to the marriage partnership can a partner truly gain the other, rather than surrender to the other or demand the surrender of the other. The persons of a partnership should feel the joy and the exigencies of their delicate and profound communion and offer their virginity in love to the other for God's predilection of children for their partnership.

Partners worship each other by giving their most and their best to each other in recognition of their mutual splendor. Partners worship God by offering their dynamic partnership and their children to God for the glorification of God.

The unifying function of sexual activity and God's indissoluble and unalterable marriage covenant are obviously absolutely incompatible with any involvement of any third person. They rule out completely not only polygamy and polyandry, but infidelity and divorce.

Such a marriage partnership supposes an agreement on a plan of life that is totally mutual; one plan of life that involves all facets of life for partners. Nothing is to be excluded from their developing partnership. Their agreed on plan of life must be built on espousing God's designs for their marriage partnership and on trust in the generosity of divine providence to supply adequately and even abundantly for the needs, welfare, and happiness of the partnership and the children of the partnership.

Since God created man male or female, an individual male or female is incapable of generating new life. A marriage partnership is a new reality, a moral person, established by God's marriage contract and that new reality is the proper subject of the responsibilities of marriage, including those regarding the generation of new life. Since God has made the marriage partnership capable of generating new life, only the partnership, not the individual person of the partnership, can be the subject of the rights and responsibilities proper to married state. The partnership must accept its God-given responsibilities of being completely open to accepting new life from God and of carrying for that new life with the generous self-sacrificing love of a devoted mother and father.

The children of the partnership are gifts from God not from Mother Nature. Their children are signs of the particular predilection God has for their partnership. A child is not his or her child, but first of all God's child. The partnership has the very grave obligation of dedicating its children to God. Since the partnership is merely the cause of the conception of a particular child, while God is the efficient cause of the child's being or person, the child belongs first of all to God. Parents have the honor and dignity of conceiving children who are always true genetic brothers and sisters of the God-man, Jesus Christ. Partners must recognize that, in the plan of God, their children were from eternity predestined by God to become true genetic brothers or sisters of the God-man and further predestined, through baptism and divine adoption, to becoming adopted children of the Heavenly Father. The best possible and most acceptable dedication Catholics partners can make of their child to God is the offering of their child for baptism in the Church of Jesus Christ.

Every marriage partnership is the privileged fundamental unit of society and for this reason human society cannot long endure without flourishing marriage partnerships and families. The welfare of marriage partnerships and families must have first priority in civil law ordering or governing society for the common good of society. Any injury to the honor, welfare, and stability of the family is also an injury to the common good of society. No civil society may passively tolerate promiscuity, adultery, divorce or homosexuality. A civil society's even passive neglect of the true welfare of families forecasts the impending doom of that civil society.

Jesus, when questioned about the legitimacy of divorce and remarriage, rejected divorce and remarriage and reminded his questioners that Adam had proclaimed the oneness of the flesh in the beginning as the reason God never permits divorce for the sake of remarriage. In Adam's view a person can no more divorce his or her marriage partner than a person can disown his own flesh or body. Jesus proclaimed the same by saying that the partners God has joined and made one by his indissoluble marriage covenant no one must attempt to separate. Since a husband and wife are not the complete cause of their marriage partnership coming into being, they must not endanger or attempt to dissolve its unity.

Jesus' resorting to Genesis in support of the indissolubility of marriage gives an interesting clue to who wrote Genesis and when what he wrote about took place. "He said to them, 'For your hardness of heat Moses allowed you to divorce your wives, but from the beginning it was not so.'" Mt 19:8. Adam said, "That is why a man leaves his father and mother and clings to his wife, and the two of them become one body." Jesus says Adam said this in the beginning not at the time Moses wrote it. This implies that Moses was having visions of what went on at the creation. Moses was having visions that were supernatural reenactments of what happened to Adam and what Adam really proclaimed at his marriage to Eve.

The marriage covenant, which God drew up for mankind in

the beginning, is indissoluble by man but not indissoluble by God. The bond of every marriage partnership ends at the death of one of the partners because the partnership itself has perished or has ceased to exist. Death dissolves every marriage partnership. The purpose of the marriage partnership on earth does not endure into the after life. During life God wills the dissolution of his primordial non-sacramental marriage contract only when the persons are incompatible and only for the sake of a new sacramental partnership, which has greater unity and is the source of all grace needed for the welfare of the partnership. Cf. 1 Cor 7:12-15. If God wills the dissolution of a primordial non-sacramental partnership only in favor of the persons entering a sacramental marriage partnership, then, in the will of God, sacramental marriage partnerships are indissoluble except by the death of one partner. The secular practice of divorcing for the purpose of remarrying is not the same thing as God permitting, in certain circumstances, the dissolution of a particular incompatible non-sacramental marriage in favor of the greater unity and the graces of a sacramental partnership.

St. Paul teaches that God has made the indissoluble sacramental union of a marriage partnership a prophetic foreshadowing of the indissoluble union between Jesus Christ and his Church. The indissolubility of that union is the reason for Christ's undying love for his body, his Church. A marriage's union is a symbol of the eternal union of Jesus Christ with his Church. Only in Christ's true Mystical Body can persons find the fullness of unity and identity with Christ and with God. Cf. Eph 5:31. The Church of Jesus Christ is the bride of Christ, the one and only bride of Jesus Christ. The beloved bride of Christ, the Church of Christ, is inseparable from the love of Jesus Christ and of God the Father. Under no circumstance will Jesus Christ fail to love his Church on earth, divorce his Church on earth, abandon his Church on earth or separate Himself from his Church on earth.

By their marriage partnership a husband and a wife share intimately the same life but not the same roles in marriage or in life. God designed the complementary sexual differences to be the bases for complementary roles not the same roles for marriage partners. Cf. 1 Tm 2:12. The husband has the role of head of the wife and of the family, as Christ is the Head of his Church. For this reason a husband should be the one to exercise the sovereignty God has invested in the marriage partnership which is to be exercised for the service or welfare of the partnership and the family.

The husband is the helpmate of the wife by being the provider of the material necessities for the partnership and family and must do so even at the cost of labor, drudgery, blood, sweat, disappointments, and tears. He must be the protector of his wife and family even at the risk of his life. The wife must be the helpmate of her husband. Her most specific role is that of bearing his children and, with the guidance and assistance of her husband, lovingly nurture them in the knowledge, love, and service of God, of Christ's Church and of the common good of society. No father would want to be deprived of his intimate role of assisting his wife in nurturing the physical, mental, and spiritual life of his children. St. Peter teaches that husband and wife must share their lives on earth, just as they share in the supernatural life and destiny God has given them. Cf. 1 Pt 3:7.

In Adam's teaching regarding the indissolubility of marriage can be found further evidence that the "our image likeness" of the sixth day of creation was one of the Father's eternal exact ideas of the God-man, Jesus Christ. The creation of Adam in "our image likeness" the likeness of the God-man, implies that Adam was created with the same store of infused human knowledge the Father willed to store in the human mind of his Son, the God-man. The gospels' account of Jesus teaching the indissolubility of marriage shows that both Jesus Christ and Adam shared the exact same knowledge and understanding of the nature of human sexuality, marriage and the indissolubility of marriage. For Jesus Christ quotes with complete approval Adam's statements which affirm the oneness of the marriage partnership and the indissolubility of marriage.

A marriage cannot be dissolved by any mutual agreement of the spouses or by any human authority. This is implied in Adam's words. Adam had the fullness of human authority on earth, yet he recognized his inability to dissolve a marriage partnership.

God's guidance for all men and women in all their human relationships is given to us by St. Paul. God's guidance he says requires that all older men be treated as fathers, all younger men as brothers, all older women as mothers and all younger women as sisters. Cf. 1 Tm 5:1-2.

The second chapter of Genesis contains primarily Moses' account of the visions God gave him regarding the making of the creation covenant, the formation of the bodies of Adam and Eve and their marriage partnership. The coming third chapter concerns primarily the fall of the first husband and his wife into original sin, the results of their original sin including expulsion from the Garden of Eden and mankind's restoration to a supernatural life and a supernatural destiny. In these chapters Moses is writing of what he sees and hears in visions and adds some comments on what he sees and hears for their better understanding by his readers, fallen men.

At the very end of chapter two, for example, Moses makes a most interesting and clarifying comment. The last sentence of the chapter seems completely out of place in the progress of his account of the live of Adam and Eve. He states what can only be his own private reflection on a peculiarity he noticed in the conduct of Adam and Eve living in Paradise. There Moses reflects with some surprise on the fact that: "The man and his wife were both naked, yet they felt no shame."

That there should be this revelation of the continuous nakedness of Adam and Eve at this point in his account seems out of place. For Moses' account nowhere records God informing Adam or Eve or anyone of the fact that they were naked and there is nothing in Moses' whole account of what Adam and Eve say or do that in any way indicates they were naked or were aware of their nakedness. It was only after they ate the forbidden fruit that Adam and Eve became aware of their nakedness and that God told them that their awareness of their nakedness was due to the fact that they had eaten the forbidden fruit. "Then He asked, 'Who told you that you were naked? You have eaten, then, from the tree of which I had forbidden you to eat!'" Gen 3:11.

So how could Moses have known that Adam and Eve were naked even before Adam and Eve themselves knew they were naked and so states at the end of the second chapter? It was only because Moses could see and hear Adam and Eve in his visions as they really were that he could see they were naked and was able to inform his readers of the fact that they were naked. Unless Moses would have injected in his account the fact of their nakedness and that they were not ashamed of their nakedness, all his readers would have supposed that Adam and Eve were wearing clothes.

All the while Adam and Eve were in Paradise they knew they were not clothed and were not ashamed of their nakedness. When God comes on the scene of their fall from grace God implies that they should not be aware of their nakedness for neither He nor anyone had told them they were naked. God tells them that they could have discovery their nakedness only by eating the forbidden fruit. God asks them: "Who told you that you were naked? You have eaten, then, from the tree of which I had forbidden you to eat!" Gen 3:11.

The nakedness they discover was not merely the fact that they were not clothed but also discovered the shame they began to feel because they were unclothed in the presence of each other.

The recorded reflection of Moses regarding the nakedness of Adam and Eve offers very special and conclusive evidence that Genesis was not compiled from any written source. For sources other than an eye witness to Adam and Eve living together in Paradise would have supposed they were clothed and would not have known of their shock on discovering their nakedness and shame. Since chapters two and three are a direct and immediate revelation to Moses by means of vision, Moses would have observed the nakedness of Adam and of Eve. He observed also their lack of shame in the presence of each other.

By his little comment that Adam and Eve were naked and without shame the author clearly identifies or betrays himself as a member of the fallen race of Adam. For only a fallen member of Adam's race would have taken notice of the fact that Adam and Eve were naked and without shame.

SOLUTIONS TO OTHER PROBLEMS REGARDING THE CREATION OF MAN

Although Satan was not permitted to see the origin of Adam and Eve, he nevertheless knew they were the only humans on earth at the time he discovered them in Paradise. Since Satan knew they were the only humans on earth and had learned from them the details of the creation covenant, Satan was sure he could alter God's destiny for the entire race of man. He would do that by leading Adam and Eve into the particular sin of eating the fruit of the tree of knowledge of good and bad.

Why would God have formed Adam's body from loose earth or clay rather than from a chiseled stone statue of a man? God wanted Adam to know that God was the sole and complete origin of Adam's whole being and that Adam was at the time of his creation absolutely unique, the only human in existence. If Adam had been born, he would have known his parents and others of his race and therefore would not have been unique.

Since Adam was created in "our image likeness" he had a great store of knowledge of natural and preternatural things. Adam from the first moment of conciseness knew that in the normal course of nature he should have been conceived and born of parents. From the first moment of his conciseness on rising from the ground and standing on his feet, Adam knew that such was not his true origin. God knew Adam had a special desire and need to know his origin. God therefore manifested to him his true origin. An origin he understood was consistent with his absolute uniqueness.

Immediately after forming Adam's body from dust and breathing into it the breath of life, God could present Adam with circumstantial evidence of his true origin. Immediately after forming the man body from dust God breath into that lifeless human form the breath of life. The man immediately became a living being and in the very place of his formation from dust. There only moments after receiving life God could point to the depression in the ground immediately in front of Adam and inform him that He had used the clay of that depression to form his body and then gave his body life. This would have been confirmed in Adam's own awareness of his having just begun to exist and of having just raised himself from the earth to stand on his feet. Adam could have no memory of having existed earlier or of having done anything prior to his rising from the earth.

Adam would have seen that the depression in the earth at his feet as an emptied mold, for it was of the same size and shape as his body. The awareness Adam had of himself as just begun to exist along with what God was telling and showing him was satisfactory evidence to him of his true origin. From that origin Adam knew God was the sole and complete cause of his being. Such an origin did not involve other humans and meant that Adam was or could be a unique human person.

This kind of origin was adequate assurance to Adam that his being and life were not his own property. His being and life were primarily the property of God and that God had sovereign dominion over his being and his life. Adam accepted God's sovereignty and dominion over him without question or objection.

If God would have made Adam's body from a statue chiseled from some rigid material then, even immediately after his body received life, God could not have offered Adam circumstantial evidence of this kind of origin for his body. The rubble left from the chiseling of a statue from some hard material would be of no value to proving the prior existence of a statue in the likeness of a man. In the whole scheme of things the making of Adam's body from a statue would have left less evidence for Adam to believe that God was the sole and complete cause of his being and that he was absolutely unique and under the complete dominion of God alone.

The apostle St. Paul obviously took very seriously the literal sense of Genesis' account of the origin of Adam's body. He believed that Adam's body came to be by a direct and immediate creation by God. St. Paul states that God formed Adam's body from dust and that Eve's body was formed from one of Adam's ribs. St. Paul thought that Adam's body was as directly and immediately formed from dust of the earth as Jesus Christ came to earth directly and immediately from heaven by his virginal conception and birth. He wrote, "The first man was of earth, formed from dust, the second is from heaven." 1 Cor 15:47. "For Adam was created first,

Eve afterward." 1 Tm 2:13. Cf. 1 Cor 11:8-9.

Before forming Adam's body God had formed a plan for the supernatural sanctification and salvation of Adam and Eve and of all their descendants. According to that plan Adam and Eve, from the first moment of their existence, were to possess transcendent human natures, original innocence their supernatural sanctification—a beginner's "share in the fullness of Christ". From the beginning Adam was predestined by God to a supernatural destiny, "to life on high in Christ Jesus." God did not require anything of Adam, at his creation or at any other time, as payment or as a condition for receiving God's gifts. Hence it is obvious that Adam, in New Testament terminology, was originally justified or sanctified or received his original state of innocence without faith or works or anything else.

Since Adam was the very first man and the forefather of a whole race of humans, God could contract with Adam not only for his own gratuitous state of original innocence and supernatural destiny but also for that of his wife and of all his descendants. An analysis of the second chapter of Genesis manifests that God made just such a gratuitous covenant or contract with Adam for his justification and that of his descendants. That gratuitous creation covenant was the means by which Adam received and could retain rights to all the gifts he had already received from God. That same gratuitous creation covenant was the means by which all of Adam's biological descendants, at the moment of their creation or conception, would receive and retain rights to the same gifts Adam had received at his creation.

According to that covenant all of Adam's biological descendants had rights to be conceived and born with original innocence, a home in Paradise, and a supernatural destiny in heaven. That covenant, if it had remained in effect, would have guaranteed even to us, Adam's most remote biological descendants, rights to be conceived and born with original innocence, a home in Paradise, and a supernatural destiny in heaven.

Obviously the creation covenant made with Adam was not designed to provide original innocence, a home in Paradise, and a supernatural destiny for any and all possible persons of the human species, but only for persons who were true biological descendants of Adam and his line. Any humans Adam might adopt from among any of the supposed humans that evolved from Adamites or real humans still roaming the earth as well as humans from Mars or elsewhere in the universe are excluded from benefiting under God's creation covenant with Adam. This is the reason the Church has never manifested anything but a speculative interest in evangelizing any possible humans or intellectual beings native to any of the planets of our solar system or elsewhere in the universe. Consequently, it is with more reason than merely keeping monkeys out of man's ancestral tree that the Catholic Church teaches that all men, who have lived on earth since Adam, are true biological descendants of Adam.

Notwithstanding the fact that God, in accord with the creation covenant, would directly sanctify or justify supernaturally all descendants of Adam immediately upon their creation and conception, there is nevertheless a very real sense in which Adam himself sanctified or justified supernaturally his descendants at their conception . For the creation covenant, by guaranteeing these rights to all but only true biological descendants of Adam, made all persons generated by Adam and his line eligible for a home in Paradise, original innocence, and a supernatural destiny in heaven. Hence Adam by generating descendants not only generated those descendants but also gave those descendants eligibility to receive original innocence and a supernatural destiny. It was in this very real but limited way of making his descendants eligible for justification that Adam would sanctify or justify his descendants.

It is obvious that Adam, by reason of the justifying provision of the creation covenant, through natural generation and by keeping the creation covenant could be responsible for all his descendants receiving the state of original innocence at their conception and creation. So it is likewise obvious that he could be responsible for all his descendants losing original innocence—be responsible for them being conceived and born in original sin—through being responsible for the sinful breaking of the creation covenant.

Many persons with some aptitude in science, create a problem for themselves by thinking that it is scientifically impossible for anyone to pass on to one's descendants by human generation anything but human qualities. Therefore they think human generation cannot possibly pass on to one's descendants anything of a non-natural or supernatural nature such as the grace of original innocence. Consequently, these persons find it impossible to believe that according to the laws of genetics, Adam could pass on original innocence or original sin to his descendants through their sexual generation from him or his line. These persons think that if original innocence or original sin could be passed on by natural sexual generation from Adam to his descendants, as the Church teaches, then original innocence and original sin would have to be something intrinsic or essential to human nature. If that were the case then the presence or absence of original innocence would have to be a gene or something that functioned like a gene in natural sexual generation. If these persons had sufficient aptitude in the science of theology when seeking a solution to these problems, their aptitude for the natural sciences should not have led them to abandon the certainty of Catholic Doctrine regarding the transmission or propagation of original innocence or original sin by human generation.

These persons confuse completely the requirements of the laws of genetics with the contractual or legal requirements regarding the passing on of hereditary rights to descendants by human sexual generation. These persons appear to lack an understanding of how the creation covenant and human generation working together could pass on to the descendants of Adam rights to the grace of original innocence along with rights to a supernatural destiny. If they had that awareness then they could understand also how, after the breaking of the creation covenant, human generation can pass on original sin to all Adam's descendants. The actual efficient cause of that supernatural sanctification is always and only God's efficient causality.

As an example, one might take the case of a child born to citizens of the United States in some foreign sovereign country. Their child according to the civil law of the United States will have all the rights of a citizen of the United States even though born outside the United States. In this case civil law and natural human sexual generation together pass on the rights of citizenship to persons born outside the United States even though the rights of citizenship are not something intrinsic to a human nature or to the process of natural human sexual generation. In this way all persons born of Adam or of his genetic line could be conceived and born with rights to a home in Paradise, original innocence, and a supernatural destiny by means of human sexual generation in connection with the creation covenant God made with Adam.

In exactly the same way, persons born of Adam or of Adam's line, after the breaking of the creation covenant, would not be conceived and born with rights to a home in Paradise, original innocence, and a supernatural destiny, for the creation covenant was no longer in effect. Consequently when the creation covenant is not in effect all persons conceived by human generation from Adam's line are conceived and born in the state of original sin.

One reason so many do not believe or ignore the Church's precise doctrine that original sin is passed on by human generation is that so many are ignorant of the very existence of the creation covenant with its terminating condition that makes that doctrine of the Church understandable. That ignorance is the reason the creation covenant never enters into their considerations when discussing the transmission of original sin to all the descendants of Adam.

Another problem results from Genesis implying God performed painless surgery on Adam when removing one of his ribs by first putting Adam into a deep sleep. It would seem appropriate to ask: How could Moses have known, what medical science has discovered only recently, that it is possible to put a person into such a deep sleep that even the great violence surgery does to a person's body would not arouse the person from that deep sleep? How could the author of Genesis have known that surgery performed on a person in a deep sleep is completely painless? The taking of a rib from Adam's body only after putting him into a deep sleep manifests that man, in his pre-fallen condition, could suffer physical pain, in particular the pain that would be involved in the physical removal of a person's rib. One might wonder what is the significance of God choosing to use deep sleep rather than acupuncture or hypnosis as a means for freeing Adam from the pain associated with surgery? Would Moses have understood these later procedures without receiving an explanation from God?

Moses could have known of this painless procedure only by observing that Adam was in a deep sleep and that Adam did not appear to suffer any pain while God physically removed one of his natural ribs. This indicates that the visions God gave Moses were so close up and realistic that Moses could observe Adam's remaining asleep during the procedure. Moses implies that avoiding causing Adam pain was the only reason God had for putting Adam into that deep sleep.

By reporting this procedure of God performing painless surgery on Adam Moses most certainly intended to report that Eve's body had a very real physical origin from Adam's body, not some mythical, symbolical or metaphorical origin from the body of Adam. It should be noted that the making of Eve from a rib of Adam most definitely rules out any evolutionary origin for the first woman and should imply the same for Adam. Adam's concern for his true uniqueness on becoming aware of Eve's origin was not in doubt.

Moses ends the telling of God removing one of Adam's ribs with: "He [God]...closed up its place with flesh." By reporting that God closed up the place with flesh, Moses would seem to imply that, after this surgery on Adam, he could not see any displacement caused by the removal of the rib. It might also imply that Moses could not see any scar on the body of Adam where the rib had been removed. This would seem to imply that not even Eve, when examining Adam's side later, could see that Adam was missing a rib or part of a rib. All of this would mean that Adam was the first person to undergo not only painless surgery but also excellent corrective or cosmetic surgery?

Adam knew God had formed all the animals from dust or loose ground. That implies that God must have informed Adam of that fact for all the animals were formed from dust before Adam was formed from dust. These stated facts lead all of us to conclude that none of the animals or man had evolved. We are told that all species of animals, like Adam, were directly and immediately created by God from dust.

Commentators, who believe in the theory of evolution of species, have not grasped or have chosen to ignore all the evidence in the creation chapters for the non-evolutionary origin of the animals and plants and especially the non-evolutionary origin of man. Some persons prefer to see in the man's origin from dust outside Paradise evidence that Genesis even teaches the evolution of man. Some hold that Genesis, in stating that all the animals were formed from dust, teaches that all life evolved from some primordial slime or goo outside Paradise. These persons hold that after the evolutionary process had produced some very primitive humans, homo sapiens, that two such humans wandered into Paradise, if there ever were such a real place, and became Scripture's biological father and mother of a whole race of humans on earth.

If Genesis intended, by informing fallen man that Adam's body was formed from dust, to teach fallen man that Adam had evolved, then God's declaration that Adam at death must return to the dust from which he was taken, at death Adam and every individual must return to their pre-evolutionary condition of nonexistence. For Adam did not really exist in any way before his formation from dust. Such a conclusion is absolutely opposed to and repugnant to revealed truth and to Catholic doctrine about the ultimate end of man. In this way too Genesis not only calls into question any evolutionary origin for man, but also the very validity of the theory of the evolution of species.

Scientists consider any new theory valid only when it explains certain facts their former theory or theories cannot explain in any way, or if the new theory produces new valid formulas and equations, or if it points out facts that had gone unnoticed under their former theories. Einstein's theory of relativity replaced Newton's physics of the universe for just such reasons. Relativity manifested new truths and produced many new things for our age of nuclear energy. It produced the valid and awesome equation $E=mc^2$

If the theory of evolution of species can not explain the origin and existence of a single species, much less can it explain the origin of millions of species. It is not true that the theory of evolution explains what cannot be explained in any other way, nor is it true that it points out truths that would otherwise have gone unnoticed, nor does it or can it make any valid predictions. Hence there are no adequate or justifying reasons for believing in its validity and in an evolutionary origin for man.

The many predictions made by the early proponents of the theory of the evolution of species that many fossils of intermediary forms of life or missing links, no less than fossils of real species, would be found in Cambrian and post-Cambrian rock. All their predictions have turned out to be completely false. For the fossil record does not contain one fossil of anything that can be considered a missing link, even though the fossil record contains many fossils of a vast array of real species. This fact is one of the dirty secrets evolutionists want to hide from everyone.

If the theory of the evolution of species were valid not only must many missing links or intermediary forms have evolved and existed in the past, but there must exist at the present time also living links or intermediary forms of life. According to the theory there must exist now living links between present real species and species about to come into existence. Yet today there is to be found no one willing to point to any living plant or animal and dare declare it a living link to a species about to come into existence. The only witness to the whole history of life on earth, the fossil record, declares that not a single missing link has ever existed in the past and declares just as emphatically missing link will ever exist in the future.

It is important to note that scientists never find it necessary, indeed will not tolerate abandoning even temporally a single exception to inviolable laws or principles of science to explain anything of fact. Why then does the promotion of this theory of the evolution of species alone demand of scientists that they abandon, at least temporarily, inviolable laws or principles to support something the theory merely proposes to be fact? Hence the theory of evolution of species appears not only unscientific but also anti-scientific. A person's toleration of even a single exception to an inviolable law or principle of science calls into question that person's competence in his science or his sincerity or both. The need for this solitary exception and the fact Genesis teaches that the origin of Adam and Eve was a direct and immediate creation by God. That leaves the theory of evolution of species as dead as the flat earth theory.

The theory, therefore, should be buried as a dead wrong theory of the bad science. All past dead theories and beliefs were based on incorrect observations of things or on what conceivably might or might not have happened. They were not based on what careful observation finds to be fact or on true conclusions of what could or could not have happened, or on what the very reliable fossil record declares happened and did not happened.

Men can easily be mistaken and so deceive themselves in respect to a particular position. The earth appears to be flat and uncritical observers may believe it to be flat, but such uncritical observations of the earth do not prove the earth is flat. The ability of species to undergo very limited change or modification and the fact that certain species appear only slightly different from certain other species has given rise to the belief that species can and do evolve. Such assumptions and assertions are completely devoid of factual evidence and there are no known laws of science or nature that would permit a change of species. All natures are in fact immutable or unchangeable!

It was ignorance about the true nature of the seemingly small differences among similar species that led Charles Darwin and his followers to think that similar species could and did evolve from similar species. Many have thought that simple single celled living species could and did evolve into other simple single celled living species and even into slightly more complex single celled living species or even into multi-celled living species. This simple celled concept modern science has shown to be a vastly over simplification of reality. Science now knows there is no such thing as a simple cell. Science now knows that the DNA molecules in every living cell make every living cell unimaginably complex. So complex in fact that if there were a process of evolution of species, that process of evolution could not possibly have produced the many millions of real species even over unimaginably long periods of time. The production of all the specific differences in earth's vast array of species by the process of evolution would require a span of time that is unrealistic to a material world or universe. Hence evolution of species does not have any basses in science or in careful observation of facts.

The theory of evolution of species must be considered the product of too simplistic observations, pseudo-science, bad science or science fiction. The Catholic Church is still taking unjustifiable bad rapes because some of her past prelates backed the "bad science of their day". This is true especially of inaccurate astronomical observations, the misunderstood astronomical observations and the bad astronomy espoused by some of the Church's prelates. Prelates who were thereby misled into opposing the cosmology of Galileo and into censuring Galileo, not putting him to death as some uninformed contend.

Today many Catholics in the field of education, even in so called Catholic religious education, are again exposing the Catholic Church to a new tidal wave of unjustifiable accusations and again taking bad raps for the acceptance and the promotion of the godless theory of evolution of species. Those educators teach evolution instead of teaching and promoting the biblical origin of all things including the biblical origin of man. That biblical teaching is that all species were directly and immediately created by God.

If Adam had evolved, he and his race could never be free from fear of attack, for other humans, who had already evolved as well as humans that would be evolving from pre-Adamites or Adamites or any real humans. These might at any time attack them in their Paradise. Moreover does not the very command of God to Adam to subdue the whole earth imply that the whole earth was uninhabited by humans and that the whole earth was available exclusively to Adam and Eve and their race? If the command does not imply that, then this command of God is an implicit command for Adam and his race to subjugate or annihilate any and all humans on earth not of the race of Adam and Eve.

If scientists would have performed tests on Adam and Eve, only days after their creation, to determine their biological or chronological ages, those tests would not have shown their true chronological ages to have been merely a matter of days. The biological age of persons born and living in Paradise was destined to remain constant once it reached maturity, for the fruit of the tree of life would have kept them in the state or condition of perpetual youth. This shows, once it is conceded that there is an omniscient and almighty Creator, that it is no longer possible to determine with certainty by such tests the true chronological age of the universe or of anything that came into existence by the direct creation of God. The reason is the very real possibility and probability that God created many creatures, like He created Adam and Eve, at a predetermined age or physical development. As an example, consider what problems could be encountered in determining the true age of the individual trees in Paradise and elsewhere on earth at the time God created those trees. Did not God create trees of different ages when He created trees on the third day?

Deliberate direct creation of all things by a purposeful God is a truth opposed to many ancient religious beliefs and much modern thought. Direct creation is opposed to such ancient beliefs as polytheism, dualism, eternal matter, intrinsically evil matter, nihilism and astrology, for all such beliefs inculcate in man a meaninglessness and insignificance for all living things and for humans in particular. Deliberate creation by God is incompatible with the atheistic theory of the evolution, which imposes the same meaninglessness and insignificance on all human life not merely on life that does not meat a quality of life set by man.

The theory of the evolution of species was and still is basic to the justification certain persons offer for the atrocious actions and goals of political and social engineers. Many of these persons have sacrificed and are still willing to sacrifice many tens of millions more of humans to achieve their goal of merely hastening the supposed evolutionary development of man. These persons attempt to hasten the evolutionary development to produce or produce earlier supermen, the super race, the soviet man, the master race, the coming perfect man, and the new agers mindless inevitable evolutionary development of man and all things into gods or even into one single god. These are elitists who think the world today is four hundred percent overpopulated and these too many billions of people need to be eliminated. These elitists think they could justifiably eliminate or exterminate the overpopulation of the earth.

The atheistic theory of evolution is basic also to accepting and promoting the practices of euthanasia, mass suicide of cultists at the instigation of cult leaders, the making of laws that would forcefully sterilize persons or abort unwanted babies or kill the so-called unfit, [the unfit as thought they were unfit to be called human] and the many kinds of experiments now being performed in laboratories on human embryos and some stem cells. These abuses will continue and multiply as more persons are disposed to plan and act in accordance with their belief in the theory of the evolution of species, including especially the human species.

By now readers should be aware that the creation of everything and the supernatural destiny of creatures—everything God has created, has done and will continue to do forever and extra—what is outside God—are the result of only one act of will of God the Father. The Father's will to incarnate His Divine Son as the God-man of our race. All of this is implied in the first article of the Apostles Creed. "I believe in the Father Almighty Creator of heaven and earth.

Hence our prayers of praise and thanks to God must be: We praise and thank you Father for willing first of all, before all and above all to incarnate your Son forever as the God-man of our race. For his incarnation Father you created first the universe the heavens and the earth. You prepared the earth for the first man and woman of our race. You created them in the image likeness of your foreseen most Holy and Beloved God-man. They were created in the splendor of preternatural and supernatural gifts and given an eternal destiny of sharing in the unfathomable riches of the God-man's.

Father you made a paradise to be their home on earth until their ascension to the eternal paradise of vision and union with You their Father.

Chapter 4

CHAPTER THREE OF GENESIS

THE FALL OF MAN: WHY WOULD SATAN TEMPT ADAM TO EAT FROM ONLY ONE CERTAIN TREE?

From the time the first great sign appeared in the sky on the first day of creation, Satan knew that God intended to Incarnate his Son as the transcendent God-man of a race of transcendent humans. Most bitter and extremely enraged over the transcendent God-man's predestination to be the Supreme Head of all creation, Satan became the most furious enemy of the God-man, his Immaculate Mother and the great good fortune God intended for Adam and his entire race.

From the first day of creation, therefore, Satan was expecting God to implement the intentions He manifested in the first great sign. After the creation of the animals, Satan felt that God was about to create the first man and the first woman and incarnate his Son as the God-man.

God concealed from Satan the precise manner, place and time of the origin of Adam and of Eve. From the moment Satan first spied Paradise and the man and the woman living in it, Satan suspected that the woman might be the woman of the first great sign and that the man was her Son, the Incarnate God-man.

Judging from their appearance, Satan might very well have thought that the man, the transcendent Adam, was the transcendent God-man and that the transcendent woman was the mother of the transcendent God-man. Remember, Adam and Eve had been made in "our image likeness", the Father's mental model for the Incarnate God-man, and therefore their appearance and their condition was like that of a transcendent Incarnate God-man. In the visions Moses had of them, Adam and Eve appeared godlike, magnificent like a transcendent Incarnate God-man. A psalm says of

God-man, "You have made him little less than the angels, and crown him with glory and honor. You have given him rule over the works of your hands, putting all things under his feet." Ps 8:6-7.

Because Satan was not certain regarding the identity of the man and the woman, Satan continued spying on them to learn with certainty from them first of all their true identity. Satan had his ears open to their conversations and soon learned their true identity. Satan discovered he had mistaken the first Adam for the second Adam and the first Eve for the second Eve.

By continuing to spy on them Satan learned of the existence of the creation covenant. The plan God had for the man to become the male progenitor of a whole race of human on earth, the existence of the creation covenant and its provisions for Adam and Eve and their entire race. All of these things were a complete mystery to Satan except for what Satan learned from the first great sign. Satan learned from them that everything the creation covenant provided Adam and Eve at their creation the covenant would provide also for all their descendants at their conception. He learned that the creation covenant could be broken or terminated by Adam deliberately eating the fruit of the tree of knowledge of good and bad.

Satan understood that if the covenant were broken not only Adam and Eve would suffer immediately the loss of all rights to Paradise, the transcendence of their human natures, their original innocence and supernatural destiny, but also that all their descendants would suffer the same losses. From the moment of the breaking of the creation covenant, Adam's generating of descendants would no longer pass on to his descendents eligibility for rights to any of God's gifts, especially not the rights to original innocence and the supernatural destiny. Adam and all his descendants would no longer be friends of God. His descendants would be conceived and born outside Paradise and without rights to transcendent human natures, original innocence and supernatural destinies. All of Adam's descendent would inherit instead original sin, sickness, disorders of all kinds and death. These evils would then be Adam's legacy for all his descendants.

On learning the particulars of the creation covenant, Satan saw in Adam and Eve and their descendants a great opportunity to extend his obstinate rebellion and hatred of God to an entire race of humans. He could do so by merely having Adam and Eve deliberately eat fruit from the tree of knowledge of good and bad. By eating that fruit they would deliberately reject God's dominion over them and that would terminate the creation covenant. Satan determined that he would deprive Adam and Eve and all their descendants of their rights to a home in Paradise, to transcendent human natures, to the state of original innocence—their beginner's "share in the fullness of Christ—and their predestination to a supernatural destiny—"to life on high in Christ Jesus.

To accomplish these things it would not do to present Adam and Eve with fruit of the tree of knowledge of good and bad and have them eat it by telling them the lie that it was fruit from some other tree. If Adam ate that fruit under false pretences the creation covenant would not be broken or terminated.

Satan knew Adam would break or terminate the creation covenant if Adam did nothing more than eat deliberately fruit from the tree of knowledge of good and bad. Satan determined to do whatever was within his evil genius and powers to trick Adam and Eve into deliberately eating the fruit of the tree of knowledge of good and bad. Satan knew he would have to be most cautious in approaching them in his attempt to carry out his most wicked intentions regarding them and mankind.

The third chapter of Genesis can be understood only if readers are aware of the existence of the creation covenant, its terminating condition of not abstaining from the fruit of that tree. For their proper understanding of the third chapter readers must also be aware of the covenant's provision that all persons by their physical sexual generation by Adam and his line were automatically eligible to receive rights to original innocence and to a supernatural destiny. Readers without knowing these things can not understand how and why in the account the mere eating of the fruit of the tree of knowledge of good and bad could have such terrible consequences for Adam and his entire race. Satan could not achieve his purpose by leading Adam and Eve into committing just any sin, but by committing one specific sin, the sin of eating the forbidden fruit, for only by eating it could they break or terminate the creation covenant. This explains why Satan had to be so insistent on Adam and Eve eating the fruit of that one particular tree, the tree of knowledge of good and bad.

Satan clearly understood that Adam and Eve would eternally doom not only themselves but also their entire race by their eating of the fruit from the tree of knowledge of good and bad. Satan understood that Adam and Eve by deliberately eating that fruit would implicitly reject God's dominion over them and by rejecting God's dominion over them, they and all their descendants would come under his dominion in his most evil kingdom.

Satan determined that he would by every manner of deception and false promise trick Adam and Eve into eating the forbidden fruit; trick them into violating the covenant's one and only condition that would break or terminate the creation covenant. However, Satan foresaw that their dooming of themselves and their entire race would be eternal only if God did not have a plan to restore Adam and his race to divine favor. God might have some such secret plan by which they could again receive God's gift of supernatural salvation. For God was free to reestablish Adam and his entire race in his favor and friendship and that God was free to do so in any way He chose.

At the very time Satan was tempting Adam and Eve, he could not be certain whether God had or didn't have a secret plan for the resanctification or rejustification of Adam and his race. Consequently, Satan could not be certain that the breaking of the covenant would result absolutely in forever depriving Adam and his race of God's favors and friendship. He could be certain it would absolutely doom them to death. The implications of the content of the second great sign raised some questions and doubts in the mind of Satan that God did have a conditional plan for man's rejustification and salvation.

Satan had good reason for hoping that their loss of God's friendship would be eternal, for Satan could not forget how unforgiving God had been and continued to be towards him and all his fellow demons on the occasion of their sin of rebellion and rejection of God's dominion. "Did God spare even the angels who sinned? He did not! He held them captive in Tarus consigned them to pits of darkness, to be guarded until judgment." 2 Pt 2:4.

Adam and Eve did not know that God the Father had a secret plan to reestablish them and their entire race in his favor and friendship if they lost his favors by eating the forbidden fruit. They did not know of the secret plan the Father had formed and would put into effect for their redemption if they failed to keep his command. God had kept secret his own wise council that pertained to his plan to redeem fallen man through the redemptive work of his Son the God-man. God would put his plan into effect only if the man should be so unfaithful as to disobey, deliberately break the creation covenant and doom himself and his entire race. "God's secret plan as I have briefly described it was revealed. When you read what I have said you will realize that I know what I am talking about in speaking of the mystery of Christ, unknown to men in former ages but now revealed by the Spirit to the holy apostles and prophets." Eph 3:3-5: cf. 1 Cor 2:7-11.

SATAN DEVELOPS A STRATEGY TO TRICK ADAM INTO BREAKING THE COVENANT

Satan knew that God could not be so unfaithful as to break the creation covenant, which He had initiated and consummated with Adam, so Satan had no choice but to attempt to lead them into sin. Satan felt certain he could achieve his objective of deceiving Eve and tricking Adam into eating the fruit of the tree of knowledge of good and bad and so have them terminate the creation covenant. This was a challenge Satan was ready and most eager to accept.

In his continuing spying on Adam and Eve in Paradise, Satan discovered, as he had hoped, that Adam and Eve had no knowledge of his existence or of personified evil, a person head and leader in all efforts at instigating everyone into doing evil. Satan knew he would be greatly aided in accomplishing his perverse plan and goal because his evil reputation had not preceded him to Paradise or into the conscious awareness of Adam and Eve. Satan's plan would take full advantage of the unwary Adam and Eve to more easily deceive and trick them into breaking their agreed-upon creation covenant with God.

Satan was aware of one very delicate problem he would have to face and overcome in his attempt to trick and deceive Adam and Eve. Readers too need to be aware of this very delicate problem for the sake of correctly and more completely understanding Satan's manner of tempting Adam and Eve. No one reading the third chapter should be under the illusion that the forbidden fruit was forbidden because the fruit itself possessed properties that were in any way harmful to the physical, mental or supernatural life of Adam or Eve. Satan knew the lush fruit of that tree was sufficiently enticing to Adam and Eve that God could make abstinence from it a test of their loyalty to Him and of their obedience to his commands.

Satan's plan presented him with the delicate problem of how he might best conceal his true identity and evil intentions when approaching them to present his promises and his proposed action. Satan knew that he must first conceal from Adam and Eve his true identity. This would be no special problem if Satan could present himself as another human person, disguise himself as another human.

ADAM'S UNIQUENESS PRESENTS SATAN WITH A VERY SPECIAL PROBLEM

Satan's problem is not explicitly mentioned by the author but is so obviously implied by the author of the third chapter of Genesis that he didn't need to be explicit about it. If persuading Adam and Eve to eat the forbidden fruit for his purpose of breaking the creation covenant were Satan's primary objective, all readers might seriously wonder why Satan would not have come up with a more suitable presentation of himself than that of a talking serpent. In particular why would Satan not have come to Adam and Eve disguised as a human person? Here as always Satan is not stupid or half-hearted in his determination to have Adam and Eve break the creation covenant.

Satan realized above all else that he must not present himself to Adam and Eve as another human and therefore must not even disguise himself as a human. The reason is that God had impressed on Adam and Eve the truth of their absolute uniqueness. Before the creation of Eve, Adam believed he was the only one of his kind, the only human person in existence. Hence Satan realized if he were to present himself to Adam and Eve in Paradise as another human person, that his very disguise would be an insurmountable obstacle to achieving his planed purpose and ultimate goal of tempting them. Satan knew Adam and Eve would immediately perceive any third human, not a true descendant of theirs, to be in contradiction not only to their uniqueness but also his very existence would be an infringement on the exclusive rights they and their descendants received from God. A third human would immediately cause Adam and Eve to regard that person a most grave direct threat to the exclusivity of all theirs and their descendants' rights under the creation covenant. For Adam and Eve rightly considered themselves the exclusive owners of Paradise and the entire earth and of all God promised and gave them and all their future descendant by the creation covenant.

According to the creation covenant, which Satan planned to have Adam and Eve break, any third human not a true descendant of theirs, should not even exist on earth. Adam and Eve rightly thought of themselves, in view of their uniqueness and the creation covenant, the sole owners and possessors of Paradise and the whole world. The very existence of a third person not a true descendant of theirs would be seen to nullify their covenant with God, that God was reneging on his creation covenant with them.

We should understand that if this were not the situation Satan faced what better disguise for Satan to assume than that of polished liberated gentleman completely his own master to successfully incite Adam and Eve to think how much better off they would be free from the restrictions God had so arbitrarily imposed on them.

It was this predicament that necessitated Satan's disguising himself as a serpent rather than a human person. This predicament testifies directly to the uniqueness of Adam and Eve as the only humans on earth at the time and indirectly testifies to the non-evolutionary origin of man.

The preservation of the belief of Adam and Eve in their absolute uniqueness as humans, the exclusivity of their and their descendants right under the creation covenant to Paradise as their permanent home, to the entire world and to the many promises of God are reasons for believing that God also in his dealings with Adam and Eve, did not appear to them in human form. The only way God could come them in human form would have been to appear as the promised God-man, whom they knew would one day be one of their descendants. But if God would have appeared to them in the form of the God-man, Satan might also disguise himself as that God-man. But then Satan, in the disguise of the God-man, would come with a message that was in contradiction to that of God and of his God-man.

Satan needed a disguise that would permit him to approach Adam and Eve without causing them to suspect that his intention was to trick them into deliberately break God's creation covenant with them. Satan of course did not want them to have any suspicion about the veracity of his words or the worthlessness of the promises he would be making to them.

Moses begins his account of the temptation and fall of man from grace of God with the words: "Now the serpent was the most cunning of all the animals that the Lord God had made." This statement is key to understanding the reason Satan decided on the particular disguise he would assume when tempting Adam and Eve. This statement of Moses implies that Moses had been keenly observing Adam and Eve. He saw they were spending some of their time observing, studying and comparing the bearing and behavior of the different kinds of animals in Paradise. From those observations Adam and Eve had concluded that serpents were the most cunning of all the animals God had made. Serpents along with birds and some animals had limited access to Paradise. Nothing would prevent birds, for example, from coming to rest on the trees of Paradise

"Now the serpent was the most cunning of all the animals that the Lord God had made." This statement is key to understanding the reason Satan decided to assume the disguise of a serpent. Serpents appear quite powerless and defenseless and therefore would need to be wiser and more cunning than other animals in order to survive on their own. As one of the wild animals of Eden a serpent was entirely dependent on its native abilities to survive. Some animals depended on Adam and Eve to look after them for their greater welfare or wellbeing. These were the domesticated animals of Paradise. Adam and Eve considered serpents to be undomesticated animals.

In this situation Satan decided that a serpent would be his very best disguise when approaching and tempting Adam and Eve. In the disguise of a wise and cunning serpent concerned with the well-being of Adam and Eve. As a serpent Satan could present himself as a more experienced resident of Eden. Both Satan and Adam knew God had created the animals before creating either man or Paradise. Some animals had free access to Paradise. In the disguise of a serpent, Satan could present himself to Adam and Eve as their newly found friend who had knowledge from the experience of a longer life on earth than Adam and Eve. He had more experienced than they in their relation with God.

Satan could and would show them that he didn't any longer considered himself bound by the restrictions of God's commandments. As a serpent in Paradise Satan could pretend not to be hostile to them but a domestic willing and able to be considerate toward them.

Adam and Eve had no reason to be on guard against any machination or deception by any creature. They were the only humans on earth and had no knowledge of Satan or any creature on earth with the ability of thought even though animals manifested different degrees of intelligence. In the disguise of a serpent Satan could claim to have lived longer in Eden and on earth than Adam and Eve and consequently was more completely familiar with the needs and conditions of creatures living inside and outside Paradise. He could pretend to know that God at times disregarded the best interests of creatures living outside Paradise and could be expected to be disregarding the best interests of those living in Paradise as well.

Satan would present himself to Adam and Eve as "Garden Smart" and even "God Smart" and that he was willing to use his smarts and experiences to help them gain for themselves some advantages they were already deprived of and aware of. Advantages coming from knowing the whole truth about God, his covenant and everything about Paradise and in particular the tree of knowledge of good and bad. Satan would present himself as one eager to help them secure for themselves a greater justice, freedom and happiness than God and his creation covenant would permit them.

On many occasions Adam and Eve had observed the bearing and the actions of the animals in Paradise. It might very well be supposed that Satan, in preparing for the deception and seduction of Adam and Eve, had days before tempting them actually disguised himself as a serpent and had gain their attention and admiration by performing cunning antics. The serpent might even have eaten fruit from the tree of knowledge of good and bad in their presence without suffering any evil effects. In this way Satan, in the disguise of an antics-performing serpent had already gained the attention of Adam and Eve. That was a plus in any attempt to convince them that he, along with all animals living everywhere, had already successfully liberated themselves from the restrictions God had imposed on them.

Success in seeking and securing that liberation especially made him competent to counsel them how they too might free themselves from the restrictions God had imposed on them by his command that they abstain from eating fruit from all trees in Paradise. If Adam and Eve were freed from those restrictions, they and their descendants could enjoy the full potential of life in Paradise and in the entire world. That liberation and freedom and their consequences would be something for which Adam and Eve and all their descendants would be eternally grateful to him.

In this way Satan planned to make things appear to Adam and Eve as though God were at fault and that God was in fact as unfair to them as He was to other creatures. Satan knew he could count on Adam and Eve understanding that, if God had been lying to others and dealing unfairly with them then God could not be their true friend and should not be trusted and served by them.

In such a situation Adam and Eve should know, according to a higher moral law, that they were free to ignore those restrictions and their agreement with God. If Adam and Eve did not heed Satan's pleading then obviously they and their entire race would forever suffer unjustifiable restrictions on their freedom, welfare and happiness by continuing to keep God's covenant and his commands or orders. They could surely understand that if they had agreed to God's creation covenant under false pretenses, then they were free to repudiate that covenant in the light of their new knowledge of their situation.

In general Satan could expect that Adam and Eve would obviously see the reasonableness and wisdom of the principle that more can be gained by doing one's own will than by doing the will of another.

Satan's plan of deception and trickery included an implied appeal to the personal honor of Adam and Eve. Under the circumstances Adam and Eve appeared to others to have already lost their honor by being wimps. Out of reverence or fear of God they had permitted themselves to be dictated to regarding Paradise. They as owners of Paradise, including all its trees, had a right to eat the fruit of all the trees including fruit from the tree of knowledge of good and bad. As monarchs of Paradise and the entire earth, Adam and Eve should not have been so gullible as to believe that they would die instead of gain the knowledge eating that fruit would naturally give them.

The temptation Satan planed to use in his seduction of Adam and Eve would have four empty promises. "You will not die. For God knows that when you eat of it your eyes will be opened, and you will be like God, knowing good and evil." Gen 3:5.

Satan is here promising Adam and Eve the wisdom that would make Adam and Eve like God knowing good and evil. Only God can perceive with certainty what is truly good and what is truly evil. Adam and Eve by eating the fruit of the tree of good and bad would become like God able to perceive with certainty what was good and what was evil for them. They would then be able to decide for themselves what they should do for their welfare and what they should not do to avoid evil.

Satan promises that by eating the fruit of that tree this wisdom would be theirs immediately. "When you eat it your eyes will be opened and you will be like God, knowing good and evil." Satan's promise perverts God's intended meaning and purpose for the tree in naming the tree the tree of knowledge of good and bad. God's intended meaning was that Adam and Eve by abstaining from that fruit would experience only good, but if Adam and Eve ate that fruit they would then begin to experience evil as well as good. Here Satan deliberately changes the sense of the word know. Satan changes it from persons experiencing good and evil to persons being able to perceive correctly what is good and what is evil. Knowing what is good and what is evil is knowledge that would normally be gained by study or by experiencing what is good and what is bad.

Finally Satan wants them to think that by eating the forbidden fruit the divine prerogative of knowing with certainty what is good and what is evil would be theirs. It is in this perverted sense of knowing that Satan promises they would be like God, able to immediately perceive with certainty the difference between what is good and what is evil.

For the purpose of more easily seducing both of them Satan would pick a time when both were near or under the tree of knowledge of good and bad and he himself eating fruit from the tree. Eating its fruit in their presence would imply that he had been enjoying the tree's lush fruit and doing so without the least fear of any evil consequences to himself. This pretense would convincingly demonstrate that the eating of the fruit did not have the dire consequence of sickness and death for him and therefore could not mean sickness and death for them.

Thus Satan's eating of the fruit would demonstrate to them that what he was saying and promising them was the truth. They like he would not die and they would have the divine knowledge to perceive with certainty what was good and what was bad.

Readers should not overlook the fact that there were reasons why Adam and Eve might believe that the mere eating of the fruit would give them such knowledge. First, it was God Himself not they who had given that particular tree the name tree of knowledge of good and bad. Second, Adam and Eve were aware that they already had two kinds of knowledge or knowledge from two different sources. They were very aware that from the beginning they possessed a great store of knowledge and that they had it without ever undergone any learning process. For example, Adam and Eve were aware that from their very beginning they possessed knowledge of a language and had the ability or skill of understanding and speaking it fluently. They had knowledge of that language without having learned it. Adam and Eve were also fully aware that they had knowledge and understanding of the nature of a great number of thing, such as: poverty, prosperity, property rights, marriage partnership, sexuality, parenthood, family life, love, faithfulness, obedience and even death. They had that knowledge without any study or any experience of them.

Adam and Eve were aware also that they had another kind of knowledge. Knowledge they acquired through experience, the process of learning by observing things. It was in this way they learned that the serpent was the most cunning of all the animals.

Part of the deception in Satan's promise is the implication that eating by itself was one way of gaining knowledge. By doing no more than eat that fruit they could gain for themselves the necessary and great knowledge of being able to determine instantaneously what is good and what is bad. In effect Satan was promising them an entirely new way of gaining knowledge or wisdom. That way was as simple and easy as eating a certain fruit.

Satan was promising that just like seeing and hearing were ways of gaining knowledge, so eating the right food was also a why of gaining knowledge. Adam and Eve knew they did not have the wisdom or knowledge of instantaneously knowing what was good and what was bad for them, so there was some knowledge to be gained by eating that fruit. It is true; we do gain some knowledge just by eating.

Satan promises that eating that fruit would immediately give them the wisdom of perceiving a particular conduct as either good or bad for them. "The moment you eat of it your eyes will be opened and you will be like gods who know what is good and what is bad." Gen 3:5. For these reasons the promises of their newfound friend did not appear unreasonable at least to Eve.

Satan planed to challenge both Adam and Eve at the same time. At a time when both were near or under that tree, because then their desire for gaining that new knowledge instantaneously and the immediate availability of that fruit would work together to shorten their time for deliberation and thus increase the probability they would eat the forbidden fruit.

One day when Adam and Eve were near the tree, this serpent approaches them and surprised Eve by talking to her. "The serpent asked the woman, 'Did God really tell you not to eat of the trees in the garden?' The woman answered the serpent: 'We may eat of the fruit of the trees in the garden; it is only about the fruit the fruit of the tree in the middle of the garden that God said, 'You shall not eat it, lest you die.' But the serpent said to the woman: "You certainly will not die! No, God knows well that the moment you eat it your eyes will be opened and you will be like gods, who know what is good and what is bad." The woman saw that the tree was good for food, pleasing to the eyes, and desirable for gaining wisdom. So she took some of its fruit and ate it [Eve, knowing that for the purpose of securing the wisdom promised by the serpent that both would be like gods that Adam also would have to eat the fruit]; and she also gave some to her husband [challenging her husband to either eat it or call the friendly serpent a liar], and he ate it." Gen 3:1-6.

Adam should have noticed and perhaps did notice that when Eve ate the fruit her eyes were not opened immediately. The fruit did not immediately do for her what Satan had promised.

At this point Eve has already committed three sins. First, she foolishly permitted herself to be seduced by a talking serpent. Second, she ate the forbidden fruit. Third, she, contrary to the command of God, severely challenges Adam, in view of the fact that she did not die or suffer any harm as a result of eating the fruit, by giving him that fruit and asking him to eat it.

If only Eve would have eaten that fruit, the creation covenant would not have been broken. The text explicitly states that it was only after Adam had eaten the fruit that the eyes of both were opened and both became aware of their nakedness. Only by breaking the covenant would they immediately lose what was given to them by the creation covenant. "Then the eyes of both were opened, and they knew that they were naked." Gen 3:7. The apostle Paul confirms this: "Then as one man's trespass led to condemnation for all men, so one man's act of righteousness leads to acquittal and life for all men. For as by one man's disobedience many were made sinners, so by one man's obedience many will be made righteous [made not merely considered righteous]." Rom 5:18-19. "Therefore as sin came into the world through one man [Adam and Eve are not one man] and death through sin, and so death spread to all men because all men sinned." Rom 5:12.

Adam and Eve reacted to Satan's disguise, pretenses, lying words, insinuations, promises and challenge exactly as Satan had hoped. They listened, insufficiently deliberated, and then proceeded to eat the fruit. They thereby broke the creation covenant by violating its one and only invalidating or terminating condition; the condition that they not eat the fruit of that tree.

Adam and Eve immediately began feeling the consequences of their breaking the creation covenant. They understood they had deprived themselves of their rights to all the gifts of God and that God simultaneously with the breaking of the creation covenant took back rights to all the gifts to which they no longer had any rights after their termination of the creation covenant.

Satan's success in achieving his purposes against man by means of lies is the reason Satan has been called "a liar from the beginning" and has been given the name "Father of lies". Cf. Jn 8:44.

Genesis manifests how immediately Adam and Eve suffered their losses by stating that their eyes were immediately open and they saw they were naked. They immediately became ashamed of their nakedness, for they immediately began to feel the shameful rebellion of their flesh. Hence it was that they began immediately to sow fig leaves together, the only material available to them, for the making of loincloths to cover their nakedness. Painfully and too late Adam and Eve realized that they had not become like God able to judge correctly what was good and bad for them. Eating the fruit did not give them the wisdom or the competence to decide correctly and with certainty what was good and what was bad for them. By giving in to the temptation offered by Satan, Adam and Eve were led into making a judgment contrary to the expressed will of God and they then proceeded to do what was gravely immoral in their circumstances.

"It was not Adam who was deceived, but the woman." 1 Tm 2:14. "My fear is that, just as the serpent seduced Eve by his cunning, your thoughts will be corrupted and you may fall away from sincere and complete devotion to Christ. I say this because, when someone comes preaching another Jesus than the one we preached, or when you receive a different spirit than the one you received, or gospel other than the gospel you accepted, you seem to endure it quite well." 2 Cor 11:3-4.

The Mosaic account supposes that Satan, Adam, and Eve knew that the tree of knowledge of good and bad in the middle of Paradise was the only tree of its kind in existence inside or outside Paradise. If it were not the only one of its kind, Satan knew Adam and Eve would want to test his promise of gaining that kind of knowledge by eating the same kind of fruit from another tree of the same kind. Running that test would not be a direct violation of the condition of the creation covenant. If that testing did not immediately give them the promised wisdom, they would then have discovered that the serpent was lying for Satan promised that the natural result of eating that fruit would be that kind of knowledge of good and bad.

Since neither Adam nor Eve nor Satan would be so stupid as not to think of conducting this test, we must suppose there was only one tree of its kind in Paradise or anywhere outside Paradise. If there were other trees of the same kind Adam and Eve might very well have already eaten that kind of fruit without experiencing any effect. Adam and Eve would have known that Satan was lying to them for then they would have already gained that promised knowledge. The only reason the eating of the fruit of that particular kind of tree could have had such dire consequences was that eating fruit from that particular tree was the terminating condition of their creation covenant.

This kind of analysis of the literal sense of the second chapter of Genesis establishes the existence of the creation covenant and that it is the covenant by which human sexual generation by Adam and his line would pass on original innocence to all Adam descendants. In the absence of that covenant generation by Adam and his line would necessarily pass on original sin. The same analysis of chapter two explains the Church's doctrine that original innocence would have been passed on by human generation and also explains why original sin is now passed on by human generation.

The creation covenant is the basis for our Catholic belief that if Adam had not sinned every one of Adam's descendants would be born with a transcendent human nature, a permanent home in Paradise, conception and birth in the state of original innocence, freedom from suffering, sickness, death and having an eternal supernatural destiny in heaven. However, Adam did sin and broke the creation covenant and as a consequence everyone is now born without a home in Paradise and in the state of original sin.

Such a creation covenant would seem to be the explanation, in view of Pope Pius XII's criticism of the opinion or theory of evolution, of how original sin has come to every descendant of Adam at conception and birth. "Now it is in no way apparent how such an opinion can be reconciled with that which the sources of revealed truth and the documents of the Teaching Authority of the Church propose with regard to original sin, which proceeds from a sin actually committed by an individual Adam and which through generation is passed on to all and is in everyone as his own." H G No. 37.

The covenant with its invalidating condition explains how original sin is now passed on by sexual generation to generation after generation. The covenant explains also how God could justly impose such an interminable penalty on the entire race of Adam and Eve for an act so morally indifferent as eating good fruit from a particular tree. Everyone can clearly understand how Adam and Eve could have brought these severe penalties upon themselves and their entire race by their breaking of the creation covenant.

Reason fails to see any equity or justice in the very severe penalties God imposed on Adam and Eve and their entire race for the violation of so minor a command of God. For that reason many commentators find it impossible to believe how that particular command of God was nothing more than a command to abstain from eating the fruit of a certain tree in Paradise. Hence they think that the command of God and the sin Adam and Eve committed had to be something of a much more serious nature than merely violating a command forbidding so insignificant and morally indifferent an act as the eating good fruit from a certain tree.

Commentators have not refrained from speculating what that much more serious command and sin of Adam and Eve might have been. Some speculate that God's command forbade Adam and Eve engaging in any sexual activity. Others speculate that Adam and Eve might have engaged in some sexual perversion instigated by the serpent or that they might have engaged in some sexual perversion with the serpent.

One opinion advances the speculation that the knowledge of good and bad, symbolized by the fruit of the tree of knowledge of good and bad, was knowledge or understanding of sex, which the eating of that fruit would have given them. The reason given for holding the speculation that this command of God dealt with something of a sexual nature is that Adam and Eve, upon doing what was forbidden, immediately discovered that they were naked.

A much more sensible speculation would have been that the eating of the fruit would have deprived rather than given them knowledge and understanding of sex. Why would God's command have been a command forbidding them wholesome knowledge of sexual matters? For God had not only deliberately created them male and female, infused them with a correct knowledge and understanding of sex, marriage, family life, but also gave Adam and Eve to each other in marriage and commanded them to multiply and fill the earth?

The problem with all speculations about that command involving something of a much more serious nature is that those speculations really do not solve or explain anything. Rather they create difficulties to making good sense of the whole story of the temptation, the life Adam and Eve had been living in Paradise and an obvious reason why expulsion from Paradise would have been of any help to Adam, Eve and their entire race.

Genesis implies that Adam and Eve, in virtue of their being created in "our image likeness", had full knowledge of sex and marriage and that eating of the fruit could not have added anything to the knowledge they already had of sex and marriage. For creation in "out image likeness" implies they were created with the knowledge Jesus Christ, who, at his Incarnation as the God-man, possessed all knowledge regarding all things, including all matters of sex.

The speculations and suppositions of commentators about a much more serious command than not eating the fruit of the tree might seem to justify the very severe punishment God inflicted on Adam and Eve. However, a more serious command would be totally incapable of justifying, in the eyes of men, the very severe penalty or punishment God inflicted on all the descendants of Adam and Eve who had no part in the commission of the sin of Adam and Eve.

What is being proposed here about the temptation of Adam and Eve, original innocence, original sin and its consequences will be found to be entirely and clearly in accord with the doctrine taught by the Council of Trent. That Council taught: "If anyone asserts that the transgression of Adam injured him alone and not his posterity, and that the holiness and justice which he received from God, which he lost, he lost for himself alone and not for us also, or that he, being defiled by the sin of disobedience, has transfused only death and pains of body into the whole human race, but not sin also, which is the death of the soul, let him be anathema." Denz., No 789.

Pope Pius XII in Humani Generis taught that there is an obvious conflict between the theory or opinion of the evolution of man and the Church's doctrine of original sin. He wrote: "For the faithful cannot embrace that opinion which maintains either that after Adam there existed on this earth true men who did not take their origin through natural generation from him as from the first parent of all, or that Adam represents a certain number of first parents. Now it is in no way apparent how such an opinion can be reconciled with that which the sources of revealed truth and the documents of the Teaching Authority of the Church proposes with regard to original sin, which proceeds from a sin actually committed by an individual Adam and which through generation is passed on to all and is in everyone as his own." H G No. 37.

The second chapter's making of the creation covenant with its invalidating or termination condition is the basis for the great tragedy that befalls man in the third chapter of Genesis. Moses begins the telling of the story of this great tragedy with the words: "Now the serpent was the most cunning of all the animals that the Lord God had made." In these circumstances and in view of Adam and Eve's opinion regarding the cunning of serpents, it appeared to Satan that his best option was to disguise himself as a serpent when approaching Adam and Eve. In the disguise of a serpent, Satan would be seen by Adam and Eve as one who had a right to roam Eden and Paradise and could possibly have an interest in the general welfare of everyone living in Eden and in Paradise. Their perception of serpents as the most cunning of all the animals endured to the extent that Jesus would admonish his apostles to be "as wise as serpents and simple as doves." Mt 10:16.

GOD ARRIVES ON THE SCENE OF MAN'S FALL FROM GRACE

Genesis indicates that Satan, still in his visible disguise of the serpent, waited in Paradise for God to arrive on the scene of man's fall from grace. Satan was gleeful in his expectation that God would take the same unforgiving attitude toward Adam and Eve for their sin of rebellion as God had taken towards him and all his demons for his and their sins of rebellion. For their sins Satan and his demons, without any sign of ever receiving forgiveness from God, were hurled down to the earth by the good angels. "Did God spare even the angels who sinned? He did not! He held them captive in Tartarus—consigned them to pits of darkness, to be guarded until judgment." 2 Pt 2:4.

Satan was encouraged in his expectation of God being unwilling to forgive Adam and Eve. For Satan observed for the first time fear of God in the talk and conduct of Adam and Eve. Adam and Eve, out of fear of God and divine retribution, were attempting to hide themselves from God in Paradise even though they knew Satan would be only too willing to reveal their hiding place to God. For this and other reasons Adam and Eve must have attempted to drive the serpent from Paradise but were unable to do so. The fact that Adam and Eve would even consider hiding from God in Paradise implies that Paradise must have been rather large.

Satan was determined to wait on the scene in the hope of learning first hand for himself of the complete and permanent deprivation of Adam and Eve and their entire race of all right to God's gifts. He wanted to see for himself God formally and permanently depriving them of all his gifts, witness their expulsion from Paradise forever, imposing on them of the penalty of physical death. Satan knew as well as Adam and Eve that their spiritual death had been instantaneous on their eating the forbidden fruit. Satan hoped God would be no more forgiving toward Adam and Eve's rebellion than He was toward his rebellion and that of his demons. Satan waited on the scene for he wanted to learn also whether God had a plan for the resanctification or rejustification of Adam, Eve and their race; a plan for restoring to them and their descendants all they had lost by breaking the creation covenant. If God had some such plan Satan wanted to know it in detail so he might know what to do to hinder man's resanctification and prevent his salvation.

Before the time of man's fall from grace, the only source of knowledge Satan had about what course of action God might possibly take was the first and second great signs that appeared in the sky on the first day of creation. In that second great sign the huge red dragon, Satan and his kingdom, failed in their attempt to kill the Incarnate God-man at his birth in order to prevent man's redemption, resanctification or rejustification and salvation.

Satan waited for he didn't want to be ignorant or uncertain regarding any specific divine plan or decree of intervention, if any, the secret councils of God had formed regarding fallen man's destiny. Satan wanted to learn, if possible, whether in God's secret councils there would be a renewing of the broken creation covenant or the making of some new covenant with Adam for his and Eve's resanctification or rejustification and that of their entire race to be. Whatever God's intention Satan was determined to do everything possible to his evil genius and power to counter God's action for man's sanctification and salvation.

If God renewed the broken creation covenant or made a new covenant with Adam, Satan would again attempt to lead Adam and Eve into breaking the renewed creation covenant or any new covenant God would make with Adam. If Adam and Eve should again break the renewed creation covenant or any new covenant God might in no way be forgiving towards any second rebellion of Adam and Eve. So Satan might yet achieve his purpose of permanently subjecting all or some men to himself in his most evil kingdom.

When God arrives on scene He demands to learn from Adam what had happened, what Adam had done and why. Adam confesses first to fearing God because of his disobedience and attempt to hide from God because of his nakedness. His confession of nakedness is God's reason for immediately accusing the man of having eaten the forbidden fruit for that was the cause of he and his wife experiencing nakedness.

The man attempts to excuse himself from blame for what he had done by placing the blame on Eve, for he confesses that he ate the fruit only after the woman God had given him gave that fruit to him and challenged him to eat it. Adam wants God to know that he and Eve had eaten that fruit in the hope of obtaining what the lying serpent promised. God then begins to question Eve. Eve attempts to place all the blame for what she had done on the serpent, for she ate the forbidden fruit only after the serpent had tricked her into eating the fruit by his lies and worthless promises. God does not accept the excuses Adam and Eve offer for their disobedience.

Their confession of guilt was their first step towards forgiveness of their sins, but only the first step to obtaining forgiveness from God. God does not question the serpent. Satan, his disguise and what he had done, were all known and foreknown by God. No questioning of Satan by God to obtain a confession of sin from Satan for the forgiveness of his sin. In the presence of Adam and Eve God curses Satan, still in the disguise of a serpent, for his part in the disobedience of Adam and Eve. After cursing Satan God curses Adam's earth because of what Adam had done. God does not curse the persons of Adam or Eve directly as He did the serpent. Instead God curses their personal realms in their lives on earth.

Contrary to Satan's expectations, God doesn't say anything explicit about either renewing the creation covenant or the making of a new covenant with Adam even though some covenant was necessary if Adam and his race were to be rejustified or to receive back any of the graces they had lost.

Satan's hopes in respect to again causing the breaking of the renewed creation covenant or any entirely new covenant with Adam, as the head of the human race, were apparently completely dashed. God apparently neither renews the creation covenant or makes any new covenant with Adam even though the protoevangelium's promised resanctification or rejustification of Adam, Eve and their race. God proclaims the profoundly prophetic protoevangelium as his divine solution to the very grave condition or situation into which Adam and Eve and their entire race had fallen in consequence of the breaking of the creation covenant.

When reading the proclamation of the protoevangelium one must carefully note what God is promising and what God is not promising in the protoevangelium. God promises to bring about two specific enmities and to place one in each of two persons. Each of these persons is directed by the enmity each received to struggle and overcome the object of his or her particular enmity. Could Adam and Eve surmise from the enmity those persons were promised their restoration to the grace of God? Would the inimical activity of those persons in some way restore to Adam and Eve and their descendants the eternal life and salvation that had been lost?

Satan was not happy that God had not explicitly decreed the restoration of the supernatural to Adam and his race, but Satan was shocked to hear God threatening him with terrible curses including the crushing of his head for what he had done. In that crushing of his head Satan would loose forever his freedom of action. A freedom of action he and his demons were permitted to retain after their expulsion from heaven. By what Satan had done Satan had tightened the noose around Satan and his demons. They will always have free will but will not always have freedom of action; the freedom to carry out whatever they would choose to do.

The resistance Satan and his demons offered to their expulsion from their dwelling places in heaven manifests that they retained free will and freedom of action. It is that retained free will and freedom of action that permitted Satan to tempt Adam and Eve. To this day their freedom permits Satan and his demons to tempt men to sin, to take possession of persons, to cause turmoil of every sort in the lives of individuals, civil society, the family of nations and even in the Church of Jesus Christ.

When coming on the scene of man's fall from grace God was not willing to abandon fallen mankind to Satan. From the proclamation of the protoevangelium Adam and Eve learn that not all had been lost. They had not completely lost the love and friendship of God, as they had feared. They learn that God is still willing to work new wonders for them and their descendants, rain down the evils of a curse on Satan and in the end empower the woman's enmity to crush Satan's head.

We may rightly ponder while looking for the reason God did not manifest the same anger, hostility and unforgiveness at the rebellion of Adam and Eve He manifested at the rebellion of Satan and all his demons. God must have some very special reason for granting the new and undeserved mercy and grace of redemption to mankind rather than abandon sinful mankind to Satan.

There were two such reasons. First, abandoning mankind would have required that the Father abandon or radically alter part of his decreed plan for the eternal glorification of his Incarnate Son, the God-man of Adam's race. For the Father had unconditionally determined that his Son become the God-man of the race of Adam and that his Incarnate Son's eternal destiny be in the eternal company and friendship of his true and real genetic brothers and sisters. "God is faithful and it was he who called you to fellowship of his Son, Jesus Christ our Lord." 1 Cor 1:9. Cf. 1 Jn 1:13.

The Father had unconditionally willed to incarnate his Son as the God-man of the race of Adam. Hence in the councils of the Father there could be no plan to create another male and female in "our image likeness" and incarnate his Son by his Son being conceived and born of a woman of that new race of humans. Rather than create another race of humans, the Father wills that the fallen race of Adam be redeemed for the sake of fulfilling his Incarnate Son's predestination to eternal friendship and fellowship with his brothers and sisters of the race of Adam. "God has not destined us for wrath, but for acquiring salvation through our Lord Jesus Christ. He died for us, that all of us, whether wake or asleep, together might live with him." 1 Thes 5:9-10. "This fellowship of ours is with the Father and with his Son, Jesus Christ." 1 Jn 1:3. These eternal determinations of the Father's councils regarding his Son, the incarnate God-man, were basic to the plan the Father had formed for his Son and was his reason for not abandoning mankind but instead decrees salvivic action on behalf of the race of Adam.

The Father therefore proceeded to proclaim the profoundly prophetic protoevangelium. He expelled Adam and Eve from Paradise, and secured Paradise against their returning to take and eat fruit from the tree of life forever.

THE MEANING AND SIGNIFICANCE OF GOD'S CURSES

First, God's curse of Satan. "Because you have done this, you shall be banned from all the animals and from all wild creatures; on your belly shall crawl and dirt shall you eat all the days of your life." Before this curse, Adam and Eve had no idea of a personified evil or of a chief of evil spirits that the words of this curse reveals. A talking serpent to be sure was something extraordinary to Adam and Eve. It was not something that would cause them to suspect that there were any evil spirits created by God and that the chief of evil spirits, Satan, had disguised himself as a talking serpent to tempt them to rebel against God.

By leading mankind into sin Satan led mankind into estrangement from God. God retaliates against Satan for this estrangement in a like estrangement for Satan. God curses Satan in his disguise of a serpent by casting Satan in the role of an eternal fugitive, a solitary outcast and banished from all the other animals. God could very aptly uses this metaphor of an outcast when cursing the serpent, because serpents are not normally social animals but loners. Serpents do not continually associate with other serpents or other animals. Serpents do not live or travel about in pairs or in small associated groups. For this reason there is no specific name for pairs or small associated groups of snakes, as there are specific names for pairs or groups of other social animals. For example, the name pride for a small associated and related group of lions, the name herd signifies a group of cattle or the name school signifies a group of fish.

Also since Satan had chosen to disguise himself as a serpent, God when cursing the serpent follows through by choosing to make the natural crawl of serpents a special sign to Satan and to all men. God decreed that the serpent's crawl be a sign or symbol of one thing to Satan and a sign or symbol of something else to mankind.

In consequence of God's curse of Satan and of God placing enmity between the woman and the serpent, Satan will find himself crawling, cringing in constant fear, dread, and terror of the woman. He will live in terror in anticipation of her heel crushing his head. The crawl of serpents on their belly, groveling in dirt and eating dust or "licking the dust" would be a prophetic sign to Satan of himself in dreadful fear and anticipation of his impending doom, the doom of the woman stalking him to crush his head. Hence Mary is rightly eulogized as the "Terror of Demons".

God intended that the natural crawl of serpents be an everlasting prophetic sign to men. The crawl of serpents God determined should become for all men an eternal symbolical reminder of God's promised deliverance from the power of Satan and an eternal sign of hope that God will be faithful to his promise of redeeming and saving mankind from the power of Satan. Genesis speaks of rainbows in the clouds of the sky in exactly this way. God informed Noah that every appearance of a rainbow in the clouds should be a reminder to him and all men of God's promise never again to destroy all flesh by another great flood. Cf. Gen 9:12.

God's curse of Satan is a metaphor based on what has always been the natural mode of travel or local motion for serpents and is no reason to suppose that prior to this curse serpents had legs and feet. As biologists and evolutionists would say, there is no anatomical evidence that serpents ever had legs or feet. Serpents do not need feet to get up into the branches of trees, for today in certain places serpents are found in trees difficult for two footed men to climb. Neither is there any empirical evidence that snakes eat dust or dirt, but, since the ancients believed snakes did eat dust, God could curse or condemn Satan, in the disguise of a serpent, symbolically to eating dust forever. "But dust shall be the serpent's food." Is 65:25.

Second, there is the curse of God regarding Eve. "I will intensify the pangs of your child bearing; in pain shall you bring forth children. Yet your urge shall be for your husband, and he shall be your master." God does not curse Eve herself, but her realms of a woman and a mother. Eve will experience difficulties in life as a woman, wife and mother of children. Eve as wife must be subject to her husband in love, bear children, and be dedicated to motherhood. In her realm or world the pains of childbirth and the difficulties of rearing children will be as characteristic of a woman as labor and sweat are characteristic of a husband protecting and providing for his wife and children.

Third, there is the curse of God regarding Adam. "Cursed be the ground because of you! In toil shall you eat its yield all the days of your life. Thorns and thistles shall it bring forth to you, as you eat of the plants of the field [not the fruit of the trees and plants of Paradise]. By the sweat of your face shall your get bread to eat, until you return to the ground from which you were taken; for you are dirt, and to dirt you shall return." Again it is not Adam himself who is cursed, but the curse falls on Adam's realm.

The ingredients of bread require much work before they are ready to be served and eaten as bread. The fruit from the various trees of Paradise required only their picking to be served and eaten. There were no thorns or thistles in Paradise to hinder Adam in his work of cultivating and carrying for Paradise. Outside Paradise Adam will find thorns and thistles hindering and making more difficult his work of procuring seeds for planting, for grinding into flour and baked and for the harvesting of produce from plants and trees for food and other uses.

Adam from the moment of his exile in the world must till the cursed ground from which his body had been formed and to which it must ultimately return. He must earn his livelihood by labor, sweat, drudgery, toil, pains, grief, tears and even blood. As a consequence of their sin Adam and Eve as well as their entire race will forever be exiled from the earthly Paradise God had specifically fashioned to be man's home in work, leisure and comfort. God's curses will always accompany men and women while they live on earth outside Paradise. All men and women will have to bear sufferings all their life long and eventually endure the ultimate pain, physical death.

By their sin of disobedience Adam and Eve deprived themselves of rights to God's many gifts except the right to their human life and their marriage. These rights were not imparted to them by the creation covenant and for that reason they could not lose those rights by their breaking of the creation covenant. Therefore after their expulsion from Paradise, Adam and Eve must remain together and live as husband and wife in the indissoluble bond of their marriage covenant.

EXPULSION FROM PARADISE

Both Adam and Eve were guilty of breaking the creation covenant. Consequently God had no choice but to follow through on his implied warning and threat of expulsion from Paradise if they would eat the fruit of the tree of knowledge of good and bad. Adam and Eve did eat the fruit and doomed themselves to expulsion and through that expulsion doomed themselves to sickness and death. To their credit even though the hearts of Adam and Eve felt greatly depressed they offered no resistance to their expulsion form their wonderful home in Paradise.

When expelling Adam and Eve from Paradise God does not overlook the obvious possibility and probability that Adam and Eve or even some of their children might deliberately and stealthily return to Paradise to take fruit from the tree of life or even from the other trees of Paradise. Expulsion implied that no one, contrary to God's new explicit command, was ever to reenter Paradise to take and eat fruit from any of the trees of Paradise. Never again would anyone be permitted to eat the fruit of the tree of life in an attempt to avoid sickness, aging and even physical death. Never again could Adam and Eve eat fruit from any of the trees they formerly enjoyed and were expected to eat for the sake of their many wondrous benefits. To prevent a single breaking of this new commandment forbidding anyone to eat fruit from the tree of life, God stations in Paradise a guarding cherubim with a fearful mighty flashing sword.

God could not permit Adam or Eve or anyone to have free access to the fruit of the tree of life for that access would have been incompatible with God's intention and decree that the sins of men deserve the penalty of physical death. God had explicitly, specifically and permanently decreed death for all man as the ultimate temporal punishment for sin. "The wages of sin is death. But the gift of God is eternal life." Rom 6:23. Accepting God's temporal punishment for one's sins is a necessary condition for anyone seeking God's forgiveness for one's sins. Just as men are tempted to sin they are tempted to ignore or even reject this requirement of accepting death for the forgiveness of ones sins. God had imposed toil and suffering as well as death as temporal punishments for sin. Therefore it is agreeable to God that all men willingly and humbly accept toil, suffering and failure as just temporal punishments for sin and that men never grumble to God or to anyone about toil, suffering and failure.

There is reason for thinking that God did not permit Adam and Eve to leave Paradise with a supply of fruit or seed from any of the trees of Paradise not merely fruit from the tree of life. Under the creation covenant Adam and Eve had rights to the fruit from all the trees in Paradise, but their breaking of the creation covenant immediately deprived them of all rights to all fruit and seed from all the trees and plants of Paradise. "Cursed be the ground because of you! In toil shall you eat its yield [not yield from Paradise] all the days of your life".

Satan came under a greater curse than Adam or Eve. Satan must crawl on his belly and eat dirt all the days of his life while trembling in fear of his head being crushed by a heel of the woman.

A person by harvesting and eating the fruit from the tree of life could maintain himself in perfect health, vigor and perpetual youth and so have no fear of death from natural causes. God did not think it wise to merely command Adam and Eve never again to eat fruit from the tree of life and then permit them to live in or near Paradise. God foreknew that Adam and Eve and even their children would be too severely tested and tempted to eat that fruit for its great and extraordinary benefits in violation of his command.

Therefore God did not merely station a angel with a visible fearful flashing sword to deter Adam and Eve from reentering Paradise and deter them from such action but also moved them to a site at a distance from the Garden of Eden. God foresaw that the children of Adam also would be tempted to return to Paradise for the specific purpose of taking fruit from all the trees of Paradise for food and taking fruit from the tree of life for the specific purpose of living forever.

God settled Adam and Eve in a place east of Eden at a safe distance from Paradise. Here again we are told God "settled" them. This implies that God had prepared a special site in which He settled them outside Paradise. God had "settled" Adam in Paradise. God's preparing of a special place for them is consistent with "The Lord God made leather garments with which he clothed them."

The author clearly states the reason for their permanent expulsion for God says to Adam and Eve at their expulsion: "Therefore, he [Adam] must not be allowed to put out his hand [as he did in the case of the tree of knowledge of good and evil] to take fruit from the tree of life also, and thus eat of it and live forever. The Lord God therefore banished him from the Garden of Eden, to the land from which he had been taken. When he expelled the man; he settled him east of the Garden of Eden. God also stationed the cherubim and fiery revolving sword, to guard the way to the tree of life."

This stationing of an armed angel in Paradise for the specific purpose of guarding the way to the tree of life forces readers of Genesis to conclude: First, that the tree of life in Paradise was a real tree. Second, that its fruit had the real and natural power of giving a special kind of immortality to man. One may also conclude that the tree was the only tree of its kind anywhere for God had decreed death for all men as temporal punishment for sin.

If this tree were not the only tree of its kind anywhere capable of making men immortal, there would not have been any point in God's new command forbidding anyone to eat fruit of that particular tree growing in Paradise and for closing Paradise to everyone. This tree was rightly named by God "the tree of life", since the eating of its fruit would in fact nutritionally or medically give humans this kind of immortality. This tree of life was the only fountain of youth that has ever existed anywhere for man.

The fact that this tree received its name "tree of life" from God and the fact that God took precautions guarding it against anyone ever again eating its fruit should lead everyone to think that the tree of life was in truth a real tree and its fruit real fruit that gave immortality men. Hence the tree and its fruit were not merely some symbols of immortality or of a good life or of God's gift of life. The fact that the fruit of this tree of life naturally caused this kind of immortality might give some scientists of today hope of possibly finding or compounding a substance that could preserve men in perfect health and perpetual youth and so restore this same kind of immortality to mankind.

God planned to create man so there would be a race of humans on which He could bestow his great and most wonderful favors and be the race of humans into which He could incarnate His Son as the God-man. He could then destine everyone of that race to live in eternal fellowship and friendship with the God-man. The irony of God giving man living in a Paradise is that God would have to impose death on man as a remedy and punishment for the sins of men.

PRELUDE TO THE THEOLOGY OF GRACE REVEALED IN THE PROTOEVANGELIUM

The setting of the creation chapters of Genesis is the setting for analyzing the protoevangelium for the theology of grace for fallen man. The protoevangelium's momentous explicit prophecies and their implications are so profound that its text requires extensive and detailed analysis. That analysis has brought to light a theology of grace that can be called a theology of grace for the third millennium.

A theological prelude to the protoevangelium is necessary for an understanding of the Father's reasons for not abandoning mankind after man's fall from grace and for God taking saving action on behalf of the race of Adam. The first reason for God's saving action is that any abandonment of mankind by the Father would have been incompatible with the Father's eternal gracious plan for his most beloved and glorious transcendent God-man of the race of Adam. The Father had predestined his Most Beloved God-man to eternal companionship and fellowship with the transcendent race of Adam in the glory of the Father's Kingdom of Heaven. The fall of man made that impossible unless the supernatural were restored to the race of Adam.

Before their fall from grace, Adam and Eve knew that everything they possessed and their predestination to the supernatural destiny of eternal companionship and fellowship with the God-man were entirely free gifts merited for them by the very Incarnation of the God-man. At the time of their deprivation of all rights to God's gifts and prior to their expulsion from Paradise, Adam and Eve understood that God was unwilling to return to them or to anyone of their race any of the entirely free gifts which had been lost in the breaking of the creation covenant. In addition the Father was unwilling to forgive either the offense of sin or the debt of dishonor done to God by any sin. God the Father made the payment of those infinite debts of reparation the condition of his forgiving any sin of man.

Instead of forgiving these debts of reparation the Father would demand absolutely the payment of these debts. The paying of those infinite debts was and is completely beyond the capabilities of men. Those infinite debts and God's demand that they be paid and man's inability to pay them clearly manifest how humanly desperate, helpless and hopeless Adam and Eve must have considered their salvation. Humanly speaking Adam and Eve, immediately after their fall from grace, could not have had any hope of supernatural salvation for themselves and their descendants. Adam and Eve realized they could never again possess God's gifts, if God did not have some very special plan of redemption to restore supernatural salvation to them and their race. For they knew they could not pay those infinite debts and pay the price of supernatural gifts for their resanctification or rejustification, the price of eternal life or the price of sanctifying grace.

Since the Father intended to resanctify or rejustify Adam and Eve and their entire race, God did not wish to expel Adam and Eve from Paradise without giving them hope of regaining their and their race's supernatural salvation. God did not want them leaving Paradise thinking that God had not made any provision for their salvation. God did not want to expel them leaving them supposing there was no way for them to be freed from their infinite indebtedness to God and God's absolute unwillingness to return anything of the preternatural or supernatural to them or to anyone of their race as a free gift.

While Adam and Eve are in their sinful or fallen condition but still in Paradise, the Father proclaims the all-merciful protoevangelium that will be the remedy for their humanly desperate and hopeless condition. Adam and Eve understand the protoevangelium to mean that God is willing to remedy their fallen condition by restoring to them and their entire race their lost supernatural life and the destiny. God is not willing to restore the lost natural and preternatural gifts or permit them to continue living in the Garden of Eden.

Since God could restore the supernatural to fallen mankind in any way He chose, He could have chosen to do so without redeeming fallen man. God could have chosen to restore fallen man to his former condition by, for example, forgiving all debts own to God in consequence of original sin and then return to them all his former gifts as entirely free gifts. In this way of saving mankind the salvation of fallen man would not be due to any redemption of mankind by the God-man.

The concept of redeeming something or someone was prominent in Hebrew religious thought and practice. The concept of fallen mankind being redeemed in the strict sense of justice, redeemed by being bought back or of someone paying the price of mankind's redemption, appears in the Old Testament and New Testaments, especially in the letters of the apostle Paul. God the Father freely chose to save mankind through redemption. A redemption accomplished by the God-man paying all debts of reparation owed to God because of original sin and all other sins and also paying the price of the supernatural life or sanctifying grace needed for man's resanctification and salvation.

The protoevangelium gives Adam and Eve hope of salvation by inferring their future redemption for their salvation. Adam and Eve understood that redemption was the only way of salvation for them and their race in view of the absolute unwillingness of God the Father to return anything preternatural or supernatural to them or to persons of their fallen race as entirely free gifts. Their redemption would have to be accomplished by God in view of the inability of mankind to pay the infinite debts own to God or pay the price of supernatural divine life. Human persons individually or collectively can not redeem the supernatural for themselves. In the redemption of mankind God would do for mankind what men could not do for themselves.

In proclaiming the protoevangelium God the Father was implying that the graces to be merited in the redemption by the God-man would be given to individual fallen men on credit. Grace would be given on credit since that grace would be merited or paid for later in the redemption. Grace would be given to individuals on the condition of each individual's faith in the God-man and his redemptive work. The Father was willing to give the graces merited in the redemption to Adam and Eve and to every individual of their race on condition that those persons would believe in their resanctification through the merits of God-man. Without faith in the redemption by the God-man no one could reasonably have any hope for his sanctification and salvation.

This faith needed for resanctification or rejustification is the basis for the Scriptural doctrine of justification by faith. "For this is the will of my Father who sent me, that whoever beholds the Son and believes in him, shall have everlasting life and I will raise him up on the last day." Jn 6:40.

The absolute unwillingness of the Father to restore anything of the preternatural and supernatural to fallen mankind as entirely free gifts still holds true and will continue to be true on the day of general judgement. That this is true is evident in the fact that there would be no need for any redemption or for a redeemer, if God the Father were willing to restore what was lost as entirely free gifts. The absolute unwillingness of the Father to restore anything of the supernatural as entirely free gifts is the reason the Father determined that payment must be made for everything. These are the very reasons the Father determined that there should be a redemption, that the God-man should pay all debts men incurred by sin and merit for mankind supernatural divine life and the supernatural eternal destiny that had been lost by original sin.

The significance of the curse God placed on Satan and the promises contained in the protoevangelium led Adam and Eve to understand that Satan would remain as inveterate an opponent of their and their descendants' resanctification and salvation as he was of their original sanctification and predestination to an eternal divine destiny.

Since God the Father willed that the redeemed supernatural graces be returned to man immediately, that willingness implies that the Father willed that the supernatural be returned to man on credit, that it be returned in expectation of full payment later by the Redeemer in the redemption. That payment would be made to God by the Redeemer and accepted by the Father on behalf of or in the name of all men. But under no circumstance is the Father willing to return to fallen men while still on earth the natural and preternatural favors granted to mankind by the broken creation covenant. For the Father had decreed that for all sinners, all men are sinners, the wages of sin must be death. Hence all must die. The Father permits suffering, sickness and death for He decreed all men be deprived of the tree of life knowing that all would die unless they ate the fruit of the tree of life. Death will be the lot of everyone living on earth until the resurrection of all the dead. The only exception will be for those living on earth at the glorious coming of Jesus Christ on the last day.

All the natural and preternatural gifts that had been granted to all men by the creation covenant will be restored to the saved in the glorification of their bodies and souls at the time of the general resurrection of mankind. For all fallen men their beginner's share in the fullness of Christ will be minus those natural and preternatural gifts. "So gird the loins of your understanding; live soberly; set all your hope on the gift to be conferred on you when Jesus Christ appears." 1 Pt 1:13. In the redemption the Father planed for mankind, the redeemer does for mankind what mankind cannot do for itself.

These demands of the Father for the restoration of mankind are the reasons the Father planned and promised a Messiah that would be a true Melchizedek, a true King of Justice. A Melchizedek with true and complete dominion over the Justice of God needed for man's rejustification or resanctification. "You are a priest forever according to the order of a Melchizedek."

The Hebrew name Melchizedek means literally "King of Justice". A true king of something is someone capable of owning, meriting, paying for and buying that something of which he is king. The Messiah the Father promised to send must be capable of meriting, buying or paying for the supernatural divine life, the "Justice of God", and capable of making infinite satisfaction or reparation for all the dishonor done to God by every sin of mankind. He must be capable of making infinite reparation for mankind's rebellion against the infinite generosity and the absolute sovereignty of God the Father. Hence the offspring of the woman must be a true Melchizedek, a true "King of Justice".

In the redemption of mankind the redeemer will satisfy all the demands of the Father for mankind's reconciliation to the Father, for mankind's resanctification or rejustification and for mankind's restoration to an eternal supernatural destiny. The Blood shed on the Cross by the Melchizedek, the redeemer, paid in full the price of the complete redemption and reconciliation of every person who lived before the redemption. These persons received forgiveness and the supernatural life on credit.

The Most Precious Blood of the Melchizedek paid in full also the price of the complete redemption and reconciliation of every person who received the graces of salvation after the redemption even if they would live and be eternally lost. The forgiveness of sins and the supernatural life these persons receive is not given on credit. "It is in Christ and through his blood we have been redeemed and our sins forgiven, so immeasurably generous is God's favor to us." Eph 1:7-8. "It pleased God to make absolute fullness reside in him and by means of him, to reconcile everything in his person, both on earth in the heaven, making peace through the blood of his cross." Col 1:19-20.

One of the reasons most interpreters of the protoevangelium start off with an incorrect understanding of the protoevangelium is that they do not have the use of a correct translation of the protoevangelium. That is the reason their interpretations cannot correctly identify the woman and the reasons for God placing enmity between the woman and the serpent, the disguised Satan. Their understanding of the protoevangelium suffers the consequences of not being able to identify absolutely the woman of the protoevangelium as Mary, the immediate mother of the God-man. One of the consequences of their non-identification or misidentification of that woman is that they have God promising to place enmity or hostility between all serpents and mankind. Some insist: "The hostility foretold is manifest in the relationship normally existing between men and serpents."

Satan, in the disguise of the serpent, is the object of the woman's enmity, of Mary's enmity and hostility toward Satan. If the hostility snakes naturally have for men were the hostility intended by God, how could that hostility do anything to redeem and save mankind? Such interpretations are made to supposedly explain the origin of the hostility existing between men and many other kinds of animals, like scorpions, lions, bears, hornets, and etc. God, as the text explicitly states, promised to place enmity between the woman and the serpent, Satan disguised as a serpent. God promised to place enmity also between the offspring of the woman and the offspring of the serpent or of Satan, not between the woman and snakes or between snakes and men.

In retrospect it is certain that the evil spirit, in the disguise of the serpent, was not just any evil spirit, but the chief of evil spirits, Satan himself. Satan considered success in achieving the downfall of mankind so critically important to his evil plans for man that he couldn't leave the outcome of tempting Adam and Eve to any of his subordinates. He thought it necessary that he undertake that endeavor himself. If the serpent were the disguise of one of Satan's underlings, God would not have addressed that underling in the manner He did; cursing him as the dominant power for evil and threatening him with the destruction of his kingdom. Adam and Eve, completely unaware of even the existence of evil spirits, must have been shocked to learn that it was the very head of all evil spirits that perpetrated their down fall.

THE CORRECT TRANSLATION OF THE MOST PROFOUND AND EXTREMLY SIGNIFICANT PROTOEVANGELIUM

The protoevangelium is a prophecy and a promise of the redemption and salvation God made in Paradise immediately after Adam and Eve's fall from grace. The protoevangelium states: "I will put enmity between you and the woman, and between her offspring and your offspring. She shall crush your head with her heel." Gen 3:15. In Paradise God proclaimed for the first time, by means of this protoevangelium, the gospel of supernatural redemption and salvation.

The word protoevangelium is Greek for "early gospel". Proto means early as in proto-type. Evangelium means gospel. The protoevangelium is the fifteenth verse of the third chapter of Genesis. The phraseology of this most prophetic protoevangelium is the most extraordinary and fascinating in the whole Bible. In the entire Bible there is no prophecy holding greater promise or covering a longer time span than the prophecy contained in this protoevangelium. Its time span is from the fall of man, shortly after man's creation, to the time of the Incarnation of the Son of God and even to the end times destruction of Satan's kingdom on earth. The destruction of Satan's kingdom on earth will be the Triumph of the Immaculate Heart of Mary on earth and will precede in time the establishment of a new heaven and a new earth in the new times of the New and Glorious Church or Kingdom of Christ on earth.

Any analysis and exposition of this most profound protoevangelium must begin with a correct translation. The most fundamental reason the protoevangelium has been so mysterious or confusing to man, its precise meaning so elusive and difficult to grasp is that for millennia the protoevangelium has suffered erroneous translations the world over. The erroneous translations have led to interpretations that are not only contradictory in themselves but also contrary to reason. There are interpretations that imply what is contrary to Christian doctrine.

The interpretations of many modern scholars have made the

protoevangelium anything but a clear, precise and certain revelation of the coming of a Messiah and of the redemption of mankind. Their interpretations have come to be little more than a confusing promise of sending a Messiah. It does not contain a promise to send anyone. There are interpretations that merely promise some vague intervention by the enmity of one or two persons (whom some suppose to be Mary and her Son because of later revelations) to achieve some kind of benefit or happiness for mankind. According to these interpretations Satan will be made to suffer by one or the other of the two persons and in that suffering and defeat of Satan the redemption and salvation of Adam and Eve and their entire race will somehow be achieved. According to these interpretations there is very little if anything in the protoevangelium that can stand as any kind of promise of a redeemer or of redemption. Yet it is just that kind of precise revelation of a redeemer that Adam and Eve were in need of after their fall into grave sin.

In this commentary there is an analysis of the protoevangelium that first answers the question how has it come about that there are translations of the protoevangelium that have very different meanings and some translations are self-contradictory in meaning. It is very disturbing to devout Catholic to learn that this very important protoevangelium has very different translations with very different meanings. This protoevangelium is considered one of the most significant passages of Sacred Scripture.

The original language of this protoevangelium is Hebrew. Hebrew was never a widely used language. After the Babylonian captivity most Jews no longer knew or spoke their Hebrew language. About two hundred and fifty years before Christ Greek became the universal language of the time. Hence the Jews of that time where in great need of a Greek translation of their Hebrew Scriptures. About the year 250 BC the Jews of Alexandria Egypt completed a Greek translation of their Hebrew Scriptures. This Greek translation became known as the Septuagint. Septuagint is Greek for seventy. Septuagint stands for the seventy scholars who are said to have made that Greek translation of the whole Hebrew Bible.

Later in the Christian era there developed a need for translations of both the Old and New Testaments in many ancient languages. There was a very early Latin translation of the Old and the New Testaments called the Old Latin translation. The most famous and perhaps best early Latin translation of both the Old and New Testaments is the Latin Vulgate of St. Jerome. St. Jerome finished his Latin Vulgate about 405 AD. This work consumed nearly fifteen years of St Jerome's life. His Latin Vulgate has recently been revised and that revised version is called the New Latin Vulgate.

Until the last decades of this past century the Catholic Church required that all approved modern language translation of the Scriptures be made from the Latin Vulgate of St. Jerome.

Most of the approved recent translations of the Old and New Testaments have been made from the rather recent critical Greek text, not the Greek LXX or the Latin Vulgate. This is the reason there are two very different English translations of the protoevangelium. One made from the Latin Vulgate of St. Jerome and the other from the critical Greek text. The fact that there are two very different translations of this most significant protoevangelium is very disturbing especially to persons who believe the Bible to be the only infallible teacher of divine revelation. For what is at issue in these two very different translations is man's need for clear prophetic Scriptural evidence of man's promised redemption and of the Catholic Church's teaching regarding the woman's or Mary's very unique and important roles in the redemption and salvation of mankind. Scriptural evidence for that Catholic Doctrine is an additional reason for determining which of the two very different translations of the Hebrew protoevangelium is the correct translation and which is the erroneous translation.

Perhaps the first and greatest cause of the contradictions, confusion, and uncertainty to be found in commentaries on the protoevangelium is the erroneous and oldest translation made from the original Hebrew, the Greek LXX translation. The long-standing general acceptance of the ancient Greek LXX and of the modern critical Greek text has resulted in its very erroneous sense being proliferated around the world by almost every modern language translation of the protoevangelium. For nearly every modern language translation of Scripture and of the protoevangelium in particular have been made from the critical Greek text.

The more recent or modern English translations made from the critical Greek text have God promising in the protoevangelium: "I will put enmity between you and the woman, and between your offspring and hers; He will strike at your head, while you strike at his heel." An English version made from St Jerome's Latin Vulgate has God promising quite the opposite: "I will put enmity between you and the woman, and between her offspring (or seed) and your offspring (or seed). She [not he] shall crush your head with her (not his) heel".

The second English translation above is from the Douay-Rheims version of Scripture. Which is a translation not based on the modern critical Greek but on St. Jerome's Latin Vulgate. Until this century nearly all approved Catholic versions or translations of the entire Bible or any portions thereof by Church Law had to be made from the Latin Vulgate of St. Jerome. The Douay-Rheims version was completed in 1610 when this law of the Catholic Church was in effect.

Obviously the translation one accepts as correct automatically determines not only the sense one accepts as the true sense of the protoevangelium but also determines how a person would answer even the most critical questions concerning any promise made of a Redeemer or of a redemption of mankind. In this matter there are no free choices. For everyone the only correct sense and understanding of the protoevangelium must be that of the correct translation of the original Hebrew protoevangelium.

In the interest of this study's avoiding many questions and problems of language, grammar and syntax, it will be supposed that either the Greek LXX or the Latin Vulgate is the correct translation of the original Hebrew protoevangelium. Consequently every modern language translation of the protoevangelium based on either of these translations will be judged to be correct or erroneous accordingly.

Why must St. Jerome's Vulgate translation of the protoevangelium be the correct translation of the original Hebrew? In the original Hebrew and all translations the protoevangelium has two parts. The first part is the same in all translations. In this first part God promises simply that He will put enmity between

Satan and the woman and between her offspring and Satan's offspring.

The second part is not the same in all translations. The text of the second part of translations made from the Latin Vulgate states "She will crush your head with her heel", while the text of the second part of the protoevangelium made from Greek translations states "He will strike at your head while you strike at his heel." This text in the English translations made from the Greek has the pronoun "he" capitalized and that supposedly indicates that the male offspring of the woman is a divine Person.

Some modern translators and commentators doubt that St. Jerome could have written "she" and "her" in this second part of his Latin Vulgate translation of the protoevangelium. They suggest that some misguided early copyist of St. Jerome's translation changed the "he" to "she" and "his" to "her".

The first reason for holding that St. Jerome's ancient Latin Vulgate translation of the protoevangelium is the correct one is that St. Jerome was a very great linguist. He was one of only a very few early Church Fathers who knew both Greek and Hebrew well. St Jerome knew several other ancient languages very well. Most early Fathers of the Church would not have been able to detect linguistically the Greek LXX's divergence from the Hebrew.

When making his Latin Vulgate translation, St. Jerome had at hand a half dozen or more different translations or versions of the whole Bible or parts of the Bible. He compared all versions available to him when making his Latin Vulgate. Since St. Jerome was an accomplished linguist and was fully competent to check the Greek LXX's translation of the protoevangelium for accuracy against the original Hebrew. He did so and rejected the Greek LXX's translation when making his Latin Vulgate translation of the protoevangelium.

The second reason for holding that St. Jerome's Latin Vulgate is the correct Latin translation of the protoevangelium is that St. Jerome was also a competent theologian. His knowledge and understanding of Catholic Doctrine must have been one of the critical factors leading him to reject the sense of the second part of the Greek LXX's translation of the protoevangelium.

The sense of the Greek LXX's second part not only stands in clear and sharp contradiction to what is the explicit and undisputed sense of the first part in every translation of the protoevangelium. Its second part stands logically in contradiction to reason, to certain truths of Christian Doctrine and to what is explicit in the gospels.

The third and best reason for holding that the Latin Vulgate is the correct translation is that St. Jerome must have seen that the sense of the second part of the protoevangelium in the Greek LXX was clearly in contradiction to its first part. This contradiction does not exist in the case of St. Jerome's Latin Vulgate.

Seeing that the Greek LXX did not conform to the original Hebrew St. Jerome kept the Greek sense of the first part but gave the true sense to the second part of the Hebrew protoevangelium in his Latin Vulgate. Why modern scriptural scholars, unlike St. Jerome, appear unable to check the Greek LXX for accuracy against the original Hebrew and make the necessary corrections in their modern language translations is astonishing!

In what way is the sense of the second part of the protoevangelium in all modern language translations made from the Septuagint or the critical Greek in conflict or in contradiction with the sense of the first part?

First the first part of the protoevangelium is the same in all translations. In all translations the first part not only places two distinct enmities between two specified persons but also and more importantly assigns a specific object each person's enmity is to pursue.

The contradiction in translations made from the Greek LXX is that in the second part the enmities are not directed against the objects assigned to those enmities in the first part of the protoevangelium. That direction is ignored or changed in the second part.

In the second part all translations made from the Greek LXX, the enmity of the woman is ignored and does nothing; doesn't do anything even to the object assigned to her enmity in the first part, namely the serpent or Satan. Since the first part places enmity between the woman and this serpent the enmity of the woman must in the second part be directed against the serpent, Satan. The Vulgate does this by stating in the second part "She will crush your head." Translations made from the Greek usurp her role and give it to the offspring of the woman. They have, "He will strike at your head while you strike at his heel". This should not be since the first part does not place that enmity between the offspring of the woman and the serpent, Satan.

The second contradiction or inconsistency between the two parts of translations made from the Greek is that the object of the enmity of the offspring of the woman has been shifted from the offspring of Satan, the object assigned to it by the first part of the protoevangelium, to assaulting the serpent as though the enmity were between the offspring of the woman and the serpent.

These translations are obviously grave mistranslation because they leave the woman and her enmity doing absolutely nothing while diverting the enmity of the offspring of the woman from the offspring of Satan to the serpent, the object assigned to the woman's enmity. These mistranslations would have the offspring of the woman vent his enmity on the head of the serpent, which is not the object of the enmity assigned to his enmity in the first part of the protoevangelium. In these translations the offspring of Satan doesn't come under assault from the enmity or hostility of either the woman or of her offspring!

The Greek translations leave the offspring of Satan untouched by any enmity or inimical activity. Yet it is precisely the enmity or inimical activity of the woman's offspring, the redeemer, directed at the offspring of Satan, that can accomplish the redemption of mankind for he is the only one capable of accomplishing the redemption. Why translators should have made and continue to adhere to such translations when it is unquestionably the offspring of the woman who is the redeemer, who redeems mankind by his enmity and inimical activity directed against the offspring of Satan. The offspring of Satan is what brought about man's lost condition.

These errors in the modern language translations made from the Greek are extremely serious. These errors first of all effectively destroy the protoevangelium's promise of redemption by eliminating entirely the redemptive role of the offspring of the woman, the redeemer. For the offspring of the woman, the redeemer cannot possibly redeem mankind by directing his hostility and inimical activity against the serpent, Satan, even if by his enmity and inimical activity he would crush the head of the serpent. Second of all, the errors of these translations deprive the woman of the roles the protoevangelium assigned to her by the enmity God gave to her. There is no choice but that the enmity God gave her must necessarily accomplish the objective of her God-given enmity.

If the enmity of the offspring of the woman does no more than strike at the head of Satan, that is, merely inflict some punish on Satan for instigating the rebellion and downfall of man, the offspring of the woman cannot in that way fulfill the role of a redeemer. For there can be no possibility of redemption in a work that merely punishes Satan. "He will strike at your head while you strike at his heel".

For these reasons alone all these translations of the protoevangelium made from the Greek must be rejected as erroneous. Hence, St. Jerome was completely justified in considering the Greek LXX an incorrect translation of the original Hebrew and in translating the Hebrew protoevangelium as he did in his Latin Vulgate.

But there is more. There are two very erroneous conclusions that immediately follow from equating the redemption of mankind with the crushing of the head of the serpent. If crushing the head of the serpent can accomplish redemption that implies the erroneous conclusion that the offspring of the woman, contrary to the Hebrew and Latin Vulgate, must not be the one to crush the head of Satan. On the other hand, if crushing the head of the serpent accomplishes redemption that would imply the erroneous conclusion that the woman is the redeemer. These are erroneous conclusions because the woman cannot redeem mankind for it is impossible for any human person to redeem fallen mankind no matter what the human person might do.

If crushing the head of the serpent accomplished man's redemption then the offspring of the woman must be the one to crush the head of Satan. That, besides being contrary of the original Hebrew and the Latin Vulgate, would leave mankind without any redemption, for true redemption can not possibly be accomplished by the woman or any human person.

These incorrect translations have been accepted because they offer an easy superficial understanding of how the protoevangelium promises a redeemer and redemption, but they in effect destroy the true promise of redemption contained in the protoevangelium. For they have the offspring of the woman assaulting Satan instead of assaulting the offspring of Satan. In these erroneous translations, the offspring of the woman never gets to the task of redeeming mankind, for he does nothing more than assault the serpent.

These erroneous translations also deprive the woman of the other very unique roles God assigned to her in the protoevangelium, the role of chief adversary of Satan and the roles of Co-Redemptrix and Mediatrix of all graces.

If severely punishing or crushing the head of Satan could accomplish redemption, then the good angels could have redeemed mankind by severely punishing Satan and his demons. Also the woman by her crushing of Satan's head could have redeemed mankind. Moreover, God Himself could have most severely punished Satan and in that way redeemed mankind without becoming the God-man and enduring crucifixion for the redemption of mankind. If Satan by enduring that punishment redeemed mankind it might be said that the sufferings of Satan, not the suffering and death of Jesus Christ, redeemed mankind!

If striking the head of the serpent implies redemption and if the redemption occurred two thousand years ago, then the striking or crushing of the head of Satan must also have occurred two thousand years ago. For two thousand years Satan has not acted as though he has had his head crushed. Why after that complete defeat does Satan still go about as a roaring lion preoccupied with leading as many persons as possible into grave sin and into hell? Why is he still engaged in protecting his kingdom by strengthening his kingdom everywhere on earth in his struggles against the woman? Why would Scripture indicate that the promised crushing of Satan's kingdom will occur in the end times for the preparation of the Church and mankind for glorious coming of Christ and the setting up of his Glorious Kingdom, his glorious Church on earth? If the Greek translations are correct the destruction of Satan's kingdom should have already occurred. It should have occurred at the time of the crucifixion? The fact is Satan and his kingdom are prospering more than ever in the world.

The complete destruction of Satan's kingdom will become necessary before Jesus Christ can set up his Universal Kingdom, because it will be impossible for Christ's Universal Kingdom to exist simultaneously with any kingdom of Satan on earth.

The promise of the coming of Christ's Glorious Kingdom still requires the complete destruction of Satan's kingdom; the crushing of Satan's head. Hence the woman obviously has not yet crushed the head of the serpent. Ending Satan's success in the world will be the Triumph of the Immaculate Mary and that triumph will occur just prior to Jesus Christ setting up his Glorious Kingdom on earth.

The promise that the woman will crush Satan's head with her heel signifies first that the woman will be involved personally in the crushing of Satan's head and second that the destruction of Satan's kingdom will be total. The heel of a human body is its most powerful crushing organ or instrument, more powerful than foot or fist. A serpent might survive the crushing of its tail or some other part of its body, but it cannot survive the crushing of its head. Thus Mary's triumph over Satan will involve the complete and permanent destruction of Satan's kingdom.

Most interpreters of the protoevangelium assume that the proclamation of the protoevangelium was simultaneous with God's first determination and promise to incarnate his Son. It is therefore most imperative for all to carefully reread the protoevangelium and so discover that the protoevangelium does not make any promise to send either the woman or her offspring. The protoevangelium promises merely enmities and where those enmities will be placed and what will be the particular object of the enmity of the woman and of her offspring. There is no direct promise in the protoevangelium of sending either of them. Hence the text of the protoevangelium supposes that God had already determined to send them and to be born of the race of Adam. From eternity the Father was determined to send his Son as a man into the world. This is especially evident in the first great sign that appeared in the heavens on the first day of creation.

It is clear that God in order to promise redemption didn't need to explicitly reveal or renew his intention to incarnate his Son as the God-man. To accomplish the redemption of man God didn't need to explicitly promise anything more than certain enmities, specify with whom those enmities would be placed and specify the objects toward which these enmities and their inimical activities would be directed.

The absolute silence of Adam and Eve on hearing the protoevangelium proclaimed indicates that they understood perfectly God's words with respect to the identity of the woman and of her offspring. If they had not understood the protoevangelium perfectly with respect to these persons they certainly would have asked for an explanation. They clearly had the opportunity to ask and God would not have been averse to giving that explanation if they did not understand the protoevangelium. A correct and precise understanding of the protoevangelium with respect to these persons was absolutely critical for Adam and Eve at that juncture. It was critical to their seeking to live a supernatural life on earth and for seeking an eternal supernatural destiny.

They could have understood the protoevangelium only because Adam and Eve had been informed before their fall from grace of the Father's determination to send this woman and her offspring into the world by them becoming members of their race.

Having that information Adam and Eve, on hearing the protoevangelium proclaimed, were very pleased to learn that God, in spite of their grave sin of disobedience, was still determined to keep his promise to them of sending the woman and her offspring to become members of their race. They understood that by putting enmity between the offspring of the woman and the offspring of Satan God was going to make the already promised offspring of the woman their redeemer. Adam and Eve understood that the enmity and inimical activity of the offspring of the woman, directed against the offspring of Satan, would redeem them and their entire race.

If Adam and Eve did not already know of the Father's determination to incarnate his Son as the God-man of their race, the protoevangelium would have been as mysterious and unintelligible to them as it is to today's scholars. Scholars who do not know or believe in any eternal absolute or unconditional determination of the Father to incarnate his Son as the God-man of the race of Adam.

The same would be true of Satan if he didn't already know the identity of the woman and her offspring. The identity of the woman and her offspring were no mystery to Satan. Satan knew the identity of the woman and her offspring because he had seen them in the first great sign that appeared in the sky on the first day of creation.

MARY'S PROPHETIC ROLES OF COREDEMPTRIX AND MEDIATRIX OF ALL GRACES

It is clear that the protoevangelium gives the woman two distinct roles in the salvation of mankind in addition to the role of mother of the redeemer. As mother of her offspring, the God-man, Mary would naturally want to fulfill her role of mother with the greatest possible concern for the welfare of her offspring and for the complete success of his life's divine mission.

The protoevangelium has the woman, the mother of the God-man, being given her additional role of chief opponent of Satan by God explicitly giving her enmity, which God has also explicitly directed against Satan, not Satan's offspring. This enmity explicitly gives Mary the role of making war on Satan and his kingdom, the role of the chief adversary of Satan in the work of defending mankind. This role of chief adversary is as distinct a role as is her role of mother of the God-man.

There is no question that Mary could have fulfilled her role of mother of the God-man without being given this enmity. The enmity the woman, Mary, is to receive assigns her the task of opposing Satan and his kingdom's assaults on the Church militant and all mankind.

The successful fulfillment of this assigned role will bring about the Triumph of Mary's Immaculate Heart in the world. She will have this triumph during the end times in preparation of the Church and mankind for Jesus Christ's intermediate coming to rule in his gloriously renewed Kingdom on earth, his Church.

It was fitting that God the Father should give Mary this very specific and unique role and task of crushing the head of Satan, Satan's kingdom. For she is the only all-powerful Queen of the Universe and as Queen she alone among humans could have the power to destroy Satan's power and kingdom on earth.

One reason Catholic theologians and others find great difficulty proving from Sacred Scripture Mary's special and unique privileges is that they are absent from their incorrect translations of the protoevangelium. They are absent for the sense of the erroneous translations do not identify the woman of the protoevangelium as Mary and consequently the interpreters of the protoevangelium cannot do so either. Another reason is that these erroneous translations have the enmity of the woman doing absolutely nothing as though the protoevangelium gave her no role and therefore the woman cannot be the chief adversary of Satan. These erroneous translations do not manifest any special role for Mary, her only role is that of Mother of the Messiah.

Because these scholars accept these incorrect translations their commentaries and theological writings overlook completely the roles God explicitly gives to Mary in the protoevangelium. The roles she received from God by her God-given enmity the incorrect translations of the protoevangelium completely obliterate; the inimical roles given to the woman in the first part of the protoevangelium. These erroneous translations have the woman's enmity doing absolutely nothing in the second part of the protoevangelium.

Mary's role of intervening powerfully in the world against Satan's activities is something Mary at Fatima explicitly promised to do during the last decades of the century in which she gave her Fatima messages.

Now it should be obvious that Mary could be a most loving mother of the redeemer without the protoevangelium ever giving her the very special enmity and role of fighting against Satan and his kingdom in the defense and protection of the Church and mankind. Mary could have been a most loving mother of the God-man without the protoevangelium predicting and promising that she would have the task of crushing Satan's head, destroying Satan's kingdom on earth. A thing she does not do while she lived on earth but will do from heaven in the end times.

It should also be evident that the protoevangelium gives the woman another unique and special role that is only implicitly expressed or contained in the protoevangelium. Since this role is only implicit it is to that extent hidden and might be easily overlooked or missed by readers of the protoevangelium. The Catholic Church authentically teaches that Mary the mother of the redeemer has other very special and unique roles in the very redemption and salvation of men.

It is certain that God absolutely could have made the promise of redeeming mankind by the protoevangelium without even making any explicit mention of the mother of the redeemer. But to the extent that Mary would be an intimate associate of the God-man in the redemption of mankind it was necessary that God explicitly mention Mary when informing Adam and Eve and Satan of the redemption. This role of Mary as an intimate associate of the Redeemer in his action of redeeming mankind makes Mary the co-redeemer of mankind, the Coredemptrix.

Hence the explicit mention in the protoevangelium, the first proclamation of the gospel, of the mother of the redeemer indicates that God intended for the mother some unique role in the redemption that is entirely distinct from and in addition to the role of Mother of the Redeemer.

What is that special and unique role of Mary and how is it implied in the protoevangelium? Maternal or paternal love and concern do not confer on parents the right to be intimate associates in the work or mission of their adult offspring.

The protoevangelium's promise of redemption by the God-man would not have required any explicit mention of the mother of the redeemer, if her role in the redemption had been limited only to fulfilling her duties of mother of the redeemer. This explicit inclusion of the mother in the protoevangelium's promise of redemption indicates that, in the intention and plan of the Father, the mother be intimately associated with her Son in his divine mission and work of redeeming and saving mankind. God the Father from all eternity willed to associate the willingness of the God-man to immolate Himself by offering Himself in sacrifice on the Cross with his Mother's willingness to agree to the Father's immolation of her Son on the Cross for man's redemption and salvation.

The two great signs that appeared in the sky on the first day of creation also manifest that the mother of the Messiah would be given this role of an intimate associate of her Son. In the first great sign in the sky a woman appears who is pregnant with the God-man. The mother was given the role of an associate of the God-man in the redemption and salvation of mankind, for in the second great sign she is manifestly the mother and Queen of those who are her Son's loyal and royal subjects. "Enraged at her escape, the dragon went off to make war on the rest of her offspring, on those who keep God's commandments and give witness to Jesus." Rev 12:17.

The gospels continually manifest Mary endeavoring to fulfill her role of an intimate associate of her Son in his work and mission of redeeming and saving mankind by continually maintaining her presence at the side of her Son. She was at his side from the wedding feast in Cana, where she manifests the Messiah by occasioning his initiating his public ministry, for the Son desired that his mother should be instrumental in his initiating of his ministry. This miracle of changing water into very good wine led his disciples to believe in Him. He desired that she accompany Him especially in the final episode of his redemptive mission, the sorrowful journey to Calvary and his crucifixion on the Cross of Calvary. Above all she was intimately associated with him in his act of immolating Himself for she freely chose to remain standing beneath his cross during that immolation. In that way Mary manifested for everyone to see her consenting to the Father's immolation of her Son for the redemption and salvation of mankind

All the way to Calvary and when standing under the Cross Mary willingly consented to the Father's decree that her Son offer Himself on the Cross and she willingly consented even to that manner in which the Father willed that her Son be immolated. With Him she drank from the same chalice of great bitterness. In her role of mother she freely offered her Son, the victim in that immolation, to the Father and by her offering her Son she shared in the paying of the price of our redemption and she thereby became a true Coredemptrix.

During the days from the Ascension to Pentecost Mary was constantly with the apostles and prayed with them and later advised them during the formative years of the early Church.

She as Queen of the Church and of mankind always shares in her Son's dominion and now sits at the right hand of her Son sharing what she merited of his eternal glory King of king and as Lord of lords.

Mary like any mother, because of her great maternal love for her Son would have been interested in her divine Son's work whatever his role or mission might be and she would have rejoiced in his every accomplishment. But motherhood and maternal love and concern for her Son could not give her any right to be an intimate associate with her Son in his redemptive work and in his divine mission. Hence it had to be by a special provision of the will of God the Father that the mother of the redeemer should have and be given the role of an intimate associate of her Son in his work and divine mission of redeeming and saving mankind.

Any reader of the protoevangelium must realize that he or she should not, as many theologians do—because they are misled by erroneous translations—limit Mary's role in the redemption to only what specifically belonged to her role of mother of the redeemer. By limiting Mary's role to whatever specifically belongs to her as mother of the redeemer, persons cannot but miss or overlook or even deny the two very specific and unique roles given to her by God in the protoevangelium. Roles of an intimate associate of the God-man both God the Father and the Son freely chose to give Mary in the redemption and salvation of mankind.

From the various sets of "our image likeness" God the Father had in mind of the God-man from eternity, God the Father chose one particular "our image likeness" to be the model for his Son's Incarnation, and would use it as his model for the conception and creation of Mary. The Father's model "our image likeness' for his Son's human nature and life were models of the very best and most for the God-man. The Father and the Son determined that the Mother also should be given whatever would make her the most perfect of all creatures and would give her the most glorious of maternal roles. They determined that she should have roles that would give the most glory to her Son and to God the Father.

That implies that if nothing stood in the way of her having or being given the roles of Coredemptrix and Mediatrix that she should have those roles. Since Mary had no impediments to receiving them she must have been given them and fulfilled those roles perfectly.

Many theologians do not seem to realize that the author of the Book of Revelation, when describing the second great sign, teaches explicitly the great doctrine that Mary the Mother of the Redeemer is also the mother of the redeemed. For her to be the mother of the redeemed it was necessary that she be an intimate of the Redeemer sharing in the life, work and mission of redeemer and savior. By that sharing Mary became the mother of the Church and of mankind. "Enraged at her escape the dragon went off to make war on the rest of her [Mary's] offspring, on those who keep God's commandments and give witness to Jesus." Rev 12:17.

It is true that in Paradise God proclaimed to fallen man for the first time on earth, by means of the protoevangelium, the gospel of supernatural redemption and salvation. Theologians living in this post-redemption era having their thoughts dominated by their post-redemption theology of grace continue to persist in their erroneous supposition that the protoevangelium is or manifests the original determination and promise of God to incarnate his Son.

Most persist in this erroneous supposition even though the protoevangelium clearly does not make those promises for it limits its promises to promising only enmities, where those enmities will be placed and to specify what will be the object of each person's enmity. These theologians don't seem to realize that God the Father even before the creation of the world had determined absolutely that the woman and her offspring would become members of the race of Adam.

Since the Incarnation had first and highest priority in the intention of the Father at the time of the creation, the Incarnation of the Son could not have been conditioned on man's falling into sin and man's consequent need for redemption by the God-man. The sign that most clearly indicates or implies that the Incarnation was already decreed and was being revealed for the first time, was the first great sign that appeared in the sky on the first day of creation. The mother and her incarnate God-man are present already in this first great sign.

The manner in which Adam and Eve accepted the proclamation of the protoevangelium manifests that Adam and Eve already knew of this woman and her Son and that God had promised them that the woman and her Son when they came into the world would be members of their race.

God wills that all his great works be prophesied, announced or prefigured far in advance of their occurrences. He wills this so that man's foreknowledge of them might always testify to the greatness of God's everlasting love, that fallen man might never be without hope, and that fallen man might never be mistaken about who was the true author of those prophesied great works. "It was I who foretold them to you of old; before they took place. I let you hear of them, that you might not say 'My idol did them, my statue, my molten image commanded them.'" Is 48:5.

The time span of the prophetic protoevangelium extends from the fall of man, through the Incarnation and life of the Son of God, to the end times destruction of Satan's kingdom in the Triumph of the Immaculate Heart of Mary in the world. That triumph will come with the destruction of Satan's kingdom and culminate in the new heavens and the new earth and Jesus Christ ruling in his Glorious Kingdom on earth.

Interpretations of the protoevangelium based on the erroneous Greek translation of the protoevangelium do not manifest any true promise of a redeemer or of redemption. For these interpretations have no choice but to suppose Eve is the woman of the protoevangelium and that demands that Eve's son be the redeemer. A child of Eve being merely a human person can not redeem mankind. The only thing clear about these interpretations with their supposition is that they are clearly erroneous. Hence, it is understandable that writers of such commentaries think the protoevangelium offers merely a glimmer, as they say, of the gospel of redemption and salvation. Yet it was clear and certain to Adam as it is to us that a revelation of a promise of redemption in the strict sense of justice was precisely the kind of revelation of a redemption Adam and Eve needed after their fall from grace.

For all the above reasons it is certain that the Greek LXX, the modern critical Greek text and all modern language translations made from them do not manifest the sense the protoevangelium has in its original Hebrew. Hence St. Jerome was most certainly justified in considering the Greek LXX an incorrect translation of the original Hebrew and in translating the Hebrew protoevangelium as he did in his Latin Vulgate.

It is clear that there can be no promise of redemption in the crushing of the head of Satan, no matter who does the crushing. If that crushing is all the erroneous translations foresee being done by the woman's offspring, there inevitably arise the question, how does the protoevangelium promise true redemption?

Persons seeking an answer to this question must be fully aware that as a consequence of the sin of Adam and Eve, God the Father was absolutely unwilling to return any of the lost gifts to Adam, Eve and to anyone of their race as entirely free gifts. If man is to be saved there will have to be a true redemption of the supernatural gifts that were lost by original sin and the protoevangelium will have to indicate that the redemption would be the work of the God-man. The erroneous Greek translations do not do this.

The protoevangelium implies this kind of supernatural redemption in the promise of enmity and inimical activity of the offspring of the woman directed not against Satan himself but against the offspring of Satan. The protoevangelium implies that the offspring of the woman must be the redeemer since the woman herself cannot be the redeemer.

Modern theologians consider the role Mary is granted by the protoevangelium to be very limited. For their interpretations would limit Mary's activity, with respect man's redemption, regardless of the enmity given to her, strictly to the activity that is specifically proper to Mary in so far as she fulfills her role of mother of the redeemer. Such an explanation of the role of Mary limits it to only that activity that can be deduced as necessarily belonging to her in her role of mother of the redeemer. Her role of mother of the redeemer is real and true but it is obviously not the only role envisioned for her by the protoevangelium's promise of enmity that will crush the head of Satan.

The erroneous translations of the protoevangelium have clearly misled many people. Misled them into accepting a sense of the protoevangelium that effectively deprives the woman, the mother of the redeemer, of the role explicitly given to her by God by giving her enmity. That enmity explicitly gives her the role of adversary of Satan and implicitly a role of an intimate associate of her Son in his work and mission of redeeming mankind.

The role and task of destroying Satan's kingdom on earth is a role entirely distinct from the role of redeeming souls. In the case of Mary the role and task of destroying Satan's kingdom is distinct from her role as an intimate associate of her Son in his work and mission of redeeming mankind. If it were not, then the redeemer would have to be the one to redeem mankind by crushing the serpent's head, a thing the protoevangelium does not permit. For it assigns each of these different tasks to the enmity of two different persons. The role and task of crushing Satan's head, destroying his kingdom on earth, is just as distinct from the role of a redeemer as it is distinct from that of being the mother of the redeemer.

The erroneous translations of the protoevangelium lead also to a second very serious and erroneous assumption. As modern theologians explain Mary's role in the redemption her role is limited precisely to doing only what is proper to Mary in so far as she has the role of mother of the redeemer. They limit her role to doing only the activity that can be deduced as necessarily belonging to her as mother of the Person of the redeemer. Such an explanation of Mary's part in the redemption necessarily deprives the woman of the protoevangelium of her God-given role of Chief Adversary of Satan besides depriving her of her distinct role of the intimate associate of her Son in his work of redeeming mankind.

Despite the fact that St. Jerome gave the correct translation of the Hebrew protoevangelium more than sixteen hundred years ago, modern translations still keep proclaiming the erroneous sense of the Greek LXX and of the critical Greek texts. That is the reason modern English translations and commentaries based on them are self contradictory and do not manifest clearly the Catholic belief and doctrine concerning Mary's roles in the salvation of mankind. That is also the principal reason no adequate and solid theological base has been developed for the declaration of the dogmas of Mary as the Coredemptrix and the Mediatrix of all graces.

Some persons wonder how it can be said that Mary could be truly the Medeatrix of all graces including the graces given to persons living before the redemption. This is no difficult problem if it is understood that she is the Mediatrix of all graces given by means of the New, Eternal and Universal covenant. The New, Eternal and Universal Covenant is the means of distributing all graces merited by Jesus Christ to persons who lived before as well after the redemption. It should be obvious that if Mary was an intimate associate of her Son in the meriting of the graces of redemption, than Mary can mediate all graces given by the New and Eternal Covenant to any person whether the person lived before or after the redemption.

HOW PERSONS NAMED IN THE PROTOEVANGELIUM MAY BE CORRECTLY IDENTIFIED

The erroneous translations lead not only to confusion regarding the true identity of the persons mentioned in the protoevangelium but also to confusion regarding their roles in the redemption. Only with correct translations of the protoevangelium will it be possible to eliminate the continuing confusion and uncertainty regarding the identity of those persons and their roles.

In the writings of interpreters and commentators the identities they give to the woman, the offspring of the woman, the offspring of Satan and the person who will be crushing the head of the serpent are incorrect or very uncertain. A clear understanding of the protoevangelium can come only from the Hebrew or from a correct translation of the Hebrew protoevangelium.

Most commentators get off to a very bad start by thinking or supposing that the woman can be, in the first instance, no one but Eve. They think this since there is no other woman in the situation in Paradise and no other woman known to Satan or Adam or Eve. Consequently they think that for the making of a minimum of good sense the woman of the protoevangelium must be Eve. They, therefore, hold that the protoevangelium's primary reference to a woman must be to Eve, the only woman known to Satan or to Adam and Eve. How false this is can be clearly and easily seen for a number of reasons.

If the woman of the protoevangelium is Eve, than Eve must be the woman to crush the head of the serpent and she will have to do so very soon for Satan would be leaving soon and would be giving up his disguise of a serpent. If Eve is the woman there was no more opportune moment for her to crush the head of the serpent than at that moment following the proclamation of the protoevangelium. For Satan was disposed to remain on the scene only so long as would be required for him to learn first-hand how God would dispose of the fallen status of Adam and Eve and of all their descendants. He was most anxious to learn what God was disposed to do for them in their fallen condition or what God was disposed to do for their supernatural resanctification and supernatural destiny.

The woman chosen to crush Satan's head cannot be Eve for Satan at that time did not as yet have his kingdom or headship over evil men and he would not have it anytime before the death of Eve. The object of the woman's God-given enmity is Satan and his kingdom not this serpent or all serpents. Always bear in mind that Eve's or anyone's crushing of the head of the serpent or Satan cannot bring about the supernatural redemption of mankind.

Eve cannot be the woman to crush Satan's head, for Satan has reduced Eve to powerlessness and she appears unable to do anything effective against Satan's genius and power, much less crush his head—destroy completely and forever his power and influence as Mary will do it with her heel.

Eve cannot be the woman. How could God have chosen Eve, who had been so easily and shamefully deceived, defeated, and rendered helpless by Satan, to crush the head of Satan? God would not do anything so senseless as to promise to place great enmity and great power in the hands of a woman who was already under Satan's influence and domination as a result of the sin she had just committed under Satan's influence. If any useful purpose could be served by a promise to place enmity between Eve and the serpent, Satan, why should that promise have an implied a delay? Any hoped-for results of Eve's enmity would have to be achieved in the very near future, for the serpent will very soon disappear and Eve is going to die and her enmity and its power will perish with her. Moreover Eve did not need to be given enmity for Satan for she must have immediately after her fall at his deception conceived a great enmity for him and despised him above all.

God could make the promise of giving enmity only to the woman, Mary, the Virgin Mother of the Redeemer and Queen of the universe, who could never come under the domination of Satan not even as a result of the original sin of Adam.

It should be noted that God here uses the future tense in proclaiming the protoevangelium: "I will put enmity between you and the woman." God's use of the future tense surely indicates that the intended woman is not Eve who was present and should have been given that enmity at that time. Hence the future tense indicates that

God intended to give the enmity to a woman, who obviously did not yet exist, but would by God's choice exist in the future. That woman can be only the woman God had specifically chosen to be the mother of the Redeemer.

If Eve were the woman, it would be preposterous to think God would be promising to give her that enmity and that task in words not even addressed to her, for the protoevangelium is not addressed to Eve but to Satan. By explicitly promising only enmities and specifying the objects of those enmities, the protoevangelium supposes God had already absolutely decreed the future existence of these two persons and that they would be members of the race of Adam and Eve.

Lastly, why would God not have chosen Adam rather than Eve for the task of crushing the head of Satan if he were able? Surely there is a mystery here to be explored if either Adam or Eve were chosen by God to crush the head of the serpent.

By proclaiming the protoevangelium God is promising to prepare two persons for specific tasks that would require of each a specific enmity and that specific enmity of each would direct the person possessing it to the particular object of his or her particular enmity. In that situation the truth is that for the protoevangelium to contain the promise of redemption and salvation, didn't need to contain anything more than the explicit promise of enmities, designate the persons to whom those enmities would be given and specify the object of enmity of each person.

God obviously knew the Immaculate Heart of Mary and her great desire to do perfectly God's will in everything, including any role He would give her in the redemption of mankind in addition to the role of Mother of the God-man. From eternity God had chosen a particular woman for the role of chief adversary of Satan and intended to endow her with an enmity of the kind needed for leadership leading to an inevitable triumph in man's titanic struggle with Satan and his kingdom.

Readers of the protoevangelium must realize that they are missing these very special, unique, and important roles God freely chose to give Mary, if they perceive Mary's role as limited to what can be deduced as necessarily hers by reason of her role of mother of the redeemer. By setting such limits to Mary's roles theologians and commentators deny Mary the very special roles which the protoevangelium manifests God freely chose for Mary alone. For as the immaculate mother of the divine redeemer, she alone was most worthy of those roles.

The next question to be asked and answered regarding the identification of persons mentioned in the protoevangelium is who is the offspring of the woman? After establishing the correct identification of the woman there is no problem in correctly identifying the offspring of the woman. Since the woman is identified as the ever Virgin Mary the offspring of the woman must be her only Son the God-man, Jesus Christ.

Mary didn't have any other child than Jesus. If she had other children then the protoevangelium is nonspecific about who is the Messiah and that leaves fallen man with a very serious problem. The real and serious problem of knowing or identifying which particular offspring of the woman is the one who would be given the enmity by which he would overcome the offspring of Satan and thereby redeem mankind.

The object of the enmity of the offspring of the woman defines, at least in part, the offspring's life mission, which is that of dealing with and contending with the offspring of Satan, not with crushing the head of Satan. It is by the offspring of the woman exercising his enmity by contending with the offspring of Satan, that he will redeem mankind.

When Mary explicitly consented to becoming the mother of the Son of the Most High, who would be named Jesus or Savior, she at the Annunciation implicitly gave her maternal consent and approval to the redemptive mission of her offspring. She also gave consent to becoming his intimate associate in his work and mission. Mary implicitly consented to the Father's immolation of her offspring for the redemption of mankind. Mary, during her life on earth, constantly manifested that consent by her presence at the side of her Son during his divine mission. In the gospels she accompanies and supports him from the wedding at Cana, where and when she manifest him as the Messiah, to her presence under his Cross to help Him die.

On the Cross Jesus completed the most essential task of the mission He accepted from his Father before his Incarnation and emptied Himself of his fullness to become like other men in all things except sin. By emptying himself so he would be able to die for the redemption of all men.

Standing by the Cross Mary helped her Son die, for by her willing presence she was assuring her dying Son that she, like He, willingly consented to his Father's will that He be immolated in this horrible manner for the redemption and salvation of mankind.

Seeing the first great sign Satan learned that God had chosen to incarnate his Son as the God-man and had chosen the woman in the sign to be the Immaculate Virgin Mother of the God-man. Seeing the second great sign Satan learned of certain future consequences of his and his demon's rebellion even before they were compelled to leave heaven. God knew Lucifer and that it was his pride that turned Lucifer into Satan. God knew and revealed to all the angels by the second great sign what even Lucifer did not know about himself and his future. God knew that Lucifer, the light bearer, had become Satan, the accuser.

Satan in Hebrew literally means accuser. As accuser he would be the inveterate adversary of God and of the good angels and men. God foreknew, as the second great sign manifests, that Satan would lead many angels into obstinate rebellion against God, would instigate man's fall from grace, would establish a most perverse kingdom on earth and would instigate in the Church the great end time apostasy.

God foreknew that ultimately Satan's most perverse designs would have to be defeated and God would honor the Virgin Mother of the God-man by choosing her for that task and triumph over Satan. Mary is the chief adversary of Satan and will remain such until she crushes Satan's head with her heel. From these two great signs and the protoevangelium Satan and all the angels, the good and the bad, learn much prehistory of angels and men.

This protoevangelium is the third of God's great revelations to his creatures and might be viewed as the delayed sequel to the two great signs that appeared in the sky on the first day of creation.

The next question to be asked and answered regarding the identity of persons in the protoevangelium is how does the protoevangelium explicitly designate the woman, not her offspring, as the one to crush the head of the serpent or Satan? The answer one would give to this question would necessarily depend on which translation that person accepts as the correct translation of the protoevangelium. If one accepts the Vulgate as the correct translation then the woman is clearly designated as that person. For that translation explicitly states "She will crush your head with her heel". On the other hand the incorrect Greek LXX, the modern critical Greek and almost all modern language translations indicate that Satan's head will be struck by the offspring of the woman. These texts state: "He [not she] will strike at your head, while you strike at his heel."

Obviously the translation: "He will strike at your head, while you strike at his heel" falls far short of indicating any complete triumph over Satan by the offspring of the woman and also falls far short of manifesting any redemption of mankind. One of the obvious great faults of these translations is that they erroneously attempt to equate the offspring of the woman striking at the head of Satan with true redemption.

Readers must always be aware that if the crushing of the head of Satan could accomplish the redemption, then Satan's head should have been crushed two thousand years ago. So why then do the New Testament Scriptures indicate that the crushing of the head of Satan has yet to occur? It is to occur in the end times.

Two very erroneous conclusions follow from these translations equating the act of redemption with striking at the head of Satan. The first is that the offspring of the woman, contrary to the Hebrew and the Vulgate, should be the one to crush the head of Satan. The second erroneous conclusion following from equating redemption with striking at the head of Satan is that the woman cannot be the one to crush the head of Satan. But that, besides being contrary to the Hebrew and the Vulgate would leave mankind without redemption, since true redemption cannot be signified or accomplished by merely inflicting punishment on the head of the serpent, Satan. Even the complete crushing of his head by her heel does not indicate redemption.

If striking the head of Satan or the inflicting of severe punishment on Satan could have accomplished the redemption of mankind, then the good angels could redeem mankind by punishing Satan and his demons. The powerful woman, Queen of the Universe, by punishing or crushing the head of Satan would be able to redeem mankind. God also by inflicting some severe punishment on Satan and his demons could have redeemed mankind without the Son becoming the God-man and enduring crucifixion for man's redemption.

From the first great sign in the sky on the first day of creation, Lucifer or Satan learned that God had chosen that woman, the Queen of the Universe, to be the Immaculate Mother of the God-man. In the second great sign the huge dragon, Satan, is already the adversary of the woman and her Son. The protoevangelium confirms some of what was foretold in this second great sign. For the protoevangelium manifest that God has chosen to give the woman the very special and unique role of adversary of Satan by placing enmity between her and the Satan.

That woman also, it turns out, is to be the one to organize and lead all the forces of good in heaven and on earth in the final phase of the great struggle against Satan. That struggle will end in the crushing of Satan's head and will be her triumph over all the forces of evil. The woman will decisively and permanently triumph over Satan by crushing his head with her heel. The chief adversary of Satan is therefore the terror of demons. In the end her Immaculate Heart will triumph.

The end time's great apostasy and the end time's great struggle between Mary and Satan are revealed in the gospels and other New Testament Scriptures. Just as Satan sought God's permission to persecute Job, so on October 13 of 1884 Pope Leo XIII heard Satan seeking from Jesus Christ permission and sufficient time to destroy his Church on earth.

Thirty-three years later to the day, on October 13,1917 at Fatima Mary by the miracle of the sun manifested that she is the woman who appeared in the sky on the first day of creation by reappearing in the sky over Fatima clothed with the sun. At Fatima Mary revealed that she had come to earth to organize and to assume command of all the forces of good to defeat Satan in his determined and desperate attempt to destroy the Church of Christ on earth.

Mary is now engaged in fulfilling, as at no other time in history, this great prophecy of the protoevangelium. She is putting an end to Satan's efforts to hinder the salvation of souls and Satan's attempt to destroy the Church. Mary will put an end to both of Satan's designs by crushing Satan's head with her heel.

If an explicit promise of true redemption cannot be found in the crushing of the head of Satan, where can it be found in the protoevangelium? It should be obvious that most commentaries by modern scholars are relying on later revelations rather than on clear and certain evidence offered by the protoevangelium for their belief that Mary is the woman of the protoevangelium. Some think that the protoevangelium without the later clear prophecies offers only a glimmer of hope not a certain hope for redemption and for supernatural salvation of mankind.

For those who think in that way regarding the protoevangelium the protoevangelium is obviously no protoevangelium, no early gospel that is a clear and certain prophecy of the gospel of redemption and salvation.

Did God intend to reveal the redemption by means of the protoevangelium? If so then God intended to reveal the redemption to Satan, for the protoevangelium was addressed to him. God did not want to reveal to Satan what Satan might use to counter his plans for man's salvation. The protoevangelium in revealing the redemption does not reveal the manner of the redemption. It does not reveal, for example, that the redemption would be achieved by the Sacrifice of the Cross. If the protoevangelium contains a promise of true redemption, the offspring of the woman will have to be the one to redeem mankind, for the offspring of the woman is the Son of God and He alone would be capable of truly redeeming mankind. But how can the protoevangelium signify true redemption by the God-man, if he does no more than kick at the head of serpent, Satan? It cannot do so.

How can it be determined from the protoevangelium that redemption is the way God has chosen to restore the supernatural to mankind? The protoevangelium does not do so. It must be read and understood in conjunction with the consequences of the breaking of the creation covenant. If God is unwilling to restore any of the lost supernatural gifts as entirely free gifts to anyone of the race of Adam, then if God restores them they must be restored through a redemption. Redemption becomes an evident and an absolute necessity for fallen man only in consequence of the Father's determination that nothing of what man had lost in the breaking of the creation covenant be returned to man as an entirely free gift.

Modern scholars have studied primarily the accepted incorrect Greek translations of the protoevangelium and that has led to their glossing over this question and other difficulties in their interpretations of the protoevangelium. This glossing over is also the reason many say that the protoevangelium offers merely a glimmer of hope for man's redemption. Their explanations and interpretations fail to take into account many difficulties and fail to answer critical questions concerning the precise sense of the protoevangelium.

While seeking answers to such questions and related difficulties there is an even more fundamental question that must be asked and answered first. Scholars have failed even to ask what difference is there in the will of God regarding the giving of grace to men before original sin and after original sin?

Since the protoevangelium by itself does not manifest the completely desperate situation of fallen man it cannot give complete answers to many questions. No one can understand how truly deplorable and humanly hopeless and helpless was the condition fallen man unless one realizes that in consequence of original sin, God the Father was and is unwilling even to this day to return to everyone of Adam's race as entirely fee gifts anything lost by original sin. This is the reason God is still demanding payment for what were formerly entirely free gifts. If man is ever again to possess what were formerly entirely free gifts, those things must be redeemed or bought back. This buying back is to redeem them for mankind.

It is very true that in the end all the graces men receive in this life and the life of heaven must be seen as merited by Jesus Christ. This implies that no one can now receive or will ever receive any grace granted completely gratuitously by God. This is true because since the fall of man God the Father wills to bestow only those graces that have been merited in the redemption.

God is free to set whatever conditions He may chose for his forgiving the offenses of man's sins and for returning to men the sanctifying grace of man's original innocence, the original justice of God. If God is demanding that his formerly entirely free gifts or graces be paid for, and if man is unable to make those payments, then God must have some plan for someone to do for mankind what men cannot do for themselves. Someone will have to make those payments; the price of man's redemption, in the name of mankind and the person who makes those payments becomes the redeemer of Adam's race.

If God has requirements then persons can not come to God just as they are or be justified just as they are. There can be no supernatural justification of persons in their sins, that is, without persons first receiving forgiveness of their sins from God. The reason is that the supernatural life of grace is absolutely incompatible with a life of hatred of God or a life of grave sin. This is the reason that John the Baptist, Jesus Christ and the apostles always preached first the necessity of repentance of ones sins for a person's justification.

Why should God the Father have withheld from his very beloved first man and woman, while they were living in Paradise, the stupendously good and great news that He would incarnate his Most Beloved Son as the God-man of their race? Hence Adam and Eve could not have been ignorant of the identity of the woman and her offspring mentioned in the proclamation of the protoevangelium. They knew that the Father's very reason for creating the universe, the earth and themselves was that his Son could be conceived and born of a woman of their race.

It was the plan of the Father and the Son that the woman who would appear in the first great signs in the sky on the first day of creation would be in reality the most gloriously Immaculate Virgin Mary and that her offspring would be the Incarnate God-man of the race of Adam and Eve. It was also their plan that her offspring be crowned the eternal Supreme Head of their race and of all creation.

Perhaps when God revealed the woman and her offspring to Adam and Eve He did so by a repetition of the first great sign which appeared in the sky on the first day of creation. Thus the first and second great signs are the very first revelations of God to his creatures. The protoevangelium may be seen as the second great revelation of God to his creatures, since it was given in consequence of the first and second great signs. In the second great sign the dragon, Satan, "makes war on the woman and the rest of her offspring [all mankind]." Here in the second great sign it is revealed that Mary's divine maternity and her motherly role in the salvation of mankind are the reasons God made Mary the spiritual mother of all men. The second great sign is accompanied by the explicit teaching that men are also children of Mary. Cf. Rev 12:17.

It is inconceivable that Adam and Eve, on hearing of the woman and her offspring, would have remained absolutely silent, if they did not already know the identity of this woman and her offspring. The protoevangelium is addressed to Satan in the presence of the fallen Adam and Eve. It assures them that God the Father, in spite of their sin, is still willing to incarnate his Son as the God-man of their race. That revelation, besides relieving them of some of their worst fears, gave them hope and assurance of a possible redemption.

They understood that the enmities God would be placing in the hands of the God-man and his Immaculate Mother were enmities directed against the enemies of their salvation. They realized that the mother and her Son would be intent on the evils Satan inflicted on them and would overpower and destroy their enemies. All of which clearly indicated to them the intensity of God's willingness to restore to them and their descendants their lost supernatural salvation and destiny.

WHO OR WHAT ARE THE OFFSPRING OF SATAN?

A complete understanding of the profound protoevangelium requires a precise identification of just who or what are the offspring of Satan. Since Satan is an angel and cannot have offspring in any genetic sense, the protoevangelium's explicitly declaration that Satan has offspring leaves persons wondering who or what are the offspring of Satan. If God is not speaking in riddles here, than there must be some apparent sense, not necessarily an immediately obvious sense but a studied senses in which Satan may be said to have offspring. So who or what is the protoevangelium calling the offspring of Satan? Here the offspring of Satan has three possible meanings.

Satan, on the first day of creation, led many angels into obstinate rebellion against God. Is the protoevangelium implying that all the angels Satan induced to rebel against God and are under his dominion the offspring of Satan? Most readers understand that since there can be no true genetic offspring of Satan, towards whom the offspring of the woman could direct his enmity, consider all the rebellious angels the offspring of Satan. The erroneous translations of the second part of the protoevangelium appear to make Satan himself his own offspring, for those translations direct the enmity of the offspring of the woman against the head of the serpent, Satan himself.

It is not just translators but commentators on the protoevangelium, following the sense of the translations they accept, erroneously direct the enmity of the offspring of the woman against Satan. They do this against reason that any action of the enmity of the offspring of the woman would take against Satan or his demons can not redeem mankind. Hence these demons cannot be the intended offspring of Satan.

If the intended offspring of Satan cannot be these demons, might the offspring of Satan be all the members of the fallen race of Adam? In Scripture obstinate sinners from among men are often called the children of Satan, just as good persons from among men are called children of God. St. John teaches: "That is the way to see who are

God's children, and who are the devil's." 1 Jn 3:10. Cf. Jn 8:44; Acts 13:10. Since Satan led all mankind into original sin, might it be that the protoevangelium is calling all fallen men the offspring of Satan?

The great problem with identifying fallen mankind with the offspring of Satan is to explain how the enmity of the offspring of the woman directed against fallen mankind could redeem mankind? It should be her offspring's love not his enmity for mankind that should redeem mankind. Consequently, fallen mankind cannot be the offspring of Satan envisioned by the protoevangelium.

The only remaining possibility is that the offspring of Satan are the works of Satan, the works of Satan lead Adam and Eve to break the creation covenant and that deprived them and all mankind of the supernatural gifts of God. Any effective action the enmity of the offspring of the woman to remedy these works of Satan could restore man's lost supernatural gifts. St. John teaches: "It was to destroy the devil's works that the Son of God has revealed himself." 1 Jn 3:8.

After the redemption God the Father remains unwilling to return the supernatural as entirely free gift to fallen mankind, but is now willing to restore the supernatural to mankind by a new covenant because the supernatural has been redeemed by the offspring of the woman in the redemption of mankind.

The protoevangelium promises that the enmity of the offspring of the woman will militate against the offspring or works of Satan. In that way the offspring of the woman undoes or overcomes the offspring of Satan.

THE PROTOEVANGELIUM FORESAW THE IMMACULATE CONCEPTION, THE VIRGIN BIRTH, THE COREDEMPTION, AND THE ASSUMPTION OF MARY

Just as the Father willed the Incarnation of his Son by an irrevocable predestination and the Son consented to his Incarnation as the God-man of the race of Adam, so the Father willed divine maternity for the woman by a like irrevocable predestination to becoming that mother of the God-man and Mary consenting to the immolation of her Son. God willed absolutely the existence of the woman and her consenting to her divine maternity and mission. In the beginning the Father willed conditionally immortality for the God-man at his Incarnation, so that in consequence of Adam's sin He could also will the death and resurrection of the God-man. There would have been no need for the Father to conditionally will the death and resurrection of the God-man if man would not have sinned as there would not have been any need for his Incarnate Son's death on the Cross to redeem mankind.

From the beginning the Father willed conditionally Mary's special task of crushing Satan's head, for God the Father would not have willed them for her at all if Adam had not sinned.

The protoevangelium does not put Mary among those of the race of Adam who are in need of redemption. The words: "I will put enmity between you and the woman, and between your offspring and hers" have been erroneously understood to imply a promise of God to send Mary and her divine Son to mankind in consequence of Adam's sin. This would make the Father's willing his Son's Incarnation and Mary's existence and divine motherhood a consequence of the sin of Adam!

This is not the case for the Father from all eternity was determined to incarnate his Son as the God-man of the race of Adam. Therefore in order that mankind might be redeem God didn't need to promise anything more in the protoevangelium than what God had already absolutely decreed concerning the God-man and his mother except to promise a particular enmity and mission for the life of the woman and a particular enmity and mission for the life of the offspring of the woman.

Mary's irrevocable predestination to Divine Maternity included her irrevocable predestination to Immaculate Conception. Those graces removed from Mary even the possibility of sinning and any need to be redeemed by her Son. Mary did not and could not have lost any grace by the sin of Adam. Mary's irrevocable predestination to divine maternity, to Immaculate Conception and to eternal salvation were not in any way dependent on the creation covenant Adam terminated. They were rather the remote cause of that creation covenant with Adam.

The angels of heaven knew from the first great sign on the first day of creation of Mary's predestination and rejoiced in her and in the name she would have among them. Among the angels Mary from the time of the first great sign, even before she existed, was always the one the angels knew as the one "Full of Grace".

This name "Full of Grace" explains many things regarding Mary. When, for example, the Archangel Gabriel came to Mary for the Annunciation of the Incarnation, he addressed her: "Hail, Full of Grace, the Lord is with thee. Blessed art thou among women."

"Hail, Full of Grace" is the correct literal English translation of the Archangel's greeting found in the very venerable Latin Vulgate of St. Jerome. It is also in the Greek text of Luke's gospel. This is the reason the Archangel Gabriel did not greet Mary by her earthly name of Mary when greeting her at the Annunciation. He greeted her: "Hail, Full of Grace". It was most obvious to the angels that the Lord was with her and that she was most blessed among all women. Only the Lord God could have so completely filled Mary with grace.

Because the Father and the Son had chosen Mary to be the Mother of the God-man, they put no limits on the flow of grace into Mary's humanity and person except the limits of her creature capacity to receive grace. And it is for this very reason that Mary is not pratically full of grace but full of grace. It is the reason she has always been known by the name "Full of Grace" among angels of heaven and the rejoicing saints in heaven.

In some recent English translations we find the Archangel Gabriel greeting Mary: "Rejoice, 0 highly favored Daughter!" or

"Hail, Favored one!" These are translations so completely capricious and groundless as to lack sobriety. In them there is no hint of the reality that Mary is so highly favored by the Most Holy Trinity as to be the only woman who has ever been or will ever be so favored by The Most Holy Trinity as to be completely full of grace.

These translations do not come close to indicating how exclusively Mary has been so highly favored among all creatures or that she has given every grace to fullest extent possible to a mere creature. These expressions do not come close to indicating that Mary was so filled with grace that she became more perfect than any creature that has ever existed, that now exists or will ever exist. Her perfection in grace is so great; so perfect in grace that She will always the Most Holy Trinity's masterpiece of all creation.

Gabriel's words: "Blessed are you among [all] woman" eulogies Mary as the most blessed of all women of the past, present and future. "Highly favored daughter" does not indicate that Mary is the most uniquely blessed of all women. Calling her daughter minimizes her favor for daughters are not as highly favored as sons are by fathers or sovereigns. The translation fails to indicate that she is the most highly favored creature of God that has ever existed, now exists or will ever exist. It does not even indicate whose highly favored daughter she is. Is she merely the most highly favored daughter among the many daughters of a particularly rich and powerful man? Is she merely the highly favored daughter of her parents? Might not the fact that she is the most highly favored daughter of some couple indicate that some injustice might have been done to other daughters? If she is the highly favored daughter of the ruling king, what is so unique or extraordinary about a daughter being favored in such a way? Is she just some royal princess? "Hail, Favored one" fails to indicate some comparison with some other favored daughter or who of distinction or impotence has favored her.

Immaculate Conception and Impeccability are graces. If Mary were full of grace she must have had the grace of Impeccability along with the great of grace of her Immaculate Conception. The same reasoning may be applied to all conceivable graces so that Mary must be seen as possessing all graces in the highest or greatest degree of perfection. She posses grace in the greatest fullness possible to a creature.

Embedded in the eternal Father's plans for incarnating his Son as the God-man through a human conception and birth was Mary's predestination to existence, to being the mother of the God-man, to her Immaculate Conception and to many other graces.

The words Immaculate Conception have one obvious and one not so obvious meaning. The more obvious meaning of Immaculate Conception, the one Catholics usually think of is that Mary was without original sin or any personal sin from the first moment of her conception or existence. Immaculate Conception in this sense is what the Catholic Church has explicitly defined in her Dogma of the Immaculate Conception of Mary. "From the first moment of her conception... the Blessed Virgin Mary was kept free of all stain of original sin."

However her complete freedom from original sin at her conception and all personal sin is merely an aspect of Immaculate Conception in its other meaning. What Immaculate Conception did in, to and for Mary from the first moment of her existence—-what Mary became from the first moment of her existence—is quite another matter! Immaculate Conception in this sense means that Mary was full of grace from her conception not merely that she possess great grace and was free from all sin from the first moment of her conception. It means that Mary's humanity and person had the most complete fullness of grace possible to a creature.

Hence Mary was not merely conceived immaculate but was the Immaculate Conception. Immaculate Conception is the most glorious of all perfections possible to a creature. Her Immaculate Conception was the result of a unique divine predilection to fill her with grace to her absolute fullness. Mary is this unique reality of Immaculate Conception. Therefore Mary is the Immaculate Conception and the reason Mary at Lourdes said, "I am the Immaculate Conception".

Immaculate Conception in the first sense could have been applied to all men in as much as all persons of the race of Adam were originally to be conceived and born in the state of grace called original innocence, that is free from original sin and any other personal sin. When Mary appeared in Lourdes France, Mary identified herself most precisely to Bernadette by telling her: "I am the Immaculate Conception".

Some find great difficulty believing in Mary's Immaculate Conception in view of the broken creation covenant and the fact that she like everyone else is a true descendent of Adam and a member of Adam's race. This problem naturally arises in the minds of persons having a too exclusively post redemption theology of grace. Preredemption theology of grace is aware that immediately after God created Adam God contracted with Adam, as the head of his race, to give to Adam, his wife and all their descendant at the moment of their creation or conception transcendent human natures and the supernatural state of original innocence. By this creation covenant God predestined all men of the race of Adam to a certain degree of holiness or grace—the beginners share in the fullness of Christ—from the first moment of their conception or existence.

Since all men were deprived of their beginners' share in the fullness of Christ by original sin—deprived of the graces and favors that would have been the possession of each of Adam's descendants under the creation covenant. Hence it was to be expected that Mary too, since she is a true descendant of Adam, would have been deprived of rights to those same graces and favors at her conception; she should have been conceived and born with original sin.

However the breaking of the creation covenant can deprive only those persons of God's graces and favors who received or would receive them by means of the creation covenant. Mary was predestined to receive her absolute fullness of grace, her Immaculate Conception, not by means of the creation covenant God made with Adam, but by means of a covenant God made exclusively with Mary and for Mary alone. The creation covenant God made with Adam was not designed to give to anyone any of the unique graces Mary received at her conception. If it were so designed descendants of Adam other Mary could have received them as well!

It was necessary that the Father initiate a very unique covenant with Mary and for Mary alone. For God intended that Mary alone would be the Virgin Mother of the Incarnate God-man and for that reason the Most Holy Trinity intended Mary alone to be the mother of the God-man and to have the fullness of grace at her conception and have it forever. The creation covenant God made with Adam could not do this for Mary or for anyone. The very unique covenant God made with Mary superseded the creation covenant God made with Adam for all his descendants. The covenant God made with Mary was in no way dependent on the creation covenant God made with Adam and its breaking by Adam could in no way affect Mary or the covenant God made with Mary.

Mary's Immaculate Conception, her fullness of grace and her conception without original sin were directly and immediately dependent only on the unique agreement which the Most Holy Trinity made with Mary and with her alone and for her alone. Consequently, the creation covenant God made with Adam is completely irrelevant to Mary in everything including original sin.

It was impossible for Mary to receive her Immaculate Conception, her fullness of grace and her many other very unique privileges by means of the creation covenant God made with Adam when created by God. Therefore it is necessary for us to understand that all of Mary's great and unique graces and favors, including her Immaculate Conception, were gratuitously given to Mary by the unique agreement or covenant God made with her alone and for her alone.

This unique covenant God made exclusively with her and the graces she received were given independently of the merits of her Son's work of redeeming mankind. They were instead dependent on the merits of the very Incarnation of her Son as the God-man of the race of Adam. The grace of original innocence given to Adam and Eve and would have been given to all the descendants of Adam, were not merited in the redemption by Christ on the Cross of Calvary. They were merited instead by the very Incarnation of the Son as the God-man of the race of Adam. The very creation of all things and the continuing existence of all things were merited by the Incarnation of the Son. They were not merited in the redemption of mankind.

Catholic theologians call the grace Adam and Eve received

before original sin gratia Dei, the grace of God. They distinguish gratia Dei from gratia Christi. Gratia Christi is the grace merited by Christ for men in the redemption.

Thus Mary, unlike all men, was never exposed to losing any grace by Adam's breaking of the creation covenant. Many theologians suppose that God by using his foreknowledge did some patchwork on the creation covenant in order to preserve Mary from original sin. Such patchwork was unnecessary for in the words of the Fathers of the Church: "Mary was untouched by original sin." Mary's Immaculate Conception—in either sense—is not to be explained as a single exception in the law, in the broken creation covenant that imposes original sin on all the descendants of Adam. Mary's Immaculate Conception is rather the single exception to law by which all mankind would receive grace. Persons dependent on the creation covenant for receiving grace would necessarily loose grace through the breaking of that creation covenant. Persons who received grace by the creation covenant are the only ones who lose grace by the breaking of the creation covenant.

Everyone must understand that God made a unique covenant with Mary by which Mary alone could received grace. Her unique covenant gave Mary the fullness of grace, Immaculate Conception, along with all her other unique and most extraordinary favors. The creation covenant God made with Adam was never designed or intended by God to give the unique and very special graces only Mary would ever be given. Only if Mary would break that unique covenant God made with her alone could Mary lose any of the graces and favor given to her.

That God must have made some such covenant with Mary is evident in the fact that whenever rights to certain things are given to persons gratuitously it is necessary that those rights be given by some explicit or implicit gratuitous contract or covenant. Mary could not possess her unique and supreme degree of holiness, her Immaculate Conception and her many unique and extraordinary privileges, without first receiving rights to them by means of some gratuitous covenant or contract God had made with her alone and for her alone. She could not have received those rights by means of the creation covenant God made with Adam for that covenant was not designed to give rights to those very special and unique graces and favors God intended only to Mary.

The need for a special covenant between God and Mary is evident from the fact that Mary would not have been chosen to be the mother of the Incarnate Son, if she at any time or in any way could possibly have come under the dominance of Satan. This would have been the case if she received grace by means of the creation covenant.

Since Mary's fullness of grace included the grace of Impeccability, Mary could not break her unique covenant with God and therefore could not lose her "Fullness of Grace", her Immaculate Conception, which she possessed from the first moment of her conception.

In the theology of the doctors of the Church, Mary was untouched by original sin. If it were necessary that Mary be redeemed, as many theologians now seem to think, how can it be true that Mary was untouched by original sin? If the need for redemption on the part of the descendent of Adam is the result of each person being touched by the original sin of Adam, how is it possible that Mary should need redemption and was redeemed if she was not touched by original sin?

If Mary were in need of the graces merited in the redemption, even though she may never have been for a single moment without her fullness of grace, how would it be possible to say that Mary was untouched by original sin? If Adam and Eve were untouched by original sin, they would not have been in need of the grace merited in the redemption. If Mary were untouched by original sin, how could it be that Mary needed to be redeemed?

Mary was chosen by God to be the Mother of the God-man, because, in a divine prodigy of love, God stooped to her profound littleness and humility and chose her. Because Mary was most humble and lowly, Mary was most exalted by God's choice of her to be the Mother of his Incarnate Son. If Mary needed redemption, God, in choosing her to be the Mother of his Son, would have had to look on her with great mercy, rather than stoop to her profound littleness and humility. Mary explicitly states that God looked on her in her lowliness and that God did great things for her. In the

Magnificat Mary says that she rejoices in God her Savior, not in God her Redeemer. "My being proclaims the greatness of the Lord, my spirit finds joy in God my savior, for he has looked upon his servant in her lowliness; all ages to come shall call me blessed. God who is mighty has done great things for me, holy is his name." Lk 1:46-49.

Mary was sanctified and destined for heaven without being redeemed in the redemption of mankind. The sanctifying graces and favors Mary received from God were merited for her by her Son in his Incarnation just as the graces Adam and Eve received before their fall were merited in that same Incarnation. Mary was destined for heaven or salvation just as Adam's first predestination to sanctification was through the merits of the very Incarnation of the Son of God. So it is right to say Mary was saved by Jesus Christ but not redeemed by Jesus Christ.

Did the protoevangelium foresee Mary's role of Coredemptrix? The protoevangelium, as already explained, contains one explicit and one implied role for Mary in the redemption of all men. The protoevangelium indicates that God intended to give the woman some unique and active role in her Son's vocation and mission, the role of an intimate associate of her Son in his work of redeeming and saving mankind. In the gospels Mary manifests great maternal concern for her offspring accomplishing perfectly his divine mission.

Mary, by being the worthy mother of the Incarnate Son of God, is worthy to be intimately associated with her Divine Son in any of his activities. She is worthy to participate actively even intrinsically in the very work or act of redeeming mankind. But worthy as Mary was by being the mother of the God-man, she could not be an intimate associate of her Son in his redeeming work without the Father and the God-man willing that she be an intimate associate of her Son in his work of redeeming mankind.

The Father and the Son willed not only that Mary participate actively in the redemptive work but also participate in that work to the fullest extent possible. Mary was given a role intrinsic to her Son's role of redeeming mankind by her Son associating her action with his work of redeeming mankind. He associated her human person with his Divine Person and associated her Immaculate Maternal Suffering with his Divine Sufferings. Together they offered the Sacrifice that redeemed mankind.

God would signify or manifest Mary's intrinsic participation in the redemptive work of her Son by preordaining her presence under the Cross on which He was offering his Sacrifice for man's redemption. There she continued to manifest her consent to the Father's will that his and her Son be immolated on the Cross for the redemption of mankind. While standing beneath the Cross of Jesus Mary willingly offered her crucified and dying Son to the Father to pay the price of mankind's redemption and it was accepted by the Father. While standing there Her Son united her immaculate sufferings and her willingness to have the Father immolate her Divine Son for the redemption and salvation of mankind. The Father willingly accepted his Son's offering of his Divine sacrifice united to that of Mary's offering of her Son. Mary thereby became the Coredemptrix.

This suffering of Mary was the fulfillment of Simeon's prophecy to Mary: "This child is destined to be the downfall and the rise of many in Israel, a sign that will be opposed and you yourself shall be pierced with a sword."

Many have great difficulty understanding, on theological grounds, how it was possible for God to make Mary Coredeemer or Coredemptrix. The great difficulty to understanding that must be pointed out. The great difficulty is an obviously valid theological principle of justice. There is the requirement of justice that any fruit of the redemption not be used in payment of the price of redemption.

Since this principle or requirement of justice must apply to Mary and her intrinsic participation in the redemption, it is thought that this principle would exclude any action or merit of Mary being used to pay the price of man's redemption. If any of Mary's merits were in any way the fruit of the redemption they would be unacceptable to the Father as payment for mankind's redemption. Consequently Mary cannot be Coredeemer.

Mary herself, her graces and merits, as already explained, were not fruits merited in the redemption of mankind, but the fruit the

God-man merited by his very Incarnation. Just as all the supernatural graces and favors Adam and Eve received at their creation and possessed by them before their fall from grace were not merited in the redemption, but were merited by the very Incarnation of the God-man. Consequently, this principle or requirement of justice cannot exclude Mary or her merits or her actions from being used or offered in payment of the price of redemption of mankind or from being accepted by the Father in payment of the price of redemption of mankind.

The fact that this principle does not exclude Mary from participating intrinsically in the redemption does not imply that Mary by her divine maternity had a right to participate intrinsically in the redemption and to be a co-redeemer or Co-redemptrix. Besides being worthy to participate Mary needed to be called by God and given by God the right to participate intrinsically in the redemptive sacrifice of her Divine Son.

Both the Father and the Son desired that Mary's offering of her person and her suffering be associated with the Person of her Son and his offering of Himself and his suffering for the redemption of mankind. The Father and the Son desired that the Son offer Himself and Divine Sufferings in union with Mary's offering of herself and her immaculate sufferings. They decreed that her offering of herself and her immaculate sufferings be associated with the Son's offering Himself and his divine sufferings for the redemption of mankind. Jesus Christ, the High Priest, associated Mary's person with his Divine Person and her Immaculate sufferings with his Divine sufferings in his offering of Himself in Sacrifice on the Cross for the redemption of mankind. This made Mary the co-redeemer or the Coredemptrix of mankind.

This theology of the explanations of the protoevangelium cannot be found in the theology of the two post milleniums. That is one reason the subtitle of the book is the theology of grace for the third millenium.

Did the protoevangelium foresee the death of Mary? Did Mary die? This is a minor difficulty that needs clarification in the theology regarding Mary. Some theologians think that Mary because she was free from original sin or untouched by original sin should not die. It was the belief of the early Church that both Jesus and Mary were without defect in soul and body. They were not only beautiful in bodily appearance and free from any dysfunction of soul or body and were free from every sickness and natural internal causes of death. Both Jesus and Mary, like Adam and Eve before their fall from grace, were free from all sickness and preserved in a state of perpetual youth and vigor. Some theologians have concluded that Mary could not die from any natural or internal causes and therefore should not have died.

How does one reconcile these beliefs of the early Church with the testimony of Sacred Tradition, which records that Mary died and was buried and rose from the dead in a glorified state from her tomb shortly after her death and burial. That she was assumed into heaven soul and body? Concerning Mary's death a sacred tradition records that all the apostles except Thomas were present when Mary died and that the apostles buried her at Jerusalem. Since the apostle Thomas arrived the day after her death and burial he asked that Mary's tomb be opened so he could have one last gaze on the mortal remains of the Mother of God. When apostles open her tomb it no longer contained her body but was instead filled with beautiful flowers and a heavenly aroma.

Mortality necessarily belongs to the very nature of every living being composed of a body and a soul, for the body and soul in a living person remain really distinct principles of a living being even though they are substantially united in the living being. If body and soul are completely one or identical in a living being they can not be separated, for something cannot be separated from itself. Since the body and the soul of a living mortal always remain really distinct principles even when substantially united in a living person, they can at any time be separated by some natural or supernatural cause.

When the soul and the body of a living person are separated by some natural cause the person dies from a natural cause. Mary could not die from natural causes because of her special gifts of perpetual perfect health and vigor.

The radical reason for these difficulties regarding the possible death of Mary is that many persons mistakenly want to make Mary's immortality, like her Immaculate Conception, dependent on the broken creation covenant. That creation covenant broken or unbroken and all its consequences are entirely irrelevant to the person of Mary, since Mary has always been and continues to be favored by God in everything in accord with the unique covenant God made with her alone and for her alone.

The Father's choice of Mary to be the Mother of the God-man was absolute and irrevocable. However, her immortality or mortality like many conditions of her humanity at her conception were willed conditionally by God and were conditional in the covenant God made with Mary. Mary was immortal in the sense that she, like Adam and Eve before they sinned, could not die from natural internal causes. If Mary died her death could not be due to any natural internal causes.

Mary died from another cause. It was at the moment God chose to use his almighty power to separate her immaculate soul from her immaculate body that Mary died. Since Mary died in this way her death could not have the appearance of a person dying from natural internal causes. Such a death would have the appearance of a person going to sleep. In the Eastern Rite Catholic Churches Mary's Assumption is commemorated under the title of Mary's sleep or dormition. The Western Catholic Church commemorates or celebrates Mary's Assumption, not her sleep or her death. Dormio is the Latin word for sleep. In Jerusalem on Mt. Zion across the street from the Cenacle, the place of the Last Supper, there stands today a large beautiful church dedicated to the Dormision of Mary, to the Sleep of Mary.

The protoevangelium implies Mary's resurrection from the dead and her glorious Assumption into Heaven. The resurrection and assumption of Mary normally should have occurred at the general resurrection of all the dead. Just as Mary died at the moment God chose to separate her immaculate soul from her immaculate body so also Mary's glorious resurrection occurred at the time God chose to reunite her immaculate soul with her immaculate body. That occurred in the case of Mary by a special favor of God shortly after her death

The correct translations of the protoevangelium foretell of

Mary's crushing the head of Satan with her heel. This prophecy, stating that Mary will crush Satan's head with her heel, deliberately brings into focus Mary's physical heel. Mary personally crushing Satan as though Satan's head were crushed with her heel necessitates Mary's resurrection from the dead and her glorious Assumption into Heaven Body and Soul before the general resurrection of all the dead. Since Mary is to crush the head of Satan before the general resurrection of all the dead and she could not personally crush Satan's head with her heel unless she physically rose from the dead Mary had to rise from the dead before the general resurrection of all the dead. Any crushing of Satan's head after the general resurrection would be too late to aid in the salvation of mankind. She in fact rose from the dead shortly after her death as Sacred Tradition testifies. Consequently, this prophecy of the woman crushing the head of Satan with her heel implies the truth of the Dogma of the Glorious Resurrection and Assumption of Mary body and soul into heaven.

The protoevangelium makes two points to manifest how total will be Mary's victory and triumph over Satan's headship and leadership in his kingdom. First, the protoevangelium specifies that Satan's head will be crushed. A serpent can survive the permanent crushing or loss of its tail or some notable part of its body without dying, but a serpent cannot survive the crushing or loss of its head without dying. A human person can survive the crushing or even the removal of arms or legs but can not survive the crushing or loss of his or her head.

Second, the protoevangelium specifies that Mary will do that crushing with her heel. The heel of a person is the most powerful crushing organ or instrument of the human body. It is more powerful than a blow with a fist. Hence a crushing by the person's heel symbolizes the most complete destruction possible by a human person. Consequently the crushing of Satan head by Mary's heel signifies the permanent and complete destruction of Satan's perverse kingdom. For this reason too Mary is known as the "Terror of Demons".

However Satan is an entirely spiritual being and does not have a physical head. Satan's head Mary will destroy is his symbolical head. It is Satan as the head of his kingdom. The protoevangelium by stating that Mary will crush Satan's head with her heel is saying Mary will completely destroy Satan's perverse kingdom on earth. Such destruction by her heel implies Mary's direct involvement in the complete destruction of Satan's kingdom on earth.

The destruction of a kingdom cannot be accomplished by the physical heel of Mary. Mary's real heel is symbolical of something in the world formed by Mary, belonging to Mary and under Mary's control. Something under the control and direction of Mary and dedicated to Mary for the specific task of gaining for her a permanent and complete victory over Satan, the Triumph of Mary's Immaculate Heart in the world. The physical heel of Mary is the symbol of some powerful organization or movement of Mary in the world engaged in a life and death struggle against Satan and his kingdom.

Mary's triumph will be a Triumph for Christ. Since Mary was given the task of achieving victory over Satan by the protoevangelium that victory will be more directly and personally the work of Mary than of Christ.

Mary's heel is the force and power of all humans and angels acting under her guidance and working together for the destruction of Satan's kingdom. This heel of Mary cannot be the Church of Jesus Christ, for Christ's Church is the Mystical Body of Christ, not the heel of Mary. This heel of Mary has to be something in this world established and formed by Mary. The Church, the mystical body of Christ, is completely subject to its Head, Jesus Christ, just as every organ of a body is subject to the head of the body. The Church since it is the Body of Christ is under the control of its head Jesus Christ. The Church of Jesus Christ was established by Jesus Christ and belongs to Jesus Christ, not by Mary. It cannot be under the control of Mary as the heel of Mary is under the control of Mary's head.

The protoevangelium further prophesies that Satan will resist Mary's attack. Satan will resist by attacking Mary's heel, which is Mary's powerful organization or movement on earth. Satan's resistance will be futile in the face of Satan's inevitable destruction by Mary's enmity. Members of Mary's spiritual force for good on earth can be certain of coming under attack by Satan and his perverse kingdom. For the sake of persons consecrated to Mary and under attack by Satan Mary has made her Immaculate Heart a secure refuge for them. This is the reason Mary's Heart is the Noah's ark of the New Covenant. In Mary's Immaculate Heart all her consecrated children and soldiers will live through the coming great tribulation, just as Noah and his family were safe and secure only in Noah's ark during the great tribulation of the flood.

God's prophecy regarding Mary's overpowering enmity being directed against Satan's perverse kingdom implies that God has entrusted Mary with the mission and task of overpowering and destroying Satan's perverse kingdom on earth. That crushing defeat will end forever Satan's efforts to seduce men. That crushing defeat of Satan will occur in the end times in the preparation of the Church and all mankind for Christ's returning to this earth to rule a completely renewed Church and a completely renewed humanity.

In the Book of Revelation the first great sign on the first day of creation Mary is already seen as the Great Queen of all creation. As Queen she has the power to overpower Satan and his kingdom. In that Book of Revelation Mary is the one who in the end times when Satan appears as Antichrist will enchain the huge red dragon and confine him and his demons to the bottomless pit. When Satan and his perverse kingdom have been removed from the earth in the Triumph of Mary's Immaculate Heart, Jesus Christ can immediately begin his Glorious Reign in his gloriously renewed Church, his Kingdom on earth.

The protoevangelium foresaw the number of children Mary would have. How many children did Mary really have? The protoevangelium foresees Mary as having only one child. Protestants ever since the reformation have been insisting that Jesus was not the only child of Mary. The protoevangelium makes it clear that Mary can have only one offspring for two reasons. First it speaks of the woman's offspring in the singular not in the plural. Second, if the protoevangelium's promise of a redeemer is truly real its promise of a redeemer must be specify. It must identify one particular person who will be that redeemer. If Mary will have several children the promise of her offspring being a redeemer is not specific because it does not designate which of her offspring will be the redeemer.

If Mary had more than one child then there is in the protoevangelium a very serious problem for everyone regarding the true identity of which offspring of Mary God has chosen for the placing of enmity between him and the offspring of Satan. If the woman of the protoevangelium were to have two or more offspring, then it would have been necessary for the protoevangelium to specify which of her offspring would be the recipient of the enmity directed at the offspring of Satan. If Mary has several children and the protoevangelium does not make the necessary designation of which of her offspring is to be the recipient of that enmity; the protoevangelium would then necessarily designate all her offspring redeemers. Consequently, it must be that the woman of the protoevangelium will have only one offspring or child.

If Mary would have several offspring than the protoevangelium designation of the true Messiah or redeemer would have to be invalid. Every designation is invalid unless it designates a person or thing in particular. As the protoevangelium stands, if Mary would have several offspring, it would designate all her offspring Messiahs or no offspring would be designated the Messiah or redeemer. A cooperation of several redeemers in the one redemption of mankind, besides being very offensive to Christian tradition, would be contrary to all prophecies and all recorded history.

Multiple redeemers is a very different matter than the intrinsic participation Mary had in the redemptive work of her offspring by being designated an intimate associate of her Son in the work of redeeming mankind. It was that designated intimate association that made Mary the Coredemptrix. Mary's coredemption of mankind is the real and true reason Mary became the Mediatrix of all Graces and the Church's teaching regarding Mary's privilege of Mediatrix of all Graces.

Thus the protoevangelium truly foretells that the woman, Mary, will have only one Child, her First-born Son, Jesus Christ. Which is exactly what Scripture and Christian tradition have constantly and consistently taught for the past two thousand years.

The gospels and history indicate in a number of other ways

that Jesus was Mary's only child. If Mary had a child or children other than Jesus, it is most strange that there is no evidence in the gospels of Mary ever having or caring for more than one child, her Son Jesus. In recorded history there is no evidence that any person or persons ever put forth seriously claims to be a true brother or sister of Jesus Christ or a true descendant of Mary and Joseph. It is inconceivable that any person truly a descendant from Mary and Joseph, a half brother or a half sister of Jesus Christ, would not have been most desirous of making such a claim. Also if Jesus had several such brothers and sisters why would Jesus, just prior to his death on the Cross, have given the care of his Mother to his disciple John, who, as his gospel states, took her as his own mother. John cared for Mary until her death without any known assistance or protest from any such half brothers or sisters or any attempt by such persons to assume what would have been their grave responsibility toward their mother.

The protoevangelium foresaw also the Virgin Birth of Jesus Christ. The conception of an existing person through nothing more than sexual relations is impossible and that impossibility makes untenable the reincarnation beliefs of many eastern religions. These religions do not have a God who can create or has created anything out of nothing. Like the gods of the mythology of ancient Greece and other ancient eastern nations, the gods can only supposedly change one thing into another; the changing of animals into humans and humans into animals and one human into another human. The reincarnation beliefs involve the changing of one immutable nature into another immutable nature! An impossibility! No correction or improvement here in thousands of years.

The conception of Jesus Christ had to be virginal. It is not possible for a person to reenter the womb of his mother to be born again. It is not possible for a person to be reborn or recreated a child of God "by blood nor by carnal desire, nor by man's willing it". {Jn 1:13.} More impossible is the conception of an existing divine Person to take place by mere sexual generation or for any such conception to take place without some very special divine intervention. This does not imply that no conception could be virginal but that virginal conception, if there should be any, raises the question, why would God want to cause such a conception. He established sexual relations of humans to be nature's way of causing the conception of human persons? This is the reason God has never caused it, except in the conception of the God-man.

Human sex and sexual activity have the designed capability of causing the conception of human persons. Human sexual fertility along with heterosexual activity is the only physical cause designed by God for the conception of human persons. Heterosexual relations cause the conception of a human person, but heterosexual relations are not the efficient cause of the human person coming into existence. In the conception of Jesus Christ, the union of the preexisting eternal Person of the Son of God with a human nature needed only the fertility of the virgin and the action of the Holy Spirit to be conceived. The conception of the Son of God as the God-man in the womb of Mary did require the deliberate intervention of God's almighty power. For only the almighty power of God could bring about the union of a human nature with the existing Person of the Son of God for his conception in the womb of the Virgin Mary.

The first great sign that appeared in the sky on the first day of creation implied the virginal conception of the Son of God, for in that sign the woman is already pregnant and no man has existed. In that sign the woman appears as the Queen of the universe, just as her unborn Son is the King of the universe. Just as the generation of the Son in God from eternity is without maternity so his conception as the God-man is without human paternity.

This virginal conception and birth of the God-man was something that could have been anticipated by man after the Incarnation had been revealed in the first great sign and in the protoevangelium. It apparently was not anticipated for there is nothing to indicate that such a conception for the God-man was ever thought of by man, that is, until it was explicitly revealed and foretold to man by God. Cf. Is 7:14. As already explained, Adam and Eve knew of the Incarnation and of his conception and birth before their fall from grace.

For a conception to be virginal it is not necessary that the woman herself be a virgin as Mary was a virgin at the conception and birth of Jesus Christ. Isaiah prophesied three things when he wrote that a virgin would conceive and bear a son. He prophesied that a virgin would conceive by a virginal conception, that there would be a virgin birth and that the conception and birth would be that of a son. Seven hundred years after this prophecy of Isaiah, the virgin Mary conceived and bore a Son just as Isaiah prophesied. This foretold conception happened in Mary just as Mary had been informed and promised by the Archangel Gabriel: "The Holy Spirit will come upon you and the power of the Most High will overshadow you; hence the holy offspring to be born will be called Son of God." Lk 1:35.

God withheld from Satan knowledge of when, where and by what means the enmity of the offspring of the woman would reverse the effects of his works—reverse the deprivation Satan's work of breaking the creation covenant inflicted on all mankind. God withheld from Satan also the means He had chosen to accomplish the rejustification or resanctification of Adam and Eve and of their descendants. Many specifics of the manner of the redemption were not made known until much later. Those specifics were the secrets of God's secret councils. Cf. Eph 3:5.

Satan, at the time of the first great sign in the sky on the first day of creation, learned that the offspring of that woman would be the Son of God and therefore knew that her offspring would be capable of redeeming mankind. This great sign was manifest simultaneously to all the angels for it filled the sky. It manifested that at some time the Father's Son would become the God-man by being conceived and born of a woman. The Son would remain the one and only God-man forever and would be the Supreme Head, Lord and King of all creation forever.

This first great sign revealed that the God-man would be given all authority in heaven and on earth and that He would forever exercise Supreme Authority over all creatures, including all angels and all men. "He is the blessed and only ruler, the King of kings and Lord of lords...To him be honor and everlasting rule! Amen. 1 Tim 6:14.

This first great sign on the first day of creation manifested to all the angels that the Eternal Father was requiring of all the angels that they freely, immediately and forever consecrate themselves in total service to the God-man. They were to freely consecrate themselves completely and forever to the service of the Son in his Sacred Humanity as their Supreme Head, Lord and King. Many angels refused to consecrate themselves in eternal fidelity, service and honor to the Incarnate God-man.

Satan who was originally called Lucifer by all the angels as his person, angelic nature and faculties were the brightest and most prominent light among all the angels. Lucifer is literally "Bearer of Light" in Latin.

After Lucifer rebelled against God, he immediately began making accusations against God and certain other angels. For this he was immediately called Satan by other angels. Satan means Accuser. This Accuser would very soon become successful in leading a great number of angels to rebel against God by his accusations against God and other angels.

All the angels who consecrated themselves completely and forever to service of the God-man were almost immediately eternally glorified by God. God calls these angels "day" on the first day of creation immediately after their glorifications. Satan and his demons immediately on their rebellion became darkness and God calls them "night" on the first day of creation. Cf. Gen 1:5. The good angels, by their consecration of themselves to the God-man and their separation from the bad angels and glorification by God, entered the eternal light of the eternal day that became for them an eternal day of complete and perfect happiness. For the rebellious Satan and his demons their separation from God and the good angels existence became intense darkness of confusion, uncertainty, hatred and strife.

All praise and thanks to our Almighty Father for willing first of all the Incarnation of his Son to become forever the God-man of our race. For his sake, Father, You created Adam in your mental image of your God-man and made the creation covenant with Adam for the supernatural life and eternal destiny of Adam and his race. When Adam broke your gracious creation covenant, Father, his sin was of such great ingratitude You determined that the graces lost by his sin never be returned as entirely free gifts to anyone who lost them in the breaking of your creation covenant. You, Father, determined that God-man in obedience to You redeem the race of Adam and that only the graces He merited in the redemption be made available for the salvation of Adam and his entire race. Gracious Heavenly Father You then made your new and eternal covenant for the eternal reconciliation, rejustification, sanctification and glorification of all men of Adam's race. These favors your new and eternal covenant were made available to everyone on the condition that persons believe in your God-man.

Blending of the truths of faith regarding grace into this synthesis of theology of grace has not been available during the past two millenniums, but has become the theology of grace in and for this third millennium.

THE NEW, ETERNAL AND UNIVERSAL COVENANT IS THE ONLY JUSTIFYING COVENANT FOR MAN

Before the fall of man, the creation covenant was the only means God had established for the entire race of Adam to receive God's many gifts, including the state of original innocence, man's beginner's "share in the fullness of Christ" and man's predestination "to life on high in Christ Jesus". Cf. Col 1:19; 2:13; Phil. 3:14; 2 Thes 2:14.

The creation covenant was the one and only means for establishing Adam and Eve and their entire race in their beginners' share in the fullness of Christ", and for establishing their entire race in original innocence. The only means to their original supernatural sanctity or justice and to bringing Adam and Eve and their entire race to eternal salvation, the eternal beatific vision of God in heaven. By the breaking of that creation covenant, the one and only means of grace for mankind ceased to exist, and unless God inaugurated or established a new covenant mankind would forever be without any means for their supernatural sanctity and eternal salvation. For men of themselves or by themselves cannot initiate a covenant for their supernatural sanctification and eternal salvation.

After the fall of man God first initiated the New, Eternal and Universal Covenant, then issued several curses, proclaimed the protoevangelium and expelled Adam and Eve from Paradise. These actions of God made it clear to Satan that God did not renew the broken creation covenant. If God had renewed the broken creation covenant Adam and Eve could have been permitted to remain in Paradise.

The reality of man's fallen condition and God's unwillingness to return any of his entirely free gifts to Adam or to anyone of Adam's race made clear to Adam and to Satan that there would be no salvation for anyone, unless God redeemed mankind and made a new covenant for man's salvation.

God the Father planned and decreed that there be a redemption of mankind and that only graces merited in the redemption would be made available to mankind. Unless God willed to establish a new means by which the graces merited in the redemption be made available to mankind redemption would have been useless to man.

The first and most relevant question any individual of Adam's fallen race can ask and needs answered correctly is, has God redeemed all mankind and has God established some new means or covenant by which the graces merited in the redemption are made available to every individual of Adam's race. The only correct answer to this question is that God has redeemed all mankind and has established a new covenant—the New, Eternal and Universal Covenant—as his new means for distributing to every individual the graces merited in the redemption for the supernatural sanctification and eternal salvation of men.

The graces merited in the redemption are the only graces available to mankind because in consequence of man's fall from grace God the Father determined that there would be no other graces available to fallen men. Hence it is entirely futile for anyone to contend that since God is so good and most generous to everyone seeking grace that grace will be given to him. They make this contention just as though redemption and the new covenant were unnecessary for them, at least not in this situation. These persons would in effect have God circumvent his own will by making other grace available than the grace merited in the redemption and by making a special means of grace for them by which they might obtain grace other than by means of the new, eternal and universal covenant. All of this is nothing but the futility of attempting to circumvent the will of God which has made only the graces merited in the redemption available to fallen man and attempting to circumvent God's New, Eternal and Universal Covenant as the only means by which the graces merited in the redemption are distributed to individuals.

In man's fallen situation, the next most relevant and important question everyone must ask and needs answered correctly is: what according to the will of God as expressed in the New, Eternal and Universal Covenant must everyone do to receive the graces merited in the redemption of mankind?

Putting this crucial question in New Testament terminology one asks, what, according to the will of God as expressed in the

New, Eternal and Universal Covenant, must an individual do to be justified or sanctified or receive the beginners' share in the fullness of Christ? It seeks the answer to the question what are the requirements of that new covenant for individuals to be given gratuitously the graces merited in the redemption by Jesus Christ? In other words, what must every individual do to be recreated or reborn in the image of God and so have the graces needed for eternal salvation?

In our times most people ask this same question in yet another way. They ask simply what they must do to be saved? By asking the question in this way, they show that they are almost completely ignorant of their need for redemption and their need to be saved by means of the New, Eternal, and Universal Covenant. They ask as though their salvation had nothing at all to do with any covenant or even with redemption. They ask as though they can merit salvation by what they do or that they are saved by merely asking God to save them. They ask as though asking God to save them is enough for God to effectively save them—as though their salvation was without any dependence on the redemption wrought by Jesus Christ or God's New, Eternal and Universal covenant.

The Apostle Paul gave a partial answer to this question when he declared that persons are justified by faith and not by the works of the Law. Paul's answer implies that there are requirements and conditions for justification. By this answer Paul wants everyone to realize that the reason the works of the Mosaic Covenant or the Old Law were not required for justification is precisely the fact that the Mosaic Covenant or the Old Law never was a justifying covenant. If the Mosaic Covenant or the Old Law had been a justifying covenant, than the only way a person could be justified would be by doing or by fulfilling the works of the Mosaic Covenant or the Old Law. Since the Mosaic Covenant or Old Law was not a justifying covenant, contrary to prevailing thought among the Jews of the day, St. Paul felt the need to point out God's true purpose in giving the Law. It had an entirely different purpose than giving persons the justice of God. It gave only the justice of the Law.

St. Paul teaches that faith In Jesus Christ justifies persons. Why does St. Paul so emphatically teach that persons are justified by faith in Jesus Christ? St. Paul claims that this truth was revealed to him personally by Jesus Christ. Cf. Eph 3:3-6. Jesus Christ revealed to Paul and the other apostles that faith in Jesus Christ is the condition of justification. Faith in Jesus Christ is merely the condition of justification, the only condition in the will of God and in the new covenant for a person's supernatural justification. Faith is not the only requirement for justification. Faith is the only condition of the New, Eternal and Universal Covenant for justification or supernatural sanctification or for possessing everlasting life or for being reborn in the image of God. "This is the will of my Father who sent me, that whoever beholds the Son and believes in him should have everlasting life and I will raise him up on the last day." Jn 6:40.

To learn the requirements of justification persons can go to the apostle Peter's sermon on Pentecost. Then and there the Apostle Peter gave the following answer when asked this question by certain Jews. The Jews who asked this question on Pentecost were deeply shaken on hearing St. Peter accuse them of killing their Messiah. They then ask Peter and the other apostles, "What are we to do, brothers?" Peter answers: "You must reform and be baptized, each one of you, in the name of Jesus Christ, that your sins may be forgiven: then you will receive the gift of the Holy Spirit." Act 2:37-38.

The fact that the answer given by Jesus and the answer given by Peter are different indicates that they tailored their answers to the circumstances of the persons asking that question. Each answer is correct for its list of conditions and requirements are incomplete when considering the complexity of the whole real process in the circumstances of the persons asking for justification. The statement of Jesus and the answers of the apostles are not contradictory.

The Scriptural doctrine of justification by faith alone is very different from the Protestant doctrine of justification by faith alone. The Protestant doctrine is erroneous in that it would make faith in Christ the only requirement of justification. In the scriptural doctrine of justification by faith, faith is the condition of justification. Faith is merely a condition of justification. Faith is the only condition in the will of God and in God's justifying covenant for justification. When considering only the condition of justification one may say as well that a person is justified by faith alone meaning that faith is the only condition for justification not that faith is the only requirement for justification.

The fact that there are requirements for a person's justification in addition to faith which is a condition for justification and the only condition in God's will and in new covenant for justification, is the reason the apostles answered the Jews on the first Pentecost that they must repent and be baptized for their justification. Faith in Jesus Christ is merely a condition but the only condition in the will of God and in the New, Eternal and Universal Covenant for a person's justification — for receiving eternal life or justification as an entirely free gift.

If justification or eternal life or sanctification is available to every person only by means of God's New, Eternal and Universal Covenant, then it should be obvious that persons must fulfill the requirements of that covenant for their justification — for their receiving the graces merited in the redemption for their justification or sanctification. Persons must be justified or sanctified by God's justifying covenant or they are not justified or sanctified at all.

The covenant is a new covenant because it has taken the place of the creation covenant, which was broken and became useless for man's justification and salvation. The new covenant is not the new covenant because it has taken the place of the Mosaic Covenant of Law, for that the Mosaic Covenant or Law was not a justifying covenant.

The new covenant is an eternal covenant because God established it to justify persons of Adam's race living on earth. It effectively justifies persons living at any time from the fall of man to the end of the world and beyond the end of the world for it gives eternal glory to the saints in heaven.

Justification is not identical with eternal salvation. A person's justification can lead a person to his eternal salvation. The covenant is an eternal covenant because all the graces merited in the redemption are continually made available to men at any time. The eternal life persons live in heaven or continues to receive in virtue of this New, Eternal and Universal Covenant.

The New Covenant is an Eternal Covenant because there is no time limit on its ability to continue justifying persons. It justified Adam shortly after he broke the creation covenant and it will make grace available to the very last man to born to the race of Adam. All persons who lived before the redemption actually occurred received the graces of the redemption on credit through the retroactive effect of the New, Eternal and Universal Covenant. This new covenant therefore has been the only justifying covenant in effect since the fall of man. It is ever the means by which persons in heaven keep their rights to the supernatural life they received while they lived on earth.

The New, Eternal and Universal Covenant is a universal covenant with respect to persons. By it alone can any and all persons of the race of Adam be justified. It is a universal covenant also with respect to grace, for by it any and all graces merited in the redemption are made available to persons of the race of Adam. There has never been and never will be a person on earth of Adam's race that this covenant was not designed to justify. The only exceptions are Jesus and Mary his Mother.

The condition for the justification or supernatural sanctification of persons is different to some extent under the New, Eternal, and Universal Covenant for persons in certain particular circumstances of life. They would have to be different for certain persons in certain particular circumstances, since God does not desire that anyone of Adam's race should be lost. God wills that He overlook certain requirements that a person through no fault of his cannot fulfill. The requirement of baptism is one such requirement.

Some persons may not be responsible or culpable for the condition in which they find themselves. Babies who die in the womb or are aborted or die before gaining the use of their reason can receive their justification by means of the new, eternal and universal covenant but on different requirements. In the mind and will of God a person invincibly ignorant of a certain requirement or is temporarily unable to fulfill some certain requirement for his or her justification may temporally be excused from it.

A person's concern for attaining correct answers to what is indispensable regarding God's new justifying covenant for his or her justification must be for that person a concern above every other concern. That concern must hold first and highest priority in the intention of that person. If it does not hold highest priority the person knows he must reform his evaluation of things and strive earnestly to discover the truth and then fulfill every provision of the New, Eternal and Universal Covenant for his or her justification.

Striving for the correct answers to indispensable requirements can be relatively easy or extremely difficult. The easy and prudent way is the way of the early believers in Jesus Christ. These believers gained faith's certainty about such matters by simply asking questions of the infallible teaching authority of the apostles and by firmly believing the answers they received from the apostles. Today, the answers to those same questions are available from the same infallible teaching authority, the Magisterium of the same Church of Jesus Christ.

The early believers had only the Old Testament Scriptures to read and study for discovering Biblical answers to questions regarding their justification and eternal salvation. The New Testament Scriptures had not yet been written. The very earliest believers in Jesus Christ could ask Jesus Christ those same questions. Later believers asked those questions of their infallible God-given teachers, the apostles.

These disciples of the apostles found believing the answers of the apostles easier than trying to fulfill or live them. That too was as Jesus taught: "If a man wishes to come after me, he must deny his very self take up his cross, and begin to follow in my footsteps. Whoever would save his life will lose it, but whoever loses his life for my sake will find it." Mt 16: 24-25.

People of today have the same two ways of discovering the truth or of having the truth available to them regarding God's way of justifying persons. The same answers are still given to the same questions by the Sacred Scriptures and the same infallible teacher, the true Church of Jesus Christ.

The much more difficult and not nearly as certain a way of arriving at correct answers to questions regarding God's way of justifying persons is that of undertaking an intense, long, very careful and extensive study of Scripture, especially the New Testament Scriptures. This difficult way will involve discovering the true reasons, which in the early Church gave rise first to the controversy over justification by faith or by works of the Law. It will involve discovering and defining precisely the nature of many problems involved in that controversy and understanding precisely the answers Jesus Christ gave and the answers the apostles gave under the infallible guidance of the Holy Spirit.

Persons willing to travel the difficult way of studying with great objectivity correct translations of Scripture are not guaranteed arrival at the correct answers to these extremely important and difficult questions, for everyone is too subject to the frailties of his fallen human nature. The great difficulties to be encountered in that endeavor is one reason Jesus Christ gave infallible teaching authority to the apostles and that infallible magisterium was given only to his Church, the Catholic Church.

Human frailty is just one of many reasons why persons singly or jointly with others make mistakes even in careful pursuit of truth when seeking merely facts while engaged in scientific research. Willingness to go the difficult way cannot guarantee anyone a correct understanding of the issues involved in the early Church's long controversy over whether justification is by faith alone or by the works of the Law of Moses. That should be evident from the many contradictory answers different persons and groups have espoused after having gone that long hard way. The many different answers arrived at by different individuals and groups make it obvious that the difficult way has many hidden pitfalls for fallen man.

The espoused different and even contradictory answers arrived at by various persons prove the inability of almost anyone to correctly answer all the questions involved in the problem of how persons are justified under the new covenant. This is true even of those persons who claim to have gone that long and difficult way seeking and relying on the assistance of the Holy Spirit. Hence the most prudent way for everyone is the way of being willing to believe the infallible Magisterium of the Church. Jesus Christ did not blunder when He gave his Church the mission of teaching with certainty the entire gospel of salvation to all men. "Those who hear you hear me."

A clear and certain demonstration of all Scripture's answers to the many questions involved in the justification by faith controversy in the early Church would, without doubt, end the Catholic vs. Protestant controversy over justification by faith alone. That controversy has continued for the past five centuries. In an effort to settle that controversy individual and groups of Catholics and Protestants have been engaged in a common study of it for years and decades. They apparently have come upon an impasse that is no better than a completely unsatisfactory scriptural and theological draw. Neither side agreeing to the others total view of justification and of justification by faith.

THE FONDEST DESIRE OF JESUS CHRIST FOR ALL HIS GENETIC BROTHERS AND SISTERS IS TO SHOW THEM THE FACE OF HIS AND THEIR FATHER

"IN THE BEGINNING WAS THE WORD"
"HE IS BEFORE ALL ELSE THAT IS"
"IN HIM EVERYTHING CONTINUES IN BEING"

Chapter 5

CREATION IN THE NEW TESTAMENT

THE NEW TESTAMENT ACCEPTS THE LITERAL SENSE OF THE CREATION CHAPTERS OF GENESIS

Genesis has given such a completely adequate account of creation of all things out of nothing that the inspired authors of the New Testament saw no need to give a supplementary account of the creation. These New Testament authors frequently quote Genesis' literal sense with approval when teaching the creation of all things by God. The inspired New Testament has thereby explicitly affirmed the accuracy and adequacy of the literal sense of Genesis' account of creation. Genesis' literal account is an account of the origin of all things by a direct and immediate creation of all things out of nothing by God. The only thing the New Testament adds to that account of the executive order of creation is the priority the incarnation had in God's order of intention at the creation of all things. For the New Testament manifests the reason God began to create, why He created all things and the reason He intends to keep all things in existence forever.

Before stating God's order of intention in the creation of all things, it would be well first to list New Testament quotations from Genesis and in that way manifest the New Testament's approval of the litteral sense of the three creation chapters of Genesis.

QUOTATIONS FROM THE NEW TESTAMENT REGARDING THE ORIGIN OF THE UNIVERSE

God created all thing and did so by his word alone:

"All raised their voices in prayer to God on hearing the story: 'Sovereign Lord, who made heaven and earth and sea and all that is in them.'" Act 4:24.

"For the God who made the world and all that is in it, the Lord of heaven and earth does not dwell in sanctuaries... it is he who gives to all life and breath and everything else." Act 17:24-25.

"God, the creator and sustainer of all." Eph 3:9.

"In him everything continues in being." Col 1:17.

"He sustains all things by his powerful word." Heb 1:3.

"Through faith we perceive that the worlds were created by the word of God, and that what is visible came into being through the invisible." Heb 11:3.

"All brought into being by the word of God." 2 Pt 3:5.

"He first created the universe." Heb 1:2.

"God's work was finished when he created the world [and every thing on it]." Heb 4:3.

"Everything God made is good." 1 Tm 4:3.

"Have you not read that at the beginning the Creator made them [man] male and female." Mt 19:4.

"In him everything in heaven and on earth was created... all were created through him and for him." Col 1:16.

"O Lord our God, you are worthy to receive glory and honor and power! For you have created all things; by your will they came to be and were made." Rev 4:11. Cf. Rev 10:6.

QUOTATIONS FROM THE NEW TESTAMENT REGARDING THE ORIGIN OF MANKIND

"For Adam was created first." 1 Tm 3:19.
"For Adam was created first, Eve afterward. 1 Tm 2:13.
"The first man was of earth, formed from dust." 1 Cor 15:47.
"Man was not made from woman but woman from man." 1 Cor 11:8.
"From one stock [some translate one man] he made every nation of mankind to dwell on the face of the earth." Acts 17:26.

QUOTATIONS FROM NEW TESTAMENT REGARDING MAN'S CREATION IN GOD'S IMAGE LIKENESS

"Then we use it [the tongue] to curse men, though they [men] are made in the likeness of God." Jas 3:9.
"Those whom he foreknew he predestined to share the image of his Son, that the Son might be the first-born of many brothers." Rom 8:29.
"All of us... are being transformed from glory to glory into his very image." 2 Cor 3:18.
"You must put on that new man created in God's image." Eph.24.
"Out on a new man, one who grows in knowledge as he is formed anew in the image of his Creator." Col 3:10.
"Just as we resemble the man from earth, so shall we bear the likeness of the man from heaven. 1 Cor 15:49.
"All that matters is that one is created anew." Gal 6:15.

QUOTATIONS REGARDING THE ORIGIN OF SEX AND MARRIAGE

"Have you not read that at the beginning the Creator made them male and female. 11 Mt 19:4.

"At the beginning of creation God made them male and female." Mk 10:6.

"For this reason a man shall leave his father and mother and shall cling to his wife and the two shall be made into one." Eph 5:31

"Let marriage be honored in every way and the marriage bed to kept undefiled, for God will judge fornicators and adulterers." Heb 13:4.

"A wife does not belong to herself but to her husband, equally, a husband does not belong to himself but to his wife." 1 Cor 7:4.

QUOTATIONS FROM NEW TESTAMENT REGARDING THE ORIGIN OF SIN AND DEATH

"Therefore, just as through one man sin entered the world and with sin death, coming to all men in as much as all sinned... I say, from Adam to Moses death reigned, even over those who had not sinned by breaking a precept as did Adam." Rom 5:12-14.

"If death began its reign through one man because of his offense..." Rom 5:17.

"It was not Adam who was deceived but the woman. It was she who was led astray and fell into sin." 1 Tm 2:14.

"It was not Adam who was deceived but the woman." 1 Tm 2:14 Cf. 2 Cor 11:13.

"The wages of sin is death." Rom 6:23.

THE NEW TESTAMENT'S DIFFERENT PERSPECTIVE ON CREATION

Many commentaries on the creation chapters of Genesis leave their readers with the impression that the New Testament doesn't have its own distinct perspective on creation. They suppose that the New Testament, because it accepts and often repeats what Genesis explicitly taught concerning the creation of all things from nothing in six days, necessarily has the same perspective on creation, as does Genesis. This is not true. Genesis teaches the perspective of God's executive order of creation. In that executive order, God first creates the heavens and the earth, then everything on earth, and last of all creates man in "our image likeness".

The New Testament teaches the perspective of God's order of intention at the creation of all things. In this order of intention, the New Testament gives first and highest priority in the intention of the Father to the Incarnation of his Son as the God-man of the race of Adam. That Incarnation is the divine motive for creating all things. Hence the God-man is the final cause of the creation of all things and of man being created in the image of the God-man. Man was created like the God-man, Jesus Christ.

THE PROBLEMS OF BEGINNINGS AND THE AGENTS OF CREATION

Ignorance of the different specific perspectives on creation in the Old and New Testaments has led to the scriptural problem of beginnings and the problem of whether the Father or the Son was creator as opposed to all three Persons of the Trinity creating all things.

Since both the Old and the New Testaments must teach the truth regarding creation, there arises the specific problem of how Genesis can state that in the beginning God created the heavens and the earth and the New Testament can state that the Word was in the beginning? Genesis would have us believe that God created the heavens and the earth first, while the apostles St. John and St. Paul would apparently have us believe something quite different. St. John wrote: "In the beginning was the Word [or Logos], the Word was in God's presence and the Word was God." Jn 1:1. Logos is a Greek word that means a word. St. Paul even more emphatically declares: "He [Jesus Christ, the God-man] is before all else that is. In him everything continues in being." 1 Col 1:17. Here in this text "before all else" has to mean first of all or in the beginning. "God has spoken to us through his son... through whom he first created the universe." Heb 1:2.

Some commentators note to some surprise of readers the fact that both Genesis and the fourth gospel begin with the same identical phrase "In the beginning". However these commentators do not appear to be in the least concerned that these identical phrases can be for many readers the very serious problem of God saying one thing in Genesis and saying something very different in the gospel of John and in the letter to the Hebrews. How can God inspire statements that clearly appear contradictory?

There can be no solution to this problem of these two beginnings being in apparent contradiction without first making a determination as to whether there is here a question of two different beginnings or one and the same beginning. If one and the same beginning that would imply a contradiction regarding what God created first of all or in the very beginning. If these are different beginnings, then two questions arise. What are those different beginnings and how can the same thing have two beginnings?

First, are these beginnings the beginning of the same thing, the heavens and the earth? "In the beginning" cannot refer to the beginning of God or the beginning of eternity, for neither God nor eternity had a beginning. Therefore beginning or beginnings in question must be the beginning or the beginnings of created things, the beginning of things outside God or some other kind of beginning. The beginning of created things or of things ad extra began when God determined that there should be a beginning of things outside God or an ad extra beginning of thing by God actually creating things outside God. Creatures, even though theoretically might have existed from eternity, still had to be created and have a beginning.

The solution to this problem of beginnings, in its scriptural and philosophical aspects, is to be found by clearly distinguishing God's order of intention from God's executive order or order of execution. These are entirely different orders and persons must understand also that things can have priority in each of these entirely different orders. Creation had a beginning in each of these orders.

Every project of an intellectual being must have two beginnings. Since God is an intellectual Being, God's project of creating things must have had two beginnings. The creation of the universe had one beginning in God's order of intention and another beginning in God's order of execution. In the order of execution things had their beginning when God actually began creating things.

Things have a beginning in God's order of execution and another beginning in God's order of intention. The perspective of God's executive order in creation is reflected in the first two chapters of Genesis. The perspective of God's order of intention in creation is reflected in the prologue of St. John's gospel and in certain passages of St. Paul's letters, his letters to the Ephesians and Colossians in particular.

The "In the beginning" of Genesis 1:1 is the beginning of creation in God's executive order, while the "In the beginning" in the prologue of St. John's gospel is the beginning of creation in God's order of intention.

Consideration will be given to distinguishing these orders and the priority things have in each after solving the Scriptural and theological problem of how God the Father and God the Son, the God-man, are each alone rightly the cause of the creation of all things.

THE PROBLEM OF GOD THE FATHER AND THE SON EACH BEING THE TOTAL CAUSES OF CREATION?

St. Paul often states that the Father is the Creator and that everything came to be in, through, and for the Son. In the Apostles' Creed we proclaim God the Father to be the Creator of heaven and earth, and that his only Son became man for our salvation.

Thomistic philosophy and theology teach that only by all Three Persons of the Trinity acting together as one Person can God be the efficient cause or agent of creation. Hence, according to this Thomistic teaching supposedly, neither the Father alone nor the Son alone can be the efficient cause of creation. This Thomistic teaching maintains further that there can be no instrumental cause in the act of creation. The God-man, for example, cannot be the Father's instrumental cause in the creation of all things. The concept of creation of all things from nothing itself implies that there cannot be an instrumental efficient cause for the creation of anything. In creation of something from nothing there is nothing to which an instrument could be applied.

Commentaries appear to ignore completely this problem of Scripture and the Creed apparently contradicting Thomistic philosophy and theology on this point of the Trinity of Persons and not the Father alone being the Creator. There is complete silence in all commentaries on this aspect of the problem of who are the agents or efficient causes of creation.

Commentators can easily gloss over this problem for in the understanding of nearly everyone God is the Creator of all things and that both the Father and the Son are God. Hence the implied solution to this problem of the creation of all things by the Father or by the Son of God can be as simple as: before the Son became man He was God and created all things along with the Father and the Holy Spirit.

Many appear satisfied to let persons think in this way in spite of the fact that a careful reading of relevant texts of the New Testament make it abundantly clear that the God-man, the Incarnate Son of God, also was the cause of the creation of all things. "The Word [the God-man] was God... Through him all things came into being and apart from nothing came to be." Jn 1:1-2. St. Paul wrote: "In him [the God-man] everything in heaven and on earth was created... all were created through him, and for him. He is before all else that is. In him everything continues in being." Col 1:16-17.

Some catechisms would want to resolve this problem by the mental process of attribution. These catechisms explain that, "To the Father are attributed the works of omnipotence, and particularly the creation. To the Son [are attributed], the works of wisdom, and particularly the redemption." Why authors of catechisms should have proposed attribution as a solution to this problem is not clear, for it is clearly no solution to the problem?

Both Scripture and the Apostles' Creed clearly teach that in some real sense the Father alone is the Creator, just as the God-man alone is the redeemer. Some persons attempt to resolve this problem by their mental attribution solution, which is that all Three Persons of the Trinity did the work of creating all things, (were the agents or the efficient causes of creation) but that the work of creating all things is merely attributed to the Father alone. Attributed to the Father alone even though it is the work of all the Persons of the Trinity working together or simultaneously in the creation of all things!

If they apply this mental attribution solution in the same way to the work of redemption as they do with the work of creation they would make redemption the work of the Three Persons of the Trinity and merely attribute the work of redemption to the Son alone. But is this really what Scripture and the Creed teach regarding Jesus the God-man alone being our redeemer? The Catholic Church certainly has not taught that all Three Persons of the Trinity were incarnated and redeemed mankind. The Catholic Church teaches that only the Son became incarnate and shed his Blood for our redemption and for those reasons is the redeemer. The Church teaches that the God-man, the Son of God, is truly the only redeemer and that He redeemed mankind by the shedding his Blood on the Cross. This surely indicates that the work of redemption is not merely attributed to the Son, but is the work of the Son alone!

If all three Persons of the Most Holy Trinity acting together as one Person are the direct and immediate efficient cause of creation how can the Creed teach that the Father is the Creator? " We believe in the Father almighty, creator of heaven and earth." Is this attribution teaching in conflict with the New Testament teaching that the Father created all things and that all things came to be in, through and for the Son? Does the New Testament teach that either the Father or the Son by acting alone was the efficient cause of creation? Is the solution to reading of the New Testament teaching that the Father alone and the Son alone were each individually a different kind of complete cause of creation?

First, all should know that a person can be the complete cause of something either in the ontological order or a cause in the moral order or in both orders. A person becomes the efficient cause of something when he intends to do a certain thing, move a rock for example, and then moves the rock physically by applying his physical force to the rock.

A person can be also the moral cause of something by ordering or commanding another person to do that certain thing, move the rock. Then the person ordered to move the rock by applying his physical force to the rock moves the rock. That person thereby became the efficient cause of that rock being moved. While the person giving the order is the efficacious moral cause of the rock being moved. A father by commanding his children to do certain things becomes the efficacious moral cause of what his children do under orders while his children are the efficient causes. The same person can be the moral cause and the efficient cause of moving the rock by deciding to move the rock and then applies his physical strength to the rock and so causes the rock to be moved.

If God the Father alone determined, decreed and ordered the creation of all things, then the Father alone is the efficacious moral cause of the creation of all things while Trinity of Persons become the efficient cause of creation. The Father being the only Person to give the command that the universe be created is the sole moral cause of the creation of the universe. It is for that reason the Creed rightly teaches that the Father is the Creator of the heavens and the earth. The Persons of the Trinity at the Father's command create the universe and for that reason are the efficient cause of the creation of all things.

In this way, creation is not merely attributed to the Father, but the Father is truly the sole efficacious moral cause of the creation of all things and therefore the Father is the Creator of heaven and earth. Therefore the Church rightly teaches in the apostle Creed, "I believe in God the Father Almighty Creator of heaven and earth."

If the God-man is neither the sole moral cause of creation—did not decree or order the creation—nor the sole efficient cause of the creation of the universe, how is it possible for the God-man to be the cause of creation? How can the Apostle Paul declare: "In him everything in heaven and on earth was created, things visible and invisible, whether thrones or dominations, principalities or powers; all were created through him and for him." Col 1:16. The apostle St. John teaches the same as the apostle Paul. He wrote: "Through him all things came into being, and apart from him nothing came to be." Jn 1:3. How can the apostle John teach that all things came to be through the Word or God-man, if the Word or God-man was neither the sole efficient cause of creation nor the moral cause by ordering or commanding the creation of all things?

These apostles can declare that all things were created or came to be through him, the God-man, because they are teaching that the God-man was the sole and complete final cause of the creation of the heavens and the earth and all things in them. They understand that the reason the Father commanded the creation of the universe was that the Father wanted his Son to become the God-man and that He become the God-man by being conceived and born of a woman of a race of humans living on this earth. It was therefore for the sake of his Son becoming the God-man that the Father commanded or ordered the creation of the heavens and the earth and everything in them.

The Father did not want to incarnate his Son by creating only one human nature and then unite the Person of the Son to that human nature. The Father wanted his Son to become the God-man by being conceived and born of a woman. The Father did not want to create just one woman and have his Son become the God-man by being virginally conceived and born of that woman.

Because the Father desired his Son to become the God-man in

this way, by being conceived and born of a woman belong to a race of humans on earth, the Father decreed and commanded the creation of the heavens, the earth and a race of humans on this earth. In accord with that decree of the Father the three Persons of the Trinity efficiently caused the creation of the universe, the earth and a race of humans on earth.

Some may be led to ask, how could the Incarnate Son, the God-man, be the final cause of creation, when the God-man was not a reality at the time of the creation of the heavens and the earth? Do not causes have to exist in order to cause something? That is absolutely true of every kind of causality except final causality. The thing that is the final cause in order to be a final cause needs to exist only as an object of desire in the intention of the person, who is the moral cause.

How the God-man could be the final cause of the creation of all things is an insurmountable problem for persons who hold that the Son would not have become the Incarnate God-man, unless the Son were to become the God-man for the purpose of redeeming mankind. It would not be possible for the Incarnate God-man to be the final cause of creation, if He would never exist and would not be the object desired by the will and intention of the Father when commanding the creation of all things.

Little wonder then, when it is thought that the fall of man and the redemption of man were sine qua non conditions in the will of the Father for the Incarnation of the Son, that many persons would confuse the final cause of creation with the efficient cause of creation. For they can be completely complacent in thinking merely that the Son in his Divinity, before becoming man, was, along with the Father and the Holy Spirit, the efficient cause of creation.

What had first and highest priority in the intention of the Father, when He gave the command that there be the creation of the heavens and the earth, was the Incarnation of his Son as the God-man, the final cause of creation. If the Incarnation of his Son as the God-man of the race of Adam had first and highest priority in the intention of the Father when decreeing the creation of all things then the God-man is the sole final cause of creation. "In him [not by him] everything in heaven and on earth was created... all were created through him and for him. He is before all else that is. In him everything continues in being." Col 1:16-17. "For from him, through him and for him all things are. To him be glory forever. Amen." Rom 11:36.

WHY THE FATHER WILLED TO INCARNATE HIS SON AS THE GOD-MAN

All Christians agree with Scripture that the Son of God became the God-man of the race of Adam, because his Father willed that His Son should do so. On several occasions Jesus made it perfectly clear to the Jews of his day that He came to earth out of obedience to the will of his Father. Jesus repeatedly taught that his Father sent Him and that He came down from the Father in heaven to do the will of his Father on earth. Hence, it should be absolutely certain that this will or command of the Father was the reason the Son became the incarnate God-man, the God-man of the race of Adam. He could not become the God-man of the race of Adam, unless he was conceived and born of a woman of the race of Adam.

Since the Son became the Incarnate God-man out of obedience to the will of his Father, Christians, over many centuries, have wondered whether the Father would have willed or commanded his Son to become the God-man of the race of Adam, if Adam would not have sinned. Many theologians are still puzzled over the question and are of two opinions.

Theologians could not find any text of Scripture, which explicitly taught either that the Father willed absolutely the Incarnation of his Son or set the fall and redemption of man as conditions for the incarnation of his Son, they resorted to texts which assigned tasks to the God-man. Texts that assigned tasks to be carried out by the Son on becoming the God-man for any implication that would or would not be required the God-man. They hoped in this way to determine whether the Father willed the Incarnation absolutely or set the fall and redemption of man as conditions sine qua non of the Incarnation of his Son as the God-man of the race of Adam.

There are many texts in the New Testament which teach that the Father sent the God-man with specific tasks to be carried out by Him while He lived among men on earth. "The Son of Man has not come to be served but to serve—to give his life in ransom for many." Mk 20:45. Cf. Mt 20:28. "Christ Jesus came into the world to save sinners." 1 Tm 1:15. "God did not send his Son into the world to condemn the world, but that the world might be saved through him." Jn 3:17. Jesus Himself said: "The son of Man has come to search out and save what is lost." Lk 19:10. Cf. Mt 9:13. The angel said to St. Joseph: "She [Mary] is to have a son and you are to name him Jesus because he will save his people from their sins." Mt 1:21.

During past centuries great doctors of the Church have reflected on these and other texts yet they nevertheless held two contradictory opinions. Some held the opinion that the Father willed absolutely to incarnate his Son as the God-man and others held the opinion that the Father willed the Incarnation conditionally, specifically on the conditions of man's fall into sin and on man's need for redemption by the God-man. Today, this issue is hardly debated even though both opinions are still held by theologians. The Magisterium of the Church has not yet formally decided on an answer to this question.

The Thomistic school of theology has inferred from the purposes or tasks the Father commanded his Incarnate Son should carry out while on earth, especially the redemption of man, that the Father conditionally willed the Incarnation of his Son. Consequently these theologians hold that the Father willed the incarnation because of man's fall from grace and to satisfy man's need for redemption. These Thomists hold that the fall of man and the redemption of man were sine qua non conditions in the will of the Father for incarnating his Son as the God-man of Adam's race. They, therefore, hold that the Son would not have become the God-man if man had not sinned and were not in need of redemption to be accomplished by the Sacred Passion and Death of the God-man.

The Scotistic school of theology holds the opposite opinion. The opinion that the Father willed the Incarnation unconditionally or absolutely. These Scotists realized that the Father did not make the task of redeeming mankind from sin a condition sine qua non of his Son's Incarnation. Consequently these theologians hold that the Father willed and commanded his Son to become the Incarnate God-man of the race of Adam whether Adam sinned or did not sin or whether man would or would not need to be redeemed by the God-man.

The Scotists teach that the Incarnation, since it is the most sublime of all God's works ad extra, could not have been willed or intended by the Father on any condition ad extra. This does not prove what it is intended to prove, namely, that the Incarnation was not willed conditionally, instead it proves that nothing ad extra, even the salvation of mankind, could have been a condition sine qua non in the Father's will for incarnating his Son. Hence, it would seem that the only condition or conditions the Father could have set for his Son's Incarnation as the God-man of the race of Adam would have been that the Son Himself consent to his Incarnation as the God-man of the race of Adam.

Theologians, in addition to looking into Sacred Scripture for evidence for either opinion turned also to the creeds of the Church, especially the Nicene Creed, to discover reasons for holding either opinion. One professor of Sacred Scripture when asked whether the sin of Adam and the redemption of mankind were conditions sine qua non of the Incarnation took refuge in this Creed to indicate the affirmative. He quoted the Nicene Creed in Latin: "Qui propter nos homines, et propter nostram salutem descendit de caelis." Who on account of us men and our salvation descended from heaven.

Some professors of Sacred Scripture and Sacred Theology understand this "Who for us men and for our salvation descended from heaven" to mean that the redemption of mankind was a condition sine qua non of the Son becoming the God-man of our race. Even though they used the Creed in this way they apparently failed to realize that the creed explicitly states two purposes for the Son becoming the God-man, but redemption is not one of them. Moreover, in attempting to turn this text of the Creed into evidence for a conditional incarnation of the Son, these persons make the word salvation mean redemption. The word salvation has a wider application than redemption. Before man's fall from grace all man were destined for salvation without any need for redemption. Only after the fall of man from grace has man's salvation been dependent on man's redemption. Only in the case of fallen mankind does the salvation of men depend on redemption.

The first explicit purpose or task of the Incarnation of the God-man specified by this Creed is "on account of us men". That it was for some good of us men that the Son became the God-man. The second explicit purpose or task specified in the creed is man's salvation. Here the redemption is not explicitly one of the purposes of the incarnation. Here the Creed's placing of the conjunction "and" between "on account of us men" and "our salvation" implies that the Father sent the God-man for some good of man besides the good that is man's salvation. However, the Creed does not point out anything that is the good "on account of us men" in addition to the good that is man's salvation. Here "us men" and "our salvation" has to mean for the good of the race of Adam, for it has to mean that the Father sent his Son to become the God-man of our race for some good of our race. What specific good of our race could be the "on account of us men" for which the God-man was sent? Since the Creed does not indicate what was that specific good, the piety of some suggests, that that specific good could have been the task of teaching the good news of salvation to us men and giving us men his good example for the practice of all the virtues, especially the most necessary of all virtues, true charity.

Professors of Sacred Scripture and theology, who rely on the above quotation from the Nicene Creed to lend certainty to their opinion that the Father willed the Incarnation conditionally, conveniently ignore the line preceding it, which states: "Through him all things were created." Could this line be teaching that our very creation, in addition to the decree for our original sanctification and salvation, was dependent on the merits of the very incarnation of the God-man? Does not Scripture teach that our creation was dependent on the Father's intention to incarnate his Son as the God-man, when it states: "Through him all things came into being, and apart from him nothing came to be." Jn 1:3. "For from him, through him and for him all things are. To him be glory forever. Amen." Rom 11:36. If the very creation of everything was for the sake of incarnating the Son as the God-man of our race, how could the Incarnation have been dependent on the later fall of man from grace and the redemption of mankind?

The Thomistic opinion that the Son would not have become the God-man, if man had not sinned and man was not in need of redemption by Him, raises some profound and obvious questions in view of other revealed truths. Here then are some of those serious questions challenging the very validity of that thomistic opinion:

First, if the Incarnation of the Son would not have been willed except for the purpose of redeeming mankind, why would the Son have retained his human nature after redeeming mankind by his death? Why would He not after dying on the Cross or when returning to his Father, have cast off his human nature forever? If, on the other hand, the redemption were not the condition sine qua non of the Son becoming the God-man, than it would have been expected that the Son would have returned to the Father retaining and treasuring forever his Most Sacred Human Nature.

Second, if the Incarnation were not willed absolutely by the Father there could not have been an eternal absolute determination of the Father that the God-man be the Eternal Supreme Head of all creation.

Third, if the Son were not to become man unless mankind fell into sin, how could God have decreed from all eternity that man be created in the likeness of the Incarnate God-man? For there would not have been that God-man to be the model after which men were to be created? Man could not have been created in "our image likeness", God's mental likeness of the transcendent Sacred Humanity of the God-man, for that transcendent God-man would not have existed unless man had sinned. The determination that Son should become the God-man of the race of Adam would have been subsequent to and dependent on Adam's falling into sin. Would that not imply that the Son, when becoming the God-man, was modeled in the image of sinful Adam, instead of the transcendent man being modeled after the transcendent God-man? St. Paul says that it was because of the sin of Adam that the Father determined that the Son, when He became the God-man, should become like us in all things.

Fourth, if the redemption of mankind were the condition sine qua non of the Incarnation, why would the Father have willed to bestow on his Incarnate God-man many unique and exalted roles to be exercised by Him in addition to that of redeemer? Roles which are in no way dependent on or related to his role of redeemer of mankind? Why, for example, would the Father have decreed from all eternity that the God-man be his First-born and therefore heir of all things? Why would the Father have from all eternity given the God-man the role of Supreme Judge of the angels in the general judgment, if the Son were to become the God-man only on the conditions that man sinned and sinners were to be redeemed by Him? The Father's will and plan from all eternity that the angels be judged by the God-man, Jesus Christ, demands that there be the Incarnation of the Son, even though man would not have been created or would not have sinned. This general judgment was necessary in either case in view of the fact that every angel and every man would have to be judged in order to receive his particular rightful eternal reward from God. In other words, the God-man's role of King and Supreme Judge of the angels could never have been dependent on or related to his role of Redeemer of mankind.

Fifth, how could St. Paul have written that the Father decreed from all eternity that his Incarnate Son be his First-born and the Supreme Head of all creatures, unless there were an absolute decree of the Father that the Son become the God-man. Not merely a decree that the Son become the God-man on conditions that man fall into sin or that man be redeemed by the Incarnate God-man? Cf. Col 1:15.

Sixth, how could St. Paul have written that the Father decreed from all eternity that the very creation of everything be through, in, and for the Incarnate Jesus Christ, unless that decree to create had been preceded by a decree of the Father to incarnate the Son as the God-man? Does not the Father's choosing to create man through, in, and for his Incarnate God-man imply that the Father decreed the Incarnation of his Son as the God-man before and independently of his decreeing the creation of man and the universe? Cf. Col 1:16-17.

Seventh, how could the Father from the beginning have chosen men for grace and salvation through, in, and for Jesus Christ, before the world began without that choice or decree of the Father being preceded by the decree to incarnate his Son as the God-man of the race of Adam? "Through him all things came into being, and apart from him nothing came to be." Jn 1:3.

Eight, if, as indicated by the first great sign in the sky on the first day of creation, God tested all the angels by commanding them to consecrate themselves unconditionally and forever to the service of the Incarnate God-man as their Supreme Lord. How could that testing have any binding power, unless the Father had already decreed absolutely the Incarnation of his Son as the God-man?

Ninth, if the Father decreed the Incarnation of his Son on the conditions that man fall from grace and that men be redeemed by the God-man, how is it possible for the protoevangelium, proclaimed immediately after the sin of Adam and Eve, to contain a promise of redemption without containing the promise to incarnate the Son as the God-man of the race of Adam. It can promise redemption only because the Father had already decreed and promised Adam and Eve to incarnate his Son as the God-man of their race. It is obvious that the protoevangelium contains only the promises of certain enmities, where those enmities would be placed and who or what would be the direct object of those enmities. This explicit promise of enmities to be given to a certain woman and her offspring, without issuing the promise of sending the woman and her offspring would be senseless, if there did not already exist the Father's decree and promise of sending them. Hence the very existence of the woman and her offspring could not have been conditioned by or dependent on Adam and Eve falling from grace and on mankind being redeemed by the Incarnate God-man.

Tenth, the protoevangelium implies that Adam and Eve already before their fall from grace knew of this woman and her offspring as the God-man and that the woman and her offspring were destined to be descendants of Adam and Eve. The protoevangelium implies that Adam and Eve knew of them by the complete and absolute silence of Adam and Eve on hearing, as some suppose for the first time, of that woman and her offspring. Their complete and absolute silence would be consistent only with Adam and Eve already knowing of that glorious woman and her divine offspring. Their absolute silence on hearing, supposedly for the first time, of the revelation of this woman and her offspring as their descendent would be inconceivable with any lack of previous knowledge of them becoming their offspring. This proclamation of the protoevangelium carried very great assurance and hope for Adam and Eve that God, in spite of their rebellion, was still going to keep his promise to them of sending that glorious woman and her divine offspring to them by them becoming members of their race.

The reason Satan knew and immediately understood that the woman of the protoevangelium was Mary the Mother of the God-man was that he had already encountered that woman. He was forced to confront that woman in the first and second great signs that appeared in the sky on first day of creation.

Eleventh, the hypostatic union of a Divine Person with a created human nature is the most perfect communication of divinity ad extra and gives the greatest possible external glory to the Most Holy Trinity. If the hypostatic union of the Person of the Son with a human nature were decreed only on condition that man sin and that man be redeemed by the Incarnate God-man then the greater would be dependent on the lesser. Then the most extraordinary and most glorious of all God's works in time and eternity would have been decreed dependent on man sinning and man being redeemed by the God-man! Why would God will to make his most extraordinary decree and most extraordinary work for his greatest possible external eternal glory dependent on man sinning or on man being redeemed by the Incarnate God-man?

The principal reason that many do not believe that the Father willed the Incarnation of his Son as the God-man of the race of Adam absolutely is that this truth is not explicitly taught in Scripture nor is it taught in a way that it could easily be deduced from Scripture. The reason is the same reason many other truths implicitly taught in Scripture are not as well known or believed as are truths explicitly taught in Scripture or easily deduced from Scripture. This is the reason the truth that Jesus' death redeemed mankind, explicitly and repeatedly revealed or taught in Scripture is held or believed by all Christians. On the other hand, many truths concerning Mary, such as her Immaculate Conception and her Assumption soul and body into heaven, which are only implicitly revealed or taught in Scripture, are not known or believed by all Christians. They are held and believed by all Catholics because the Magisterium of the Catholic Church has always diligently taught them to Catholics.

The writer of this study has taken the position that the Father absolutely or unconditionally willed the Incarnation of his Son as the God-man of the race of Adam. He has taken that position not because he is a Scotist, but in spite of the fact that he has been trained in the theology of St. Thomas, who apparently held that the Incarnation was conditioned by the fall and redemption of mankind. He has taken the position because of the clear evidence for it in Sacred Scripture, both the Old Testament and especially in the New Testament Scriptures.

That clear evidence in Scripture has apparently gone unnoticed by most theologians and commentators even though it is a definitive answer to what has been for so long a most puzzling question. The principal purpose of this chapter is to conclusively demonstrate from Scripture that the Father did not set the fall and redemption of man or anything else as a condition sine qua non of the Incarnation of his Son as the God-man of the race of Adam. Therefore the Son would have become the God-man of the race of Adam, whether man sinned or did not sin.

THE FATAL FLAW OF ALL PAST ARGUMENTS OPPOSED TO GOD THE FATHER WILLING ABSOLUTELY THE INCARNATION OF HIS SON

Before presenting more explicit evidence from scripture that answers this most puzzling question, it would be very helpful for readers to understand that all the arguments based on tasks the Father imposed on the God-man to be carried out while on earth to prove that the Father willed the Incarnation conditionally, have one fatal flaw. That fatal flaw is that the Incarnate God-man would have been able to fulfill any task imposed on Him by the Father, whether the Father willed his Son's Incarnation conditionally or absolutely except those that couldn't have been imposed unless man sinned. Therefore, any argument, which might attempt to prove from tasks imposed on the Incarnate God-man by the will of the Father, must be fallacious. For this reason any real proof, that the Father willed absolutely or conditionally the Incarnation of his Son, must be based on something other than tasks the Father imposed on the God-man. It must be based on the high priority the Incarnation had in the intention of the Father when commanding the creation of all things.

UNDERSTANDING THE PRIORITY THINGS HAVE IN THE INTENTION OF PERSONS

Since the Son became the God-man and came to earth in obedience to the will of the Father, it will be necessary to review a few particulars about volition and the similarities of human volition to divine volition.

The New Testament manifests that the Incarnation had first or highest priority in the intention of the Father when in the beginning the Father decreed the creation of the universe, the earth, the race of Adam and the eternal supernatural salvation of mankind. From the beginning, the Eternal Father decreed the ultimate in eternal glory and dominion for the God-man and that mankind share in that eternal glory of the God-man.

In this matter of understanding human volition, there must be an understanding of the fact that a person does only those things he plans to do or intends to do and that a person always does things in a certain sequence. A person does things in a certain sequence because of the high priority the person has given to some particular thing he intends to achieve. The first and highest priority a particular thing has in the person's intention is the reason he begins doing things to achieve that thing and also begins doing them in a certain sequence or order.

A person intending to build a new house must give building his new house first and highest priority in his intention otherwise the house will not be built. He understands also that by giving first and highest priority in his intention to building his new house he will begin doing all the things he must do for his house to become a reality. He realizes that he must do things in a certain sequence or order if what has first and highest priority in his intention will be achieved or become a reality.

He understands that having given first and highest priority in his intention to building that house he will begin doing all the things he must do and will begin doing them in a certain sequence or order. The high priority the new house has in the young man's intention causes him to do those things he must do for his new house to become a reality; he begins to arrange for the making of the blue prints of his new house, to select a suitable site on which to build his new house, to allocate funds for contracting with persons for clearing the site and obtaining materials and skilled labor. That first and highest priority will determine indirectly also what the young man will not be doing if those other things are seen as impeding his plans for the construction of his new house.

He does these and many more things in a certain sequence, because he understands that only by doing all of them and doing them in that sequence can his new house become a reality.

The same young man might also intend to become president of the United States and to exercise that office for the good of all. The high priority the office of president has in the young man's intention is the reason he begins doing whatever he thinks will assure him the outcome of being elected to the office of president. He therefore educates himself in a certain way, joins a political party, becomes as active as possible in his party's politics, does outstanding work in every political job or position given to him, and curries the favor of all persons of influence and power.

He plans what to say and do and what not to say and do so he can win for himself the nomination of his political party and the necessary votes in the general election. He studies to project on the public and on voters an image of himself as a person completely competent and deserving of the people's trust and their vote. He does all these things in a certain order, because he understands that doing them and doing them in that order is necessary for winning his party's nomination and the office of president in the general election.

The high priority a person gives to a certain thing in his order of intention is the reason a person commits himself, in his order of execution, to begin doing certain things, doing them in a certain sequence and at set times. The person realizes that only by doing all of them in that way can he achieve what has first and highest priority in his intention.

This young man has had to give one high priority in his intention to constructing his new house and another high priority to being elected resident of the United States. In order for him to begin striving to achieve both high priorities, he must see his striving to achieve those priorities as compatible. If striving to obtain both priorities is seen as incompatible in his life, the young man will then have to choose to give highest priority in his intention to achieving the one he intends to achieve first of all, most of all, and above all or he will have to abandon one entirely.

Incidentally, it is only when a person truly gives first and highest priority to something in his intention that a person becomes truly completely dedicated to that something. A person becomes truly dedicated to God only by giving first and highest priority, without any conditions, in his intention to honoring God, to learning and believing God's revealed truth, to repenting and doing penance for his past sins and doing all the works of God's law of love. Every person is obliged to give this kind of first and highest priority to the service of God or the person has not truly completely dedicated himself to God. A saint is a person who has dedicated himself to God by having the intention of doing God's will first of all, most of all, above all and without any conditions. It is this kind of self-dedication or consecration that all persons are obliged to make of themselves in the service of God and in the hope of achieving sanctity.

From the above examples of how human volition works it is obvious that knowing what has first and highest priority in another person's order of intention, one can know and predict what things and in what order another person will be doing things in his order of execution. Knowing another's order of intention is to know in advance what that person's order of execution will be. Knowing what another person holds in highest priority in his intention reveals what the persons will be doing, what order he will be doing things and when he will be doing them. Conversely, by observing what things a person is doing in his order of execution, the sequence in which he does them and when he does them, it is possible to determine with certainty what has first and highest priority in that person's order of intention.

Finally, in this matter of volition it is important to note that the priority something has in a person's order of intention is reversed in that person's order of execution. There is a philosophical principle, which states: What is first in the order of intention is last in the order of execution. This principle of volition too can be understood best by illustrations.

The person, who has given first and highest priority in his order of intention to building a new house for himself for the purpose of living in it, does not begin in his order of execution by immediately beginning the work of constructing his new house. He begins his order of execution by doing those things that need to be done before he can begin the work of actually constructing his new house. He doesn't begin by getting ready to paint. He begins by drawing up blue prints, selecting and buying a desirable site or lot, allocating necessary funds for buying the lot and contracting with persons to clear the ground and obtaining the materials and skilled labor needed for construction of his new house. Last of all, in his order of execution, he begins the actual construction and painting his new house. On its completion, he furnishes it and begins living in it. In this illustration, living in his new house, although it was desired first of all in the person's order of intention, is last in his order of execution.

God too in doing anything ad extra must give first and highest priority in his intention to some particular thing. God the Father gave first and highest priority in his intention to incarnating his Son as the God-man of the race of Adam when creating the universe and all things in the universe. God committed Himself to doing things in a certain sequence and at certain times in his order of execution, so that He could achieve what had first and highest priority in his intention, namely the Incarnation of his Son as the God-man of Adam's race. Genesis' account of creation gives God's executive order of creation.

The first and highest priority God the Father gave to incarnating his Son as the God-man of the race of Adam is the reason God the Father began doing things in his order of execution. He began by first creating the universe. He created the heavens, the earth then Adam and Eve and finally incarnated his Son the God-man of the race of Adam by his Son's conception and birth from a particular woman of the race of Adam.

Our young man willed the completion of his new house absolutely or unconditionally. Anything a person wills first of all and with the highest priority is not willed conditionally to other things. Hence, if the Incarnation of the Son had first and highest priority in the intention of the Father when creating all things the Father did not will the Incarnation on any condition. Hence not on the condition of man's fall from grace and not on man needing redemption by the God-man.

The only thing that needs to be shown to prove that the Father willed the Incarnation unconditionally or absolutely is that the Incarnation had first or highest priority in the intention of the Father when the Father created the universe, the heavens and the earth and Adam and Eve. The Incarnation had that first and highest priority in the intention of the Father if the universe, the heavens and the earth and the race of Adam were created by the Father in preparation for the Incarnation of his Son as the God-man of the race of Adam.

IN SCRIPTURE THE INCARNATION HAS FIRST AND HIGHEST PRIORITY IN THE INTENTION OF GOD THE FATHER

There are two texts of Scripture in particular, which most explicitly deal with the order things had in the intention of the Father when creating all things. These texts teach that God the Father gave first and highest priority in his intention to incarnating his Son as the God-man of the race of Adam. These texts declare that the God-man and his eternal glorification were the Father's reason or motive for creating all things and for doing everything God the Father has ever done and intends doing ad extra. These texts therefore teach that the Incarnation was not conditioned or made dependent on man sinning or on the God-man redeeming mankind.

The first of these texts is from the prologue of St. John's gospel. St. John begins with the declaration: "In the beginning was the Word; the Word was in God's presence, and the Word was God. He was present to God in the beginning. Through him all things came into being, and apart from him nothing came to be." Jn 1:1-4.

Here St. John is teaching that the Word was first in the line or at the beginning of all things in the Father's order of intention. The Word obviously was not first in God's order of execution but first in his order of intention. The Incarnation was not the first thing God did ad extra. Hence St. John is saying the Word was in the beginning. The Word had first and highest priority in the intention of the Father. Hence he can say that it was through the Word, which is the Father's mental image of the God-man, that all things came to be and apart from Him nothing came to be. The only way all things could have come to be through the Word or the Father's mental image of the God-man would be for the Word or the image of the God-man to be the final cause of the creation of all things. The only way a non-existing thing, the pre-incarnate God-man, can cause anything is by it being a final cause. For a final cause to be the cause of anything it need exist only as the object of desire in the will of a person. The only way something in the intention of the Father could be the efficient cause of all creation is for it to have first and highest priority in the intention of the Father who is the moral efficacious cause of everything ad extra.

What is first in the order of intention is last in the order of execution. The fact that the Incarnation was the last thing in God the Father's planned order of execution means it was first in the Father's order of intention and had highest priority in the Father's order of intention. "Apart from Him nothing came to be" implies that the Incarnation of the Father's Son had first and highest priority in the intention of the Father.

If the Word, the image of the God-man, did not have first and highest priority in the Father's intention, then things, if they came into existence, would have come into existence apart from the Word, the Father's mental image of the God-man. But St. John explicitly states the contrary by writing, "apart from him nothing came to be." How would it be possible for everything to owe its existence to the Word or the image of the God-man if the Word or the image of the God-man did not have first and highest priority in the intention of the Father at the Father's creation of all things? Only by the Word being the final cause in the Father's intention to create everything?

Since the Word cannot be the efficient cause of the creation of all things, all things could owe their existence to the Word, the Father's mental image of the God-man only by the Word or the image of the God-man having first and highest priority in the intention of the Father when the Father ordered the creation of all things. For the Word to be the cause of the creation of all things and of everything God does ad extra, the Word would have be the final cause of the creation of all things and everything God does ad extra.

The second text is in St. Paul's letter to the Colossians. There St. Paul also teaches that in the Father's intention for achieving his Son's Incarnation as the God-man of the race of Adam, the incarnate God-man was the cause of everything coming into being and for everything continuing in existence. He wrote, "He is the image of the invisible God, the first-born of all creatures. In him everything in heaven and on earth was created, things visible and invisible, whether thrones or dominations, principalities or powers; all were created through him, and for him. He is before all else that is. In him everything continues in being." Col 1:15-18.

Here St. Paul is explicitly teaching that achieving his Son's Incarnation as the God-man of the race of Adam the Father caused the creation of everything through the God-man. The Father could do that only by the Incarnation having first and highest priority in the Father's order of intention. St. Paul declares: "He [Jesus Christ] is before all else that is." Col 1:17. By saying, "Jesus Christ is before all else that is" St. Paul certainly did not intend to say that the God-man, the Incarnate Son of God, the God-man of the race of Adam, existed before all else that is. This before all else must mean before all else in the intention of the Father, for He certainly was not before all else in the Father's order of execution.

Moreover St. Paul wrote elsewhere that Jesus Christ became man in the fullness of time. That fullness of time was obviously long after the heaven and the earth were created in the beginning. What is first in the order of a person's intention is always last in the person's order of execution.

Because the God-man had first and highest priority in the intention of the Father, St. Paul, like St. John can teach that the God-man was the reason or the final cause not the efficient cause of everything coming into existence. He was the cause of everything coming into existence by being the final cause of the creation of all things. The God-man could be the final cause of all things only if He had first and highest priority in the intention of the Father at the creation of all things. For the God-man, like anything else that would have had first and highest priority in the Father's intention would be the final cause of the Father creating the heavens and the earth.

Here St. Paul besides insisting that the God-man is the final cause of the creation of all things insists that the God-man is the final cause also of all things continuing in existence. "In him everything continues in being". Col 1:17.

There is still a third text that teaches but not so explicitly that the Father created all things to incarnate his Son as the God-man of the race of Adam. "In times past, God spoke in fragmentary and varied ways to our father through the prophets; in this, the final age, he has spoken to us through his Son, whom he has made heir of all things and through whom he first created the universe." Heb 1:1.

These apostles can declare that all things were created or came to be through him, the God-man, because they understood that the God-man was the only and complete final cause of all creation. They understood that the reason the Father commanded the creation of the universe and everything in it was that his Son might become the God-man of the race of Adam by being conceived and born of a woman of that race of humans on the earth. To incarnate his Son in this way the universe had to be created and a race of human be created and continue to exist on this earth at least until the God-man would be born. Also all things would continue to exist forever for the God-man is the final cause of all things continuing in existence.

Some may be led to ask, how could the Incarnate God-man be the final cause of creation, when the God-man had not yet become a reality at the time of the creation of the heavens and the earth? Do not causes have to exist in order to be the cause of anything? That is absolutely true of every kind of causality except final causality. The being that is the final cause in order to be a final cause needs to exist merely as an object of desire in the will and intention of the person who is the moral efficient cause of something.

Thus the Incarnation of the Father's Son as the God-man of the race of Adam was the first incentive and object of everything God the Father has ever done and continues to do ad extra. The Incarnation of the Son was that on account of which the divine intelligence and will ventured outside themselves into the realm of the ad extra, into creation.

The only reality ad extra God the Father has ever willed for its own sake has been the Incarnation of his Son. Everything the Father has ever willed was willed either as a means to incarnating his Son or as a means to the God-man's perfect eternal glorification. For the Father has made his First-born, the God-man, heir to all things and the Supreme Head of all creation forever.

The priority the God-man had in the Father's order of intention had been God's secret until God revealed it. God revealed this specific secret or mystery to St. Paul. St. Paul fittingly calls this secret the mystery of Christ. After God revealed this mystery to him, St. Paul could not be more insistent on preaching this mystery to others until they understand it fully. He wrote: "God has given us the wisdom to understand fully the mystery, the plan he was pleased to decree in Christ." Eph 1:9. "God's secret plan as I have briefly described it was revealed. When you read what I have said, you will realize that I know what I am talking about in speaking of the mystery of Christ, unknown to men in former ages but now revealed by the Spirit to the holy apostles and prophets." Eph 3:3-5. "I became a minister of this church through the commission God gave me to preach among you his word in its fullness, that mystery hidden from ages and generations past but now revealed to his holy ones. God has willed to make known to them the glory beyond price which this mystery brings to the Gentiles—the mystery of Christ in you, your hope of glory." Col 1:25-27. The mystery of Christ "in whom every of treasure of wisdom and knowledge is hidden" Col 2:3. Cf. Col 1:5-9.

When St. Paul understood that the Incarnation of the Son as the God-man and the God-man's perfect glorification had first and highest priority in the Father's order of intention, he understood immediately how true it would be to say that the Father created all things in, through and for the God-man. St. Paul understood that the Incarnation was the final cause of everything that has ever occurred or will ever occur in God's order of execution.

There are other texts in the New Testament, which teach that the Incarnation had first or highest priority in the intention of the Father at the creation of all things, but they do so only implicitly. They imply that the creation and the continued existence of all things depend on the Word or the Incarnate God-man. "For from him through him and for him all things are. To him be glory forever. Amen." Rom 11:36. "Whom he has made heir of all things and through whom he first created the universe." Heb 1:2. "This is what we proclaim to you: what [Jesus Christ] was from the beginning [first in the Father's intention], what we have heard, what we have seen with our eyes, what we have looked upon and our hands have touched." 1 Jn 1:1. "For us there is one God, the Father, from whom all things come and for whom we live; and one Lord Jesus Christ through whom everything was made and through whom we live." 1 Cor 8:6.

In the Book of Revelation Jesus gave St. John a wonderful play on words which is based on the difference between these orders: "I am the Alpha [in the order of intention] and the Omega [in the order of execution], the First and the Last, the Beginning and the End!" Rev 22:13.

There are many texts written by St. Paul about what God has done for man and has in store for man that are quite unintelligible. Unintelligible unless they are read with the understanding that whatever the Father willed to create or wills to continue doing in the present or in future is always willed by Him either in view of the Incarnation of his Son or for the sake of the God-man's eternal glorification. That perfect glorification of the God-man is the God-man's absolute fullness, his perfection as the God-man, his Supreme Headship over all creation and the God-man's destiny to share his life in friendship with the eternally saved in heaven.

As an example of one such unintelligible portion of Scripture, one might sight this lengthy passage from Ephesians: "Praised be the God and Father of our Lord Jesus Christ, who has bestowed on us in Christ every spiritual blessing in the heavens! God chose us in him before the world began, to be holy and blameless in his sight, to be full of love; he likewise predestined us through Christ Jesus to be his adopted sons—such was his will and pleasure—that all might praise the glorious favor he has bestowed on us in his beloved. [After the sin of man] it is in Christ and through his blood that we have been redeemed and our sins forgive, so immeasurably generous is God's favor to us. God has given us the wisdom to understand fully the mystery, the plan he was pleased to decree in Christ, to be carried out in the fullness of time: namely, to bring all things in the heavens and on earth into one under Christ's Headship. In him we were chosen; for in the decree of God, who administers everything according to his will and counsel, we were predestined to praise his glory by being the first to hope in Christ." Eph 1:3-12. "Though he was in the form of God, he did not deem equality with God something to be grasped at. Rather, he emptied himself and took the form of a slave being born in the likeness of men. He was known to be of human estate, and it was thus the he humbled himself, obediently accepting even death, death on a cross! Because of this, God highly exalted him and bestowed on him the name above every other name, so that at Jesus' name every knee must bend in heaven, on earth, and under the earth, and every tongue proclaim to the glory of God the Father: JESUS CHRIST IS LORD." Phil 2:6-11. Read Col 1:11-20; Heb 1:3 to 3:6; 1 Cor 2:16 with the same purpose in mind.

That the Father now and in the endless ages of eternity to come will delight to do all things in, through and for his Incarnate Son is best seen in a text from St. Paul. In that text Paul teaches that God the Father will keep on keeping things in existence forever for the glory of the God-man. "In him everything continues in being." Col 1:17.

In addition to these texts from the New Testament, there are the Old Testament texts. In particular there is the protoevangelium, which implicitly reveals that the Incarnation was willed absolutely by God before the fall of man. With the benefit of the hindsight offered by the New Testament, we are able to see clearly from the protoevangelium that the Incarnation had already been revealed to Adam and Eve before they sinned. Hence the Father's decreeing of the Incarnation could not have been conditioned by man sinning and by man's need for redemption by the Incarnate God-man.

The protoevangelium has been unwittingly and almost invariably interpreted to mean that at the fall of man from grace the Father for the first time formed his intention to incarnate his Son as the God-man and then promulgated the protoevangelium with its promise of redemption. The obvious fact is that a careful reading of the protoevangelium, proclaimed immediately after the fall of man from grace, does not contain a promise to incarnate the Son as the God-man nor a promise to send the woman and her offspring as is supposed by many.

The protoevangelium by promising, "I will put enmity between you and the woman and between her offspring and your offspring" explicitly promises nothing more than to place enmity between the woman and Satan and between the offspring of the woman and the offspring of Satan. These promises fall far short of a promise of God to incarnate his Son as the God-man.

Clearly by this protoevangelium God intended to establish the woman in her role of chief adversary of Satan and to establish her offspring, the God-man, in his new role of redeemer of mankind. Thus the protoevangelium indicated at the time of its proclamation that the Father had already revealed to Adam and Eve the coming Incarnation of his Son as the God-man of their race. This is indicated by the absolute silence of Adam and Eve regarding the identity of the woman and her offspring on hearing of the woman and her offspring. Their silence forcefully suggests, in the complete absence of any request to know their identity, that Adam and Eve already knew the identity of this woman and of her offspring. They would have learned of them by a special revelation of God, for those persons were to be the two most exalted personages that would ever be born to their race. Why should God have keep from Adam and Eve knowledge of this most glorious Mother and Queen and that she would be the Mother of the Incarnate Son of God. Knowledge of them would have been a very special joy to Adam and Eve even before their fall from grace.

Perhaps it was during one of the earliest of God's routine visits to Adam and Eve in the Garden Paradise at the breezy time of the day that God revealed to them his intention of incarnating his Son as the God-man through his conception and birth from a woman of their race. That early revelation of the woman and her offspring made it easy for the fallen Adam and Eve to believe what God had just promised in the protoevangelium. The proclamation of the protoevangelium, immediately after Adam and Eve fell from grace, gave Adam and Eve, in spite of their serious offence to God, great assurance of God's willingness to forgive them and of God's faithfulness to his promises. These routine visits and God's revelation to Adam and Eve of his promise to incarnate his Son suggests that God would continue his routine visits to Adam and Eve and their descendents in Paradise until the actual Incarnation of the Son as the God-man of their race.

It should be carefully noted that the protoevangelium foresaw more than the newly decreed role of redeemer for the offspring of the woman, for it also gave the woman the special role of invincible adversary of Satan in the defense of the Church and mankind. In that role the woman will crush the head of Satan. This crushing of the head of Satan must not be equated with redemption, as the Greek translation of the protoevangelium would seem to do.

All the angels saw the great sign in sky on the first day of creation. The identity of the woman and of her offspring who appeared in the first great sign was obvious to them. The angels understood the purposes of the first sign, for immediately after its appearance a majority of the angels consecrated themselves by an unconditional commitment of submission and eternal service to the offspring of the woman, the Incarnate God-man, King of kings and Lord of lords. They understood also that they owed a similar commitment to his Mother, the Queen of the Universe.

Satan and his crowd of rebellious angels refused to make this consecration of themselves to their King and to their Queen. The rebellion of these fallen angels was a most serious sin and God immediately ordered the faithful angels to forever evict them from their places in heaven.

ST. PAUL CONTRASTS THE GOSPEL OF GOD WITH GOSPELS OF THE WORLD, OF THE NEW AGE OF MAN, OF THE FALSE RELIGIONS AND OF ATHEISM

St. Paul saw in the absolute fullness of Christ a limitless treasure for man—the treasure of the unfathomable riches of Christ's inheritance, an unlimited inheritance because it is limited only by the unlimited almighty of power of God. He saw in it the source of every good, great consolation and of limitless hope for all fallen mankind. "To me... was given the grace to preach...the unfathomable riches of Christ and to enlighten all men on the mysterious design which for ages was hidden in God [the Father], the Creator of all things." Eph 3:8-9. cf. Rom 16:25. "There is, to be sure, a certain wisdom which we express among the spiritually mature. It is not a wisdom of this age, however, not of the rulers of this age, who are men headed for destruction. No, what we utter is God's wisdom: a mysterious, a hidden wisdom. God planned it before all ages for our glory. None of the rulers of this age knew the mystery [of Christ]; if they had known it, they would never have crucified the Lord of glory. Of this wisdom [of the unfathomable riches of Christ man's sharing in the fullness of Christ] it is written: 'Eye has not seen, ear has not heard, nor has it so much as dawned on man what God has prepared for those who love him.' Yet God has revealed this wisdom to us through the Spirit." 1 Cor 2:6-10. Cf. Eph 1:9; 3:3.

What makes the true Christian gospel an overwhelmingly good for mankind is its predestination of mankind to sharing in the eternal absolute fullness of Christ, the benevolence of what is limithless. Man's share in the absolute fullness of Christ is man's sharing fully in the unfathomable riches of Christ's inheritance as the Almighty Father's First-born. The gospel is a great mystery and only its proclamation, accurate interpretation and understanding can enlighten all men concerning the most gracious designs of God the Father for everyone of Adam's race. Knowledge of that mysterious gospel, which for ages it was hidden in God but revealed to Paul, brought comfort to St. Paul in all his concerns for others. He wrote: "I wish their hearts to be closely united in love, enriched with full assurance by their knowledge of the mystery of God—namely Christ—in whom every treasure of wisdom and knowledge is hidden." Col 2:2-3. Cf. Rom 16:25-27; 2 Cor 4:4.

Clearly those who promote Christianity as a religion or a faith that has some positive good news for mankind are not promoting true Christianity. Those who preach the kind of Christianity that has for its goal the fulfillment of the self of every individual or that merely fosters ever greater temporal benefits for individuals and for mankind in general are promoting the religion of the age, the religion of the rulers of this age, the religion that attempts to reconcile the desires persons have for all the world can offer and the urges of the flesh with God's plan and intention for the supernatural salvation of mankind. Such a christianity worships man as god. It even worships the environment of men and even evil spirits. These promote a religion that worships "Mother Nature or Mother Earth". She is mankind's only true best friend and benefactor while it ignores that wicket "Father Time" who despoils everyone of everything Mother Nature has given them.

The greatest frustration of the promoters of that kind of christianity is their gospel's inability to move the powerful and the wealthy to generously or sacrificially share their wealth and power with the most needy. Their kind of christianity has adopted the theology of liberation and the worship of the god of every satisfaction. Many of its duped followers do their best to preach peace while at times doing their best to carry on violent revolution to force their dreams on everyone. These profess to have the greatest love for all mankind but cannot stand individuals. No one could be more headed for destruction then these, for "Wisdom like this does not come from above. It is earthbound, a kind of animal, even devilish, cunning." Jas 3:15. "Their glory is in their shame." Phil 3:19. These proclaim the deceitful fictions of Satan and the darkness of men seeking only personal satisfaction.

Their gospel cannot compare with the gospel story for mankind. Cf. Gal 1:1-9. The true gospel comes from above, it is the revealed mystery of the unfathomable riches of Christ and assures everyone of what, "Eye has not seen, ear has not heard, nor has it so much as dawned on man what God has prepared for those who love him." 1 Cor 2:9.

THE MYSTERY OF CHRIST AND CHRIST'S ABSOLUTE FULLNESS

St. Paul often dwells on the mystery of Christ and the fullness or the absolute fullness of Christ. This mystery of Christ is the Almighty Father's eternal plan and decrees, made before the world began, that gave first and highest priority to incarnating his Son as the most glorious God-man of the race of Adam. The mystery of Christ includes the mystery of the fullness of Christ. What is the fullness of Christ? It is the Father's plan to establish the God-man in a transcendent human condition at his Incarnation and later establish the God-man eternally in a state of ultimate perfection and glory, in the eternal state or condition of Supreme Head of all creation ruling and reigning supremely at the right hand of the Father.

The secret plan of the Father for the absolute fullness of Christ includes granting Him at his Incarnation a marvelously transcendent Sacred Human Nature, the perfection of every natural, preternatural and supernatural gift; his body, soul, and human mind in a state as perfect as possible. His human intellect would be a treasure of all knowledge, all sciences and all arts. His human will a paragon of all the virtues especially charity. In addition to granting Him a marvelously transcendent Sacred Humanity, the Father planed that the God-man in his absolute fullness would be forever at the summit of communion and fellowship with all men and angels.

This mystery of the absolute fullness of Christ is the end result of the Father having decreed the most and the best of everything for the God-man as his First-born, the heir of all things, the Supreme Head of all creation, the King of kings and Lord of lords.

In that decree for the absolute fullness of Christ the Father destined men to be forever close to Christ's throne and that the God-man be in constant friendship and fellowship with all his brethren. "This fellowship of ours is with the Father and with his Son, Jesus Christ." 1 Jn 1:3. The Father always intended to give his Only Begotten, the God-man, an inheritance of unfathomable riches that can be measure only by the almighty power and infinite generosity of the Father for his First-born who will be sharing all his treasures with his brethren. The Almighty Father has promised the God-man, "The Lord said to me, 'You are my son; this day I have begotten you. Ask of me and I will give you the nations for an inheritance and the ends of the earth for your possession"'. Psalm 2:7-8.

Scripture reveals that it is the intention of the Father all men become coheirs to the absolute fullness of Christ, coheirs sharing fully in the unfathomable riches of Christ's inheritance as the First-born of his Almighty Father. Cf. Eph 3:6-8. "Yours is a share of this fullness, in him who is the head of every principality and power." Col 2:9-10. "Of his fullness we all have had a share." Jn 1:16. St. Paul understood that by men sharing in the absolute fullness of Christ, men would bring to completion Christ's absolute fullness. "In his own flesh he abolished the law... to create in himself one new man formed from us." Eph 2:15. "Till we become one... and form that perfect man who is Christ come to full statue." Eph 4:13.

St. Paul was overjoyed to know not only of his own sharing in the unfathomable riches of Christ, but also to have been chosen by God to proclaim this most marvelous good news of God to all men. "To me... was given the grace to preach...the unfathomable riches of Christ and to enlighten all men on the mysterious design which for ages was hidden in God [the Father], the Creator of all things." Eph 3:8-9. "No, what we utter is God's wisdom: a mysterious, a hidden wisdom. God planned it before all ages for our glory. None of the rulers of this age knew the mystery; if they had they would not have crucified the Lord of Glory." 1 Cor 2:7-8. Paul's joy and enthusiasm to proclaim such great good news that, as some modern scholars of the New Testament Koine Greek point out, St. Paul in his exuberance to more effectively preach the gospel intentionally violates the grammatical rules of Koine Greek.

However, these scholars fail to manifest what was the reason for Paul's unbounded exuberance. They say of Paul's preaching and writing that Jesus loved us to the extent of giving his life for our redemption.

They are not aware that the great mystery of the gospel which St. Paul preached is the great mystery of the Father intending to incarnate his Son in absolute fullness, enriched with the unfathomable riches of an eternal inheritance of his Father's infinite generosity and almighty power, and that his Father has destined all men to be coheirs in the Son's inheritance of unfathomable riches. That the Almighty Father is willing to use his almighty power to do everything and anything to add to the riches of the inheritance his First-born has and will share with his coheirs, his brethren.

ST. PAUL DETAILS FOR US THE REASONS FOR OUR SHARING IN THE UNFATHOMABLE RICHES OF CHRIST'S INHERITANCE

Because St. Paul was overjoyed to proclaim the good news of the gospel of God or of Jesus Christ he could not refrain from detailing for man as best he could the many different things the Father has done for man through, in, and for Christ. St. Paul taught that the Father chose, called, decreed, predestined, created, redeemed, saved, reconciled, justified, sanctified, gave inheritance brought to life and raised men from the dead in Christ, through Christ and for Christ. Here are some texts, which detail in part what the Father decreed and has done for man in, through and for Christ.

From the beginning the Father decreed the creation and continuous existence of everything in Christ, the God-man. "In him [Jesus Christ] everything in heaven and on earth was created, things visible and invisible, whether thrones or dominations, principalities or powers; all were created through him and for him. He is before all else that is. In him everything continues in being." Col 1:16-17.

Before the world began the Father decreed that every blessing and gift mankind would be receiving be given in and through God-man. "Praised be the God and Father of our Lord Jesus Christ, who has bestowed on us in Christ every spiritual blessing in the heavens! God chose us in him before the world began, to holy and blameless in his sight, to be full of love; he likewise predestined us through Christ Jesus to be his adopted sons—such was his will and pleasure—that all might praise the glorious favor he has bestowed on us in his beloved [from the fullness of Christ]." Eph 1:3-6.

From the beginning the Father chose mankind for blessedness in the God-man. "God chose us in him, before the world began, to be holy and blameless in his sight, to be full of love." Eph 1:4. "I continually thank my God for you because of the favor he has bestowed on you in Christ Jesus, in whom you have been richly endowed with every gift of speech and knowledge." 1 Cor 1:4-6. "In him we were chosen; for in the decree of God... we were predestined to praise his glory... In him you too were chosen; when you heard the glad tidings of salvation." Eph 1:11-13.

From the beginning the Father predestined mankind for adoption in and through Christ Jesus, the God-man. "He [the Almighty Father] predestined us through Christ Jesus to be his adopted sons—such was his will and pleasure—that all might praise the glorious favor he has bestowed on us in his beloved." Eph 1:5-6.

From the beginning the Father called mankind to holiness in Christ Jesus, the God-man. "God has saved us and has called us to a holy life, not because of any merits of ours but according to his own design—the grace [the Father] held out to us in Christ Jesus before the world began." 2 Tm 1:9. "God it is who has given you [eternal] life in Christ Jesus." Eph 3:18. "God is faithful, and it was he who called you to fellowship with his Son, Jesus Christ our Lord." 1 Cor 1:9. "I continually thank my God for you because of the favor he has bestowed on you in Christ Jesus, in whom you have been richly endowed with every gift of speech and knowledge. Likewise, the witness I bore to Christ has been so confirmed among you that you lack no spiritual gift as you wait for the revelation of our Lord Jesus Christ. He will strengthen you to the end, so that you will be blameless on the day of our Lord Jesus [Christ]. God is faithful, and it was he who called you to fellowship with his Son, Jesus Christ our Lord." 1 Cor 1:4-9.

In Jesus Christ, the God-man, all men were chosen by the Father, "For in the decree of God, who administers everything according to his will and counsel, we [Jews] were predestined to praise his glory by being the first to hope in Christ. In him you [Gentiles] too were chosen [and predestined]; when you heard the glad tidings of salvation, the word of truth, and believed in it." Eph 1:11-13. "It is in Christ and through his blood that we have been redeemed and our sins forgiven, so immeasurably generous is God's favor to us. God has given us the wisdom to understand fully the mystery, the plan he was pleased to decree in Christ, to be carried out in the fullness of time: namely, to bring all things in the heavens and on earth into one under Christ's Headship." Eph 1:3-10.

The Father decreed that fallen mankind be saved in Christ, the God-man. "God has saved us and has called us to a holy life, not because of any merit of ours but according to his own design—the grace held out to us in Christ Jesus before the world began." 2 Tm 1:9. "It is in Christ and through his blood that we have been redeemed and our sins forgiven, so immeasurably generous is God's favor to us." Eph 1:7. "He has made him our wisdom and also our justice, our sanctification and our redemption." Eph 3:18.

The Father decreed that fallen man achieve reconciliation and salvation in Christ, the God-man. "[Colossians], you yourselves were once alienated from him; you nourished hostility in your hearts because of your evil deeds. But now [according the Father's plan] Christ has achieved reconciliation for you in his mortal body by dying [for your sins], so as to present you to God [the Father] holy, free of reproach and blame. However [according to the plan of the Father] you must hold fast to faith, be firmly grounded and steadfast in it, unshaken in the hope promised you by the gospel you have heard. It is the gospel which has been announced to every creature under heaven [to all men], and I, Paul, an its servant." Col 1:16-23.

MARY'S UNIQUE FULLNESS IS LIKE THE FULLNESS OF CHRIST

Through the laws of nature and of nature's God we know that a transcendent God-man needs to be born of a transcendent human mother. The God-man in his fullness needs to be born of a mother with a like fullness. Therefore the Father predestined Mary, the Mother of the God-man, to a particular fullness of Christ at her conception and birth; the same fullness the God-man would have at his conception and birth. The fullness of the God-man would have at his conception and birth was that mirrored in a particular "our image likeness", the mental model God the Father chose to use for the conception and birth of the God-man.

The Father had many different "our image likeness" of his Son, the God-man. One "our image likeness" for each of the possible special states or conditions the God-man could have at his conception and birth and of the various stages in his human development and of the special missions of the God-man. The Father used one such "our image likeness" of the God-man as his working model when creating Adam and Eve. It was the "our image likeness" God would use as his working model in the Incarnation of his Son, if Adam did not sin. A second "our image likeness" was that of Christ emptied of his fullness. A third was the "our image likeness" the Father had of the absolute fullness of Christ, the God-man, in his eternal ultimate perfection and glorification at his right hand in heaven.

The Father had at least another set of three similar "our image likeness" of the God-man. This set of "our image likeness" the Father would use as his working model for making Mary a suitable Mother of the God-man. One from the set for each of the two possible states or conditions Mary might have at her conception and birth. These corresponded to the two similar states or conditions of the God-man at his conception and birth.

From all eternity the Father gazed with greatest predilection on Mary and chose to make her the masterpiece of all his works. The Father rejoiced to see in Mary his most perfect communication of divinity and glory to a creature. The Son chose Mary to be his Mother and rejoiced to have his Mother at his side and sharing with her forever his royal throne and universal power over all creation. The Holy Spirit united Himself to Mary with the bond of spousal love and rejoiced in his Spouse exalted forever above all creatures in heaven and on earth.

From all eternity Mary, like her Son, was predestined to reign forever. For she was predestined to be Queen of the Universe with her Son as King of the Universe. In her Divine Maternity and Queenship, Mary was always destined to share in the specific fullness of Christ at her conception in her Immaculate Conception and in the absolute fullness of Christ as the glorious Queen of heaven and earth.

We, her children, should be moved with joy at Mary's most special chrisms of holiness and purity, mercy and tenderness, glory and charity. In the plan of God the Father the Mother of the Incarnate Son of God was to be given every perfection, grace, and favor that an all knowing, loving, and almighty Father and Son could deposit in her human nature and person. She was destined to possess holiness to the fullness extent possible to a human nature and person. Hence the honor and respect every creature owns Mary is so great that the only mistake possible would be to give her divine honor.

God the Father predestined Adam and Eve to existence on this earth and chose a particular "our image likeness" of the God-man as his working model in the creation of Adam and Eve. In just the same way the Father and the Son chose a particular "our image likeness" of the God-man as their working model in the conception and birth of the Mother of the God-man. In this way God fashioned Mary's humanity and her divinity by grace after that of the Most Sacred Humanity of her Son in his holiness. Every created grace of the humanity of Jesus Christ was to grace the humanity and person of his most pure and Immaculate Mother.

The Father absolutely or unconditionally predestined his Son to become incarnate as the eternal God-man and to be born of a woman of the race of Adam. However the Father predestined Him only conditionally to an incarnation according to a particular "our image likeness" with its specific fullness.

Mary was absolutely or unconditionally predestined to existence and to being conceived and born of a woman of the race of Adam, but her predestination to a specific fullness of Christ was conditional. The Father intended that the God-man be conceived and born with a specific fullness or emptiness and that He be born of a woman of the race of Adam with the same specific fullness or emptiness as that of the God-man. That implies that there be created a race of humans of the same specific condition of fullness as that of the God-man. For the laws of nature and of nature's God require that the God-man be conceive and born of a woman having the same specific likeness or fullness as the God-man. That is what was in expectation and in preparation when the Father created Adam and Eve in accord with a specific "our image likeness", the Father's exact idea of a specific fullness of the God-man.

However, the creation of Adam and Eve in the likeness of a specific fullness of Christ would make only Adam and Eve share in that specific fullness of Christ. So God the Father further intended that all the descendants of Adam and Eve have the same specific fullness of Christ as Adam and Eve and that their descendants be created according to that same specific fullness that also corresponds to an "our image likeness" of the God-man.

For that reason God made a creation covenant with Adam, the progenitor of his entire race. Made a covenant that would be the means by which all persons of the entire race of Adam and Eve would have rights to the same specific fullness of the God-man which Adam and Eve had at their creation. This creation covenant was designed to give all the descendants of Adam and Eve the right to a conception and birth that made them shares in a specific fullness of Christ.

The Father's master plan for the God-man was a plan that would produce a genetic oneness of the transcendent God-man with a whole race of transcendent humans. According to that plan the whole race of humans including its God-man would descend from one man and one woman. A race and a family of such oneness could not be formed, unless the entire race and family, including its God-man, had been born from the same pair of progenitors.

The transcendent race of Adam and Eve along with the transcendent God-man were destined to be of such perfection and unity that all men would form one perfect man, all men come to full stature in the absolute fullness of Christ. "Till we become one...and form that perfect man who is Christ come to full stature." Eph 4:13. "This is the Christ we proclaim... hoping to make every man complete in Christ." Col 1:28. "To create in Christ one new man from us." Eph 2:15. "It pleased God to make absolute fullness reside in him." Col 1:19. "In Christ the fullness of the deity resides in bodily form. Yours is a share of this fullness, in him who is the head of every principality and power." Col 2:9-10. "He has put all things under Christ's feet and has made him thus exalted, head of the church, which is his body: the fullness of him who fills the universe in all its parts." Eph 1:22-23.

According to the plan of the Father every person of the race of Adam was to have the honor and dignity of belonging to the one family of man, which would include the God-man. A family in which God the Father is father of all, Mary, the Mother of the God-man and the spiritual mother of all, and all persons true genetic brothers or sisters of the God-man, Jesus Christ. Every person could then rejoice in the image of himself or herself as a true genetic brother or sister of the Incarnate God-man.

WHY JESUS EMPTIED HIMSELF? OF WHAT DID HE EMPTY HIMSELF?

The Father willed absolutely the Incarnation of his Son but that must not be understood to imply that the Father willed absolutely a particular condition for the God-man at his Incarnation. The Father intended that the Most Sacred Humanity of the God-man at his Incarnation be in one state or condition if man did not sin, and in a less perfect or in an emptied condition if man sinned. It was not the will of the Father in any case to incarnate the God-man in the absolute fullness of the glorified state or condition the God-man would have at the right hand of the Almighty Father and ruling as King of kings and Lord of lords.

If man sinned or did not sin both the God-man and his Mother would be conceived and born in a like specific fullness of the God-man. If man sinned, both the God-man and his mother would have the same condition of emptiness at their conceptions and births. The Son was incarnated in accord with the Father's "our image likeness" of Christ emptied of preternatural fullness. If man sinned, Jesus Christ would willingly empty Himself of his fullness to become the suffering servant of God in order to redeem mankind. "Rather, he emptied himself and took the form of a slave being born in the likeness of men." Phil 2:7.

As a remedy for Adam's and man's lost share in the greater fullness of Christ, their original innocence, God the Father decreed that only supernatural gifts be returned to men at their reconciliation with Him. That reconciliation of man with the Father and the restoration of the supernatural were merited by Christ in his redemption of mankind. The God-man would manifest by his Sacred Passion and Death that He was God's suffering servant. The Son's Sacred Passion and Death required that the Son, at his Incarnation, take on Himself a human condition in which He would be capable of redeeming mankind by being capable of suffering and dying. The God-man would be capable of suffering and dying if He emptied himself of his preternatural fullness.

The willingness of the God-man to be conceived and born without his fullness is what St. Paul means by Jesus Christ emptying himself. At his Incarnation Jesus did not empty Himself of his divinity or his humanity, but emptied his Sacred Humanity of its fullness by assuming a Sacred Humanity that was minus the transcendent qualities of that fullness in which Adam and Eve were created. "He emptied himself and took the form of a slave, being born in the likeness of men. He was known to be of human estate, and it was thus that he humbled himself, obediently accepting even death, death of a cross!" Phil 2:7-8. "It is in Christ and through his blood that we have been redeemed and our sins forgiven, so immeasurably generous is God's favor to us." Eph 1:7-8. "Just as through one man's disobedience all became sinners, so through one man's obedience all shall become just." Rom 5:19. "Those whom he foreknew he predestined to share the image of his Son, that the Son might be the first-born of many brothers." Rom 8:30. "This is the [God and] Christ we proclaim while we admonish all men and teach them in the full measure of wisdom, hoping to make every man complete in Christ." Col 1:28. "The life I live now is not my own; Christ is living in me. I still live my human life, but it is a life of faith in the Son of God, who loved me and gave himself for me." Gal 2:20.

The Father willed that the God-man should be emptied of his fullness only temporarily, for the Father had only conditionally willed his emptiness and had not abandoned his plan for the absolute fullness of the God-man. "Jesus, who was made for a little while lower than the angels, that through God's gracious will he might taste death for the sake of all men." Heb 2:9. Jesus even in his emptied or diminished state or condition would still be the "Head of the body, the church; he who is the beginning, the first-born of the dead, so that primacy may be his in everything." Col 1:18-19.

Jesus in his emptied condition was known as the "Son of Man" for He appeared as other men and was called the son of Mary and Joseph. When Jesus Christ calls Himself the Son of Man it is always with reference to Himself as the humble servant of the servants of God. The Son of Man is always the one "Who came to serve and not to be served."

Original sin deprived all the descendants of Adam of a specific kind or degree of fullness of Christ for their conception and birth.

It deprived them of that specific kind or degree of fullness that was the perfection of their original innocence. Original sin is the reason the Father conditionally willed that particular fullness of Christ for men, the condition of the God-man and of his Mother conceived and born in the likeness of the God-man emptied of that specific kind or degree of the fullness of Christ. Original sin did not change the Father's absolute will to incarnate his Son, but changed only the state or condition the God-man and of his Mother would have at their conception and birth if Adam and Eve sinned. After Adam's original sin Mary retained her predestination to Immaculate Conception. Both she and her Son were conceived and born empty or minus those perfections of their human natures which would have made them incapable of suffering and death. "He might taste death for the sake of all men." Heb 2:9.

The Father determined that fallen man be recreated through the redemption, but not recreated in the fullness of Christ. They were not created in the fullness Christ gave up at his Incarnation. Redeemed man's new share in the fullness of Christ is minus those natural and preternatural gifts that had been included in Adam and Eve's creation in fullness of Christ.

HOW REDEEMED MEN ON EARTH NOW BECOME SHARERS IN THE DIMINISHED FULLNESS OF CHRIST FOR THEIR SALVATION

The salvation of a sinner requires that a sinner be first reconciled to the Father and second that he become a sharer in the diminished fullness of Christ by being reborn or recreated in a certain particular image or likeness of the God-man. How do redeemed sinners become sharers in that diminished fullness of Christ or become true Christians? St. Paul answers that it is not by circumcision, as many Jews thought. "It matters nothing whether one is circumcised or not. All that matters is that one is created anew [in a particular fullness of Christ]." Gal 6:15. "Formed anew in the image of his Creator." Col 3:10. "The full redemption of a people God has made his own, to praise his glory." Eph 1:14.

Since the Father wills to reconcile and justify every sinner and to reconcile and justify them by the graces merited in the redemption, the graces of the redemption must in some way be made available to every sinner. After the fall of man from grace, no grace other than the graces merited in the redemption are available to sinners. The graces merited in the redemption are available to sinners only by means of the New, Eternal, and Universal Covenant. God the Father willed that the New, Eternal, and Universal Covenant, as already explained in the previous chapter, should go into effect immediately after man's fall from grace. Hence only by fulfilling the conditions of that covenant can sinners obtain forgiveness of their sins—be reconciled to the Father—and regain a share in the diminished fullness of Christ. The graces merited in the redemption are distributed to men only by the New, Eternal and Universal Covenant and primarily by means of the Sacraments and Sacrifice of the New, Eternal, and Universal Covenant.

Only through a sinner's reconciliation to the Father and his recreation in the likeness of the diminished fullness of Christ and by retaining it do sinners become and remain "One in faith and in the knowledge of God's Son, and forms that perfect man who is Christ come to full stature [the absolute fullness of Christ]." Eph 4:13. "To create in himself one new man from us." Eph 2:15.

No man can ever discover the mystery of the gospel, the mystery of Christ or the mystery of Christ sharing his fullness with men. Even if someone should know of the mystery of man's destiny of sharing in the fullness of Christ, that person by himself is incapable of becoming or making himself a sharer in the diminished fullness of Christ or the absolute fullness of Christ.

Because of this inability of everyone, certain Jews on the first Pentecost, deeply shaken on hearing St. Peter accuse them of crucifying their promised Messiah and were lacking that specific fullness of Christ, asked the apostles: "What are we to do, brothers? Peter answered: 'You must reform and be baptized, each one of you, in the name of Jesus Christ, that your sins may be forgiven; then you will receive the gift of the Holy Spirit [as you see we have received the Holy Spirit].'" Acts 2:38.

The road leading every sinner back to God begins, but does not end, with a sincere conversion or reformation of the sinner's life, which is accomplished in part through the person's own sincere repentance and conversion, the crucifixion and death of self. The sinner must maintain himself in his recreation, in his fullness of Christ. One's own works of sincere reform and conversion are necessary for sharing in the fullness of Christ. A person's old sinful way of life is incompatible with eternal or divine life. Conversion and repentance must change a person's old way of life to the extent that his new way of life becomes at least compatible if not totally in tune with the eternal life that is a sharing in the fullness of Christ or one's recreation in the image of the God-man.

Eternal life or the grace of justification or the life of sharing in the fullness of Christ is as absolutely incompatible with a life of personal grave sin as the life of Christ is incompatible with sin. Hence after reconciliation and recreation the life of a Christian is no longer his own life, the life he lived before his recreation or justification. He must live a life like that of St. Paul, who said of his life: "The life I live now is not my own; Christ is living in me. I still live my human life, but it is a life of faith in the Son of God, who loved me and gave himself for me." Gal 2:20.

If the Father willed to create man in the likeness of the God-man the Father wills also that a man live a life like that of the God-man.

The inability of any sinner or anyone to justify himself or even to know the condition of the New, Eternal and Universal Covenant for ones reconciliation, recreation and salvation are the reasons St. Paul taught that Jesus Christ established persons in roles of service in his Church for the saving of sinners. "It is he who gave apostles, prophets, evangelists, pastors and teachers in roles of service for the faithful to build up the body of Christ, till we become one in faith and in the knowledge of God's Son, and form that perfect man who is Christ come to full stature." Eph 4:11-13.

A redeemed sinner needs assistance from the persons in the Church who have roles of service to become and to remain a sharer in the diminished fullness of Christ. St. Paul wants to assure redeemed sinners that Jesus Christ has placed in his Church persons in service to the body of Christ, persons in the Church empowered to help and save others. "He [Jesus Christ] will strengthen you to the end, so that you will be blameless on the day of our Lord Jesus Christ [the day men will share in the absolute fullness of Christ]. God is faithful, and it was he who called you to fellowship with his Son, Jesus Christ our Lord." 1 Cor 1:8-9.

The apostle Paul, fully aware of the dangers to his converts losing their recreation in the diminished fullness of Christ or their recreation in the image of God, could not be without grave concern for his converts' stability in their Christian faith and way of life. These dangers and the instability of some of his converts amazed the apostle, for he wrote to his converts in Galatia: "I am amazed that you are so soon deserting him who called you in accord with his gracious designs in Christ, and are going over to another gospel." Gal 1:6.

To encourage and strengthen his converts St. Paul was anxious to inform them of his constant concern and prayer for confidence in their heavenly Father. He informs them what was that constant prayer to God the Father for them: "May the God of our Lord Jesus Christ, the Father of glory, grant you a spirit of wisdom and insight to know him clearly. May he enlighten your innermost vision that you may know the great hope to which he has called you, the wealth of his glorious heritage to be distributed among the members of the church, and the immeasurable scope of his power in us who believe. It [the scope of his power] is like the strength he showed in raising Christ from the dead and seating him at his right hand in heaven, high above every principality, power, virtue, and domination, and every name that can be given in this age or in the age to come. He has put all things under Christ's feet and has made him, thus exalted, head of the church, which is his body: the fullness of him who fills the universe in all its parts." Eph 1:16-23.

St. Paul wanted his converts to be so convinced of their ultimate God given Christian calling to the absolute fullness of Christ that no one would ever be able to mislead them by some supposed greater and better gospel. "Now to him who is able to strengthen you in the gospel, which I proclaim when I preach Jesus Christ, the gospel which reveals the mystery hidden for many ages." Rom 16:25. Obviously, not even God could make greater or better promises to man or predestine man to something greater or better than to share in the absolute fullness of Christ and to a life on high in Christ Jesus. "To me... was given the grace to preach to the Gentiles the unfathomable riches of Christ and to enlighten all men on the mysterious design which for ages was hidden in God, the creator of all." Eph 3:8-9. "Thus you will be able to grasp fully... the breadth and length and height and depth of Christ's love, and experience this love which surpasses all knowledge, so that you may attain to the fullness of God himself." Eph 3:18-19. "I tell you all this so that no one may delude you with specious arguments." Col 2:4. The gospel "surpasses all [human] knowledge". Cf. Phil 3:8.

The fact that the truths St. Paul preached are great mysteries does not prevent him from repeatedly assuring his converts that they are able to know and understand well this great mystery of Christ. "When you read what I have said, you will realize that I know what I am talking about in speaking of the mystery of Christ." Eph 3:4. "God has given us the wisdom to understand fully the mystery, the plan he was pleased to decree in Christ, to be carried out in the fullness of time: namely, to bring all things in the heavens and on earth into one under Christ's headship." Eph 1:9-10. "It pleased God [the Father] to make absolute fullness reside in him and by means of him, to reconcile everything in his person, both on earth and in the heaven, making peace through the blood of his cross." Col 1:19-20. "Whom [the God-man, Jesus Christ] he has made heir of all things and through whom he first created the universe." Heb 1:2.

God manifested to Adam and Eve that their transcendent humanity and supernatural divine life reflected God's wisdom and that God's works in them was worthy of his Divinity. God manifested the same to the angels. By knowing their transcendent natures and supernatural life the angels knew that they reflected God's wisdom. They saw that God's works in them and for them were worthy of his divinity. This is reason for thinking that the heavenly dwellings of the angels were most magnificent and very pleasing to them and would be so forever. The magnificence of those heavenly dwellings would have been one reason Satan and his demons refused to leave them when commanded to do so by God.

The doctrine of the mystery of Christ, the truth that the Father gave first and highest priority to the Incarnation and the doctrine that God has done everything ad extra in through and for the God-man, offer the best internal evidence of the fact that the letters to the Romans, 1 Corinthians, Ephesians, Philippians, Colossians, Hebrews and 2 Timothy were all written by the same person, the apostle St. Paul.

This mystery, the high priority the Incarnation of the God-man had in the intention of the Father, manifests that God never had any intention of creating anything independently of his intention to incarnate his Son as the God-man of the race of Adam. If the Father willed the Incarnation of his Son on the conditions that man sin and that man be in need of redemption by his Incarnate Son, that to Paul meant all creation would be without its Supreme Head, the God-man.

Because the Incarnate God-man redeemed mankind by embracing his Sacred Passion and Death men have been rightly taught to continually meditate on, wonder and marvel at the immense love of Jesus Christ the God-man. The God-man was willing to suffer crucifixion to redeem rebellious mankind so that sinners could be freed from the eternal punishment their sins deserved, be reconciled to the Father, be recreated in the image of the God-man and live forever with the Father and with Him in the Kingdom of Heaven.

But why should all men not be taught also to meditate, wonder and marvel at yet another unbounded love of God the Father for all men. It is the love the Father has for us in his Son that his command brought man into existence, his decree gave man the eternal destiny of sharing in the absolute fullness of Christ. That absolute fullness of Christ includes unfathomable riches, all the riches the almighty power of the Father can create and do for the God-man and all his brethren. It is because of this most gracious will of the Father toward his God-man and us that St. Paul wrote: "Praised be the God and Father of for Lord Jesus Christ, who has bestowed on us in Christ every spiritual blessing in the heavens! God [the Father] chose us in him before the world began, to be holy and blameless in his sight, to be full of love, he likewise predestined us through Christ Jesus to be his adopted sons—such was his will and pleasure—that all might praise the glorious favor he has bestowed on us in his beloved." Eph 1:3-6.

All men should realize that God the Father, already before the creation of Adam and Eve, was most pleased to bestow eternal existence and an eternal sharing in the absolute fullness of Christ on everyone as entirely free gifts. This the Father willed to do in, through and for his Incarnate Son, the God-man of our race. He willed to do it from all eternity and not in consequence of the fall of man or for anything man would deserve. After the fall of man the Father determined that man be reconciled and recreated only through the merits of their redemption by Christ.

If these truths were known, men could then better understand and be led to appreciate that the Father is now and has always been most pleased to grant requests or petitions of all persons of Adam's race made in the name of his Incarnate God-man.

All should know that if the Father created, chose, called, predestined, justified, redeemed, reconciled, forgave and recreated sinners in, through and for Christ, it must be certain that the Father is also always most pleased to grant the requests made of Him in the name of his Incarnate Son for his own glory and the glory of his Son, the Incarnate God-man.

Just as the Father is most pleased to grant all prayerful requests made to Him in the name of his Incarnate Son, so the Father is also most pleased to accept our praise and out thanks and our worship when we offer them to Him in the name of his Incarnate Son, and even more pleased to accept our praise and thanks and worship when offered to Him by his Incarnate Son, our Eternal High Priest.

The Church of Jesus Christ, knowing of this great predilection on the part of the Father for the Person of his Incarnate Son and everything about Him, has always very wisely offered all her reparation, praise, adoration and petitions to the Father in the name of the God-man, Jesus Christ. Jesus Christ is man's Eternal High Priest of the New, Eternal and Universal Covenant. "So that all you ask the Father in my name he will give you." Jn 15:16.

"So that all you ask the Father in my name will be given you." These words of Jesus imply the existence of a formal agreement between the Father and the Son that the Father grant whatever men ask of Him in his Name, the name of his Incarnate God-man. These words imply also that the Father intends to deny certain requests for no other reason than that those requests are not made in the name of the Incarnate God-man. This formal agreement between the Father and the Son has for its purpose the manifestation of the great love of the Father for his Incarnate Son and the Son's great love for his Father. It is in this way that the Father wants to prove to us that He loves his Incarnate Son, that the Incarnate Son loves his Father and always does the will of his Father.

Little wonder then that the Holy Spirit delights to inform us of what we will see, hear and clearly understand when we stand before the throne of the God-man in heaven. Then it will be made abundantly clear to everyone that all the marvelous things the Father decreed from all eternity were decreed through the priority the Father gave to the Incarnation of his Son when creating the universe and everything in it. "The one who sat on the throne said to me, 'See, I make all things new!' Then he said, 'Write these matters down, for the words are trustworthy and true!' He went on to say: "These words are already fulfilled! I am the Alpha and the Omega, the Beginning and the End and [the First and the Last of all things].'" Rev 21:5-6.

MAY ALL MEN FOREVER PRAISE GOD THE FATHER FOR GIVING ABSOLUTE PRIORITY TO INCARNATING HIS SON AS THE GOD-MAN OF OUR RACE, THE RACE OF ADAM. BECAUSE JESUS CHRIST WAS FIRST IN THE FATHER'S ORDER OF THE INTENTION THAT HE IS LAST IN HIS ORDER OF EXECUTION.

JESUS CHRIST
IS
THE FIRST AND THE LAST
THE BEGINNING AND THE END
THE ALPHA AND THE OMEGA

Appendix 1

THE ORIGIN OF THE UNFOUNDED DOCUMENTARY HYPOTHESIS

The skepticism of so many concerning any clear, definite and certain meaning of the lead chapters of Genesis has resulted primarily from great uncertainty regarding the origin of Genesis and the identity of its author. This skepticism continues because persistent pertinent questions go unanswered. Questions about the source of the information the author could have had about what happened at the beginning of time. This is so because, if the creation account in Genesis is the absolute truth, everyone sees that the author needed divine revelation as his source of information. Only divine revelation could enable him to assure his readers that his account was the absolute truth and not pure speculation, fiction, or myth.

If there is no evidence the author of the creation chapters was writing revealed truth in his account he cannot offer fallen man certainty concerning the origin of all things or of man. Man needs certainty to order his life. There is no possibility that any creature author could have observed the creation. For any creature to do that the creature author would have had to exist before the creation of any creature on the first day. For everyone understands that if the author wrote with the best information human genius and intuition could have afforded him, his account would at best be nothing more than speculations about a mystery. The precise ultimate origin of all things is and will always remain a mystery to the science and intuition of men.

Unfortunately many believe that the lead chapters of Genesis do not at all or do not clearly enough manifest they are a new and direct divine revelation to their human author. Catholic tradition has always considered Genesis to be biblically inspired by God and that Moses was its human author. However the reasons for the Catholic tradition that Moses was the inspired author of Genesis are unknown or are not clear. Is the reason for that Catholic tradition the fact that in the gospels Jesus seems to imply that Moses is their inspired author or is it that in Jewish tradition Moses is the inspired author of Genesis?

Whatever the reason or reasons, this commentary will demonstrate that the first chapter of Genesis manifests itself to be a new and direct revelation of God to its human author and that he was inspired by God to write the creation chapters. Opposed to all this is the documentary hypothesis.

THE DOCUMENTRY HYPOTHESIS IS SPECULATION TO DISASTER

It is inconceivable that God would not have informed the first man and woman, Adam and Eve, of the mysteries of their ultimate origin, of the universe and the mystery of their ultimate divine destiny. It is just as inconceivable that the first man and woman would not have passed on to their children and generations of descendants what God had revealed to them of the ultimate origin of man, the universe and their ultimate divine destiny. Hence it is at least conceivable, but not probable, that Genesis' account of the origin of all things by creation from nothing could have had its origin in what Adam and Eve passed on to their descendants.

It is equally inconceivable that Adam and Eve would not have informed their children and grandchildren of the wonderful life they enjoyed for a short time in Paradise. It is inconceivable that Adam and Eve would not have informed their children of the reason for their expulsion from Paradise and of the many sorrows, problems, and hardships they endured during the first years of their exile in the world outside Paradise.

Since most modern biblical scholars appear to believe in the evolution of man they do not think that Genesis' account of creation could have been successfully passed on to the descendants of Adam over millions or many hundreds of thousands of years to the time Genesis is considered to have its origin three to four thousand years ago. They find it extremely improbable or even impossible for that original information to have been preserved and passed on intact over the supposed many hundreds of thousands or millions of years from the first man to the time of the origin of Genesis.

Adam and Eve, whether man did or did not have an evolutionary origin, certainly would have passed on to their children the information God revealed to them and since their children in turn certainly would have passed that information on to their descendants, one cannot but wonder what ultimately happened to that oral tradition. Would it not have vanished from the face of the earth many thousands of years ago. One might wonder whether that tradition was corrupted through the insincerity, dishonesty and ungodliness of their early descendants to become the abhorrent ancient pagan creation myths of the pagan nations?

Today, many biblical scholars hold that the Genesis of the last three millennia had an entirely independent origin of its own. They think Genesis had its entirely independent origin in the knowledge certain early Semites began to discern about God and the origin of things and that they passed on that discerned knowledge generation after generation first in oral story form by their telling and retelling in gatherings that celebrated their peoples' past. They suppose that those stories constantly evolved or underwent change in their telling and retelling. They suppose also that those stories were understood and interpreted differently in different local communities before comminutes began to commit their different oral stories to written form. They further suppose that the early composers, storytellers and later redactors or editors of later documents were under the influence of the ancient creation myths of their neighboring pagan nations.

It is supposed by many today that Genesis had its beginnings in the speculations of the earliest Semites about God and the origin of all things. The discerned knowledge these speculators produced was preserved originally in the form of prehistoric or most ancient wisdom traditions. These traditions were in circulation in oral form for centuries before being put in written or documentary form. Today's biblical scholars think that the final editing of those supposed source documents occurred some three thousand years ago and that the Genesis of today is the final edition of those passed on redacted or re-edited ancient documents.

All these suppositions, if true, would raise very compelling and disturbing questions. Questions such as: would not such an origin and history be typical of a myth? Would not such an origin and development leave the creation account in Genesis of little value? Would not the account of creation in Genesis then be merely an account or story of certain persons speculating on the insoluble mysteries of the ultimate origin of all things and of man?

Since believers in the documentary hypothesis conceive this kind of origin for Genesis, today's believers in the documentary hypothesis cannot conceive of any one person being the author of

Genesis. Hence many modern biblical scholars are very reluctant to name any one person as the author of Genesis in the same sense that they have named other individuals authors of other ancient books of the Bible.

The proponents of the documentary hypothesis are alleging that the Genesis found in the Bible is compiled from much older documents and each written by different persons or person. They claim there is evidence for this in the many repetitions, dissimilarities and contradictions they claim to find in the creation chapters. Those repetitions, dissimilarities and contradictions are supposedly due to the different treatments the same subjects receive in the different source documents.

Hence the hypothesis has in itself the germs of its own demise. For it should be evident that no person or persons would work at editing or compiling from documents a book he knew was so flawed and contradictory as the proponents of the documentary hypothesis contend Genesis must be with its many source documents. Anyone today would certainly expect that intelligent readers would recognize those inconsistencies and contradictions and reject not only their many inconsistent and contradictory passages, but also the entire work or book.

They would be forced into rejecting the entire book as an unreliable source of truth and certainty. It is not merely that the contradictory parts were obvious nonsense, but, as far as anyone can know, all other parts are undeserving of belief and useless for that reason. This is especially true of a work so mysterious as the ultimate beginning and destiny of all things. In this way the documentary hypothesis renders the creation chapters almost completely worthless as a source of the truth and certainty persons need for the direction they must give to their lives. This is the principal reason for the skepticism of so many today regarding everything in the creation chapters and other chapters of Genesis. They hold all of Genesis has been compiled from such sources.

Since no person would knowingly write or compile a book with such great deficiencies, and if Genesis were such a book, Genesis would have no rational reason for being, should never have been composed and would never have been preserved. Since Genesis does exist, it cannot be the result of such a process and the documentary hypothesis must be prejudged on that basis alone to be without credibility.

It should be noted also that scholars, who believe in the documentary hypothesis, offer no satisfactory explanation of how or why the continuing redacting and editing of those supposed source documents should have ceased to allow for the text to become fixed or permanent. On the other hand, it should be obvious that any general awareness of a new and inspired account of the origin of all things would have put an abrupt end to that passing on of source documents, the supposed edited and compiled Genesis. Why would persons have continued to put forth the great effort required for preserving those rather useless documents?

By advancing and promoting this recently invented documentary hypothesis, biblical scholars have obviously raised up for themselves and their students towering heaps of seemingly insurmountable difficulties to determining, with any degree of accuracy or certainty, the intended meaning or sense of Genesis' creation chapters or even the truly revealed account of creation. How can modern experts and students of Scripture ever hope to determine with accuracy and certainty by means textual criticism, literary form, redaction criticism or form criticism what was the original language or specific sense of those supposed source oral stories and documents? How are they to do that when they are unable to form any consensus regarding the sense of the text of the Genesis they actually do posses?

In consequence of accepting that rather recently invented documentary hypothesis, modern biblical scholars have been speculating about some of the many great difficulties that would have been involved in any trustworthy transmission of those supposed sources documents over many centuries or even millennia. They have also been engaged in trying to identify particular passages in Genesis as lifted from one or other of their several supposed sources documents.

The more commentators have become enamored with belief in the redacting and editing of sources documents, the theory of evolution of species and the influence pagan creation myths supposedly had on persons composing, transmitting and editing the supposed source documents the more their commentaries abound in confusion, uncertainty and contradictions. The results of all these suppositions have been very detrimental to anyone trying to believe and understand anything of Genesis' entire account of the creation of all things, the origin of man and any natural or supernatural destiny God has for man. Their commentaries spread bewilderment not the clarity and certainty of revealed truth.

The particular objective of all such commentaries is always to give the creation chapters a sense that would, to the greatest extent possible, conform Genesis' supposed symbolical sense to the sense demanded by the modern science of physics and especially the theory of evolution. Such commentaries are completely bogged down in speculations which make it quite impossible for fallen man to gain any certainty regarding God's intended meaning for the creation chapters, if they should contain any divine revelation or have a meaning truly intended by God. Holders of these views suppose that the origin of man could not have been different from that of all other living beings on earth, for all living beings are supposedly the product of the same evolutionary process.

It was inevitable that the promotion of that recently invented documentary hypothesis would soon result, as indeed it has in our time, in greatly reduced expectations of ever truly determining what if any meaning was intended by God for fallen men's use as a guide for belief and action. The documentary hypothesis has subjected all of Genesis, not merely its creation chapters, to such unrestrained speculation that discovering with any certainty the author's intended meaning is now practically nil.

As a consequence of that kind of unrestrained speculation the creation chapters have been rendered incapable of nourishing the minds and spirits of fallen man with the certainty of revealed truth. The supposed symbolical sense of the creation chapters and the speculative interpretations given to them have not made the creation chapters or the whole of Genesis more acceptable as truly historical to believers or unbelievers. Completely secular societies, their media, and their institutions of higher learning do not respect Genesis as a sacred book, a book worthy of belief and especially not worthy of guiding the minds of man in matters of morality.

Because of the failure of modern biblical scholars to grasp the literal sense of the creation chapters they now claim that Exodus is of greater significance to fallen man than is Genesis. In their view, Exodus not only teaches creation by God but in addition reveals God's established covenant and Law for man, manifests the Israelites as God's chosen community, promulgates the ten commandments of God and establishes the Levitical Priesthood with its liturgical worship of the true God.

This erroneous view of Genesis' insignificance was the inevitable result of the failure of the same scholars to see that the literal sense of Genesis manifests that God made a creation covenant with the progenitor of an entire race for the justification and salvation of his entire race. The correct evaluation of Genesis manifests that man was created in the state of original innocence and the reasons men now find themselves in a fallen condition and the reason God, after man's fall from grace and the annulment of the creation covenant, made the new, eternal and universal covenant for the resanctification or rejustification of all fallen men and has given men a supernatural eternal destiny.

Their erroneous view and evaluation of Genesis and of Exodus fail completely to appreciate the fact that Exodus' covenant or Law, given at Sinai, was not a justifying covenant and that it was for that very reason, as St. Paul taught, no one could be justified by the works of that covenant or Law. If it had been a justifying covenant then the only way persons living under that covenant or Law could have been justified and reached eternal salvation would have been by the works of that covenant or Law. St. Paul wrote that the works of that Law or covenant couldn't justify anyone.

The apostle Paul forcefully taught that works cannot merit justification, that the works of the Law cannot merit justification and that the works of the Law are not even the condition in the will of God for giving justification as a free gift. He taught these truths so forcefully that the Judaizers raised the question, if the Law cannot do any of these things what good then is the Law and the keeping of the Law? It was to answer these objections that St. Paul in several of his letters expounds the true purpose and value of the Law and the reasons God gave the Law to the Israelites.

It should be noted that hardly anything could be of greater significance or value to fallen man than a sanctifying or justifying covenant. Hence hardly anything could be of greater value or significance than the existence of the creation covenant God made with Adam in the second chapter of Genesis and God's new, eternal and universal covenant implied in the third chapter of Genesis.

If Genesis' account does not contain God's explicit revelation of the mystery of the ultimate origin of all things, including that of man, how could any myth or story concocted by man offer certain knowledge of the true origin of all things and of man? The ultimate origin of all things including that of man is and always will be an insoluble mystery to the science and intuition of man. The best of theories men have been able to devise for the ultimate origin of all things would appear to be the big-bang theory and the theory of evolution. The big-bang theory tries to identify what was first. It in no why explains how the first came to be. To think it explains how things came to be would be similar to the error of thinking that matter always existed and doesn't need to be created. Neither theory can in any way satisfy man's desire to know with certainty himself, his ultimate origin and his ultimate destiny.

If the creation chapters are a new and direct revelation of God to and for fallen man then there is reason for accepting them as correct and adequate to man's need to know. The first chapter of Genesis manifests that its account of creation is a new and direct revelation from God. Only God could have known and made known or revealed detailed information about why, when, how and in what order He caused all things to come into being.

This commentary through its analysis of the text of Genesis manifests its literal sense. It gives an understanding of Genesis' account of creation based on its literal sense and that sense is consistent with a belief in an all-knowing, powerful, loving, and befriending God. A God who desired to give fallen man an account of the origin and destiny of all things and especially of man that would be most suitable or appropriate to man in his fallen condition. The information Genesis gives in its literal sense gives satisfying answers to the great need and legitimate desire of man to know himself, his ultimate origin, and his ultimate divine destiny.

Such a revelation was necessary because men continually strive for a destiny that is either a revealed destiny or some destiny of man's own choosing, a destiny based on man's very limited knowledge and understanding of his God, himself and his world. Every person needs to know his God, himself and his destiny with certainty, for man desires to strive for his hoped-for end or destiny at all times and in everything he does and to do so with certainty.

This commentary should lead readers and students of Genesis to a better realization of the many options available to God with respect to time, place, persons, and manner for revealing to fallen mankind the mysteries of the origin of a vast and complex universe. The mysteries of man's original state of innocence and to what extent man would share in the absolute fullness of the God-man's inheritance—the unfathomable riches of the inheritance the Almighty Father granted to the God-man, the Almighty Father's First-borns who would share his inheritance with all his true brothers and sisters.

It must be understood that the supposed documents of the documentary hypothesis are not to Genesis what the four gospels are to the Diatessaron. The four gospels are not hypothetical documents but real Divinely inspired documents and therefore the Diatessaron contains divine revelation. It is not composed from sources that are in any way the result of speculative, mythical and contradictory sources. Since it is composed from sources of revelation the Diatessaron has been used in the Liturgy of certain Eastern Rite Churches in place of the four gospels.